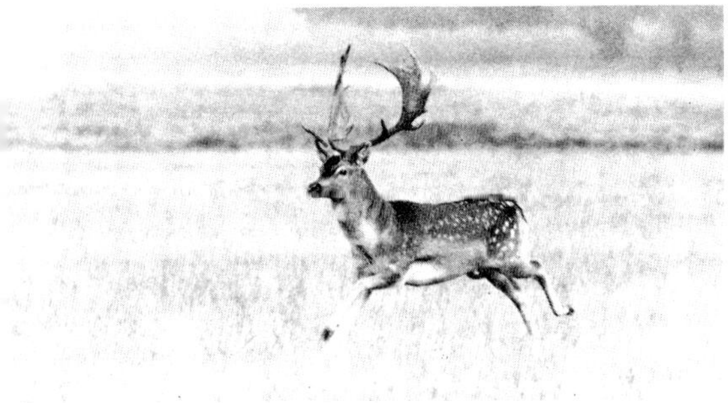

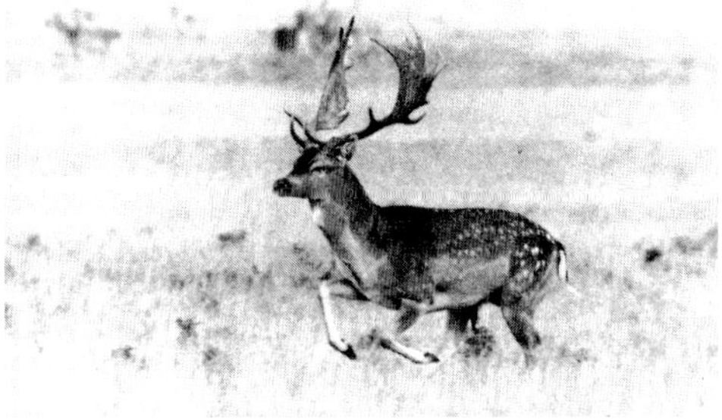

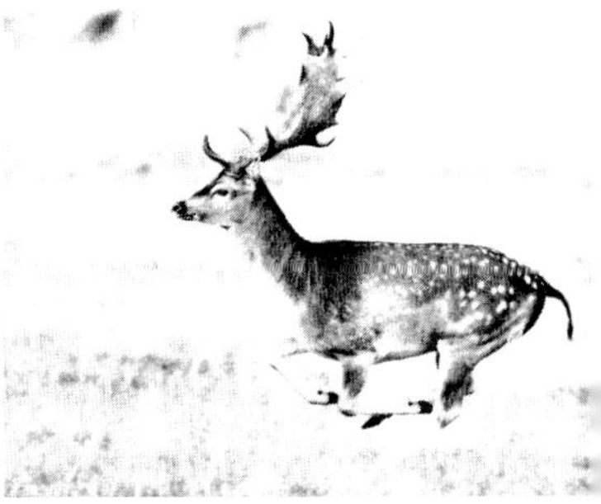

Acknowledgments

All the photographs illustrating this book were taken by J.-M. Baufle and J.-P. Varin, with the exception of the following:

M. Bailleau: p. 82; J. M. Bernard: pp. 90, 124, 139; F. Bel and G. Vienne: p. 94 top; Barry Blair: p. 101; H. Chaumeton: p. 108 bottom; A. Fatras: p. 109 bottom; W. Grossa: pp. 22, 23, 39; C. Huyghens: pp. 80, 95, 116, 120, 125, 128; P.-A. Milwaukee: pp. 55, 102 top; A. Molinier: pp. 76, 77; P. Montoya: p. 15; C. Nardin: p. 83; S. Ousoff: p. 102 bottom; K. Ross: pp. 26, 27, 62, 63, 107, 110; Y. and M. Vial: p. 109 centre; A. Visage: pp. 74, 75, 103 bottom, 127, 142 top; G. Vici: p. 43 bottom; Wagner: p. 113 top.

The above-mentioned photographs were supplied by Agence Jacana, Paris.

The publishers would like to thank The Reader's Digest Association for permission to reproduce the map on pages 146 and 147, and the World Wildlife Fund for their assistance in compiling the material on pages 148–153 of this book.

Oxford University Press, Inc.,
200 Madison Avenue
New York, N.Y. 10016
1972

First published in France by
Librairie Hachette

ISBN 019 519714 3
Library of Congress No 72 82675

All enquiries and requests relevant to this title should be sent to the publisher at the above address and not to the printer.

Printed in Holland by Smeets, Weert.

JEAN-MARIE BAUFLE

JEAN-PHILIPPE VARIN

photographing wildlife

Translated from the French by
Carel v. Amerongen

NEW YORK
OXFORD UNIVERSITY PRESS
1972

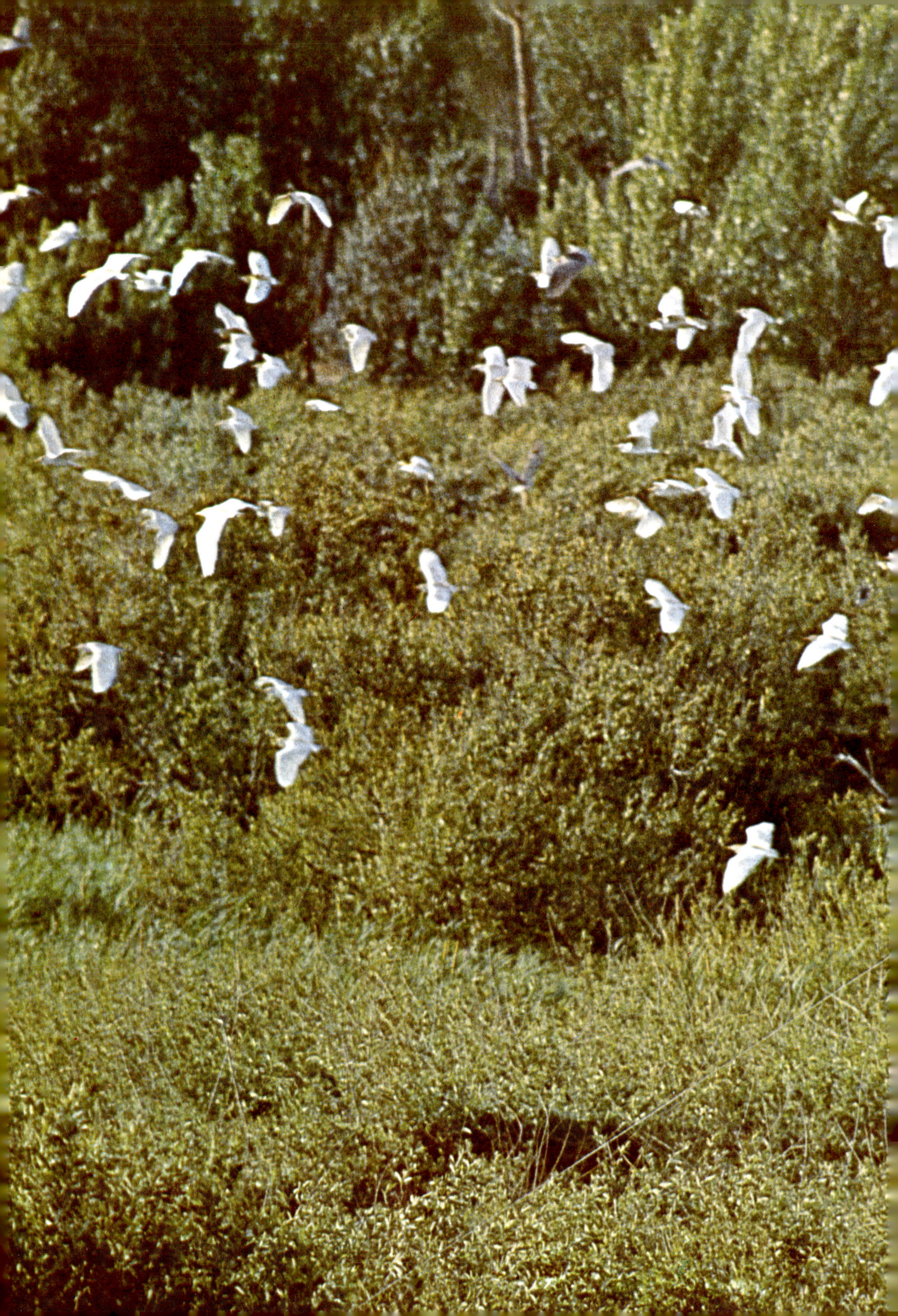

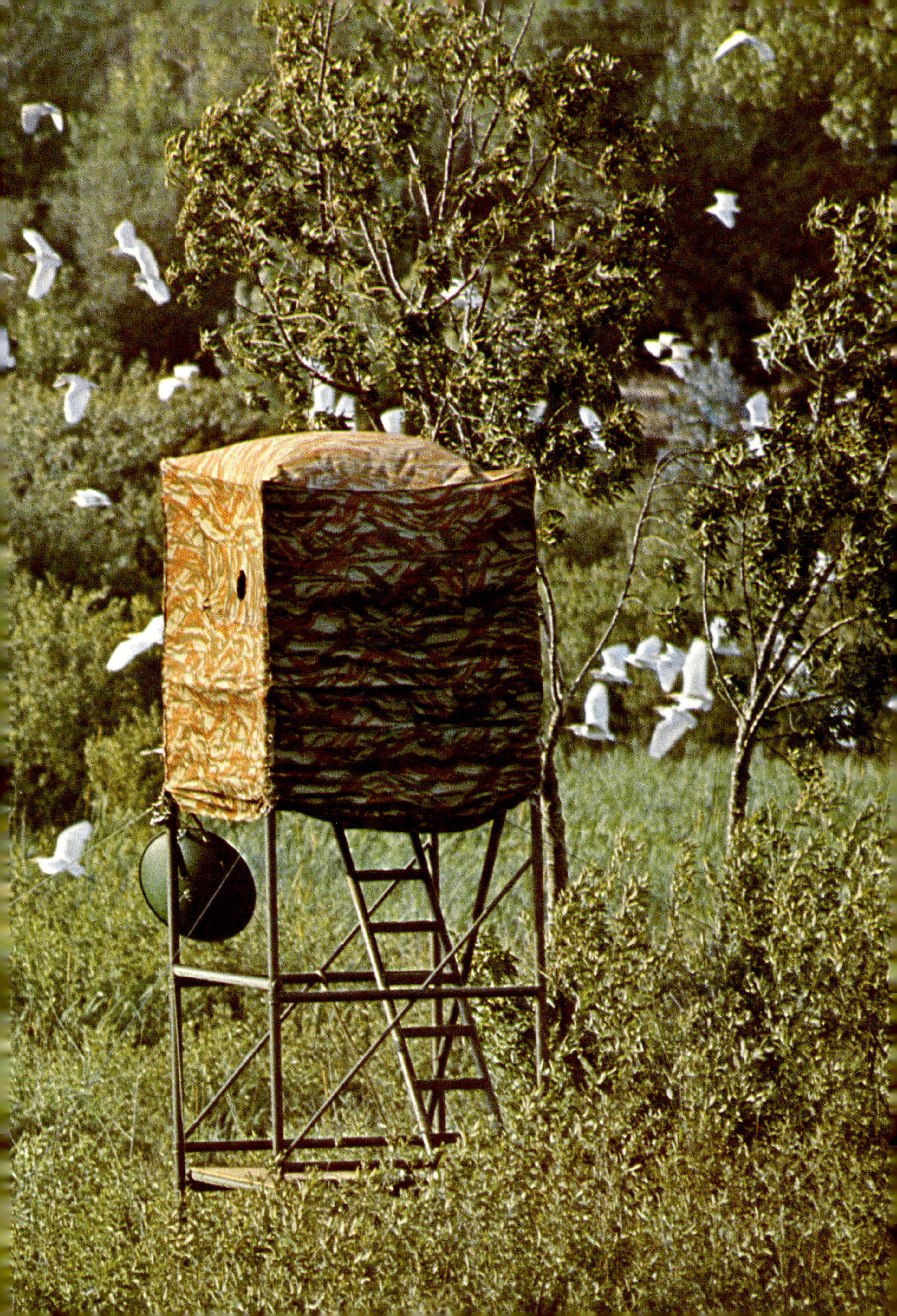

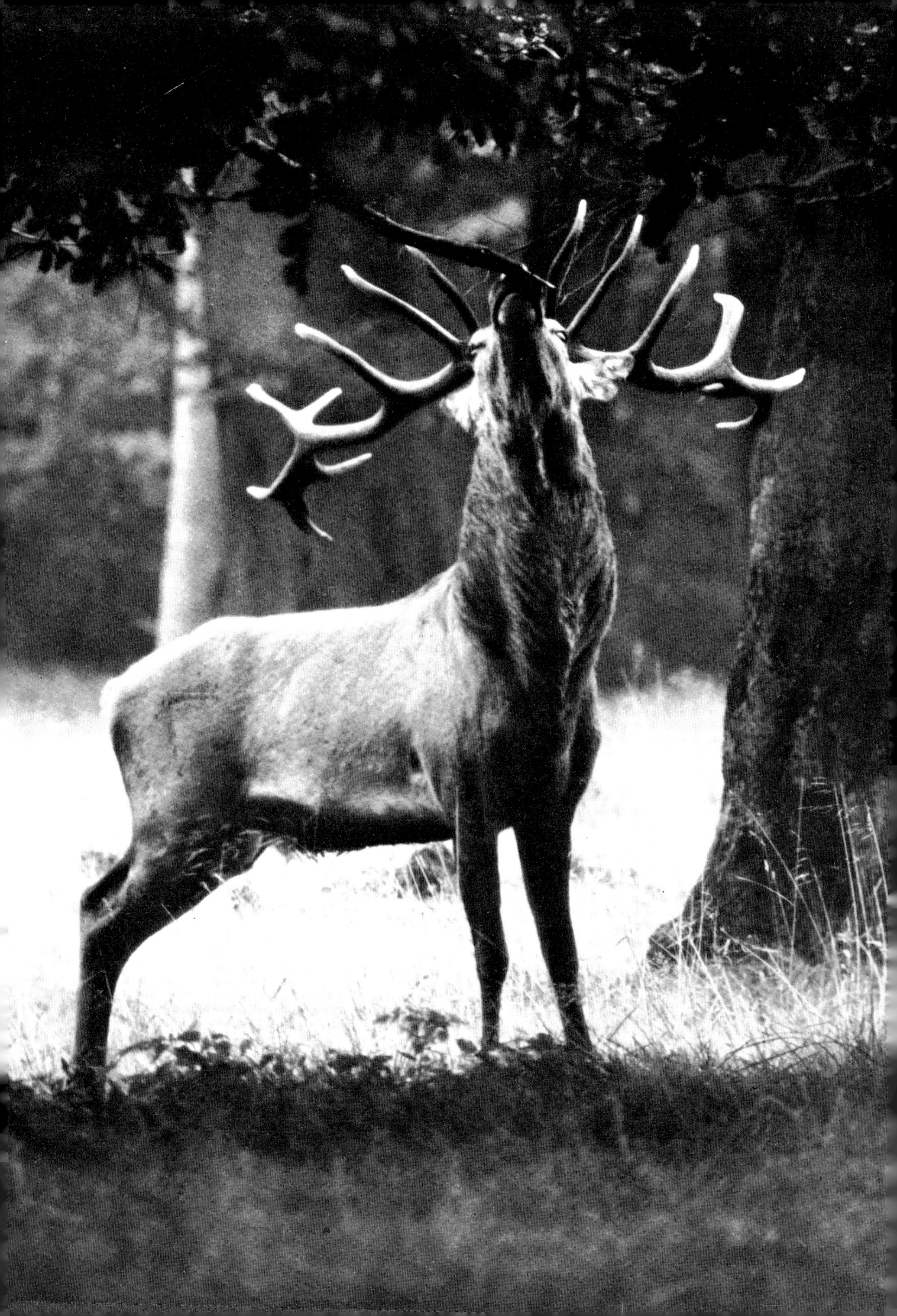

contents

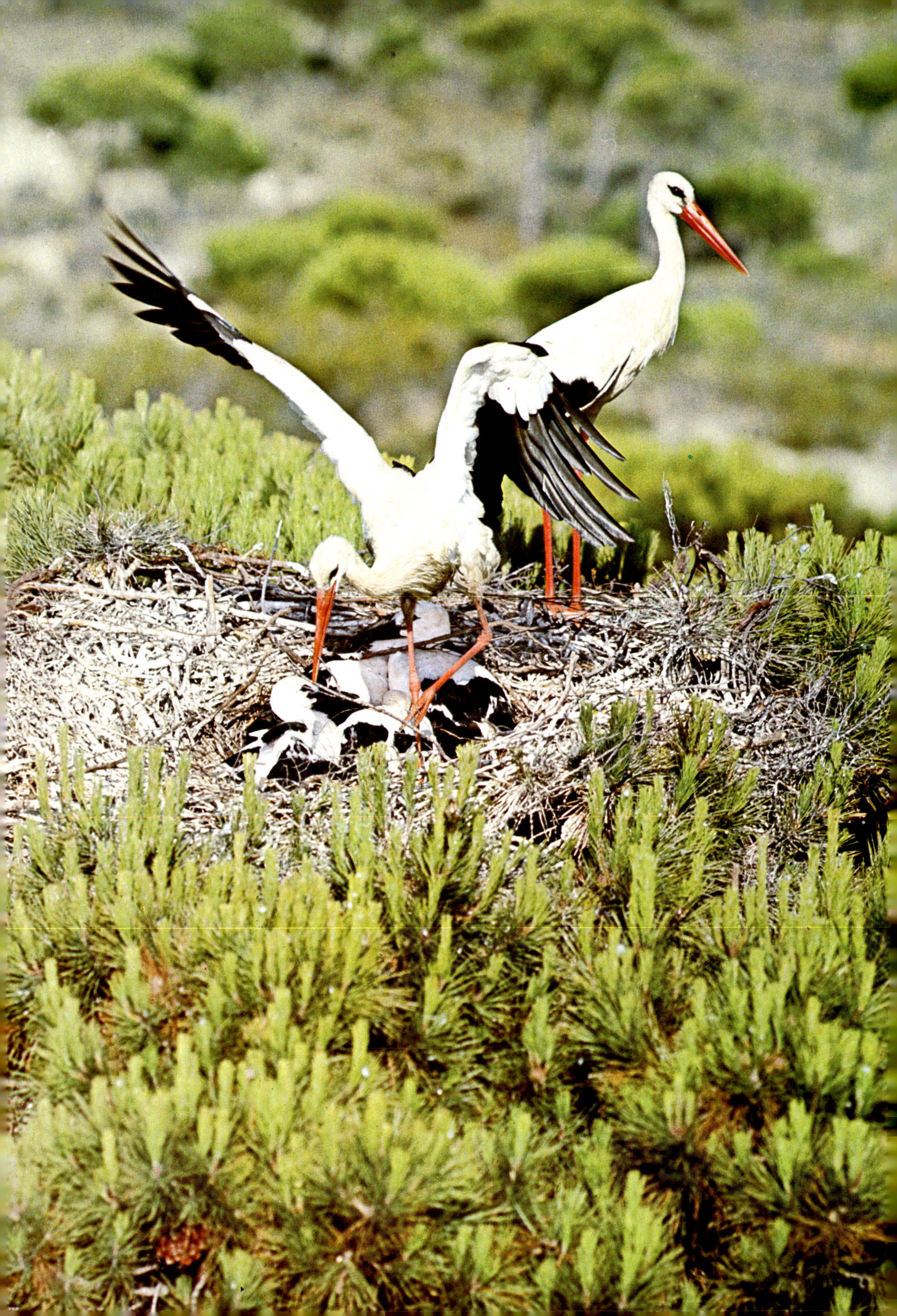

attempt at definition

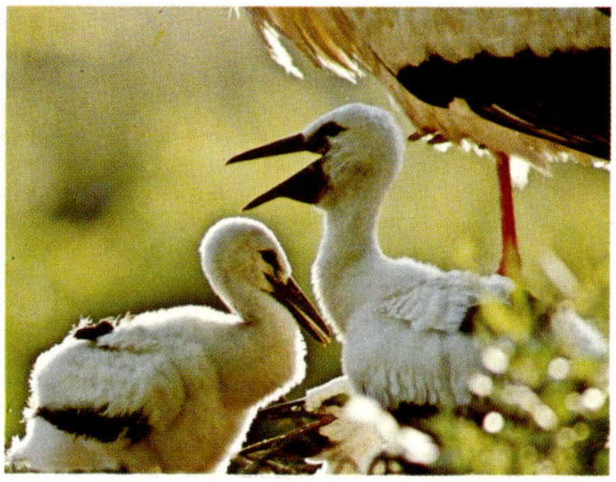

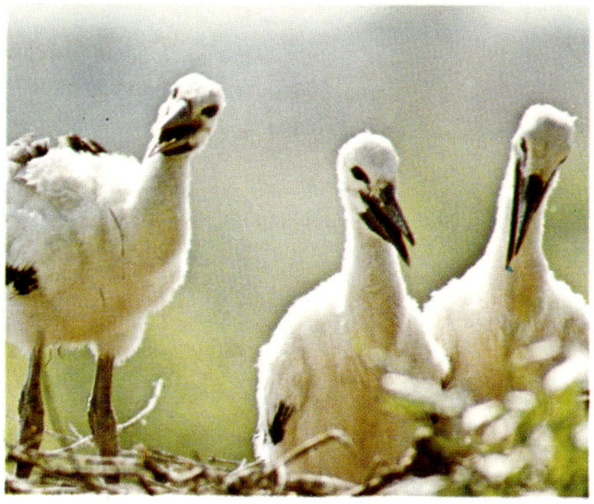

To get these pictures of nesting storks (*Ciconia ciconia*) a 21-feet-high tower with a hide on top had to be constructed. The nest was at the top of a pine tree 18 feet above the ground, and the tower had to be high enough to provide a view of the nest from above to enable the birds' behaviour to be properly observed. The position of the tower and hide was chosen with due regard to the direction of the sunlight at different times of the day.
Equipment: 35 mm reflex camera with lenses of 135 mm and 400 mm focal length.

Just what wildlife photography is and aims to do has long baffled attempts at precise definition. The activity itself is not new, but the ever-increasing interest it arouses–together with the sense of wonder that such pictures produce in people living cut off from nature in their cities of concrete and stone–is a sign of the deep respect for living creatures that has so rapidly developed in our generation.

It is indeed a long time since man himself had to carry on a daily struggle with nature for his own survival and be perpetually on his guard to protect himself against an unknown and hostile world. And through the ages that followed, man in his greed, impatience and meanness of spirit did not greatly change in his attitude to nature and its resources, which he came to regard simply as a storehouse of almost inexhaustible wealth for the plundering.

It is to the everlasting credit of the people living in this second half of the twentieth century that they have at last woken up to the importance of any action undertaken to safeguard this pristine beauty and this delicate biological equilibrium that is the source of our life.

To get to know this environment of ours intimately, with the creatures and things in it, it is necessary to observe it and love it. There is no other way. And from observing it to photographing it is just one step: to try to capture something of this dream world, existing near us and yet so inaccessible, and to adorn our walls with bloodless trophies.

The wildlife photographer is a naturalist in spirit, a scientist, a poet and a dreamer, filled with respect for life that does not belong to him, a man who wants to share his emotions and his enthusiasm with others.

Books are bringing nature home to people; films and television broadcasts on wildlife have taught an increasingly large section of the general public, with leisure at their disposal, to look beyond the city with its smog and pollution. To modern man it has become a necessity to get away from himself, his thoughts, his home, away from over-familiar and commonplace surroundings, to discover the safety valve through which he can escape from the isolation within the crowd to the freedom of a world still ruled only by the forces of nature. And what does he get in return? Solitude–but of the kind he wants, accepts, looks for–not isolation. It provides him with a fresh means of asserting his personality outside his hectic everyday world, of experiencing once again the power of his senses, of remaining at all times master of his actions and reflexes. And it is indeed hard to imagine how one could expect to define within precise limits this adventure in which all who have a desire for knowledge can participate, however much they may differ individually in temperament and tastes.

Wildlife photography is not something that people do only on desolate seashores or in the remote depths of the forest. Nearer home, too, there are worlds teeming with life–in the drop of water from the garden pond, in the patch of grass growing on the balcony, or in the aquarium by the window. Studying

Stalking mountain animals requires good physical stamina and a sense of balance. Very lightweight equipment should be used; a camera in a 'photosniper' mounting is essential, as it is seldom possible in mountainous country to find a hiding place within suitable range of the subject. The photograph below shows a group of ibexes (*Capra ibex*) coming round a ridge of rock. Equipment: photosniper with 400 mm focal length lens.

and recording the micro-universe can form an important part of this activity whose crowning achievement is the successful photograph.

At this present time, when nature has need for attentive observers and enthusiastic photographers, the concept of wildlife photography can surely not be confined, as some people suppose, solely to the photography of truly 'wild' creatures, i.e. living in conditions of complete freedom. If that rule were to be strictly and consistently applied, the distinction of being wildlife photographers could not be claimed by those who take pictures of creatures kept in any sort of confinement, however spacious, as in private game preserves, or living in woods bordered by roads, or in parks or open spaces surrounded by walls, fences or buildings, or for that matter in the great wild animal parks in Africa.

If that were so, the sea (and then only well away from protected coastlines) and the few unexplored territories that still remain in the world would be the only legitimate hunting grounds for the wildlife photographer; and only a handful of rare individuals throughout the world, who have between them taken perhaps a hundred or so pictures of truly 'wild' creatures, could be called wildlife photographers.

We could try to establish a sort of equation to define the 'freedom' of a creature living in the wild state. Thus for an animal whose territory and fleeing distance are more than, say, 100 or 200 times its own length, it could be defined,

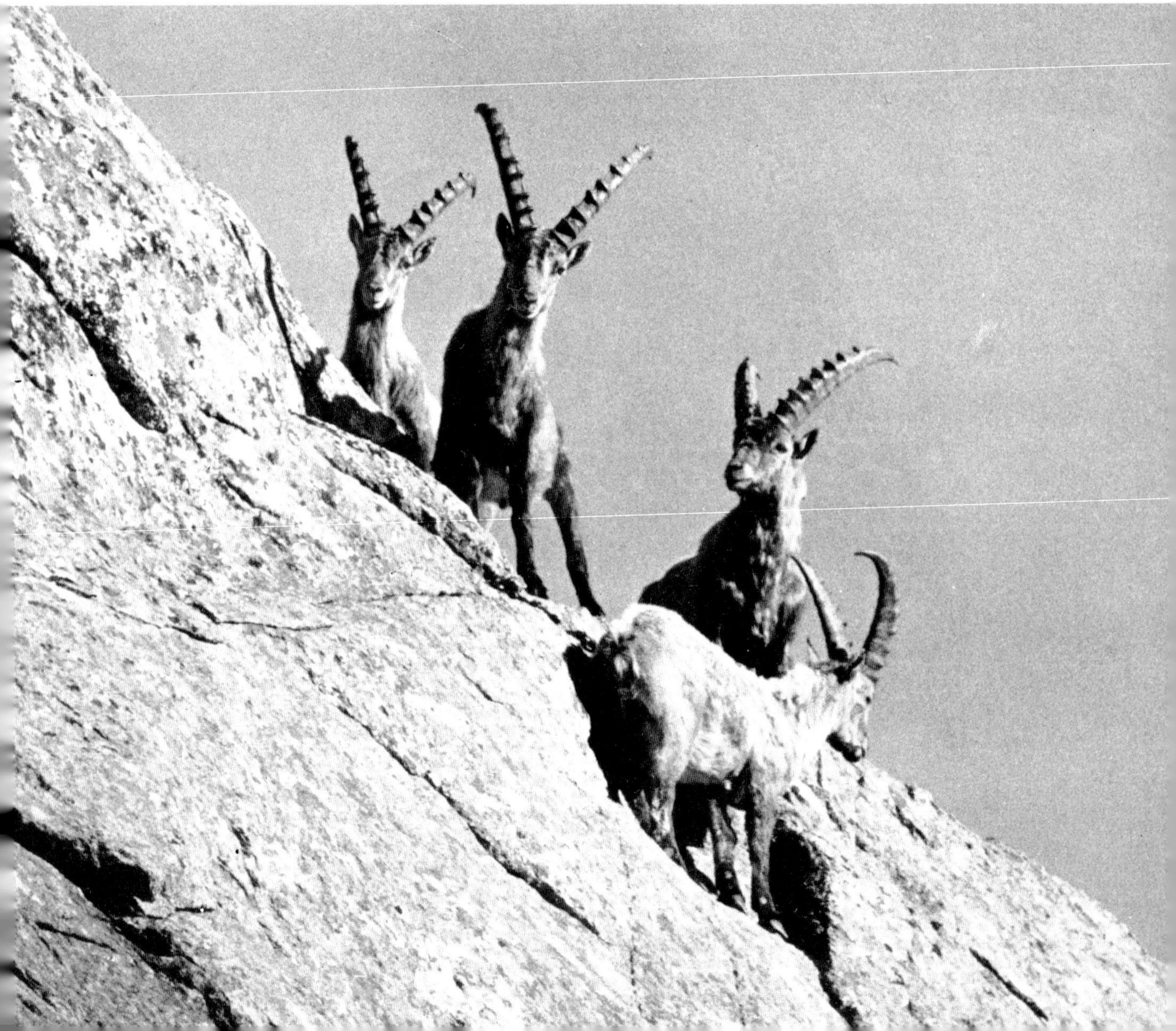

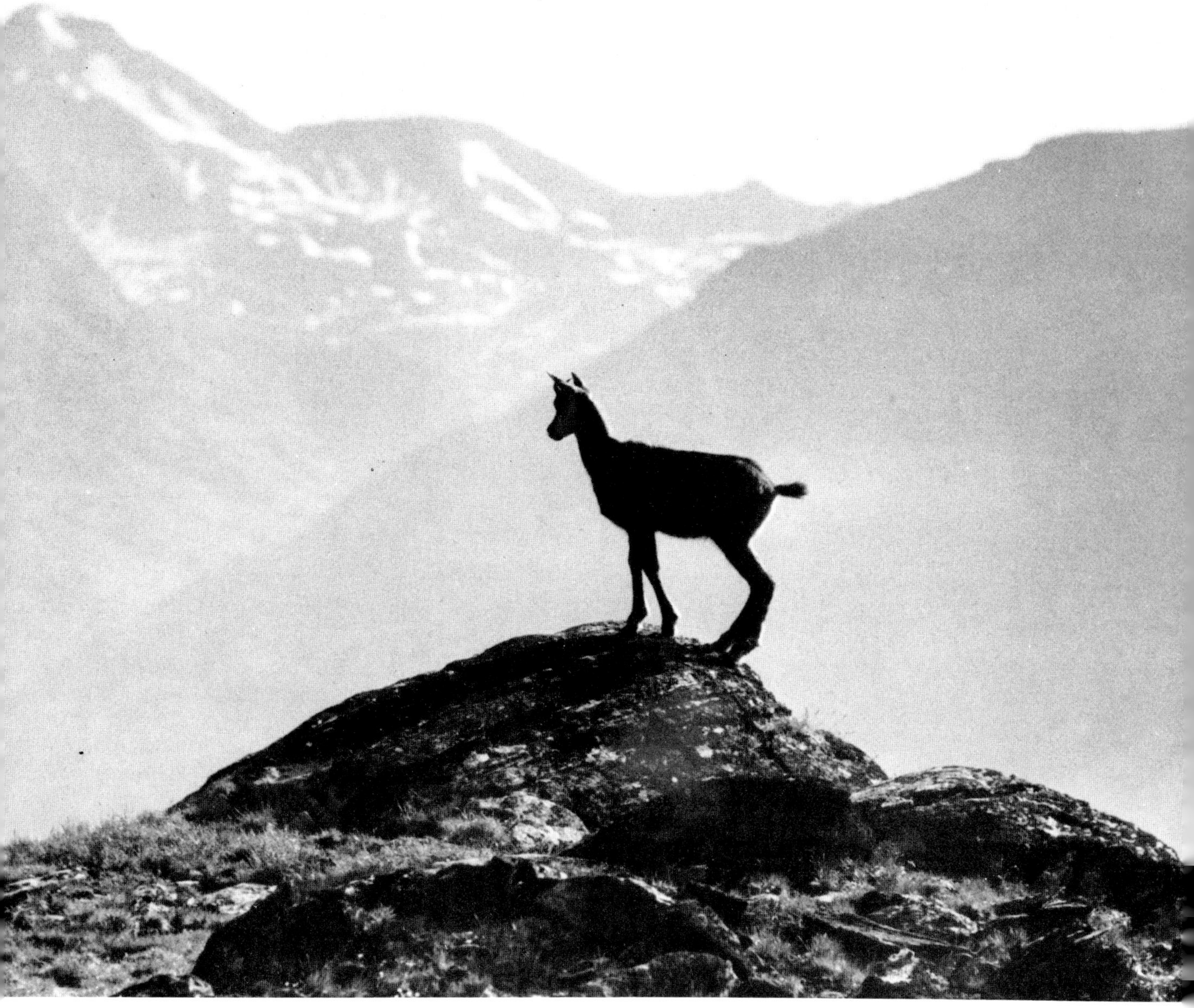

for example, as $200 \times 4\frac{1}{2}$ feet for a deer or $200 \times \frac{1}{2}$ inches for an ant. However, various corrective factors would have to be introduced, such as the acuteness of the animal's sense of smell, its absolute speed of movement, its endurance, the prevailing wind direction, etc. But all this still could not produce a criterion that we could seriously apply. In actual fact, the scope and limits of what can legitimately be said to constitute wildlife photography must depend solely on the integrity, the code of honour that vouches for the truthfulness of the picture recorded, and the good sense that every naturalist should possess.

Of course, it requires more knowledge of the environment, more physical courage and tenacity, more sheer luck to find an edelweiss, and take a photograph of the parasite that lives in it, at an altitude of 9,000 feet, than to get a picture of some drowsy mammal in a park a few miles outside one's city.

The term 'wildlife photography' has always been applied in too restrictive a sense, denoting the trophy obtained as the result of some great effort. This is a mental attitude that comes directly from that remote past when our ancestors had to hunt in order to survive. At a later period this instinctive activity of hunting became a dangerous and manly sport, a contest fought on something like equal terms, which called for a sound knowledge of the life and habits of

The chamois (*Rupicapra rupicapra*) is a very shy animal which presents a fascinating challenge to the photographer wishing to stalk it. All sorts of precautions have to be taken to allay its suspicion. This picture was taken at 6 am from a very light portable hide. Equipment: 35 mm reflex camera in photosniper mounting with 400 mm focal length; speed 1/125 sec.; aperture f 5·6; film Ilford HP4.

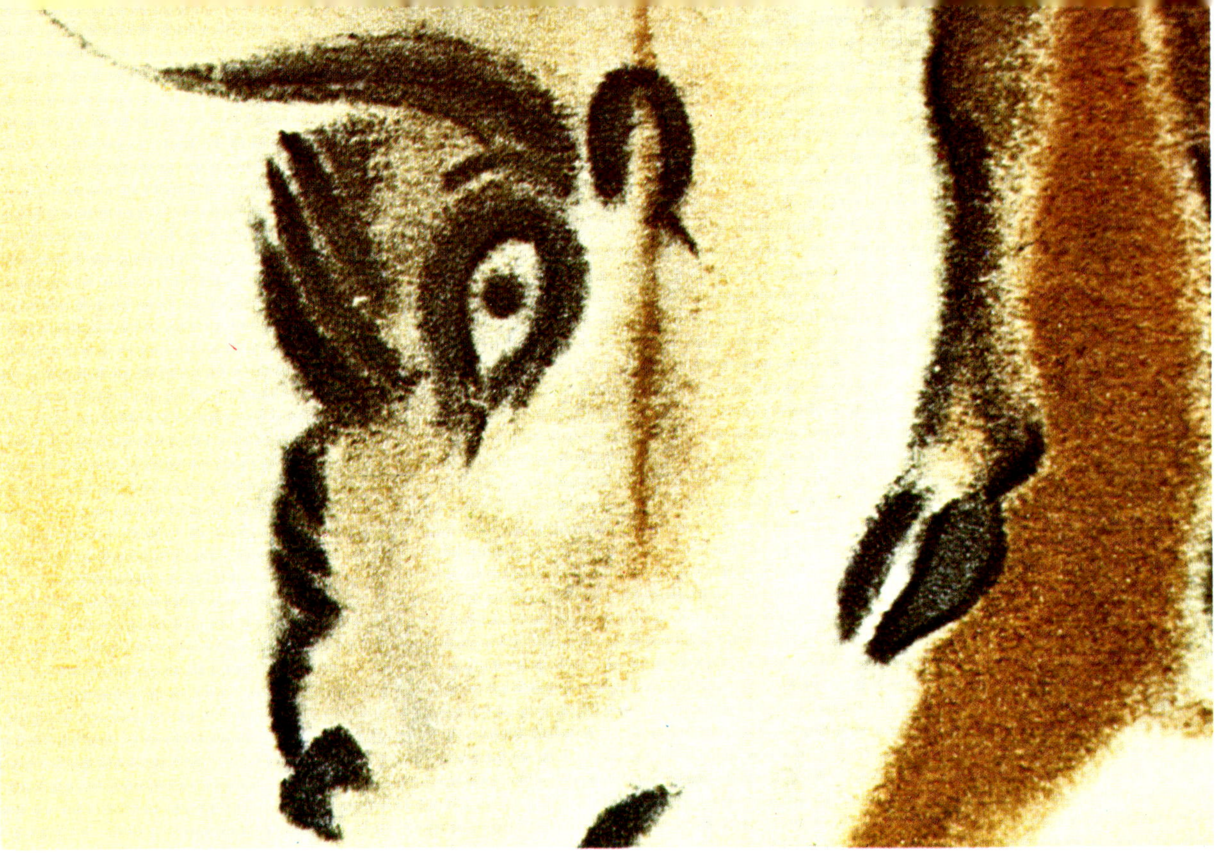

141

Primitive man recorded his first impressions of animal life by drawing or painting them on the walls of the caves in which he dwelt. The illustration shows a cave painting of an aurochs from Altamira.

The hare (*Lepus europæus*) is a very shy but also an amusing creature because of its mimetic behaviour. To approach it close enough to obtain good shots of its private habits and pattern of behaviour requires sound knowledge of this animal and a great deal of patience. But this effort will be rewarded by interesting pictures of the hare cleaning its paws, for example, or in a listening attitude, as shown opposite. Equipment: 200 mm telephoto lens; speed 1/125 sec.; aperture f 8; film Kodachrome II.

the animals hunted. Although hunting sometimes still requires much physical effort, the risk run by the hunter has virtually vanished and, by the same token, the game he hunts now no longer has anything like a fair chance. Thus hunting has lost much of its challenge and glory, and as a sport in its present form it is hardly likely to be tolerated for more than a few decades beyond our present time.

This situation is aptly highlighted in the words of Oliver G. Pike, the naturalist and photographer: 'In August, one of the foxes disappeared. It was hunted and killed by those gallant ladies and gentlemen who call it sport to chase and torture a small animal with forty well trained hounds, then when it is exhausted and almost run to death, to allow its enemies to tear it to pieces. But they tell us that the fox enjoys it all, and of course they ought to know!' (*Nature and Camera*, Focal Press, 1943.)

In the future, except when in an extreme case the selective hunting of a particular species becomes necessary, no one will dare think of taking an animal's life in its natural habitat.

There is nothing more distressing than to learn that a race of living creatures has become extinct, that a certain species has disappeared from the face of the earth. Killing will have to be restricted to animals bred for slaughter, while the trigger-happy marksman will have to content himself with shooting at artificially animated moving targets–electronic gadgets to simulate the headlong rush of the startled rabbit or the erratically swerving flight of the woodcock.

The wildlife photographer, though not in pursuit of game for the sake of killing or capture, has inherited with this hunting instinct a keen taste for individual effort, for sustained action, for the thrill of discovery. In his confrontation with the animal or bird that he is trying to portray he is striving also to regain man's long-lost confidence. This is the feeling that is uppermost in the wildlife photographer's mind–this determined quest for contact with the living creatures that inhabit nature, this need to understand and love them.

The desire to capture images, to preserve for himself and for those who share his life the record of this fleeting contact, has existed almost since man first

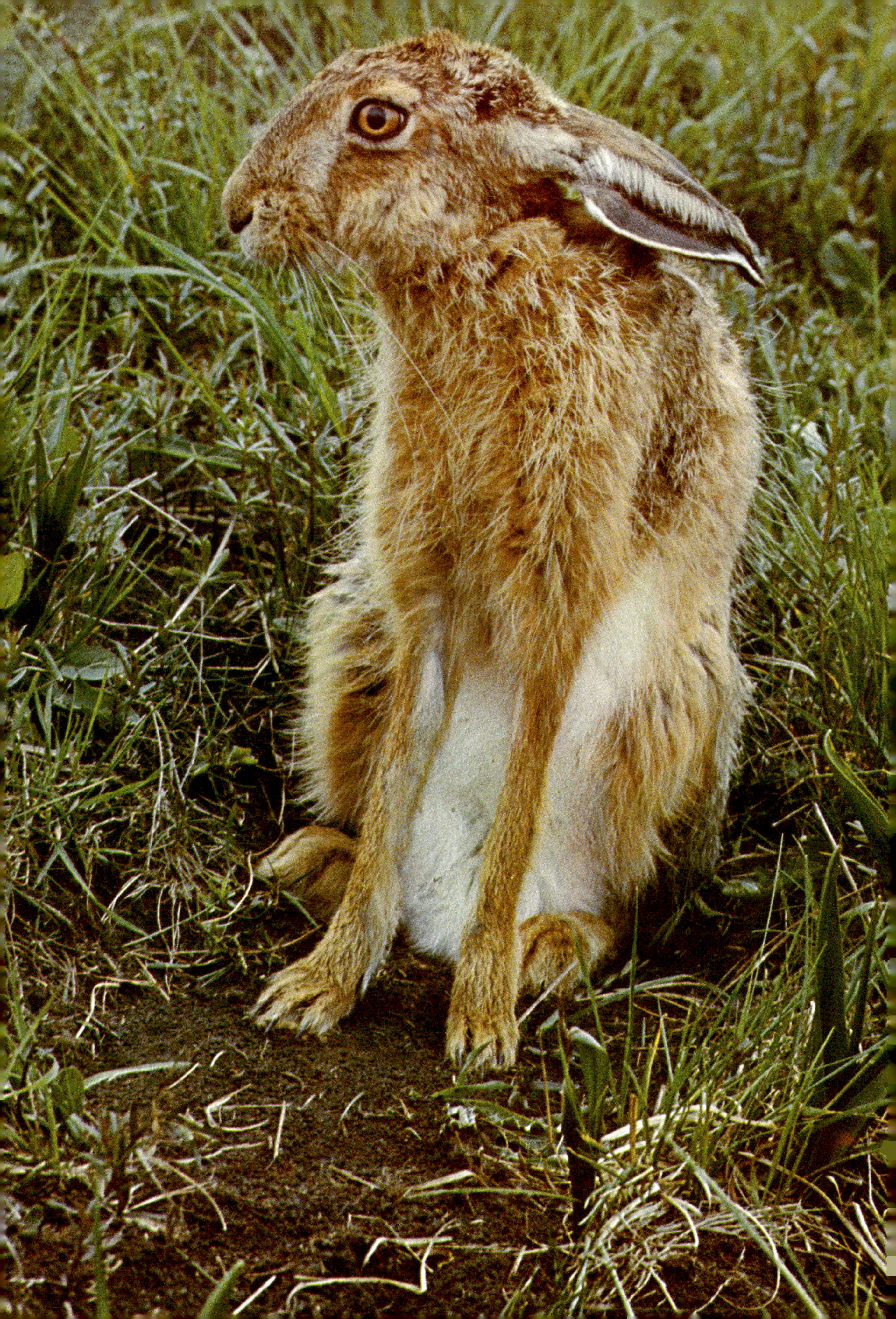

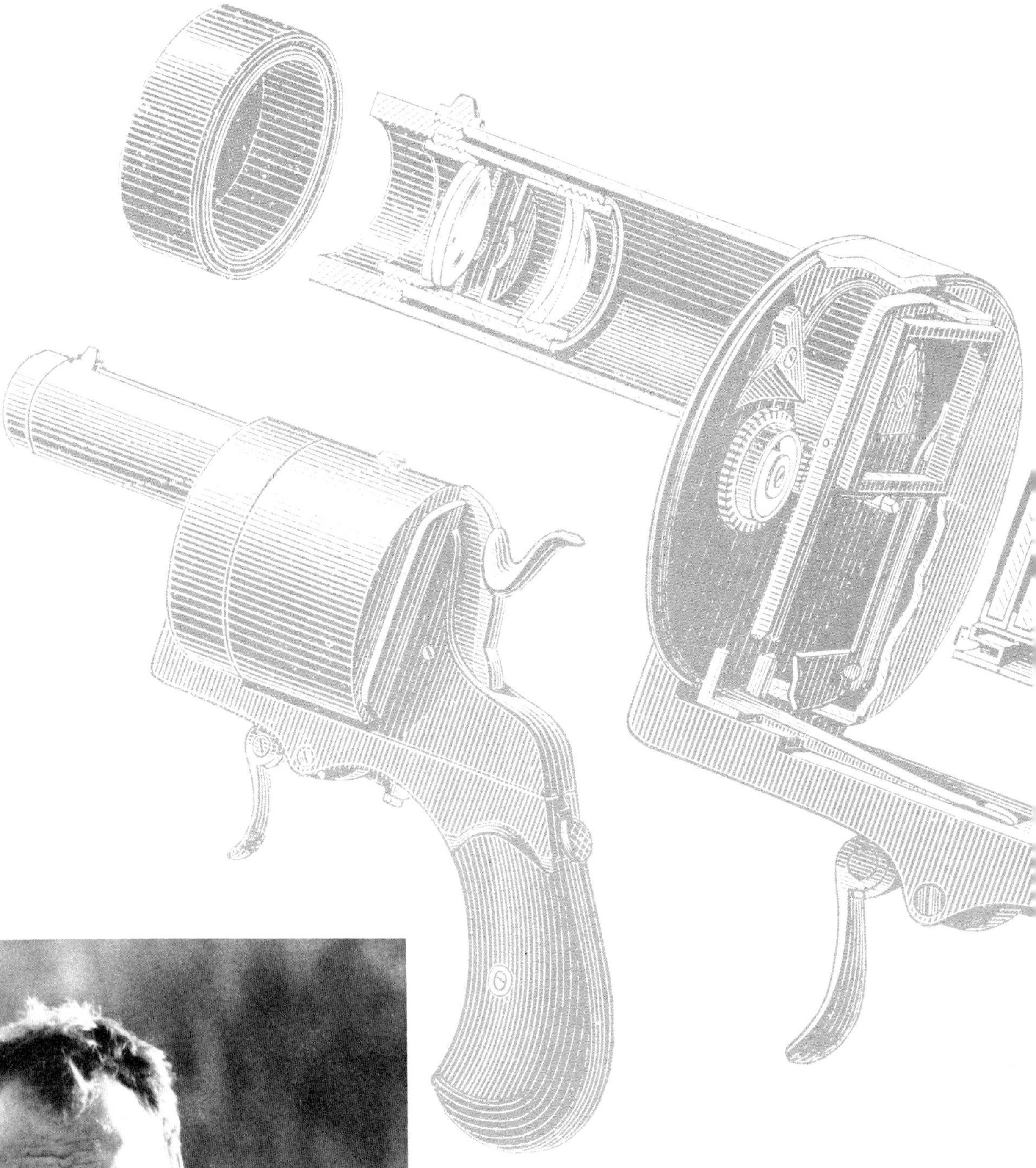

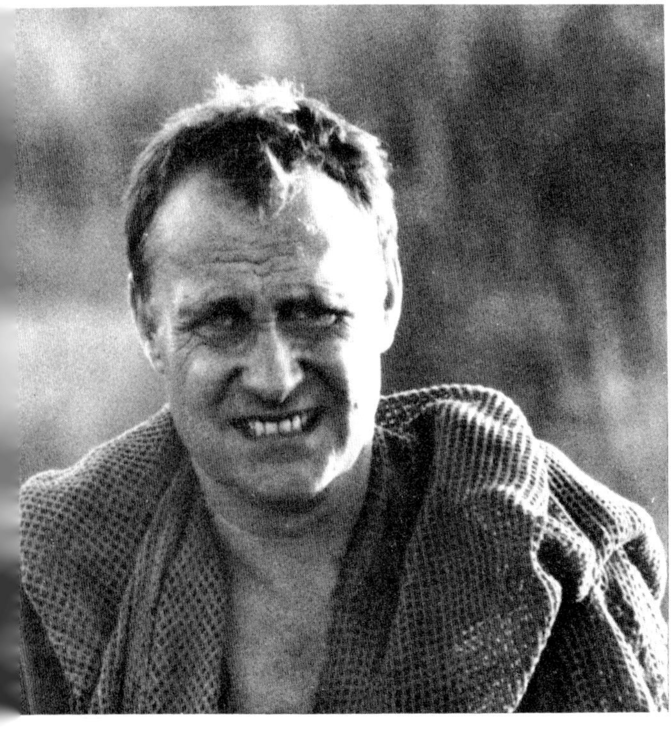

Ever since the early days of photography, enthusiasts have striven to dispense with clumsy wooden cameras and to use convenient lightweight quick-action devices for obtaining 'dynamic' pictures. An early example is this 'pistol camera' dating from 1885.

The authors of this book in 'field get-up': J.-M. Baufle (left) and J.-P. Varin (right).

emerged upon the scene. The most striking manifestations of this feeling are undoubtedly the famous cave paintings of Altamira and Lascaux. These paintings were in part also motivated by the desire of early man, that naked denizen of the forests, to become better acquainted with his equal: the animal. By painting the permanent, immobile images of those spirited and dangerous creatures on the hard rock surface, the cave dweller may have been seeking to protect himself from them; and this instinct of possession, this desire to understand, has continued to assert itself through the ages in artistic productions of astonishing diversity: sculptures, tapestries, paintings, etc.

Some photographs of live animals taken in a zoo in 1870 marked the somewhat peculiar beginnings of wildlife photography. Because of the very slow speed of the photographic plates used in those days, the animal had to be

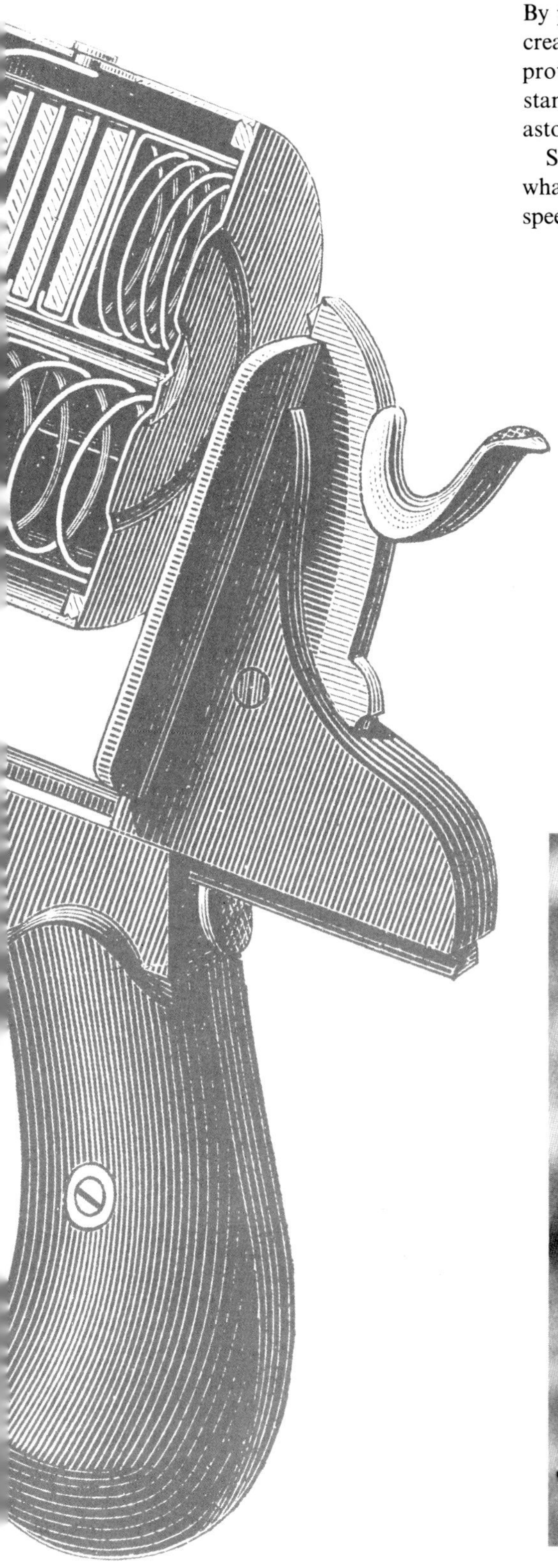

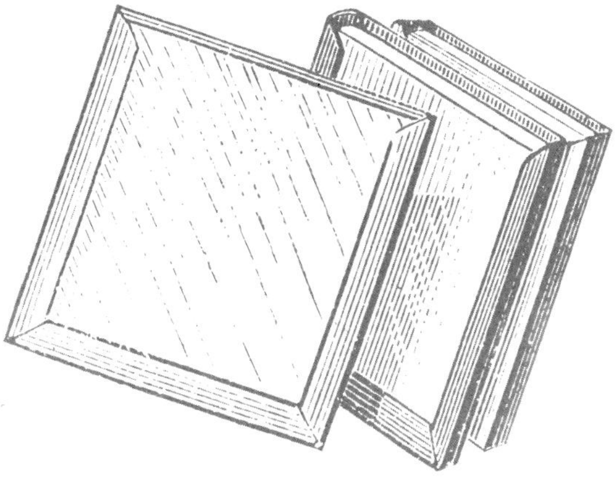

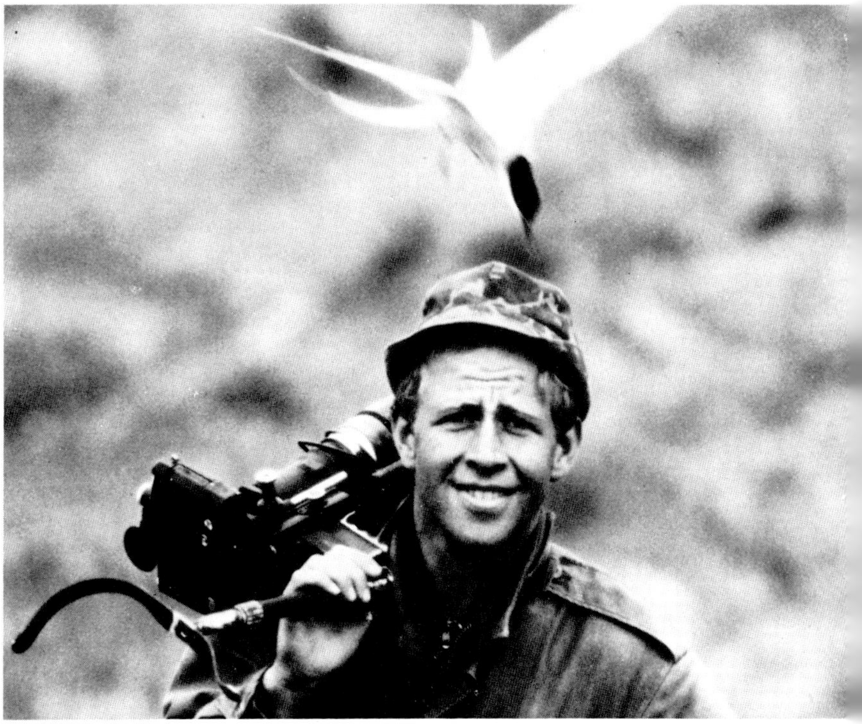

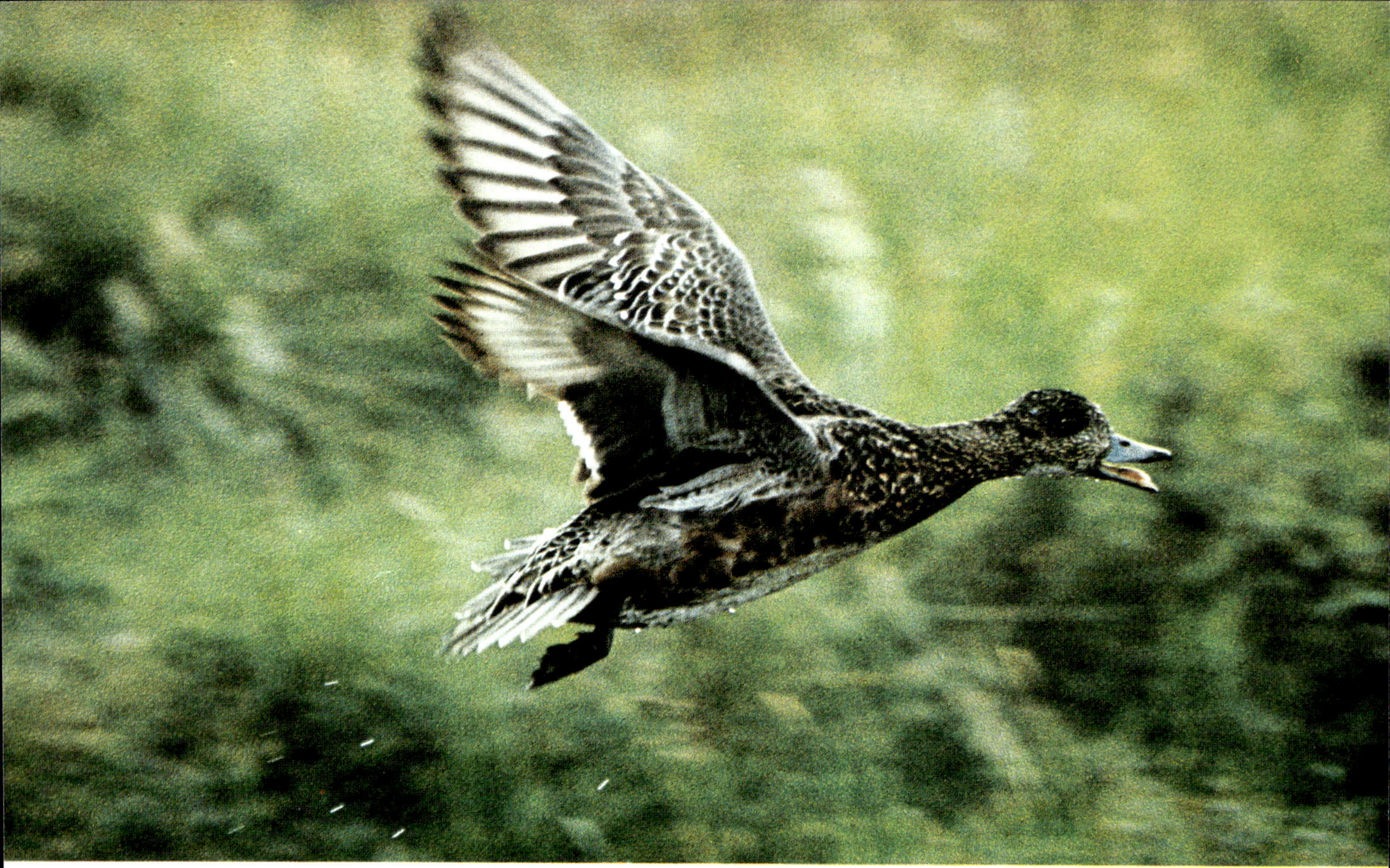

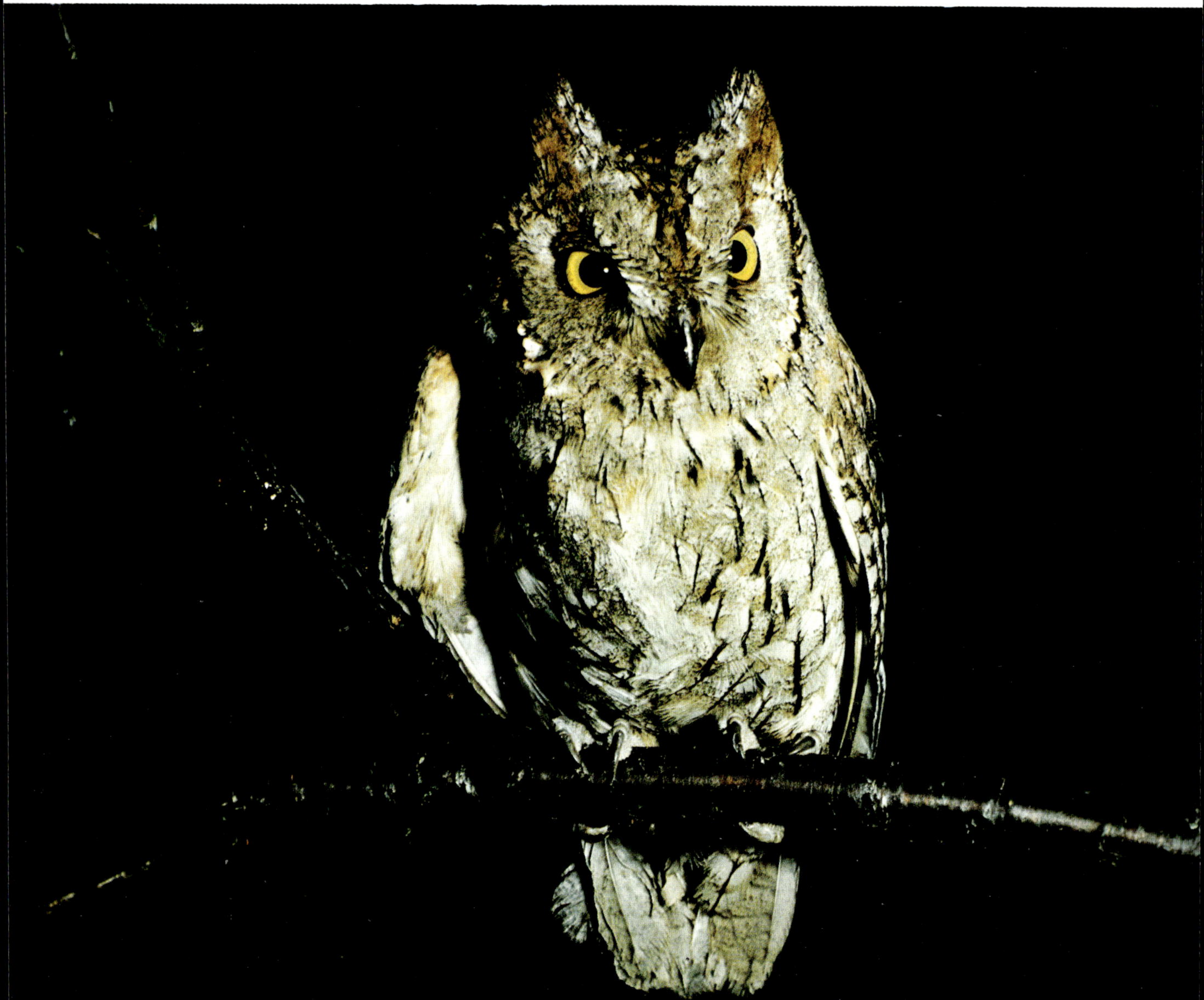

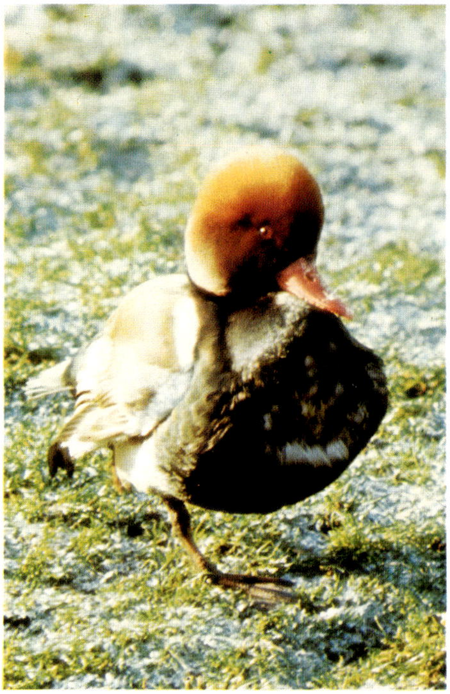

A good photograph shows its subject in a certain suitable way that reflects also something of the photographer's own personality. The camera is merely the technical means to the end: to capture fleeting impressions of scenes or events of animal life.
The horned owl (*Otus scops*), featured opposite, is a nocturnal creature and should be pictured within the context of its natural environment—the night.
Equipment: 35 mm camera with 105 mm focal length; electronic flash.
Top left: The impression of dynamic flight of this widgeon (*Anas penelope*) is enhanced by the blurred background caused by the movement of the camera in tracking the subject.
Equipment: 35 mm camera with rangefinder and 135 mm focal length; speed 1/500 sec.; aperture f 5·6; film Kodachrome II.

Above: Ducks are birds which can be observed in cold winter weather, and this red-crested pochard (*Netta rufina*) is quite at home in surroundings with hoar-frost on the ground.
Equipment: 35 mm camera with 250 mm focal length; speed 1/125 sec.; aperture f 8.

surprised and made to 'freeze' with fright by a long blast of a whistle—literally petrified for several seconds!

In 1875 Muybridge, an Englishman, using complex and expensive equipment, obtained the first instantaneous shots of a horse in gallop. The series of pictures produced by him demonstrated the scientific value of this method of photographic observation, which revealed facts that the human eye had failed to detect.

After the development of Jansen's 'photographic revolver', originally intended for celestial photography in astronomy, the French physiologist E.-J. Marey invented, in 1882, a very advanced 'photographic rifle', which is regarded as one of the forerunners of the motion picture camera. Designed for wildlife photography, this apparatus could, for example, be used to obtain pictures of a galloping horse or a bird in flight at a rate of twelve shots per second with an exposure time of 1/700 second. From the photographs taken in this way small wax models were made which, when placed in a special revolving viewer, gave a lifelike reproduction of the animal's or bird's movements.

That period, so fertile in technical research and practical applications, marked the real beginnings of the methodical exploration of nature with the aid of photography.

In 1893, Louis Boutan obtained, in the Bay of Banyuls, the first successful underwater photographs, and in 1907 Dr P. Gromier brought back from an African safari a series of pictures of animals in the completely wild state.

At about the same time the famous British photographer, Oliver G. Pike, who was the first to take up nature photography professionally, made a film entitled *In the Kingdom of the Birds* and a series of outstanding pictures of bird behaviour. His work, which was difficult because of its very novelty and the experiments that he was constantly trying out and striving to perfect in the course of his fieldwork, met with considerable success. In fact, the British school of wildlife photography was to dominate a substantial part of the first half of the twentieth century.

In that heroic period these men had to carry heavy, bulky equipment on their backs through remote and desolate country and up dizzily steep slopes in order to get near enough to a bird or animal for a good picture.

The use of large-picture formats and relatively short-focus lenses required this close approach. The pictures obtained by such methods, though somewhat static in character, are in terms of quality and precision among the finest of their kind.

In 1930, with the advent of the Leica miniature camera and 35 mm photography, the German school of wildlife photography, freed from physical restraints, concentrated on the photography of movement and was among the first to experiment with macrophotography.

It was not, however, until 1950, when Jean Dragesco developed a modern version of the 'photographic rifle', that the French, Belgians and Swiss took up this photographic challenge in earnest.

Since then, F. Merlet, G. Dhuit and younger photographers have proved that a love of nature and a passion for photography (and cinematography) could abolish the invisible barriers which had hitherto separated the various schools of photography and give us even finer pictures of the world in which we live.

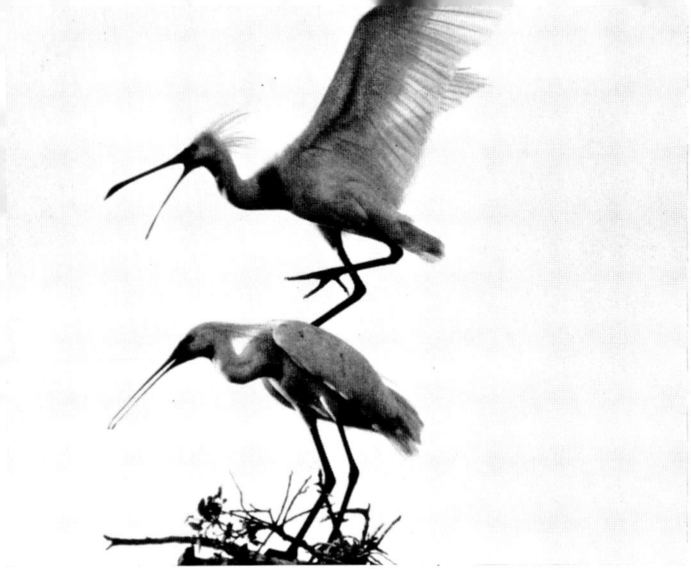
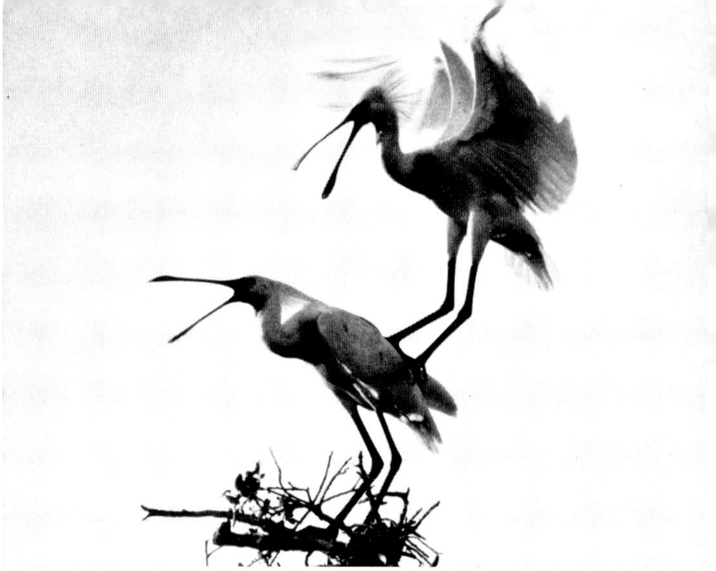
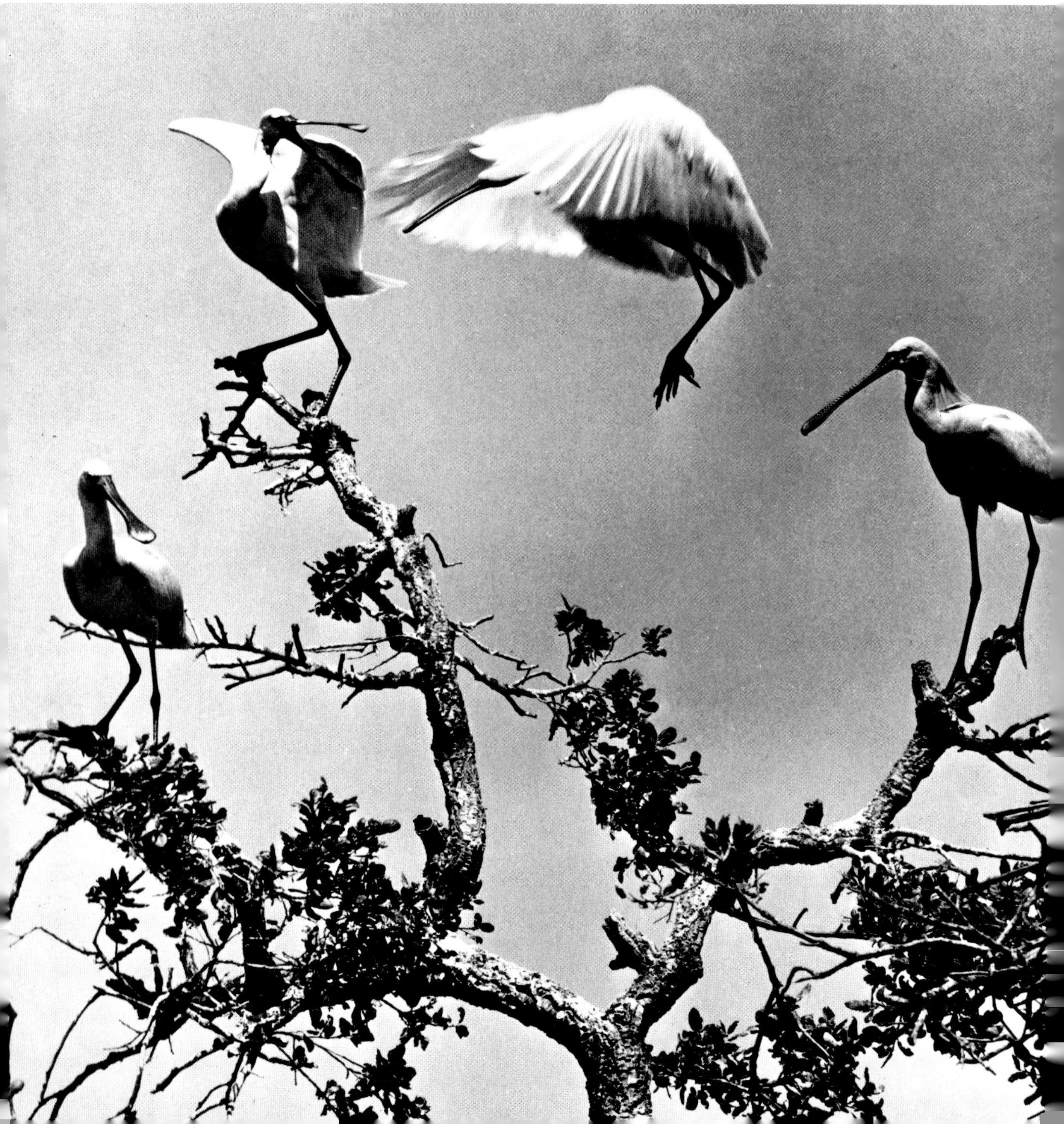

a science and a sport

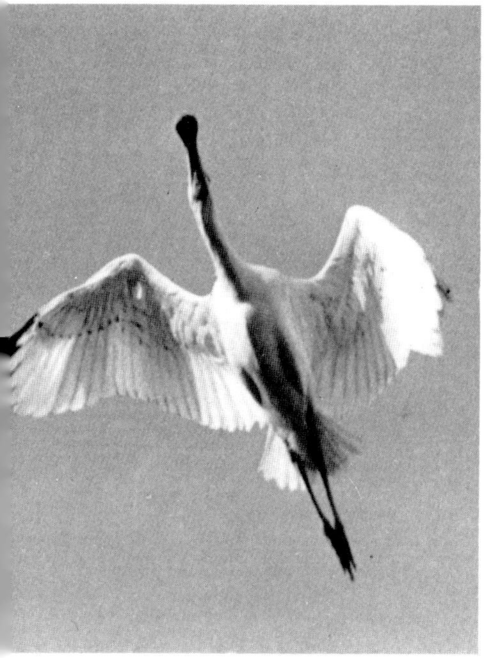

Many movements of birds or animals are so fast that the human eye cannot observe them in detail. Photography can thus be a valuable aid to the biologist engaged in animal behaviour study. The picture on the left illustrates various head and beak attitudes of the spoonbill (*Platalea leucorodia*) as a prelude to mating.
Above: Young spoonbill with full-grown plumage performing its first flight. These photographs were obtained over a period of several days from a tower 12 feet high installed near a cork oak.
Equipment: 35 mm photosniper camera and 6 cm × 6 cm (2¼ square) reflex camera.

The animal is a very different creature from ourselves. The world in which it dwells belongs only to it: it does not see with the same eyes nor hear with the same ears as we do. We must therefore take care not to judge its reactions in terms of our own; not only its senses but also its needs are different from ours. Instinct does indeed form the basis of its knowledge, but its behaviour is nevertheless more complex than what would merely be necessary for solving simple problems such as feeding, reproduction, self-protection and resting.

We have only just begun to know and understand the animal's universe. The systematic study of living creatures, their classification, has long been the naturalists' chief pride. It still forms one of the firmest corner-stones of the 'natural sciences', but biology as it used to be taught at school has left many of us with memories of a rather dull and tiresome subject. Even the most brilliant teacher too often failed to bring us close to nature, imprisoned as we were within the four walls of the classroom, where we inspected rows of dusty jars containing preserved specimens or examined poorly-mounted stuffed birds and animals or peered at mysterious charts and diagrams. How could these lifeless abstractions conjure up the beauty of the animal world for us?

As a result of systematic study, living creatures have been classified into an ascending scale which culminates in man. But comparative anatomy has to rely on so many other sciences in order to assign to each creature its precise place in this system that it is still an incomplete branch of investigation, and discoveries continue to be made.

Such discoveries tend to proceed in a haphazard and random manner, for nature is a vast assembly of creatures large and small, in which disorder and disproportion appear to reign. But this is so in appearance only. Actually, all creatures are intimately linked to one another and to their habitat, i.e. the natural surroundings in which they live.

The new science of ecology aims at gaining a better understanding of the behaviour and reflexes of an animal in a particular environment or in a specific situation. Nowadays it involves more than observations and routine experiments conducted in the laboratory: the animals are also studied in their natural habitat, that is, within the complex and fragile equilibrium that enables them to survive.

The still photograph and the motion picture are outstandingly useful aids in carrying out these field studies. With their unobtrusive and reliable techniques they provide a high degree of objectivity. Their function is not confined to checking or observation. They also constitute remarkable means of exploration and investigation in conditions where the human eye is incapable of analysing the phenomena, either because these are too rapid or too slow or because they cannot be seen in ordinary visible light.

And we consider that the naturalists, who sometimes assail the photographers with the reproach that they disturb the animals and cause damage just for the sake of getting a good picture, have their faults too – particularly their failure to learn photography. By the richness and truthfulness of the pictures it can provide, photography has in recent years made a major contribution to arousing in people an awareness of the importance of nature conservation and wildlife protection. So if only the naturalists would become photographers! The technical rules they would have to learn and apply are really not so very complex. And if only the research scientists would not take refuge in the remote privacy of their laboratories, as though nature were a museum with specimens so delicate that it must remain inviolate! For proper study of animal behaviour, those scientists should be the first in the field: through their knowledge and their respect for the environment they would also be the first to get good pictures.

The red uakari (*Cacajao cacajao*), a South American monkey, moves about in the treetops with incredible agility, leaping from tree to tree by making huge deliberate dives into space. It can sit delicately balanced on a thin branch for hours on end. Its curiously bald head is embellished by its bright red facial area.
Equipment: 35 mm reflex camera with 250 mm focal length and 6 cm × 6 cm reflex camera with 80 mm focal length.

In the last century the reproduction of photographs was still awkward and expensive, the journeys undertaken by naturalists and explorers were difficult and dangerous: to make the general public acquainted with the world of nature, they showed them collections of specimens – useful reference objects and certainly essential to comparative study. But in modern times people are broadening their minds more and more. To rouse and hold their interest, they must be made to share an understanding of this live environment by being made almost physically aware of it.

Since the experience of others can only be advantageous in achieving a rapid initiation, there is nothing to be ashamed of in going to books to learn the elements of photographic technique and the basic notions that can give guidance in discovering nature.

The observation and study of animals in captivity are also very rewarding, and, whatever the purists may think, photographing animals in zoological gardens is an excellent training school. Since zoos are usually situated in or near cities, they provide a convenient means of getting close to any particular species of animal and judging its true size, which otherwise is liable to come as something of a surprise when we turn from our books to the real thing. Also, there are then no problems of identification, as might well exist if you have to rely for your information on some too-concise handbook with illustrations consisting of none-too-good drawings accompanied by inadequate captions. And the thought of some day perhaps actually coming face to face in the freedom of nature with the species of animal which one has previously observed in a somewhat sad tête-à-tête in a zoo can only heighten the desire to photograph it in other surroundings – its own habitat.

In the zoo, too, you can learn to develop your reflexes, to react quickly; you can compare, test and perfect your equipment; and the art of composing your picture and acquiring a sense of light cannot be learned from books alone: these things require intensive practice on live subjects.

At any season of the year and any time of day the zoo is a good place for familiarizing yourself with particular features of the camera, the lenses or the films you will be using. By trial and error you can avoid subsequent failures due to use of unsuitable film, inadequate equipment or lack of experience in handling it. With this training you will later be able to choose the right method swiftly and unerringly, so that you can, in a matter of seconds, get your shot of an unrepeatable scene. Remember that every picture is unique, that even under strictly similar conditions there is never an exact repetition, and that in ten years' time the picture will still have preserved its value.

For testing your skill you should not wait only for the rarest photographic opportunities. When you choose an animal on which to practise, you will soon perceive, when you examine your negatives, that even the most powerful telephoto lens does not possess the magic powers that are commonly attributed to it.

By dint of training and constant practice, always correcting and improving

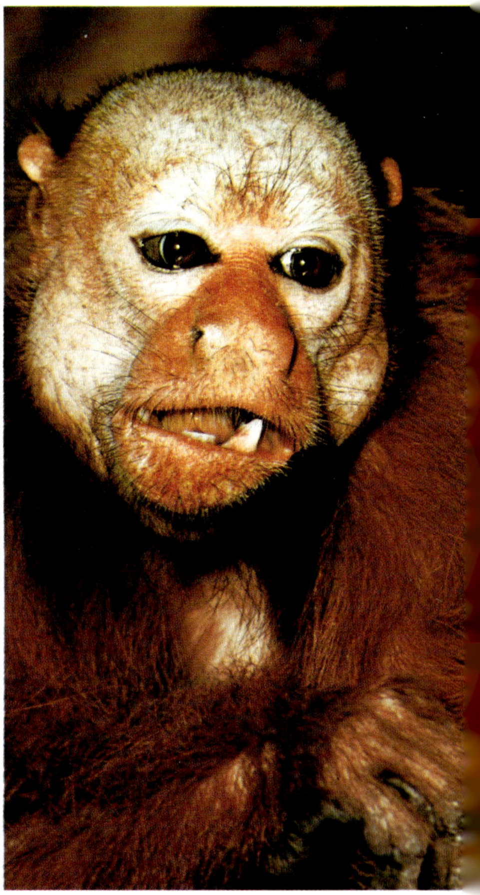

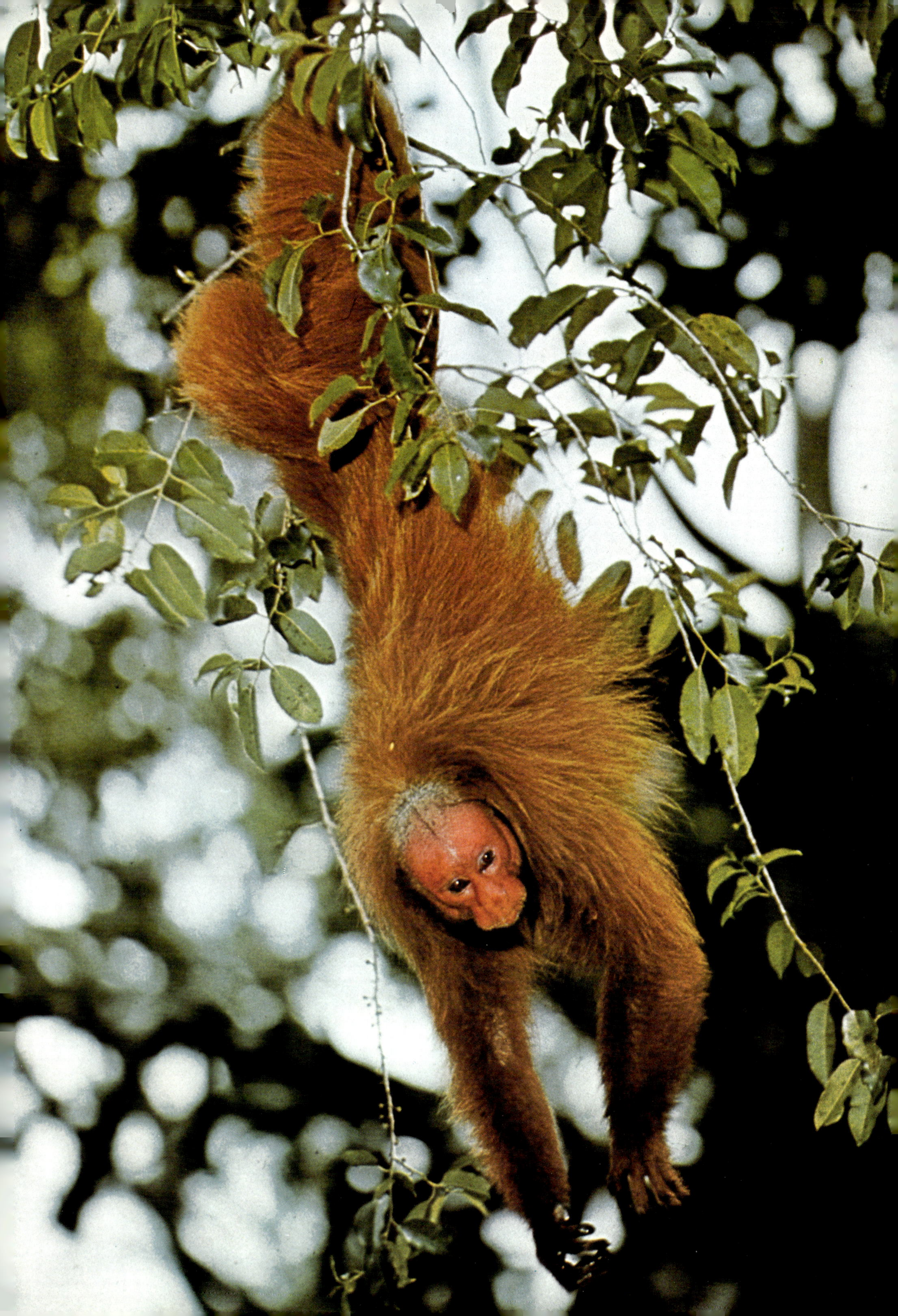

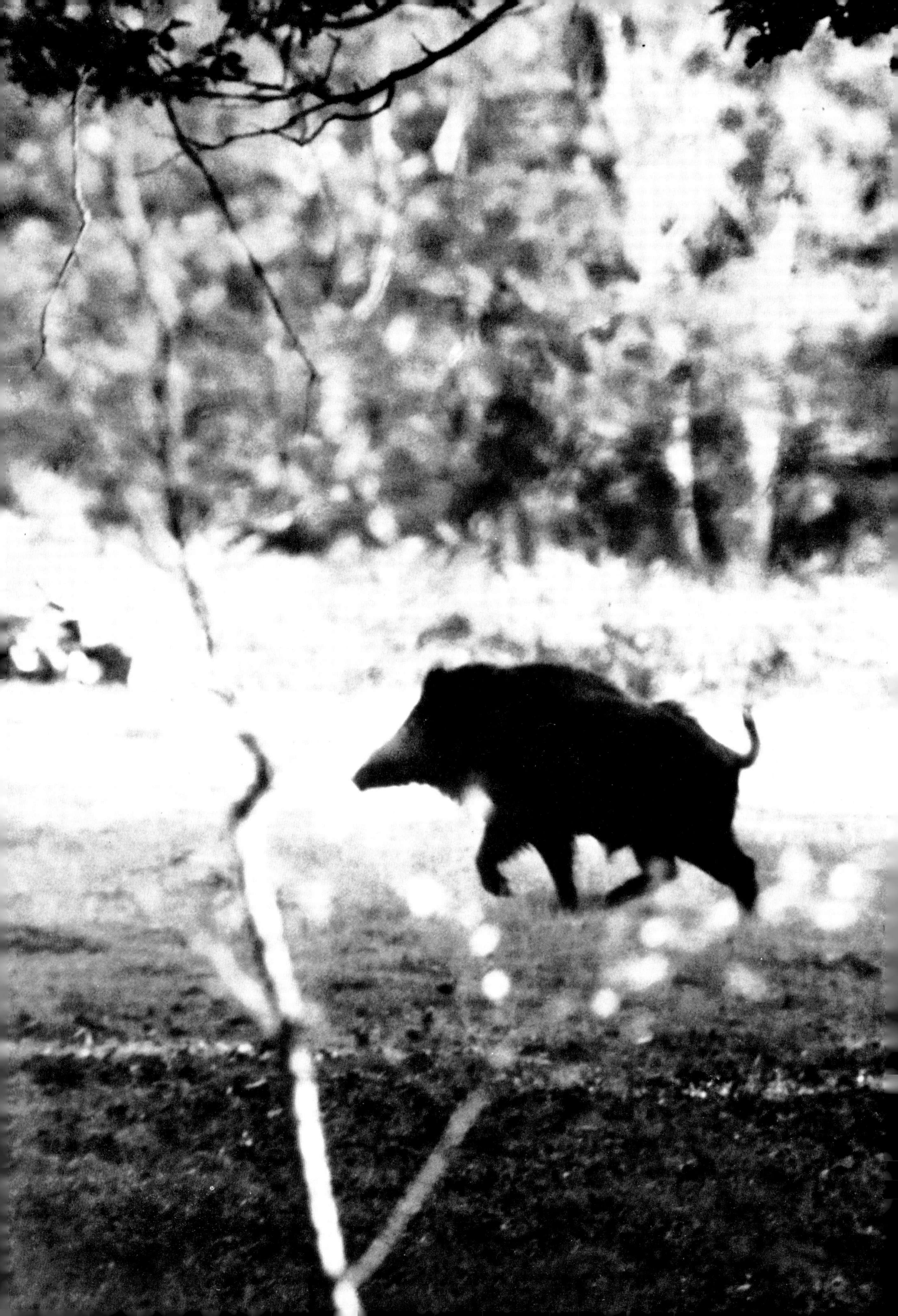

The wild boar (*Sus scrofa*) is one of the largest animals found in Europe, very savage and with no precise habits. It is very difficult to take by surprise, and meeting it is largely a matter of luck. In a locality where fresh traces of boars are found, it is sometimes possible to photograph them from a hide by attracting them to bait laid in carefully chosen places. But a good deal of patience is needed, and the outcome will always remain doubtful. The boar shown in this picture was photographed from concealment in undergrowth.
Equipment: 35 mm camera with 400 mm telephoto lens; speed 1/125 sec.; aperture f 5·6.

The picture below shows two photographers working on the same subject, one with a lens of 1200 mm focal length in order to get close-up shots of the animal when it stops, the other with a photosniper with a 400 mm lens for securing overall pictures and movement shots.

your efforts, you will become so familiar with the technique that you can forget about it and concentrate on the noble sport itself: seeking out and studying the subjects for your camera and getting good pictures of them.

You should not regard your technical equipment–which will be discussed more fully in another chapter–as all-important. In addition to some essential knowledge of biology and ecology, it is necessary also to possess strength of character and plenty of physical stamina.

To obtain interesting results, photography demands a lot of time and patience anyway, and the practice of this art in combination with nature study requires the photographer to be alert and available at all times (day or night) and anywhere (in the laboratory or in the field). We know quite a few naturalists whose passion for nature has so encroached on their lives that their success has been achieved at the expense of some major domestic upheavals.

Perseverance is necessary through the long nights of vigil in the laboratory waiting, perhaps in vain, for an animal to manifest a particular pattern of behaviour–waiting which can be as exhausting as a long tramp through thick and hostile forests. But physical endurance is something that has to be acquired in the field. You must therefore toughen yourself to stand all climates, all weather conditions, all discomforts, and prepare yourself by one excellent method of training: walking. Indeed, walking has long been–and for many people still is–man's only means of travelling on land. Quiet and unobtrusive, walking gives you access to almost any type of terrain and any altitude; and, despite the weight of the equipment you have to carry, walking is the only form of locomotion that enables you really to benefit from nature.

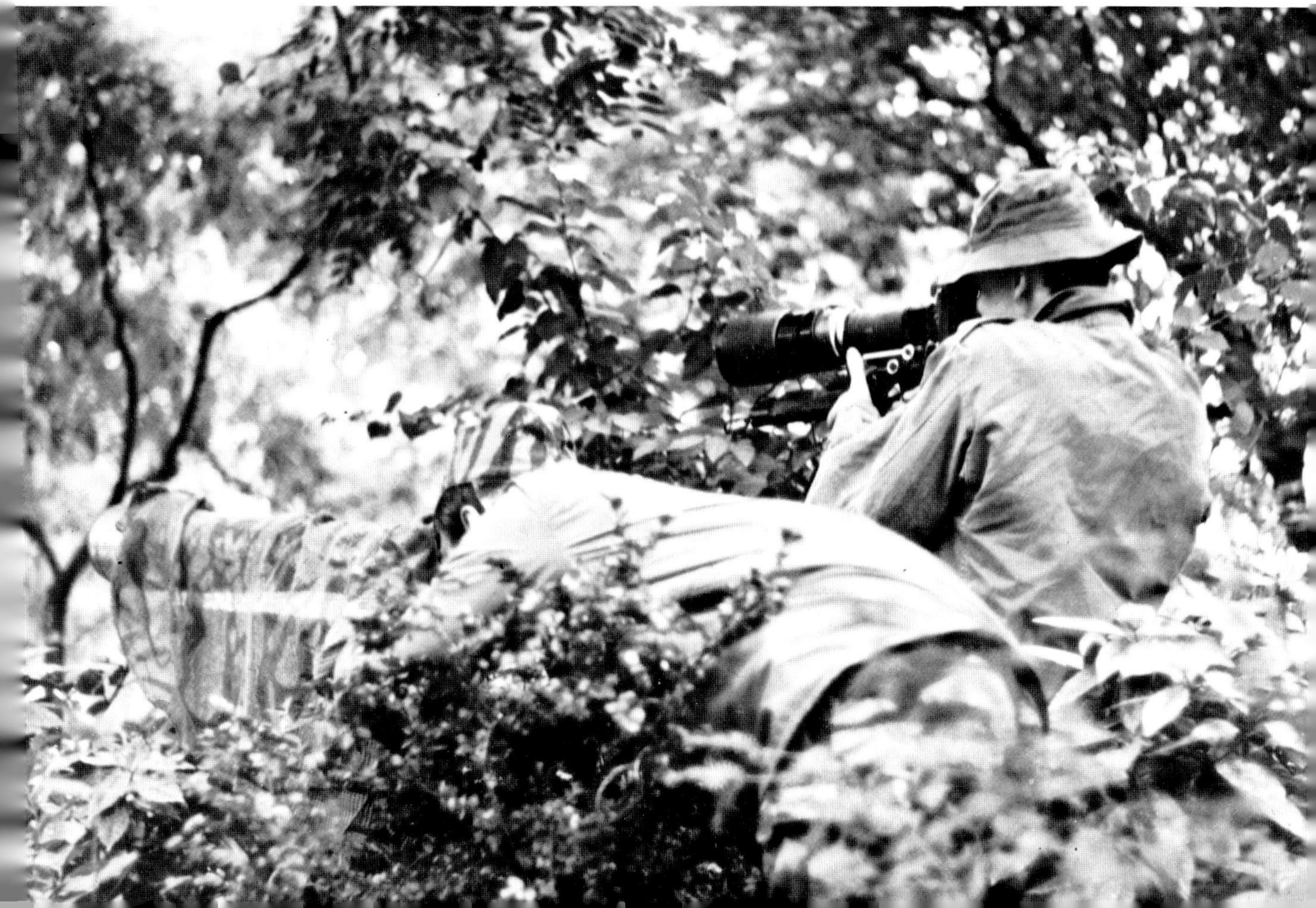

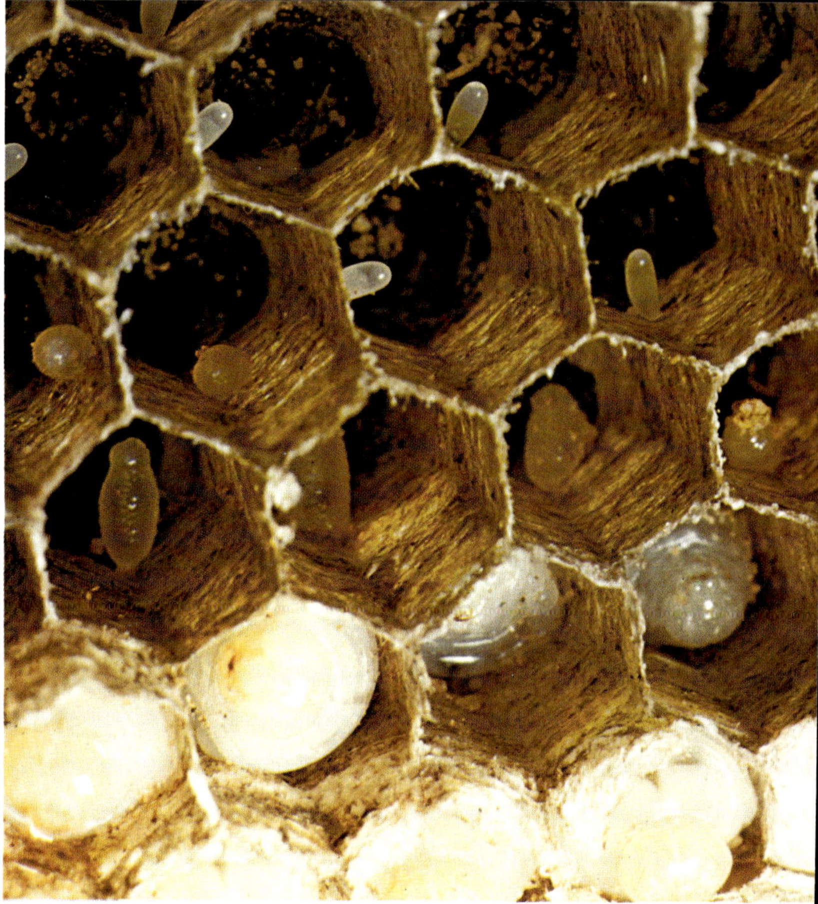

Closely related to the hornet, the wasp *Vespa sylvestris* builds a suspended nest made of a paper-like material (chewed wood fibre) in which it forms hexagonal cells like the wax cells of the honey bee. The eggs are laid in these cells. The upper photograph shows various stages in the development of the brood: the cells at the top contain newly-laid eggs; in the middle are larvae of various ages; the cells at the bottom of the picture contain larvae in process of pupation.

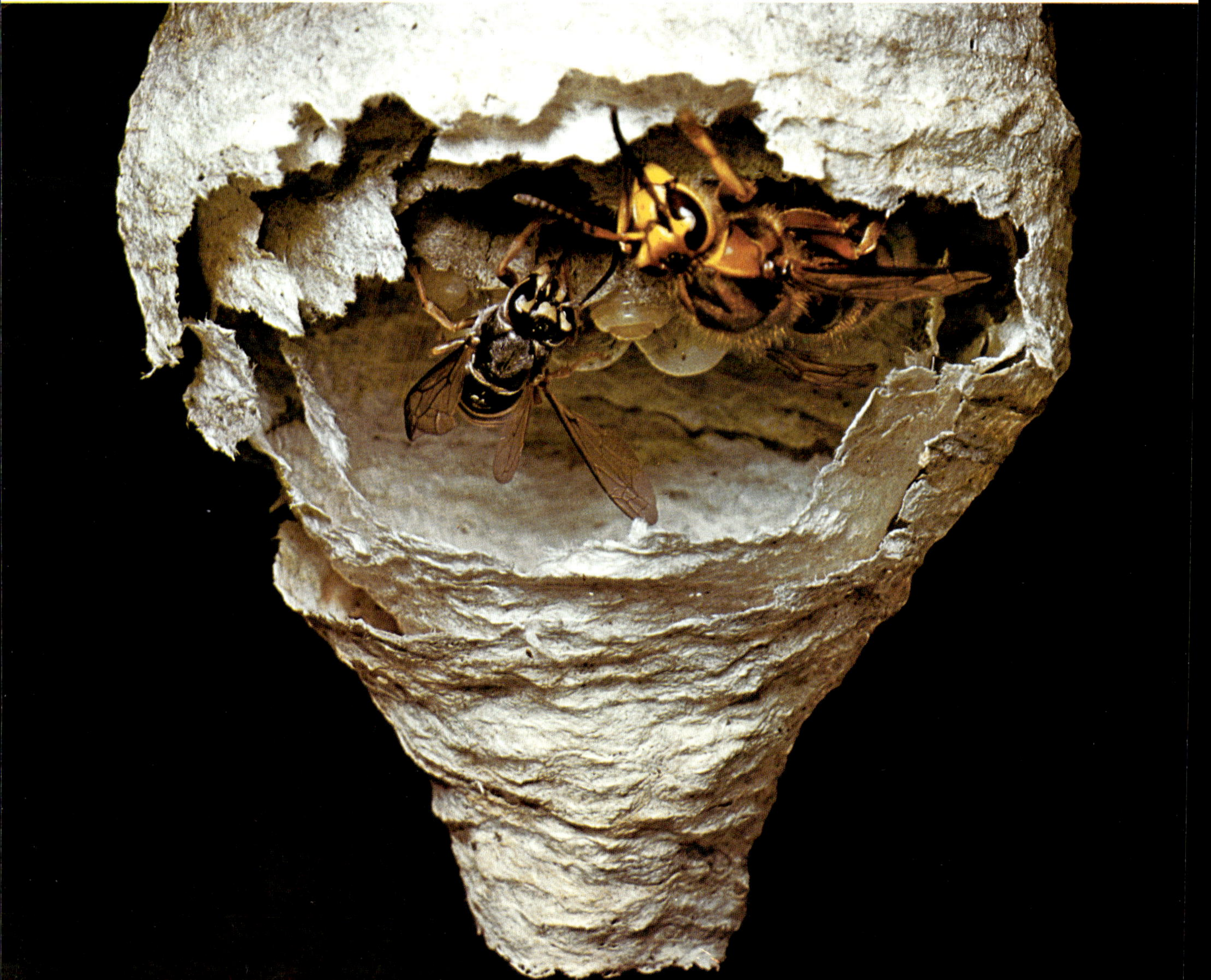

the naturalist

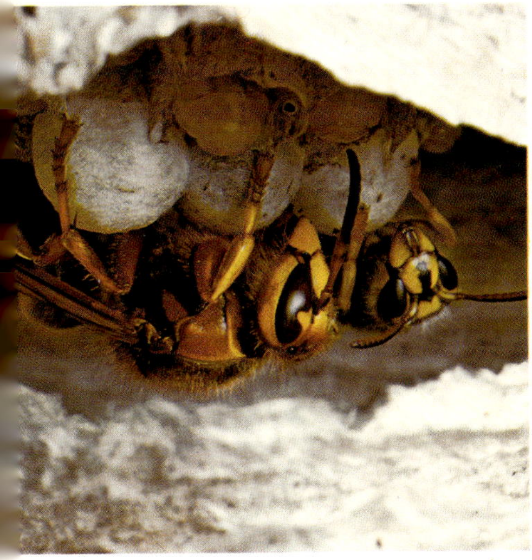

The photograph opposite shows the successive layers of paper which protect the cells from variations in climatic conditions. The entrance to the wasps' nest is at the bottom. To obtain this picture a hole had to be made in one side of the nest.
The photograph above shows another species of wasp (*Vespa omissa bischoffi*), a nest parasite.
Equipment: 35 mm reflex camera with bellows and 50 mm focal length; electronic flash; aperture f 16.

Isolated behind his cases of collected specimens or dashing about in frenzied activity, butterfly net in hand, the naturalist used to be regarded as a simple and naïve creature, a figure of fun.

Nature was, in a sense, 'handed to him on a plate'. Prior to his day, the resources of nature had been utilized only for the cultivation of crops or as a supply of game for hunting. But later, after the forests and the earth's agricultural resources had been intensively exploited, people came to regard this same nature as a place of repose where they could seek refuge from the stresses and strains of city life. Thus they attributed to nature a noble function, a means of healing many a broken heart, of fulfilling many an escapist dream. But you cannot appreciate it truly and deeply if you do not, at some stage, begin to take a closer interest in the things to be found in it and the living creatures that inhabit it. You must ask questions in order to get beyond mere simple curiosity, and observation alone is not enough for obtaining a proper understanding of nature.

You are not born a naturalist. You have to become one by patient effort and steadfast purpose; and before you start any activities in the field, you should study the environment and the climate in which you will be operating, determine every feature of the biotope,* find out about the ties that govern the biological interrelationships. All this is absolutely essential as a preliminary to setting out in search for the animal or bird you intend to photograph. From the network of relations between all these factors emerges the discovery of the food chains that link the plant to the animal world and also interlink the various animal species. For example, certain species of bird feed on insects which destroy plants, but those birds themselves fall victims to small carnivorous mammals or large birds of prey. These predators are in turn killed off and their bodies absorbed by carrion-eating creatures and bacteria. The waste products thus introduced into the soil serve as food for plants. And if you know the moment when the intervention of any particular species in this chain of events occurs, then you can – depending on the animal populations and the plants of which the biotope in question is composed – determine what species of animal you have a chance of meeting and can prepare yourself for that encounter.

*(i.e. the whole set of distinctive factors that make up an animal's environment: living organisms, effects of soil, weather conditions, etc.).

The dung beetle (*Scarabaeus laticollis*) uses the excrement of herbivorous animals to make large balls which it rolls into a spherical shape and then buries in the ground.
Equipment: 6 cm × 6 cm reflex camera with 80 mm focal length and adapter ring; electronic flash.

Right: For concealment from its enemies the stick insect (*Carausius morosus*) has the appearance and colour of the twigs among which it lives. The young stick insects are usually born by parthenogenesis, i.e. without fertilization of the female.
Equipment: 6 cm × 6 cm reflex camera; illumination by incandescent lamp; speed 1/60 sec.; aperture f 11.

While you are extending your knowledge, backed up by your own notes and personal observations, you should be thinking of how you are going to treat the subjects in which you are interested. Although you may not intend actually to specialize, it may be that you will prefer to concentrate on a particular species of animal or bird or on a particular biotope because you feel attracted to it or because you may not have the time or the resources to tackle too vast a range of subjects.

It is not only the larger mammals or rarer birds that merit inclusion in the wildlife photographer's collection. Of course, it may not be so exciting, but even a close study of 10 square yards of open country can be a fascinating experience. And anyway, a single picture such as is often obtained in a chance encounter with some wild creature is by itself hardly a sufficient means whereby the naturalist can communicate his impressions. The setting of the animal in its habitat, re-created by a series of documentary photographs, is as important as the finest portrait of the animal itself. The countryside, plants, flowers, fungi and trees will form the basis for a reasoned synthesis of these pictures. Besides an open eye and a sound knowledge of biological science, the good wildlife photographer will need enthusiasm and patience.

And even more than enthusiasm he must possess confidence–confidence in

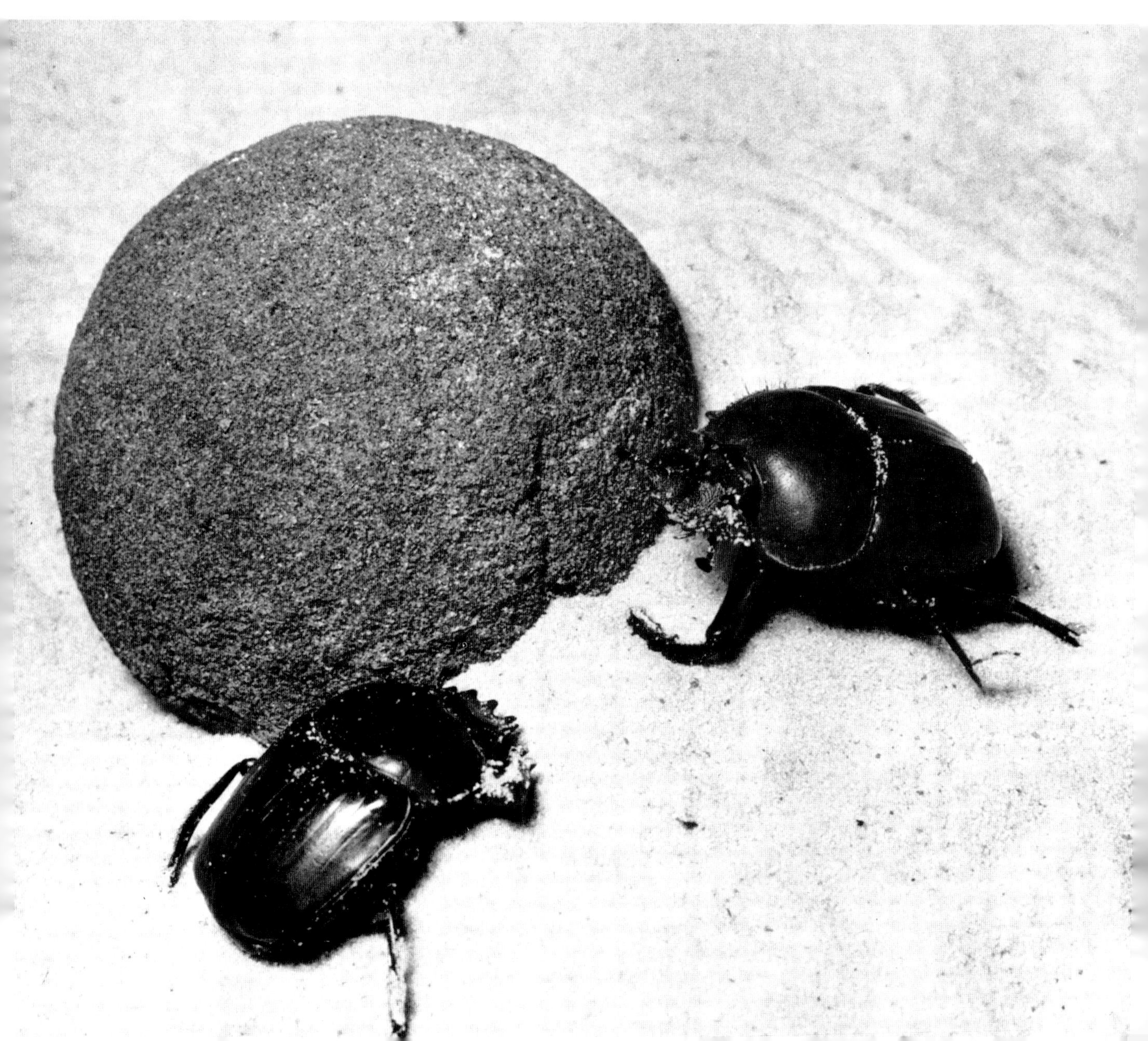

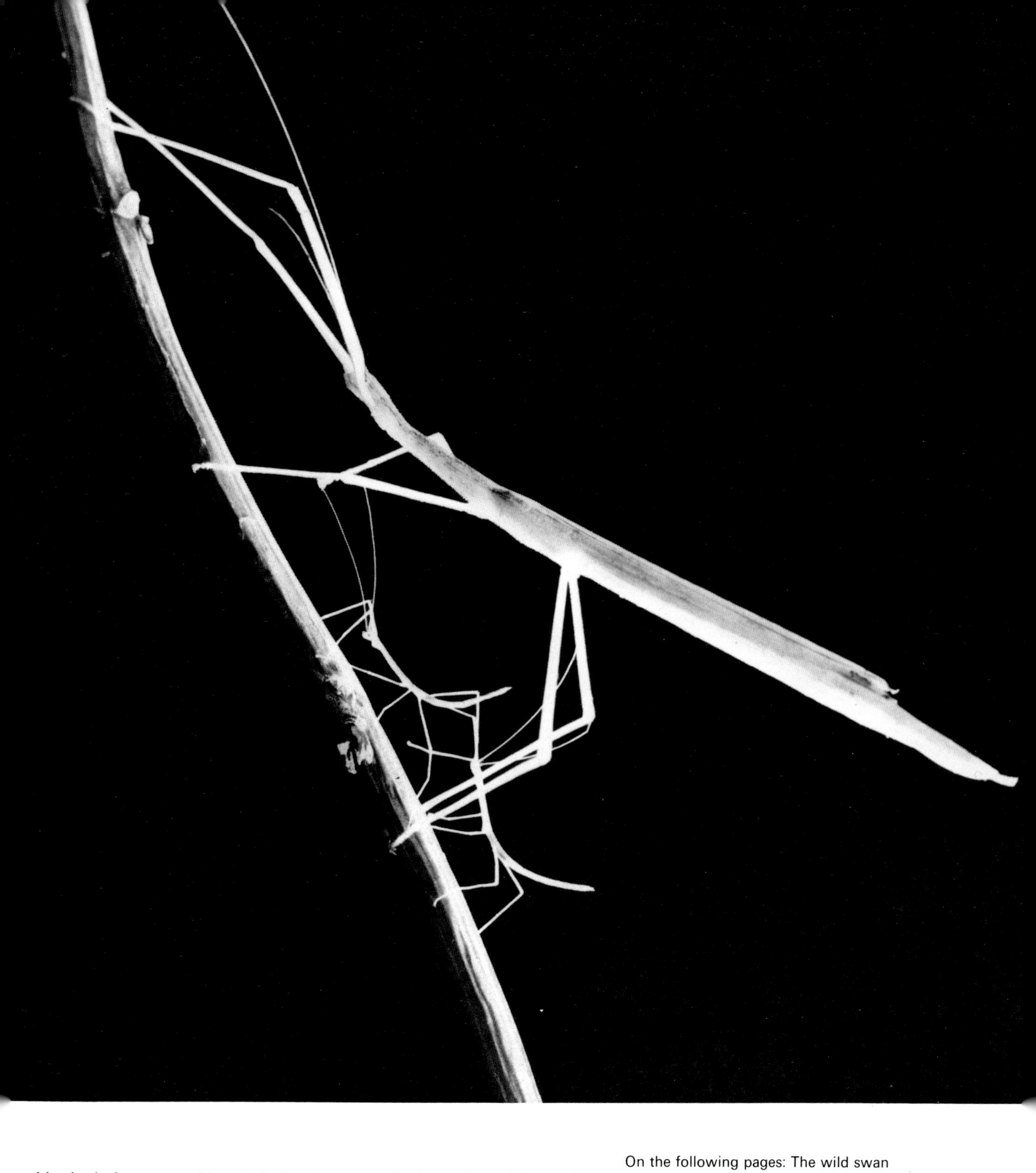

his physical resources, his technical equipment and, above all, confidence with regard to the animal that he means to confront in its territory.

The animal reacts instinctively; it has no notion of your fine sentiments. However, animals in their natural surroundings, when approached with caution so as not to disturb or frighten them, are usually dangerous only when their line of retreat is cut off.

And you must have confidence in your good luck–always an essential ingredient for achieving success in the field.

On the following pages: The wild swan (*Cygnus cygnus*), which has a wing-span of about 6 feet and weighs over 13 lb, lives in northern latitudes. It often nests beside very small pools in the tundra, just large enough for it to alight and take off.
Equipment: 35 mm camera in photosniper mounting, 400 mm focal length; speed 1/250 sec.; aperture f 5·6.

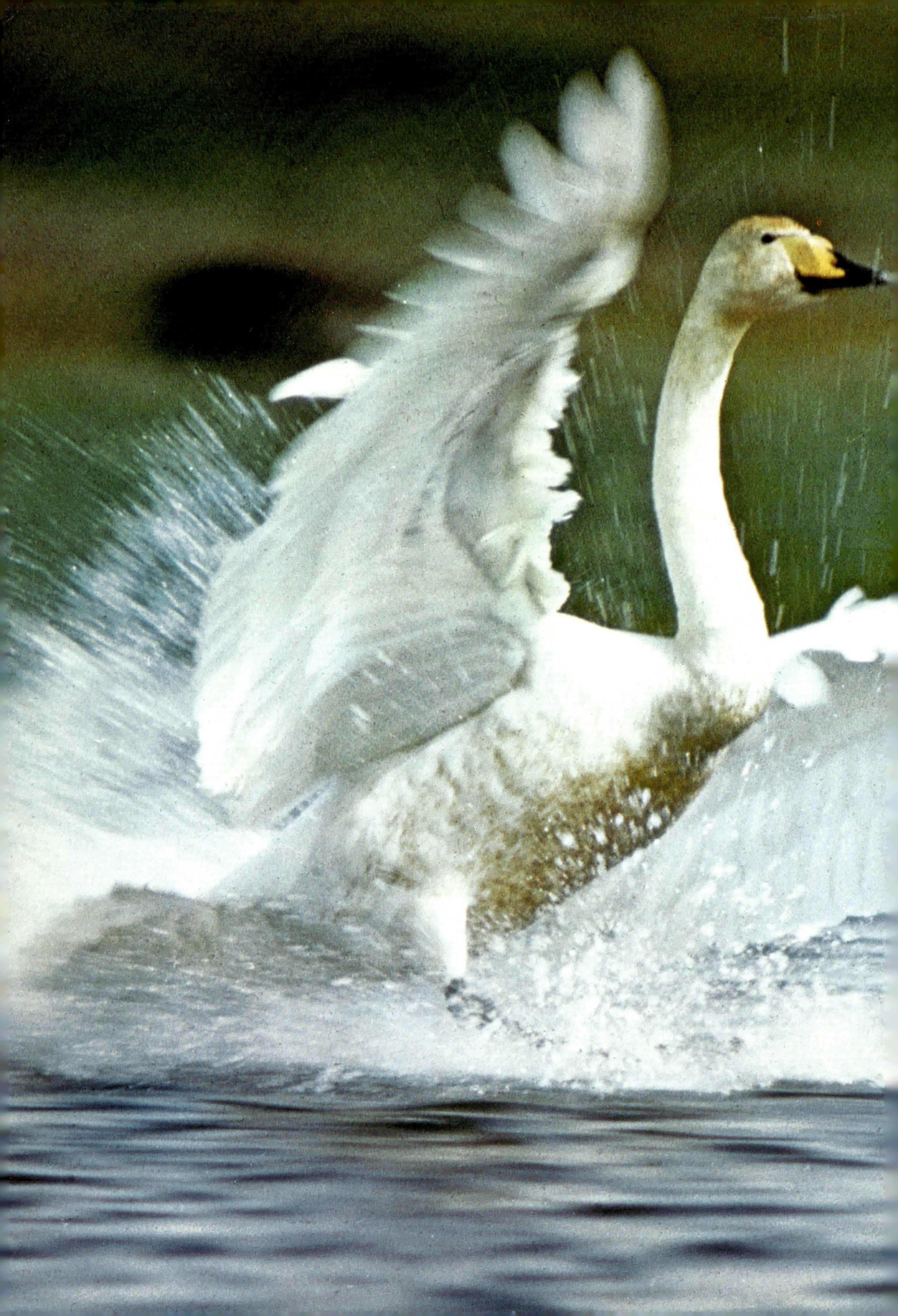

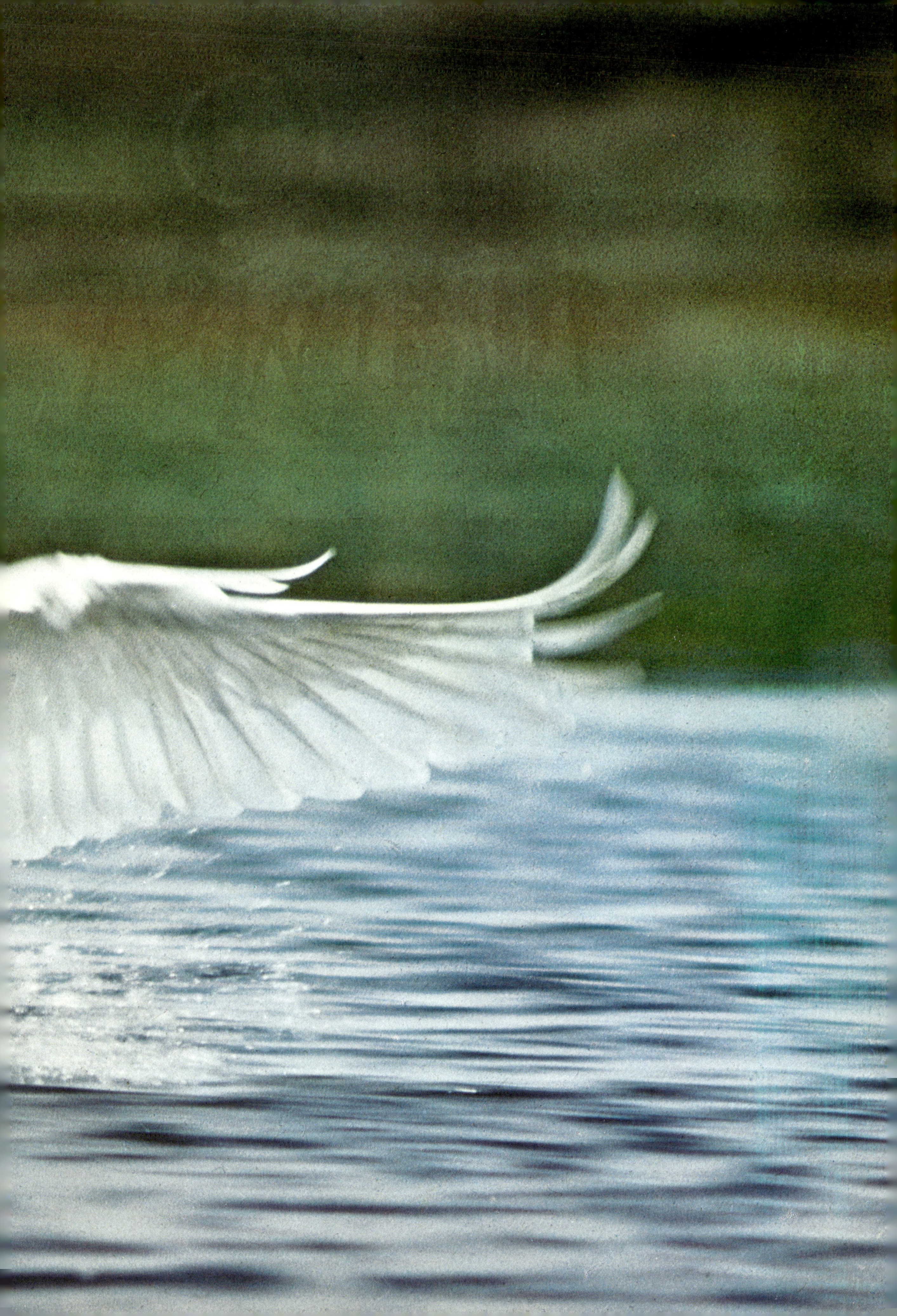

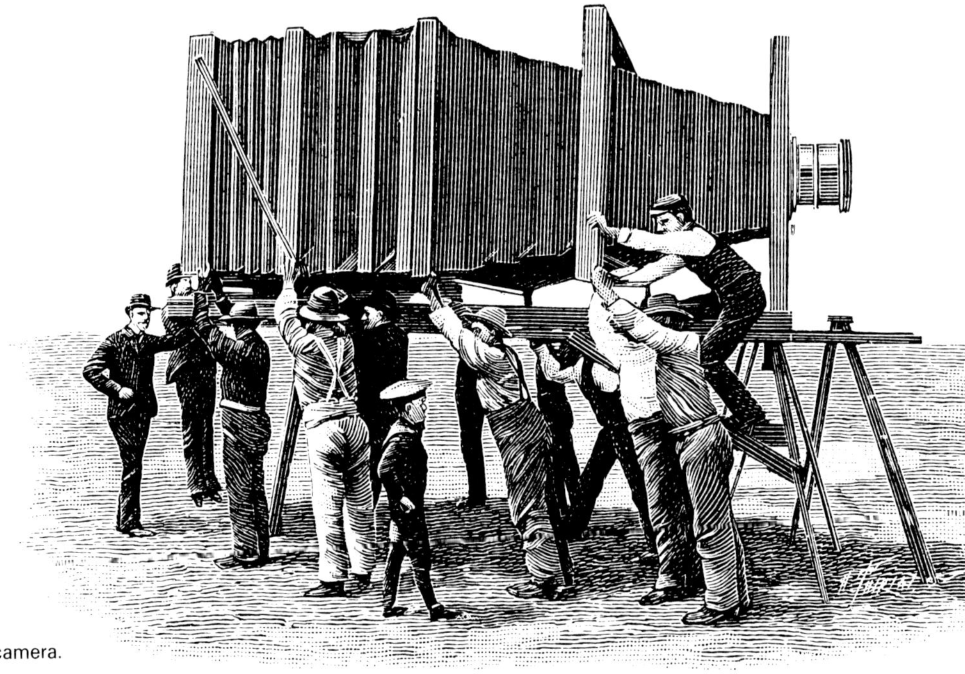

Monster camera.

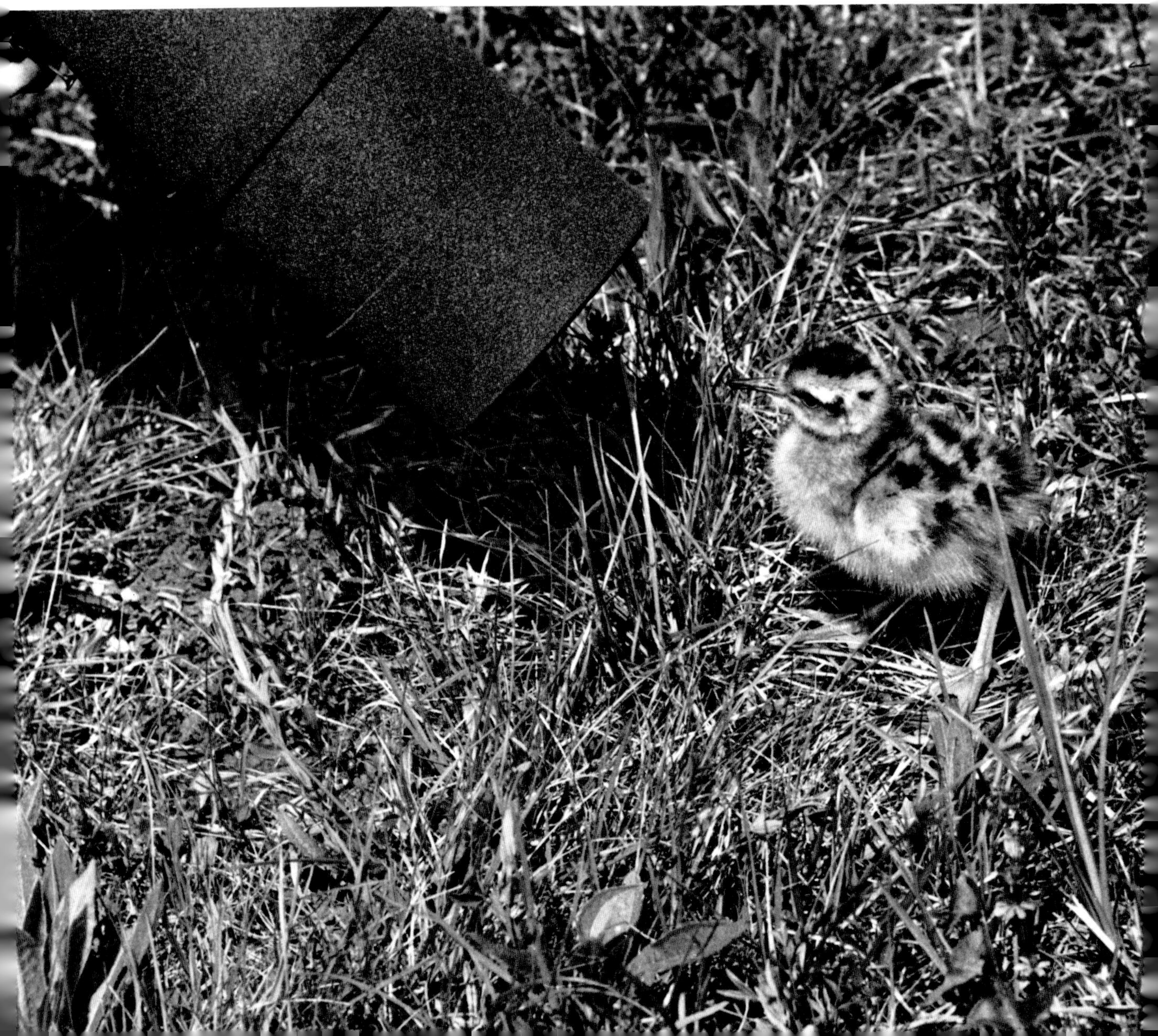

equipment and techniques

Choosing a technique and a means of expression

The choice of a technique in wildlife photography will depend first of all on your own personality and secondly to an almost equal extent on the ideas that you want to express and communicate.

A motion picture is not just a rapid succession of static images producing an impression of animation – it is a reconstruction of real life – but it often requires such elaborate means and effort that it is harder to get a ten-minute sequence of film of sustained interest than a series of good still photographs.

Hundreds of hours spent amidst nature have taught us that it is virtually impossible to obtain high-quality shots in both media – cine and still – at one and the same time. One of the techniques will inevitably have to be sacrificed to the other.

The equipment and methods are different for the two media, and it must be borne in mind that sound recording, now an essential accompaniment of cine film, further complicates the work and adds to the load of equipment already encumbering the wildlife photographer anxious to move about unobtrusively.

It is indeed possible to combine all three techniques, i.e. still photography, cinematography and sound recording, but then it will be necessary to decide for each day, or for each half-day, which of these techniques you are going to use. And you must stick to your choice, even if it means missing some opportunities of getting exceptional shots in the medium which you happen to have 'left at home' on that occasion. The choice is all part of the game of chance.

The photographer's personality, his psychological make-up, also matters: he should know his own limitations and the most suitable way to express his feelings, i.e. the way to capture and reproduce with the aid of some lifeless and complex equipment a particular instant in the life of an animal in its natural environment.

Some people see life in black and white, others in colour; some translate it into words or sounds, others view it in static images – condensations, as it were, of fleeting visions and impressions – and others again prefer the medium of cinematography, which can provide visual images and sound that come closer to reality. Without adopting too rigid a degree of specialization, which would tend to impose too tight limits, it is nevertheless necessary to choose a method suited to your tastes and your physical capabilities. From the start of your

The first photographs of natural history subjects were directly inspired by the art of painting. Around 1850 Louis Rousseau, a member of the scientific staff of the French Museum of Natural History, published a set of animal pictures based on photographic reproductions. He corrected the imperfections of the process and created a kind of composite art, half photography and half painting, which took advantage of the pictorial precision of the new technique. The 'monster camera' illustrated at top left was used in 1890.

apprenticeship you will thus, by more or less conscious stages, arrive at a degree of knowledge, training and skill that will reflect your temperament.

With a few friends we recently went on a safari in Africa, a photographic safari. We were all crowded together in one vehicle and took shots of the same subjects, under the same conditions and from the same angles. Yet none of the photographs obtained on this trip resemble one another. Each photographer had used the lens with the focal length that he considered to be best suited to the subject, each had used a different shutter speed, and–most significantly–each had released the shutter at the instant he judged to be most favourable to within a fraction of a second.

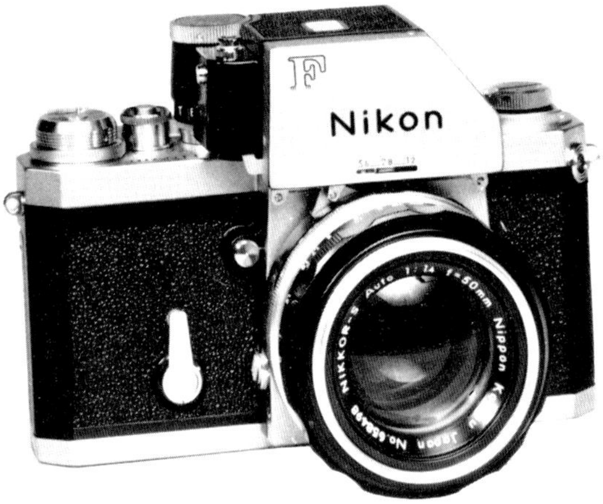

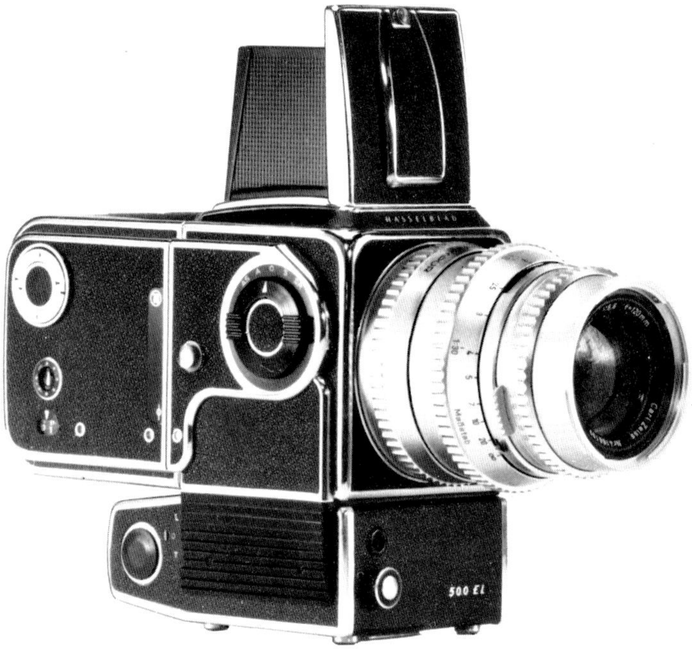

Nikon F. 35 mm camera with built-in CdS meter. Range of speeds: 1 sec. to 1/1000 sec. Here shown equipped with standard lens of 50 mm focal length. This camera can be fitted with electric motor drive (12 volts dc).

Hasselblad single-lens reflex camera, size 6 cm × 6 cm, with interchangeable lenses. Here shown equipped with built-in electric motor and 120 mm lens. The magazine holds perforated roll film for 70 shots.

The camera

The camera is not all-important. Its only function is to capture an emotion, the image of a fleeting instant. You must not attribute magic powers to it, however sophisticated an instrument it may be. The format (size of the negative) is not of much importance, nor is the mechanical or (in modern cameras) the electronic equipment. A famous experiment proves this: some years ago a leading manufacturer of photographic materials lent ten of the world's greatest photographers each a box camera. This was the simplest type of camera, with a very elementary lens (meniscus) and only two light settings (sunshine and overcast). The photo-

Main photographic sizes and their diagonal dimensions

Size	Approx. diagonal
24×36 mm (35 mm)	45 mm
4×4 cm (127)	60 mm
6×6 cm ($2\frac{1}{4}$ sq)	85 mm
6×9 cm	105 mm
9×12 cm	150 mm
13×18 cm	220 mm
$2\frac{1}{4}\times3\frac{1}{4}$ in	100 mm
$3\frac{1}{4}\times4\frac{1}{4}$ in	135 mm
4×5 in	160 mm
$4\frac{3}{4}\times6\frac{1}{2}$ in	200 mm
5×7 in	220 mm
7×9 in	280 mm

Image field for 24 mm× 36 mm size of negative as related to the scale of reproduction

	Scale	Image field
REDUCTION	1:10	24 ×36 cm
	1: 5	12 ×18 cm
	1: 3	8 ×12 cm
	1: 2	4·8× 7·2 cm
	1: 1	2·4× 3·6 cm
ENLARGEMENT	×1·5	1·6× 2·4 cm
	×2	1·2× 1·8 cm
	×3	0·8× 1·2 cm
	×4	0·6× 0·9 cm
	×5	0·5× 0·7 cm

graphers were requested to show what they could do with such unpretentious equipment. The results were the ten best pictures ever obtained with this type of camera.

The photographer familiarizes himself with his camera rather like a motorist getting to know a new car, so that after a few hundred miles he knows its good and its bad points. He has 'become one with his car'. In the same way, your camera should become a kind of extension–a valuable and fragile extension–of your own personality.

Of course, from the outset you are going to be impressed by this marvel of precision engineering, its finish, its fine chromium-plated parts. But after you have shot a few trial rolls or spools of film and experimented with various subjects in their natural surroundings, you will be surprised to discover that the design of the camera does not exactly conform to the requirements of your shots. You will ask yourself questions and feel misgivings: for example, your camera may have a rather dim viewfinder which makes it very difficult to compose your pictures quickly; or it may have protruding parts that get caught in your clothing just when you are about to release the shutter; or putting a fresh film in the camera may be an awkward and time-consuming operation.

The camera manufacturer (or the dealer) whom you may ask about these things will doubtless tell you that their customers demand equipment of up-to-date technical design (perhaps provided with a range of gadgets) and that it is his aim to sell an inexpensive and, as far as possible, universal camera.

We shall revert to these particular problems, but it must be admitted that wildlife photography is still a relatively little-practised branch of the art and that at the present time it is hard to conceive a camera designed specially for that purpose, except at a price that would be prohibitive to all but a fortunate few.

The fact is that there is no such thing as the perfect camera; but this should not deter the wildlife photographer from striving after that ideal, and with the ingenuity and skill with which he can turn his hand to many things he may indeed succeed in contriving and making that rare, well-nigh 'personalized' apparatus which will most faithfully render his moods and feelings.

The choice of a camera is directly linked to the photographic format–the size of the negative–that you wish to use. This applies both to still photography and to cinematography. There are many different sizes, but these can for practical purposes be grouped into three main classes: miniature sizes, ranging from 24 mm×36 mm to 6 cm×6 cm ($2\frac{1}{4}\times2\frac{1}{4}$ in); intermediate sizes from $2\frac{1}{4}\times3\frac{1}{4}$ in to 4×5 in; and the large sizes 5×7 in to 8×10 in. It is preferable to work with several different sizes if you wish to practise all aspects of wildlife photography. But if you have to limit your choice to one size only, you should definitely choose the standard miniature size, the so-called 35 mm giving a 24 mm×36 mm picture (size of the negative). This format offers many advantages: handiness, light weight, reasonable price, large supply of film in one loading, great adaptability. It must be remembered that you are dealing with subjects which are on the move and that it is, both in the laboratory and in the field, therefore often necessary to be 'quick on the draw', to act quickly, using fast shutter speeds and high-powered lenses.

So we must leave the quarrel about picture format to those photographers who are technical perfectionists and attach greater importance to formal accuracy of detail than to considerations of practical convenience under field conditions. The large camera can certainly record more detail and therefore attain higher quality in terms of fineness and precision of the image. But at the same time it is awkward to use for the photography of animals in their natural surroundings because it is unwieldy and its accessories are inconvenient.

In the field, when stalking animals or birds, the 35 mm size is preferable. For equal picture enlargement, using lenses which cost less and have larger apertures, your 35 mm camera will have only half the weight of an equivalently equipped $2\frac{1}{4}$ square camera.

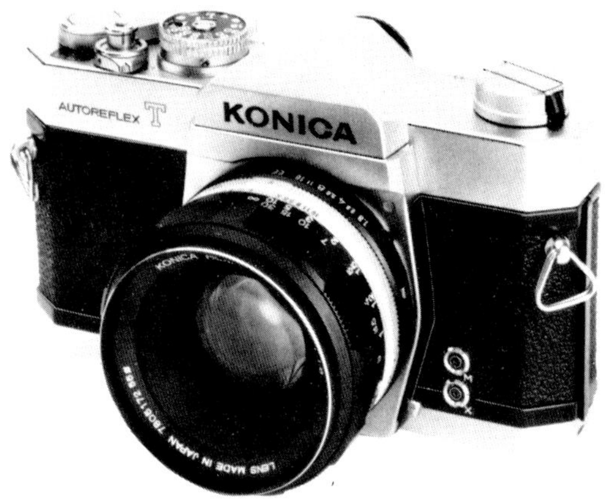

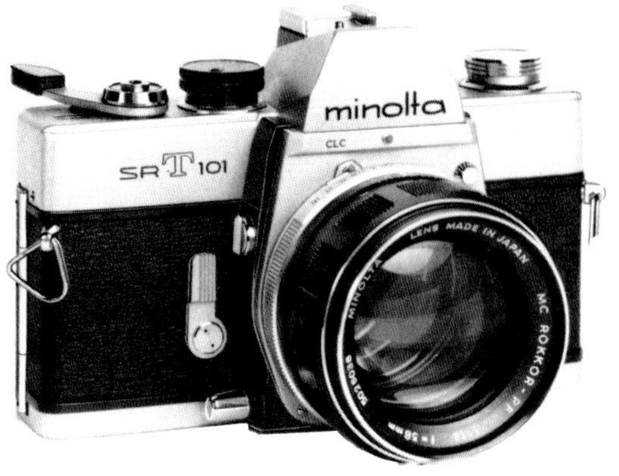

Above: Konica 35 mm single-lens reflex camera with a metering system comprising two meters enabling a fraction of the subject to be analysed for any particular focal length of lens employed.

Right: Minolta SRT 101 35 mm reflex camera with two photosensitive cells in the prism, compensated measurement of contrast and electric drive motor.

Below: Diagram of the reflex viewfinding system with full-sized image and integral exposure meter (Nikon).

1 photo-resistor cell
2 eyepiece
3 right-angled prism
4 pentaprism viewfinder
5 collector lens
6 viewing glass
7 mirror
8 lens

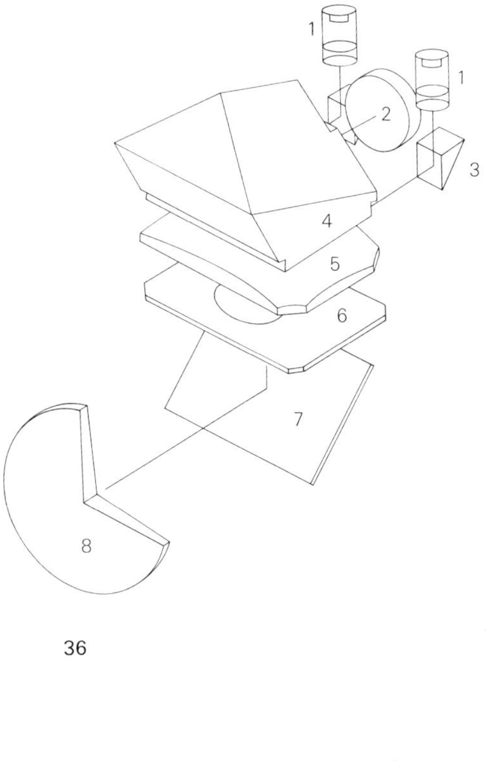

As we shall see later on, however, the choice must also to some extent depend on the wildlife photography technique applied: stalking the subject in the open or working from a hide.

For nature photography in general, and more particularly for wildlife photography, you should without any hesitation choose a camera of the single lens reflex type, this being preferable to any other viewfinding method. In a few years the reflex camera has captured about 80 per cent of the precision camera market. With such a camera the exact composition of the picture can be determined up to the very instant of shutter release, and accurate focusing is assured. These are the most decisive arguments in favour of the reflex camera. For the special applications in which we are here more particularly interested it has the further advantage of lens interchangeability, so that the lens best suited to any set of circumstances can quickly be fitted, as well as extension tubes or bellows to extend the focusing range of these lenses. Also, the reflex camera can be fitted to a microscope or to a telescope. It usually has a focal plane shutter of the roller-blind type giving a wide range of speeds up to 1/2000 second, which is not possible with diaphragm shutters.

As already stated, there is no such thing as the truly universal camera. In any case it is preferable to possess and carry a second camera, especially if you are going out into the field for days on end. For one thing, no camera is immune from mechanical trouble, and for this reason you should have a spare one with you. Also, when working under varying conditions, there is not always time to manipulate and change your lenses, and the success of your shots will suffer in consequence. A ready-to-use second camera can be a great boon in such situations. For relatively static subjects, such as nesting birds, or for photographs of the creatures' habitat in which no moving objects are included, you should, if you can afford it, choose a $2\frac{1}{4}$ square or a 6 cm × 7 cm camera – a reflex, of course – which will indisputably give you very-high-quality pictures. These cameras are generally very well equipped; some have interchangeable magazines which enable you to change the type of film during a sequence of shots. They have synchronized shutters, automatic diaphragm control and come equipped with electric motors for film transport (winding); but some reflex cameras of this size have only diaphragm shutters (as distinct from focal plane shutters) and the disadvantage that their fastest speed is generally not more than 1/500 second.

There also exist larger cameras, some of which are of the reflex type, which are seldom used for fieldwork because they are unwieldy. They are used mainly in studios, seldom for hand-held camera work, since they are designed essentially for mounting on firm stands or tripods and for operation at relatively slow shutter speeds. Such cameras are sometimes installed in shelters or hides, but can hardly be used in the sort of wildlife photography that involves stalking one's subject – real 'hunting with the camera'.

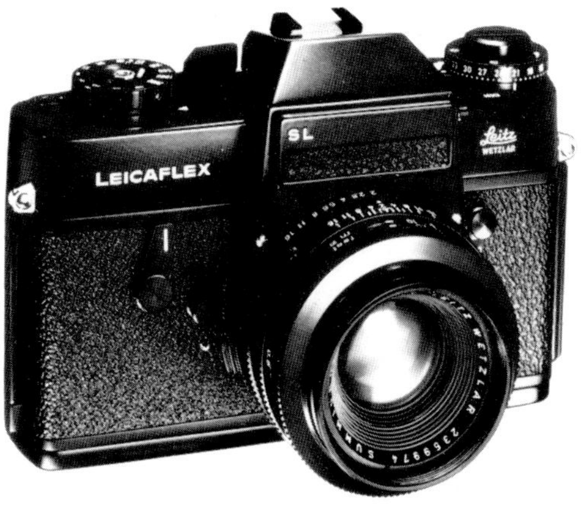

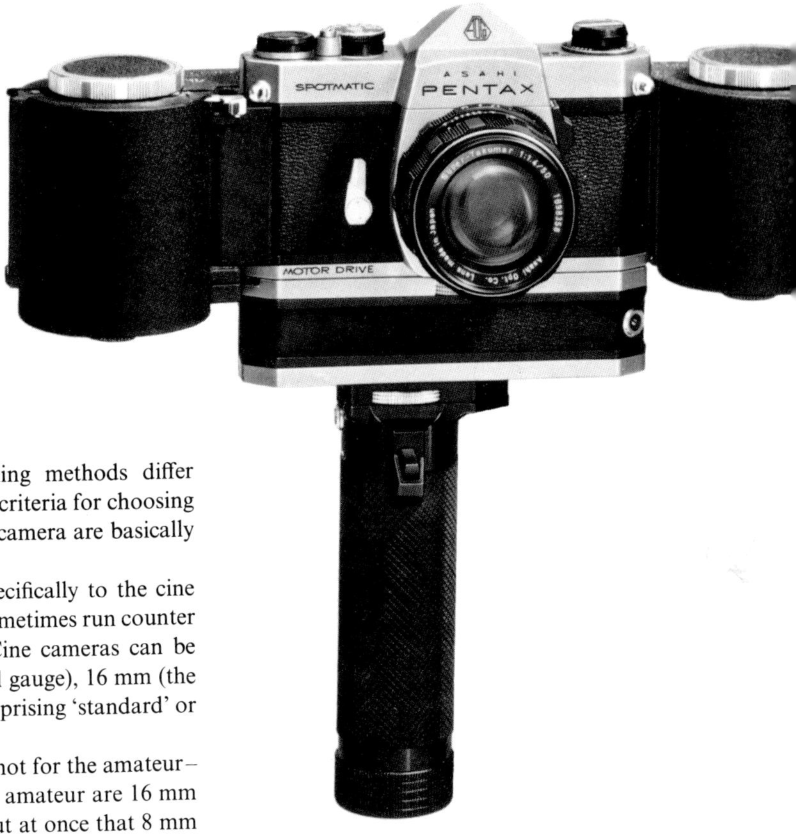

As for wildlife cinematography, although the working methods differ significantly from those of still photography, the technical criteria for choosing the format and the appropriate viewfinder system for the camera are basically the same.

Without wishing to go into considerations relating specifically to the cine camera, we shall mention the significant differences that sometimes run counter to the fundamental principles of nature photography. Cine cameras can be classified into three main groups: 35 mm (the professional gauge), 16 mm (the wider of the two so-called narrow gauges), and 8 mm (comprising 'standard' or 'double' 8 mm and 'super' 8 mm).

Because of its very high cost, the 35 mm cine camera is not for the amateur–it is for professional use only. The gauges suitable for the amateur are 16 mm and 8 mm (in particular: super 8). It should be pointed out at once that 8 mm costs only about a quarter of 16 mm per minute of viewing time, but that it cannot, as 16 mm can, be enlarged to 35 mm size for commercial projection.

Modern 8 mm and 16 mm cine cameras offer the same advantageous features and suffer from the same disadvantages as regards lack of picture stability which is apparent because of the smaller picture area. In their more sophisticated versions they are equipped with a range of technical features and refinements

Above left: Leicaflex SL 35 mm reflex camera with built-in exposure meter. Speeds 1 sec. to 1/2000 sec. Adaptable for electric motor drive.

Above right: Asahi Pentax Spotmatic 35 mm reflex camera with CdS exposure meter, here equipped with electric motor drive and magazine for 250 shots.

Below: Section through the Leica SL showing the path of the light beam through the camera.

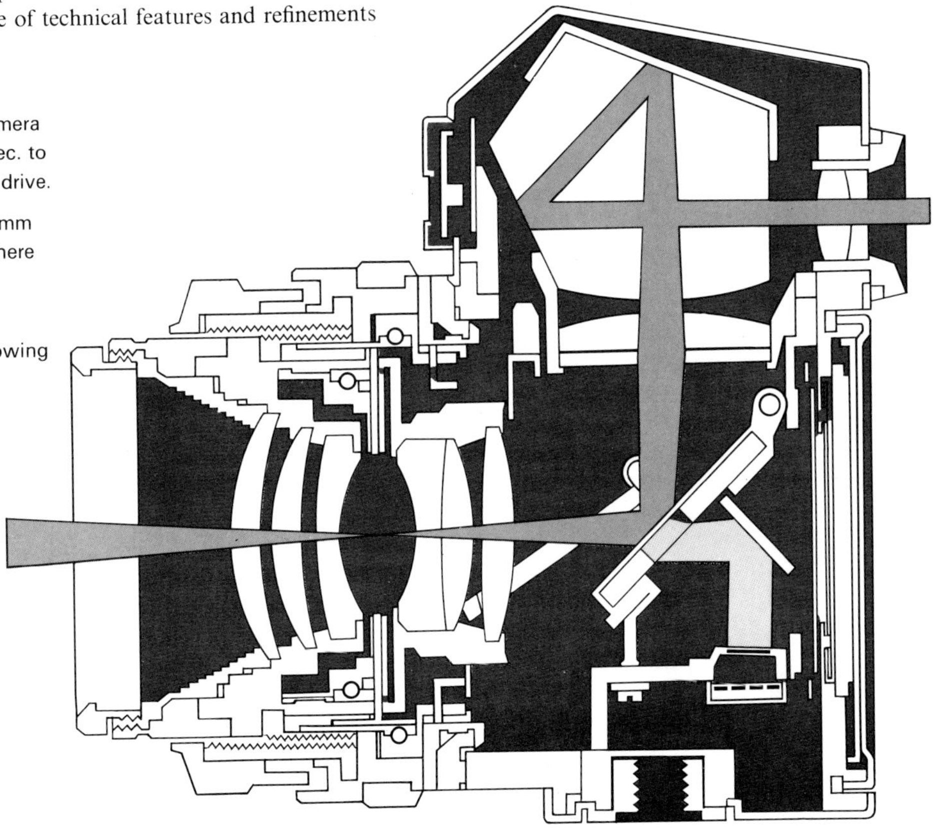

Leicina reflex Super 8 mm all-electronic cine camera, electric-powered zoom lens, through-the-lens metering.

Beaulieu fully automatic reflex cine camera for 16 mm film in magazine holding 200 ft of film, electric-powered zoom with automatic diaphragm control.

Opposite page: A mother gorilla and her child photographed in a zoo.
Equipment: 35 mm camera with 200 mm focal length; speed 1/125 sec.; aperture f 4.

that are the envy of many a professional cameraman using 35 mm. If your aim is merely to show your films in the family circle or informally in small groups, the super 8 format is quite adequate. But if you want to make research films or show the films at lectures or conferences, you should use 16 mm. Like your still camera, your cine camera should be of the reflex type, which is the only sort of equipment with which you can properly tackle any subject in the field or in the laboratory, with all the advantages already explained with reference to still photography–i.e. more particularly, the interchangeability of the lenses and universal adaptability of the equipment. However, one important difference between film and still shots must be emphasized: you do not 'hunt'–stalk your subject–with a cine camera except in special circumstances and then only using very high camera speeds. As a rule, the camera should be mounted on a tripod, which sometimes limits the spontaneity of the shots obtained; on the other hand, an unsteady picture which jerks about on the screen due to camera shake while filming is very objectionable to the viewer.

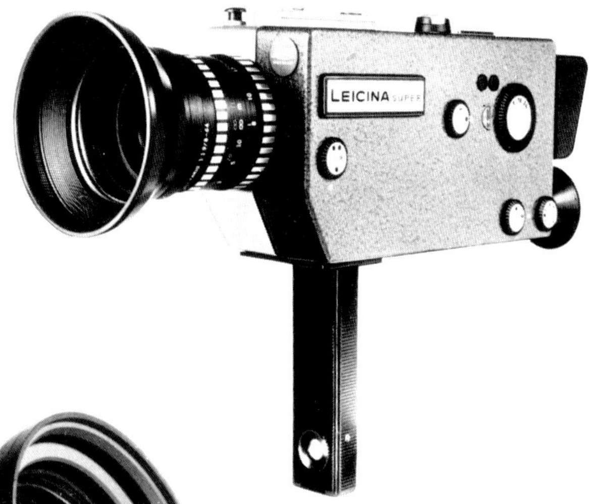

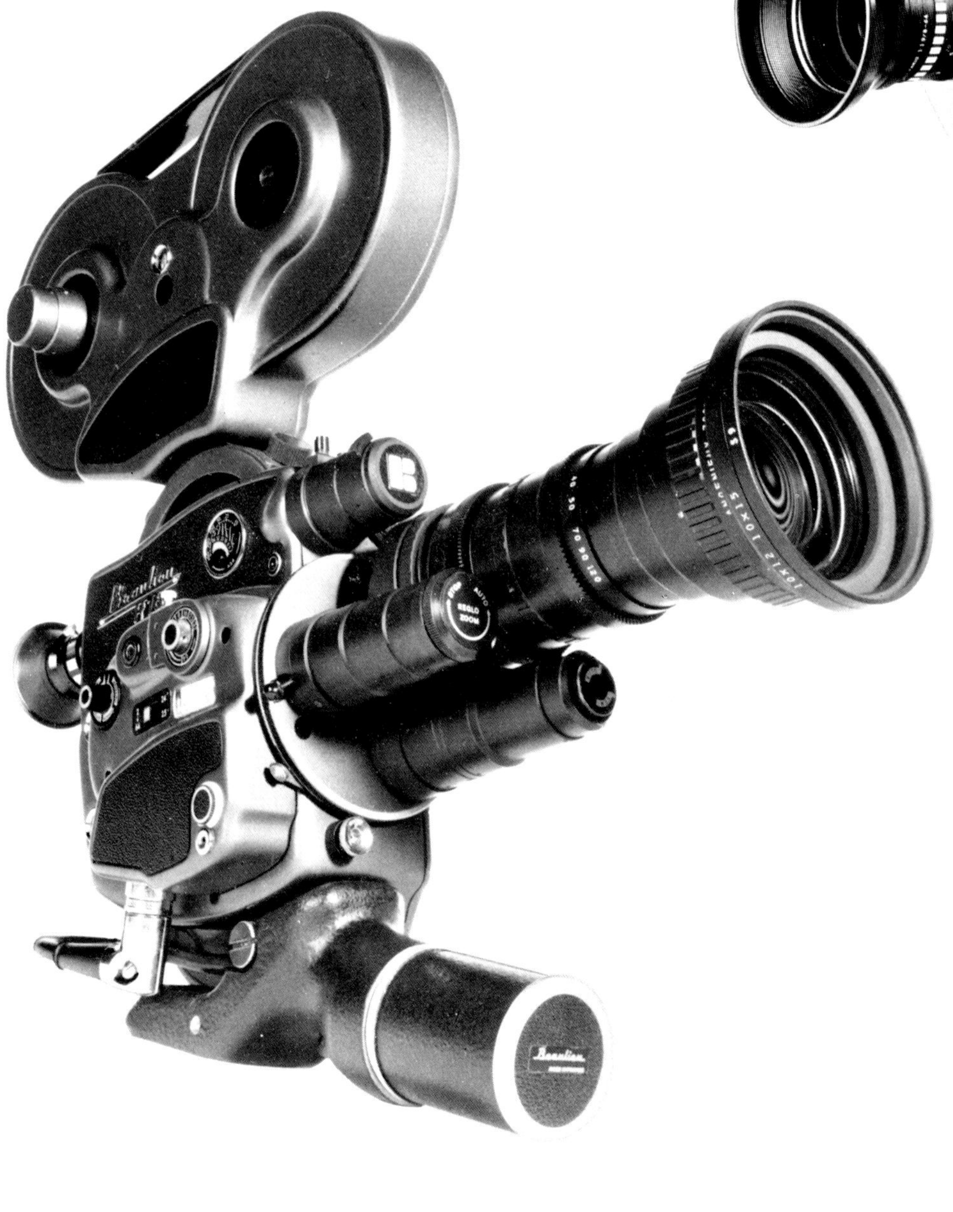

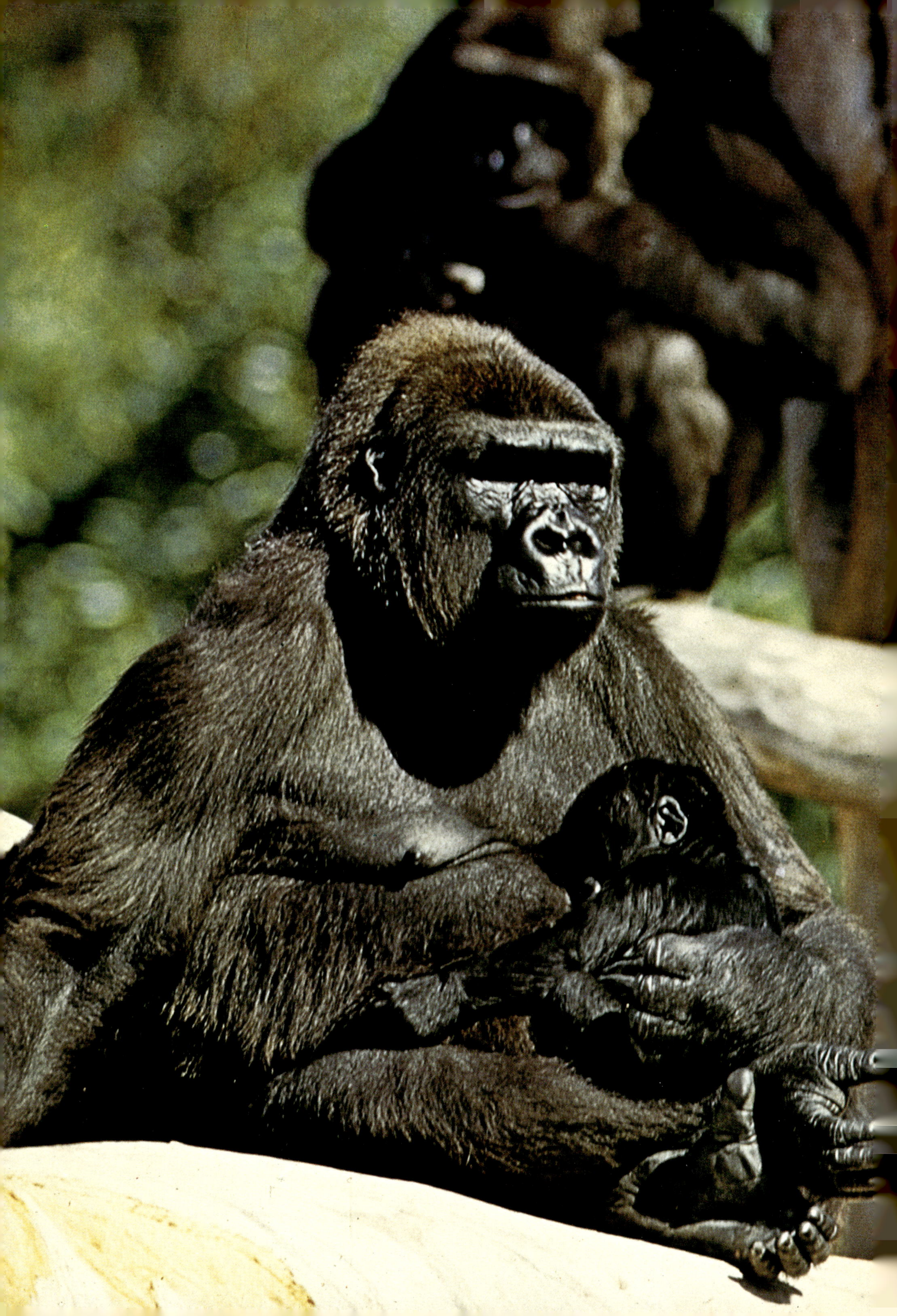

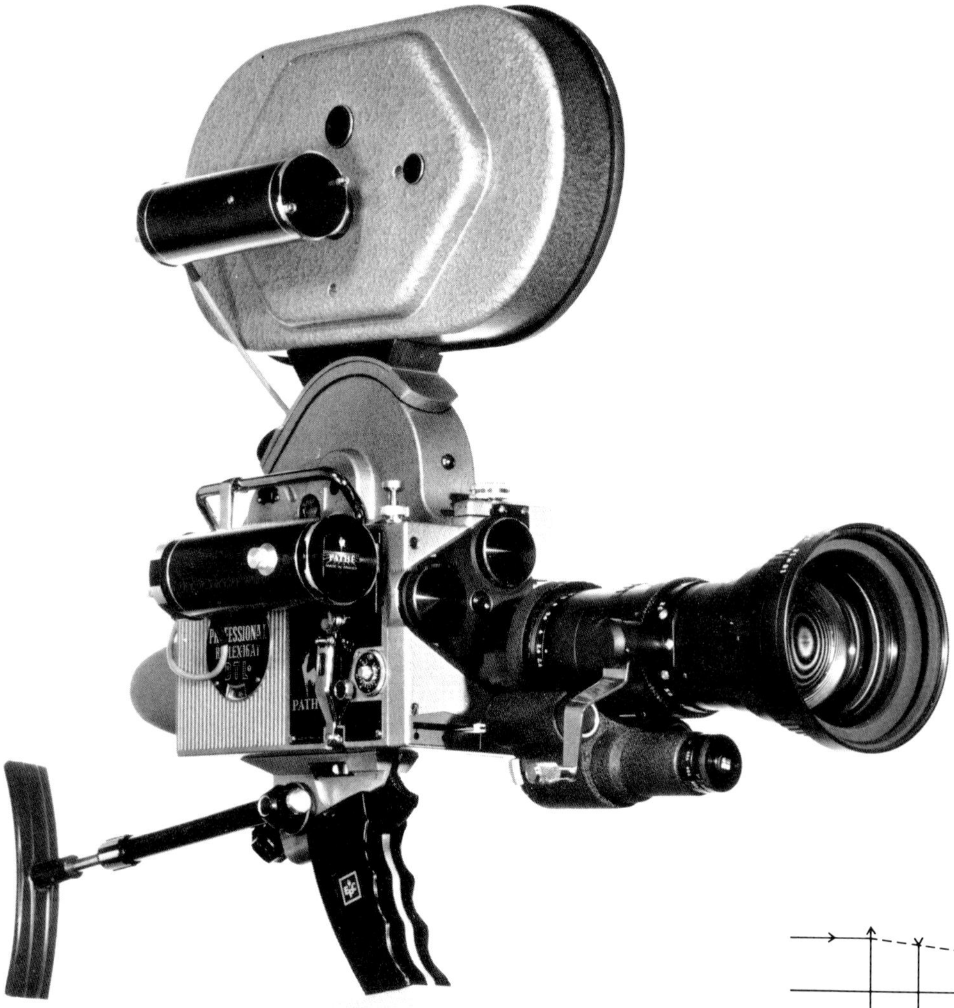

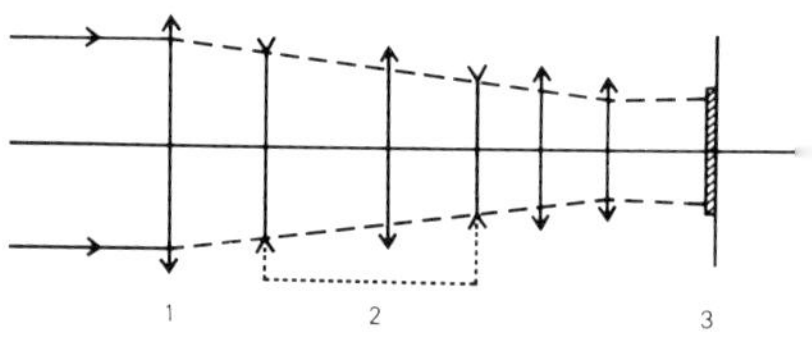

Pathé reflex cine camera for 16 mm film, with mechanical drive, range of speeds from 8 to 80 frames per second, two electric motors, 200 ft film magazine and Angénieux automatic zoom system.

The diagram on the right illustrates the principle of the zoom lens (lens with continuously adjustable variable focal length):
1 front lens
2 set of lenses mounted in travelling sleeve
3 image plane

The optical system

The lens is the most important individual feature of your equipment as far as the success of your pictures is concerned. The body of the camera is less important in that you may choose to modify it, change it and, if necessary, repair it; but the lens will remain just as the manufacturer supplied it, with all its good properties and its faults. Its price–and no high-class lens can be cheap–will limit frequent replacement.

Like the camera itself, there is no such thing as the ideal or universal lens to cope adequately with all possible uses. In theory the zoom lens, i.e. the lens of variable and continuously adjustable focal length, with its convenience and ease of manipulation, should come near to fulfilling these ideal requirements. Actually, however, the possibilities of the zoom lens are limited on account of its price, its weight and its relatively limited range of focal lengths. Such lenses are indeed used on television and cine cameras, but these are unsuitable for the larger picture area of stills, and besides, are very bulky and expensive.

In our opinion you should equip yourself with a range of at least three lenses. But if you can afford only one, then you will be well advised to get one with a focal length of 135 mm or 200 mm and an aperture (f-number) of 2·5 or 4 (for 35 mm still cameras). This is the basic lens for working in the field at a reasonable distance from the animal, holding the camera in your hands, with or without additional support. It will give you pictures that have the flavour of 'wildness' because, unless you are photographing some special kind of behaviour, you must always take care not to dissociate the animal from its environment; otherwise your pictures will look very like those you could take in a zoo, and often not nearly as good.

In order to master the technique and quickly acquire the essential minimum of knowledge and skill, it is helpful to know about the fundamentals of optics.

The lens, the essential feature of your camera, forms a real image of the more-or-less distant subject (the thing or creature that you wish to photograph) on the film in the body of the camera. This image should be as sharply focused as possible, especially with 35 mm equipment (24 mm × 36 mm picture format on the negative), and its sharpness will in part depend on the so-called resolving power, or definition, of the lens. In practice this resolving power is measured by means of special test objects comprising a series of black and white lines; it is expressed as the largest number of lines separated by spaces of line width that the lens is able to reproduce as distinct separate images. A lens is thus said to be able to resolve so many lines to the inch or to the millimetre. A good lens should be capable of resolving between 50 and 120 lines per millimetre. Another important quality criterion for a lens is its capacity to give equal quality at the centre and at the edges of the image. This quality is considerably affected by the use of the diaphragm and is more difficult to achieve with a short focus than with a long focus lens.

For practical purposes a classification of lenses into three main groups, according to focal length and angle of view, is convenient: the standard (normal focus) lens, the wide angle lens and the telephoto lens.

The normal focus lens has a focal length approximately equal to the diagonal of the negative – i.e. about 45 to 50 mm for a 35 mm camera (negative size 24 mm × 36 mm) – and an angular field of 55 degrees, which corresponds approximately to that of the human eye. (The angular field is the angle subtended at the lens by the largest object that the lens can image on the film.) Such lenses are seldom used in wildlife photography, and if you buy a camera particularly for this class

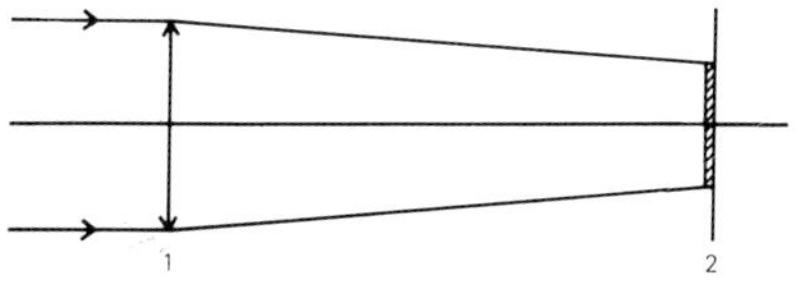

Long-focus lens
1 positive element
2 image plane

For equal focal length the telephoto lens and the long-focus lens give images of exactly the same size, but the telephoto lens is of shorter and more compact design.

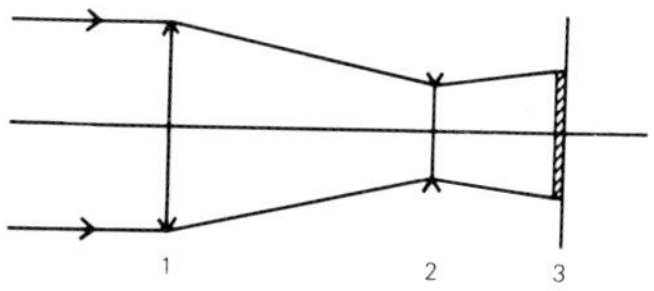

Telephoto lens
1 positive element
2 negative element
3 image plane

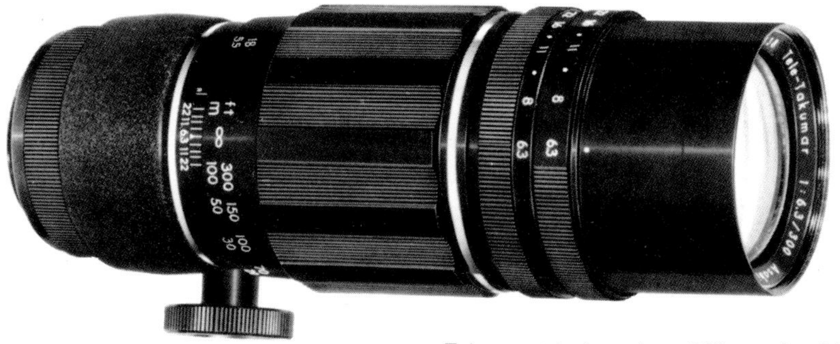

Takumar telephoto lens, 300 mm focal length

Takumar long-focus lens, 1000 mm focal length

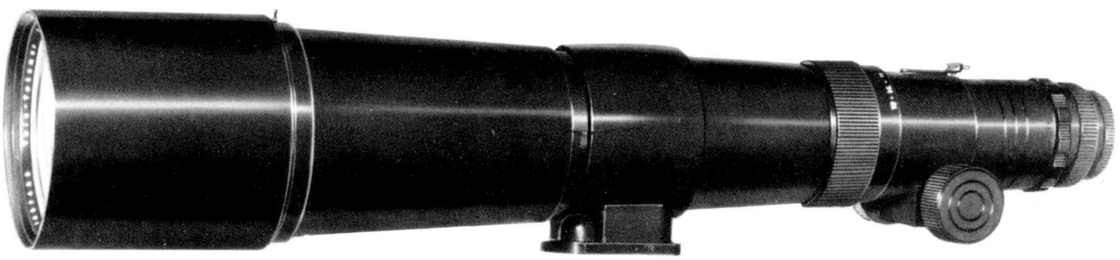

On hatching out, the young goby fish (*Gobious niger*) remain attached by their tail fins to the support on which the eggs were laid. In this photograph (enlarged twenty times) the eyes, the heart and the fins in a very early stage of development are clearly discernible.
Equipment: 35 mm reflex camera with 35 mm Micro Summar lens; flash; film Kodachrome II.

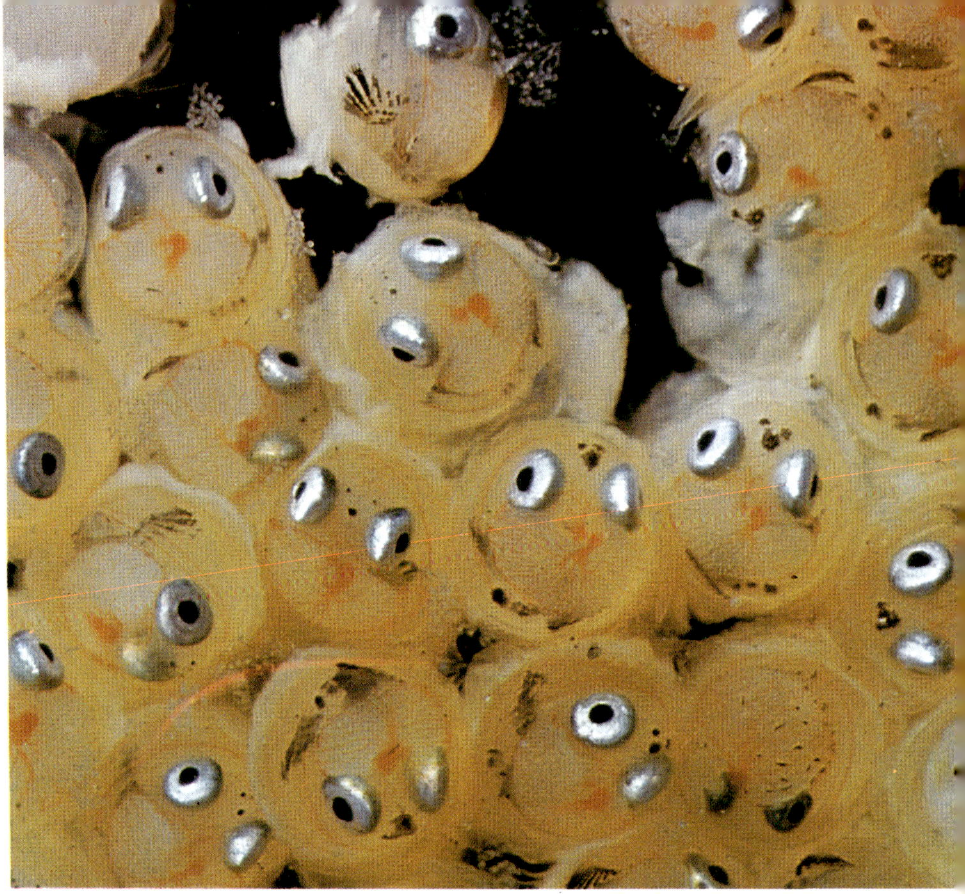

For reproduction the male and female sea urchin (*Spharechinus granularis*) discharge considerable quantities of sperm and eggs, respectively, and fertilization takes place in the water.

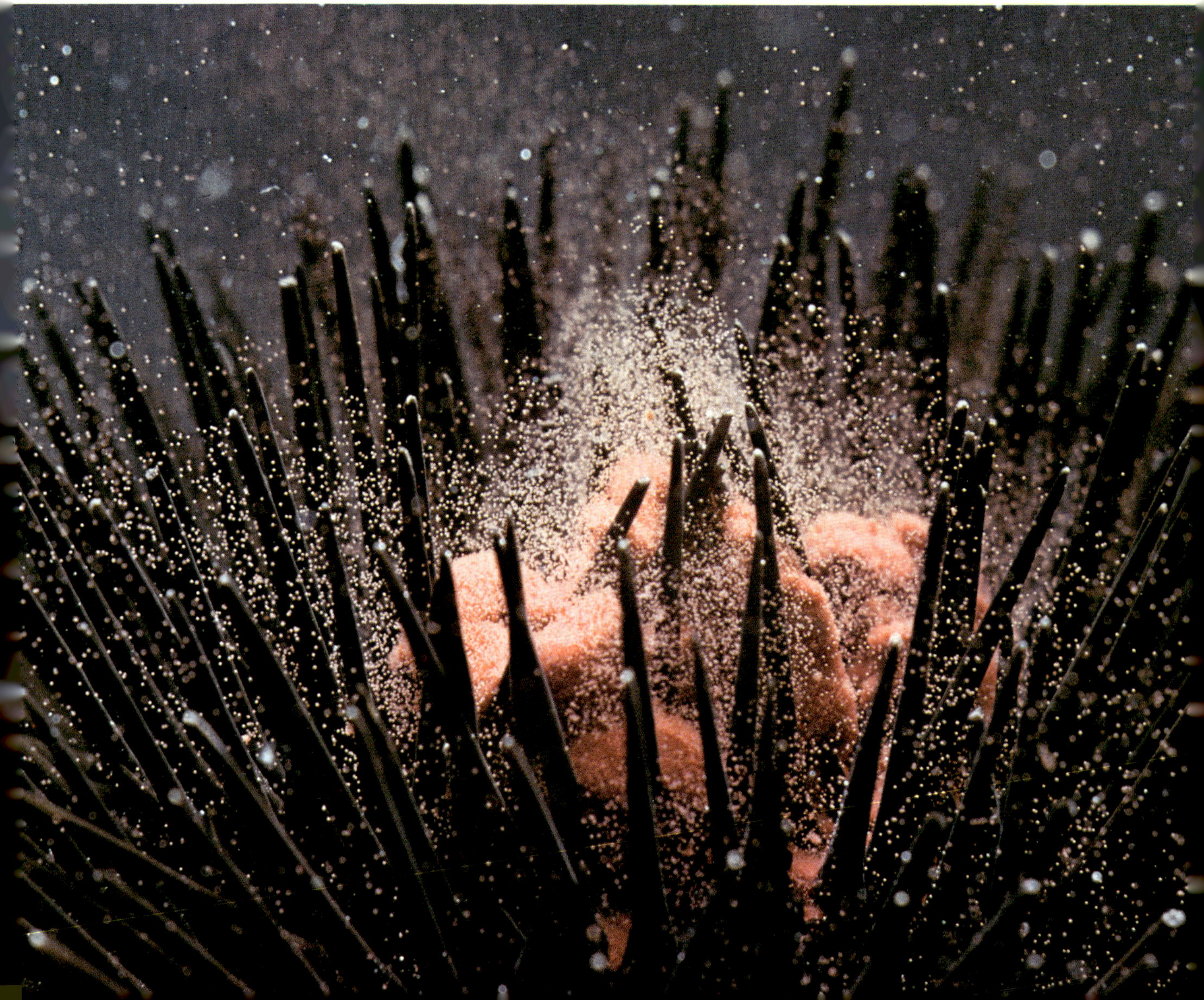

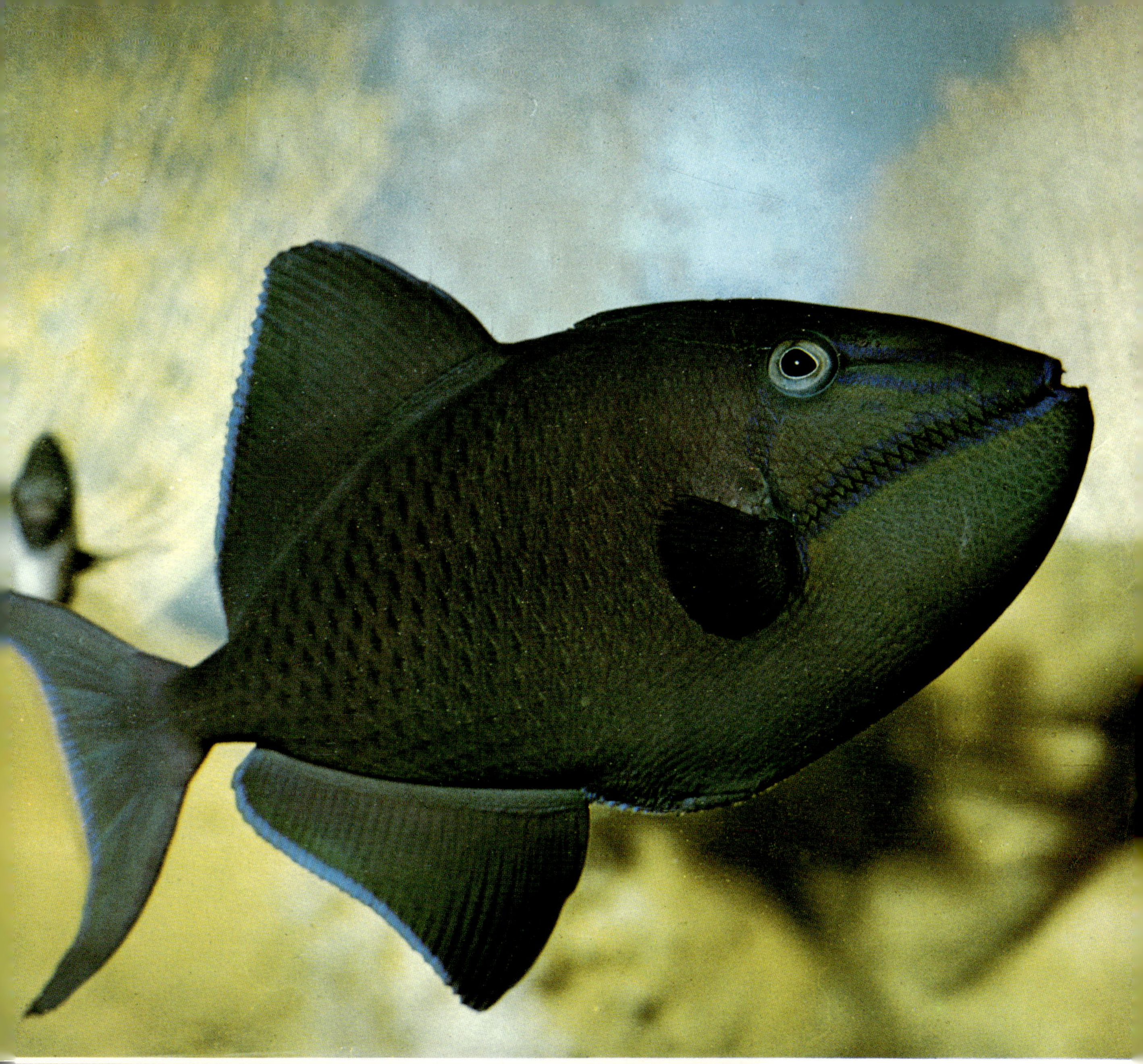

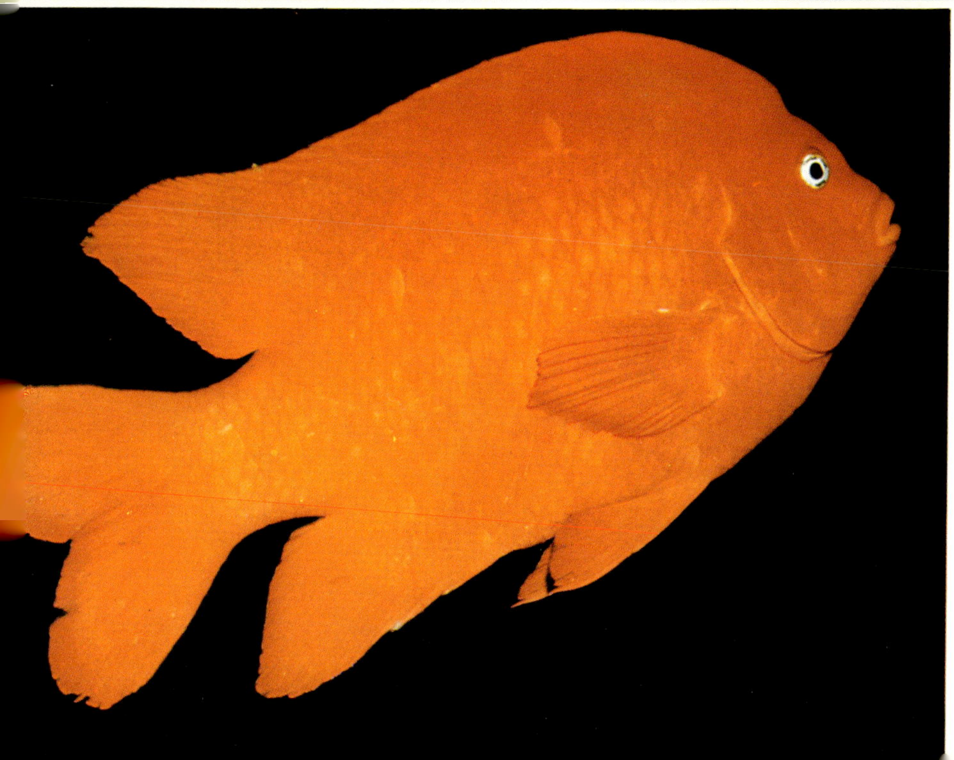

Pictured above is a balistes or trigger fish, a denizen of tropical waters which can anchor itself in the branches of corals by raising the first spine of its dorsal fin.

The fish in the lower photograph is *Hypsypops rubicunda*, which lives in temperate latitudes, more particularly off the rocky weed-covered shores of southern California.
Equipment: 35 mm reflex camera, 80 mm focal length; photographed in an aquarium using two flash-guns.

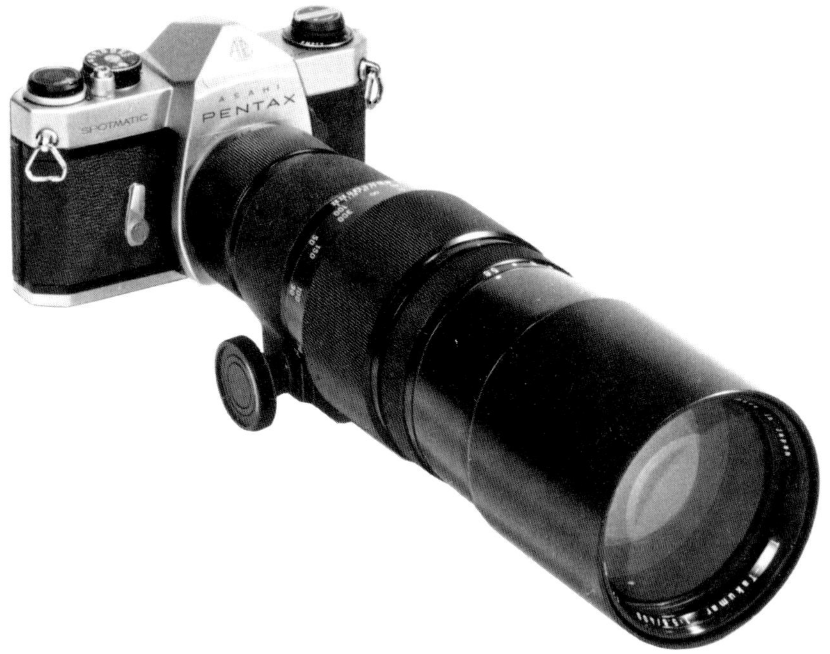

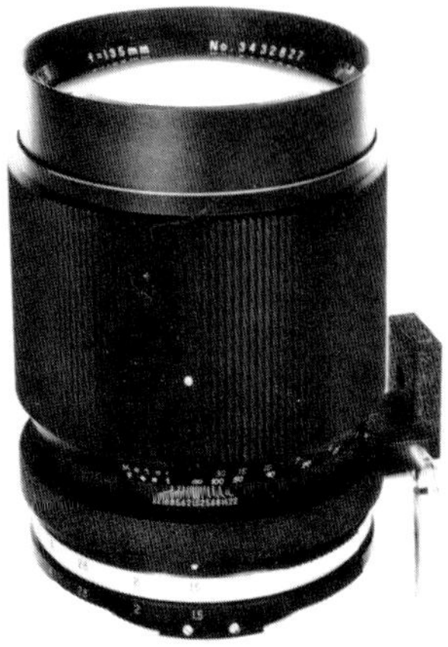

Asahi Pentax Spotmatic camera with built-in exposure meter and telephoto lens, 400 mm focal length, f 5·6.

Right: Soligor 135 mm lens, f 1·5, which can be fitted to any reflex camera.

Below: Example of a special chart for testing the resolving power of a camera lens.

Image of the object recorded on the negative

Distance from object to lens	100 m		50 m		25 m		10 m	
Dimension of the object	1 m	0·30 m	1 m	0·30 m	1 m	0·30 m	1 m	0·30 m
With a lens of 400 mm focal length	4	1·2	8	2·4	16	4·8	40	12
With a lens of 200 mm focal length	2	0·6	4	1·2	8	2·4	20	6

Dimensions on the negative in millimetres

Formula: $I = \frac{o \times d}{D}$

I : dimension on the image
o : size of the object
d : distance from lens to negative
D : distance from lens to object

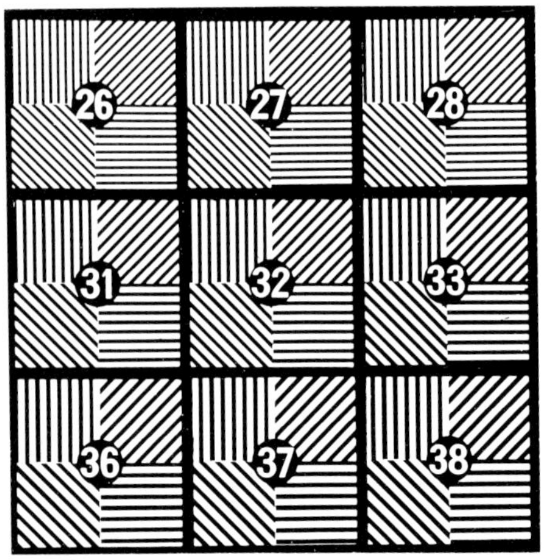

of work, you can easily do without the normal focus lens, unless it is equipped to give double or triple extension, which is very useful for close-ups.

Wide angle lenses are used in special circumstances (caves, underwater pictures, landscapes). The angular field generally ranges from 80 to 100 degrees and the focal length from 18 to 35 mm.

Telephoto lenses are available with focal lengths from 80 to 1200 mm, while the angular field correspondingly varies between 20 and 2 degrees. Such lenses are essential basic items of the wildlife photographer's equipment, both in the laboratory and in the field.

A distinction is to be made between the telephoto lens and the ordinary long focus lens, though for equal focal length the two types of lens will have the same magnifying power. The telephoto lens comprises a set of convergent lenses producing a virtual image which in turn is focused by a divergent system to form the image on the film. Thus the actual length of the lens barrel is less than the focal length, and such a lens is therefore shorter and less unwieldy than an

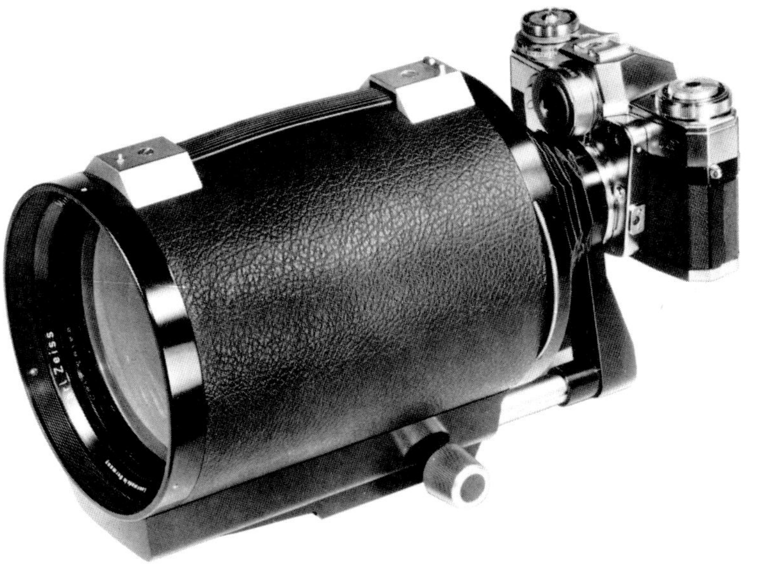

equivalent long focus lens. Telephoto lenses are generally of good quality, but are expensive and tend to be rather heavy.

The long focus lens comprises a doublet or triplet (i.e. a compound lens consisting of two or three lenses cemented together) which forms an enlarged image directly on the film. The barrel of the lens is therefore at least as long as its focal length, so that such lenses tend to be rather bulky. Against this, they are relatively light in weight and moderately priced. But in choosing such a lens you must proceed with caution, for the optical quality is often rather inferior.

Another type of lens, much less frequently employed, is the so-called mirror lens, which has an image-forming system using curved mirrors, on the same principle as that of a reflecting telescope used in astronomy. A lens of this kind is short and relatively lightweight, but has a large diameter and a fixed-aperture diaphragm (f-number 8 or 11), so that it is not possible to vary the depth of field.

Contarex camera with mirror lens, 500 mm focal length, f 4·5.

Below: 'Sniper' camera with butt and trigger mechanism, 300 mm focal length, rapid focusing system. The camera is supplied also with a 50 mm standard lens.

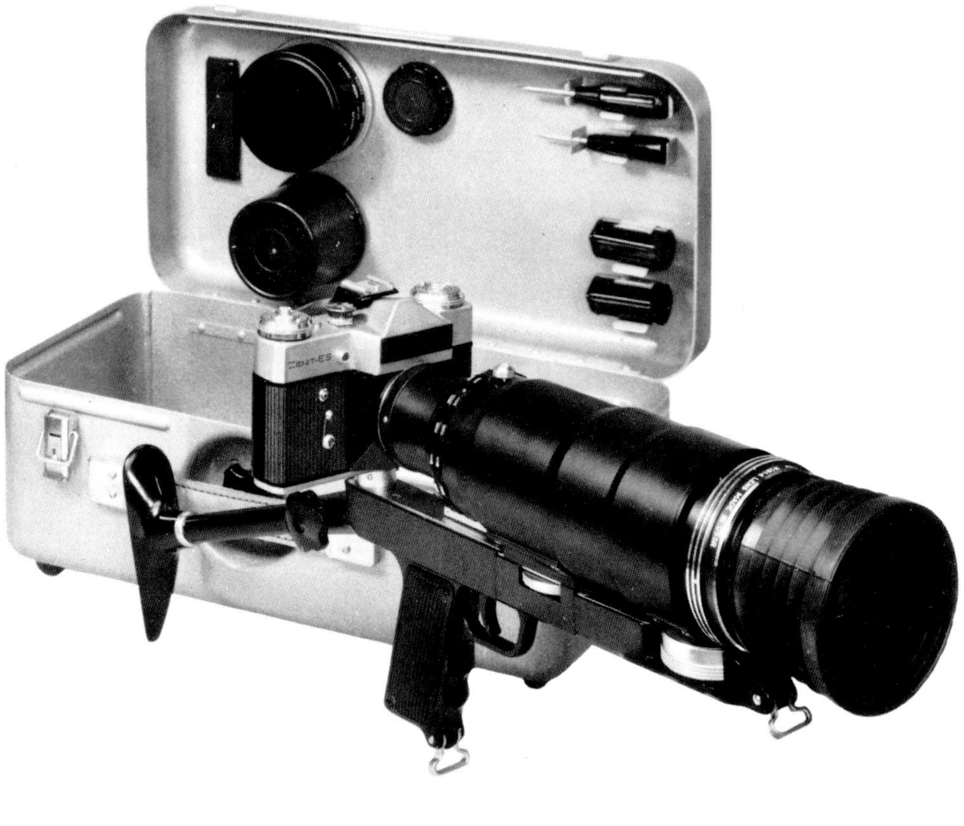

Closely related to telephoto lenses are attachments for doubling or tripling the focal length. These devices are inserted between the lens and the camera body, adding little to the overall length of the lens system. They have the drawback of causing serious loss of image brightness – equivalent to two or three diaphragm stops – and are often of poor quality.

Zoom lenses, already referred to, are variable-focus systems closely related to telephoto lenses, but their optical quality may be inadequate for photography, especially with long focal lengths.

Telephoto and long focus lenses are provided with various precision focusing systems, not always of efficient design. Alternatively, a special focusing device may be inserted between the lens and the camera body, focusing being effected by means of bellows or a double sliding tube.

The stag (*Cervus elaphus*) is the finest and wildest animal of Western European forests. In the rutting and belling season it is less shy and correspondingly easier to approach.
Equipment: Photosniper with Télyt telephoto lens, 400 mm; poor light; speed 1/125 sec.; aperture f 6·8; film high-speed Ektachrome (photograph on facing page).

The young male stags remain together until they can challenge the ageing 'owner' of a harem of females. The photograph below shows a brocket (second-year stag with straight horns) and two older males with branched antlers.
Equipment: Photosniper; speed 1/125 sec.; film Kodachrome II.

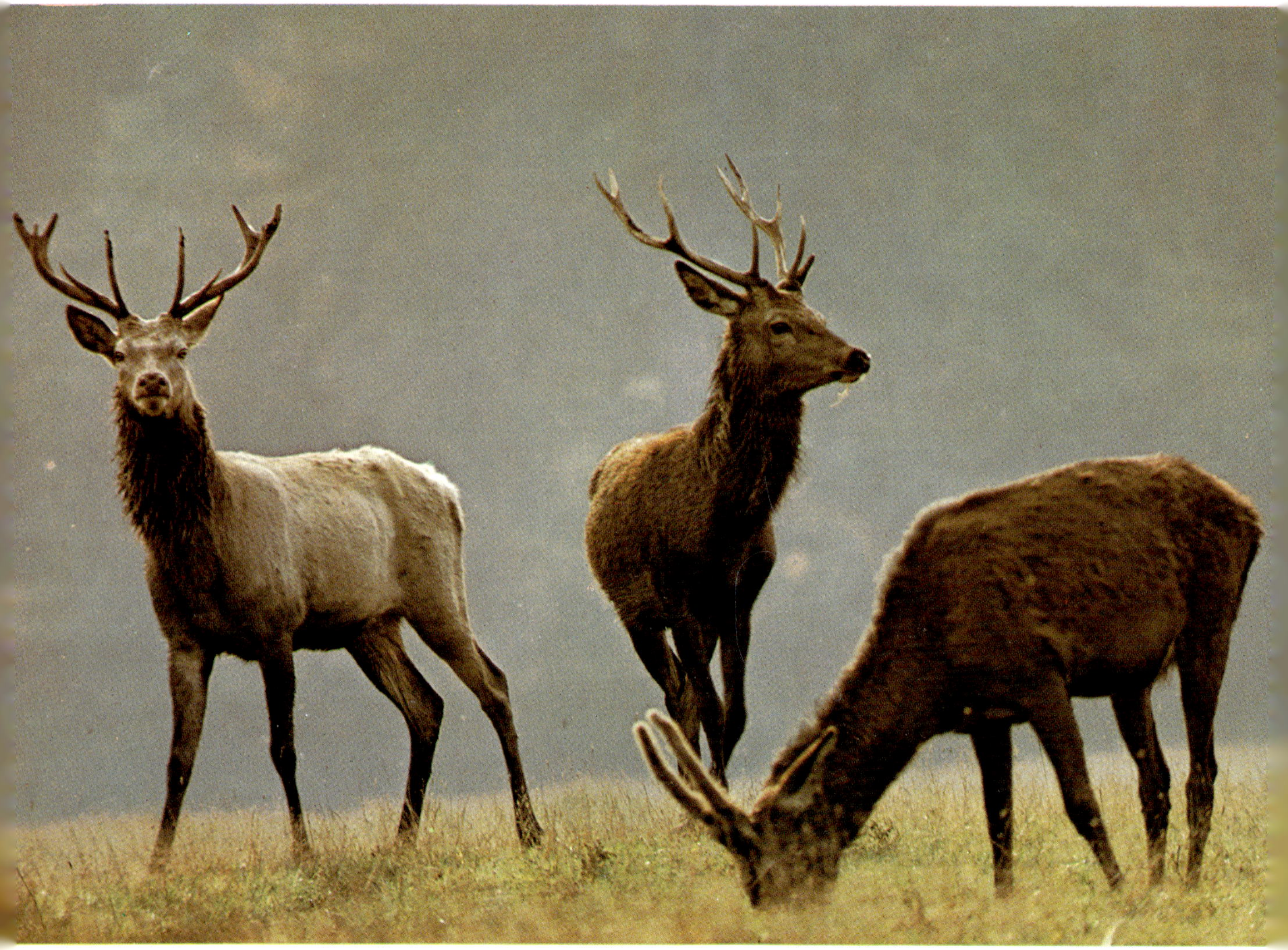

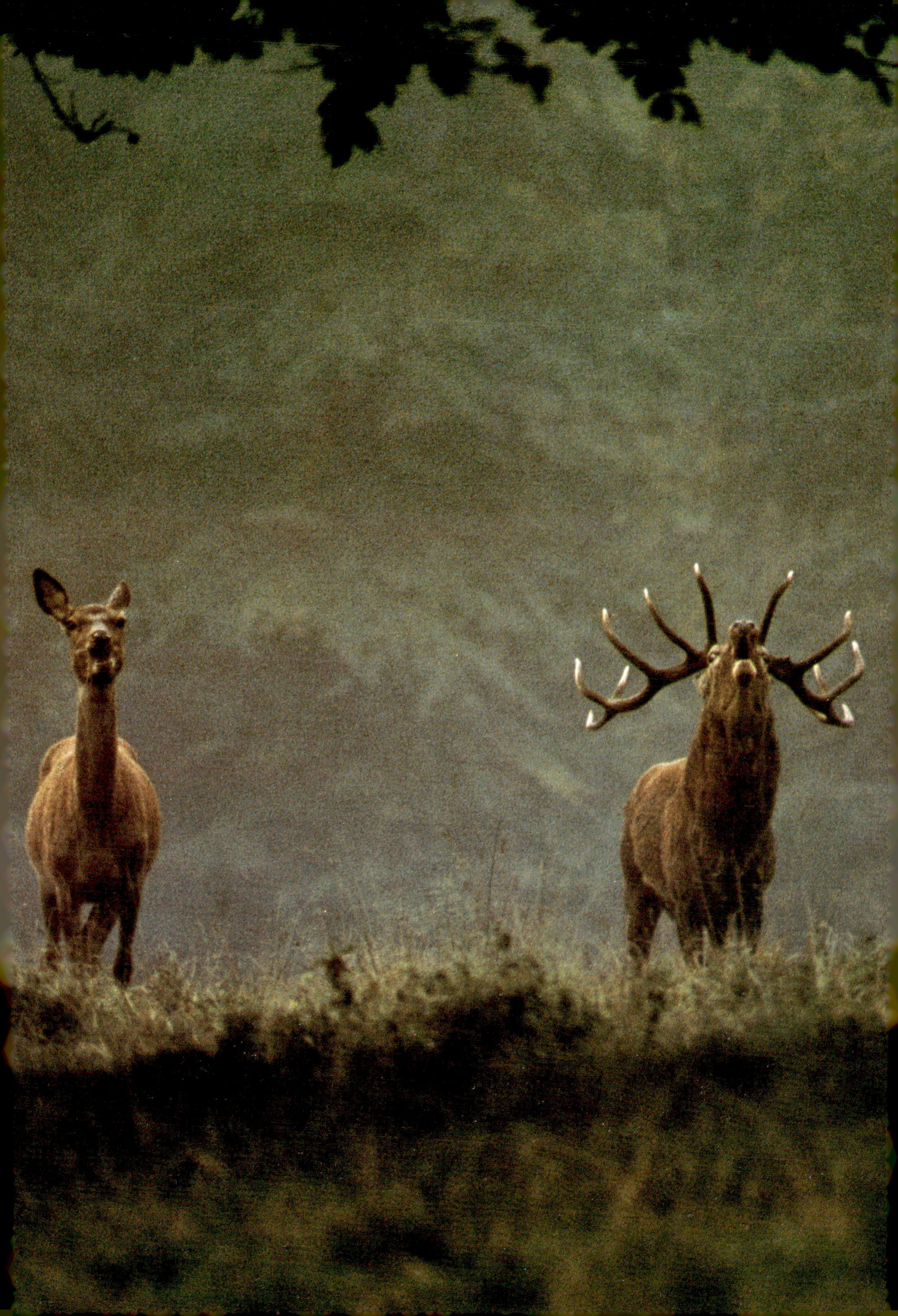

When food is scarce, as in periods of drought, the stags feed on the foliage of low-hanging branches of trees (photograph below).

In the rutting season the males utter their cries (known as belling) and engage in combat, sometimes with fatal results if adult males are fighting for supremacy where their rights to the females are concerned. However, 'real' fights of this sort are rare. In most cases the combat consists of a series of feints and ferocious-looking but not very dangerous interlockings of the rivals' antlers. Even so, such fights are difficult to observe and photograph because they mostly take place at night or at dawn in very poor light. The female stags appear to affect indifference to the outcome of the struggle.
Equipment: Photosniper, 400 mm; speed 1/250 sec.; aperture f 11; film Ilford HP4.

'Belling in the stag is a means of attracting and challenging. It bells out its joy of living . . . its mastery over the females . . . it bells when an adversary approaches and a challenge must be issued. The stag bells before and after victorious combat, in the evening, at night, in the morning and sometimes throughout the day during the two or three great days in the best years of its life.'

François Sommer

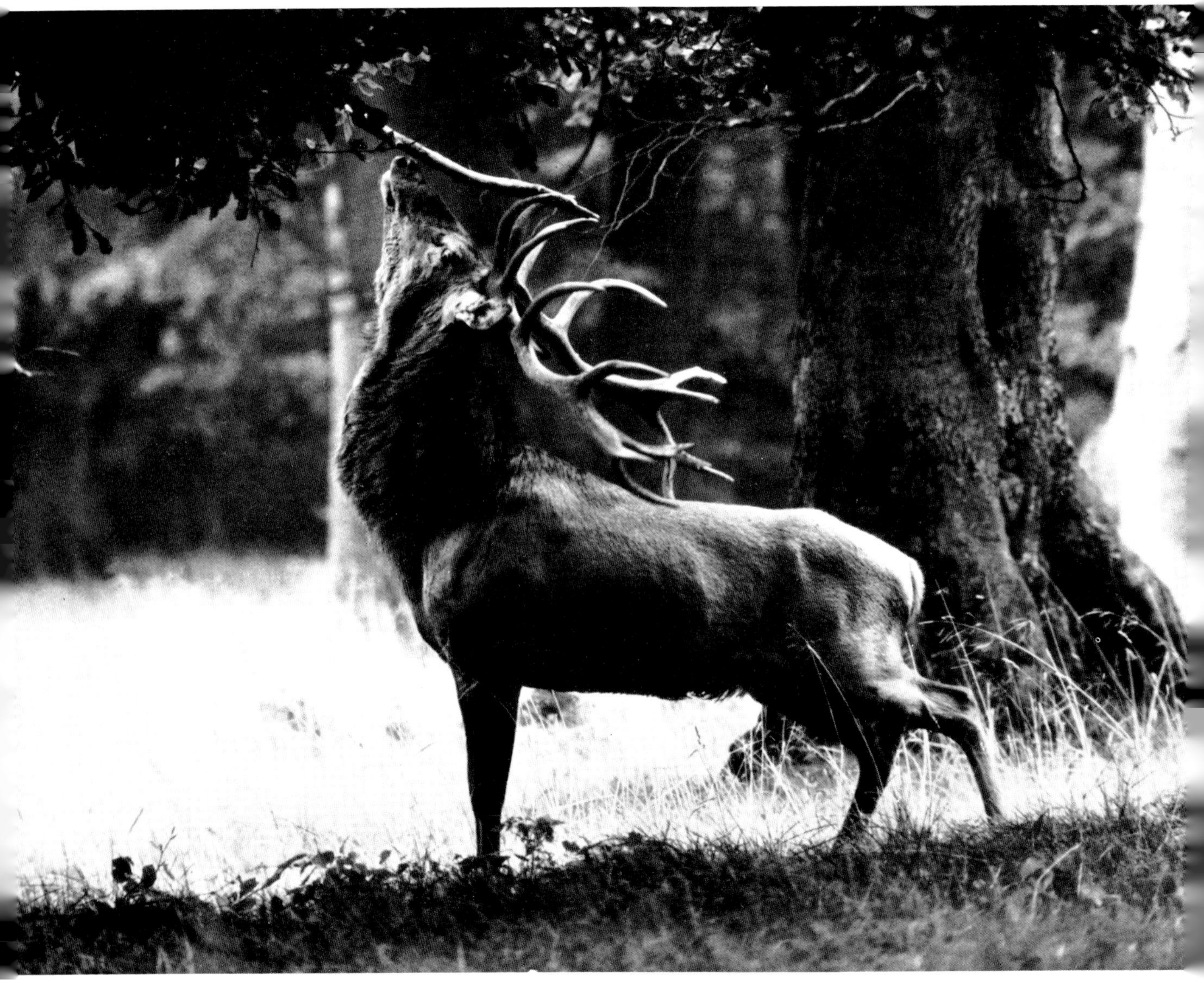

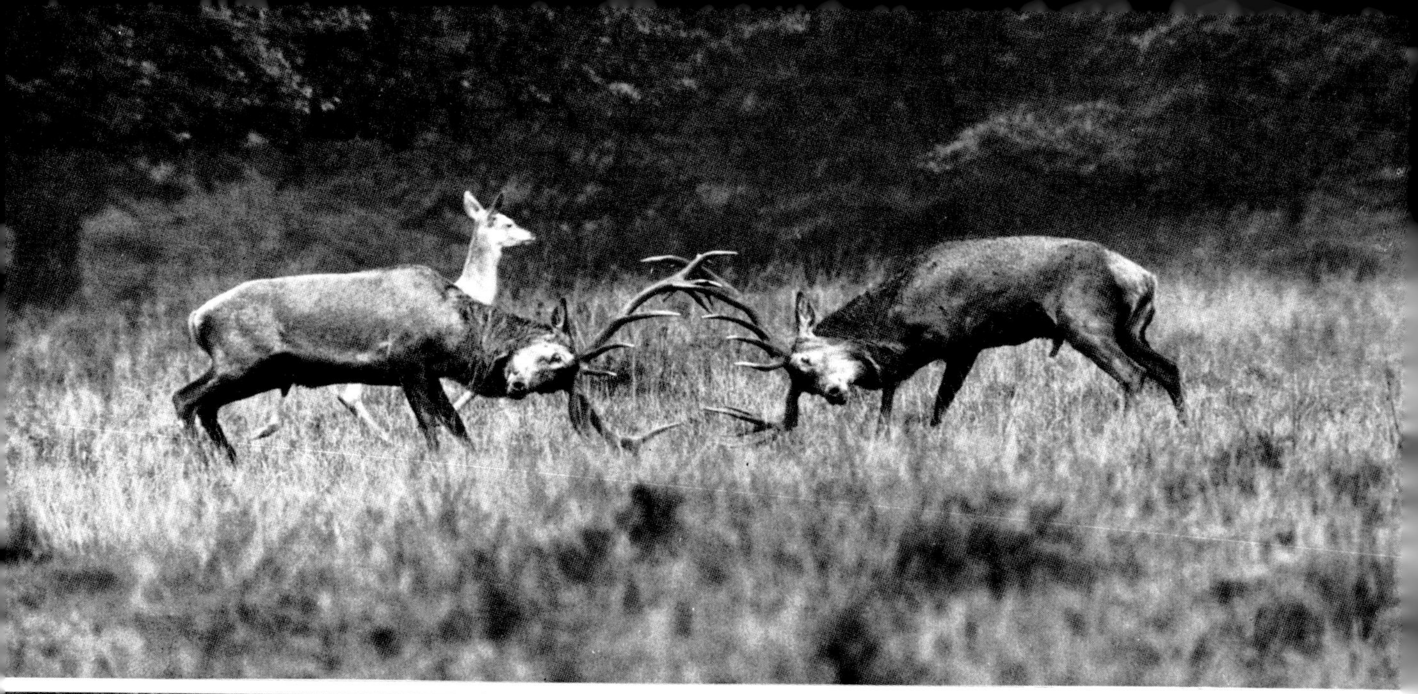

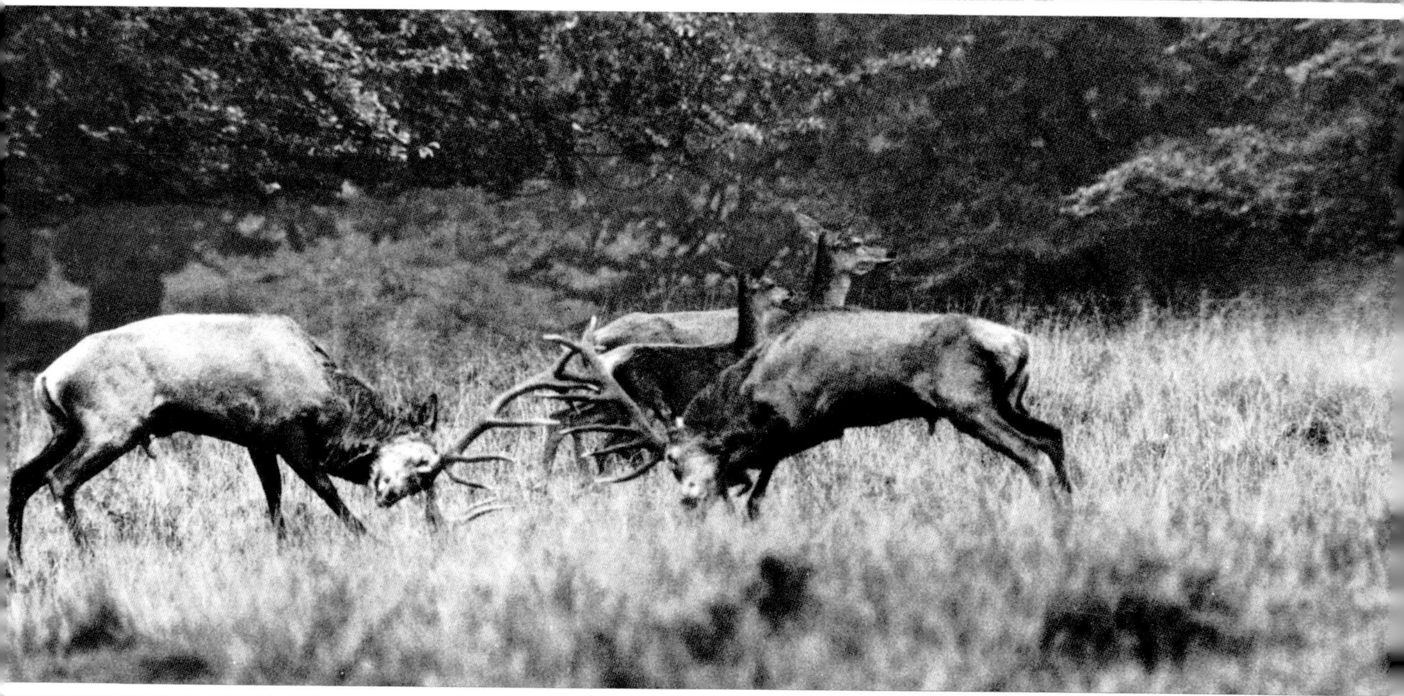

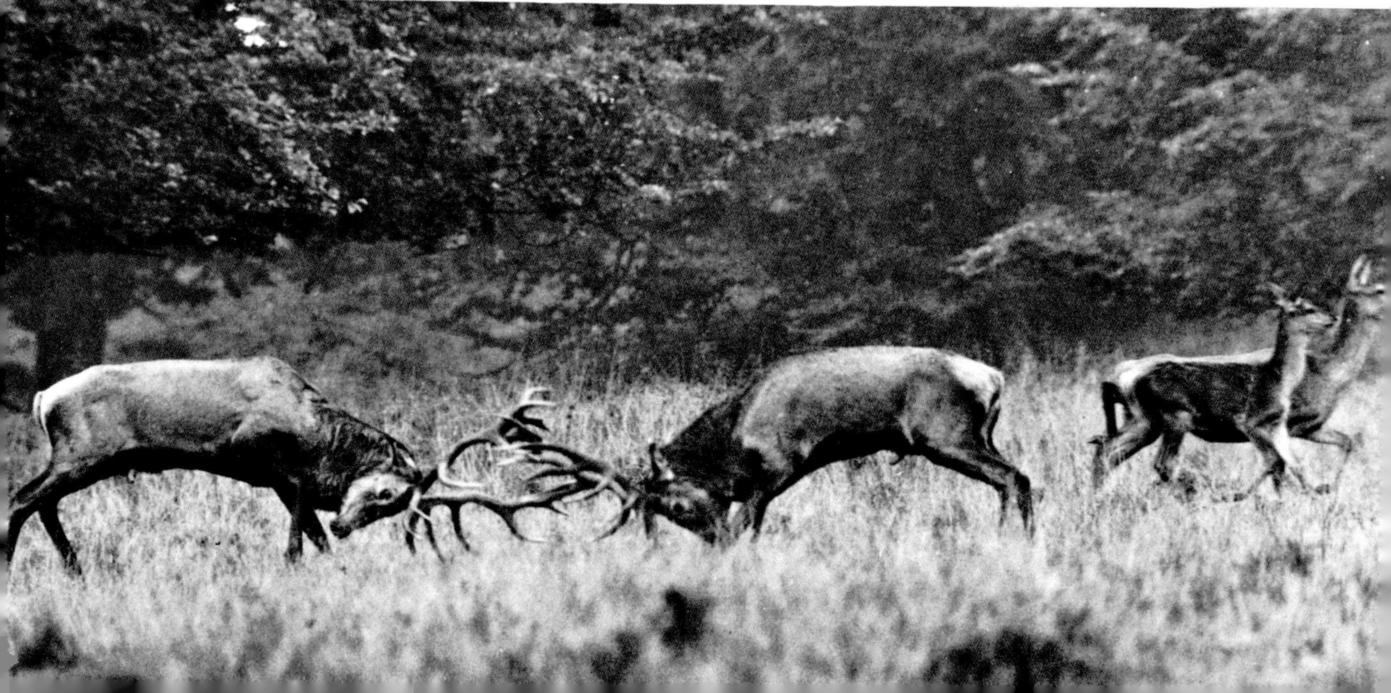

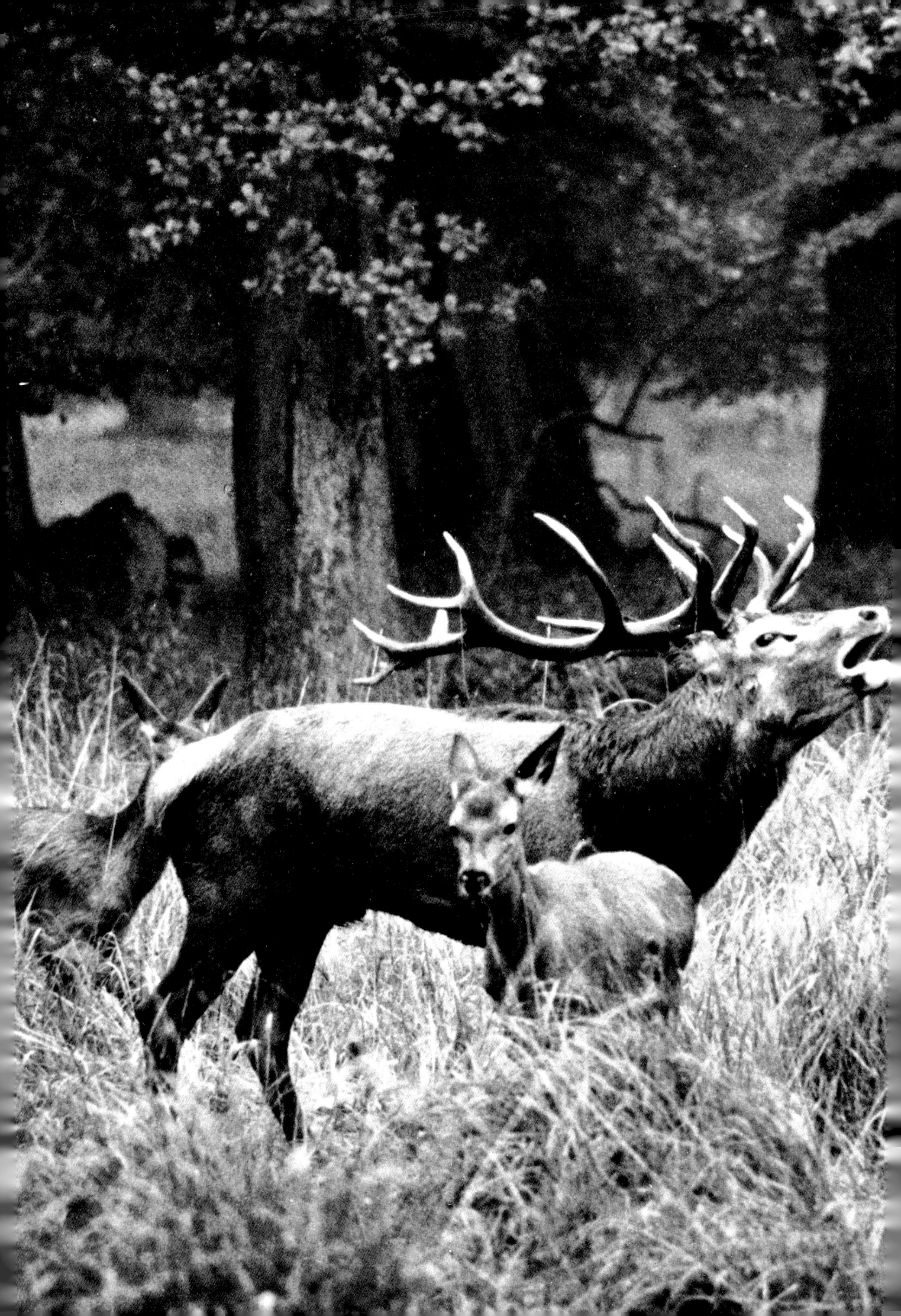

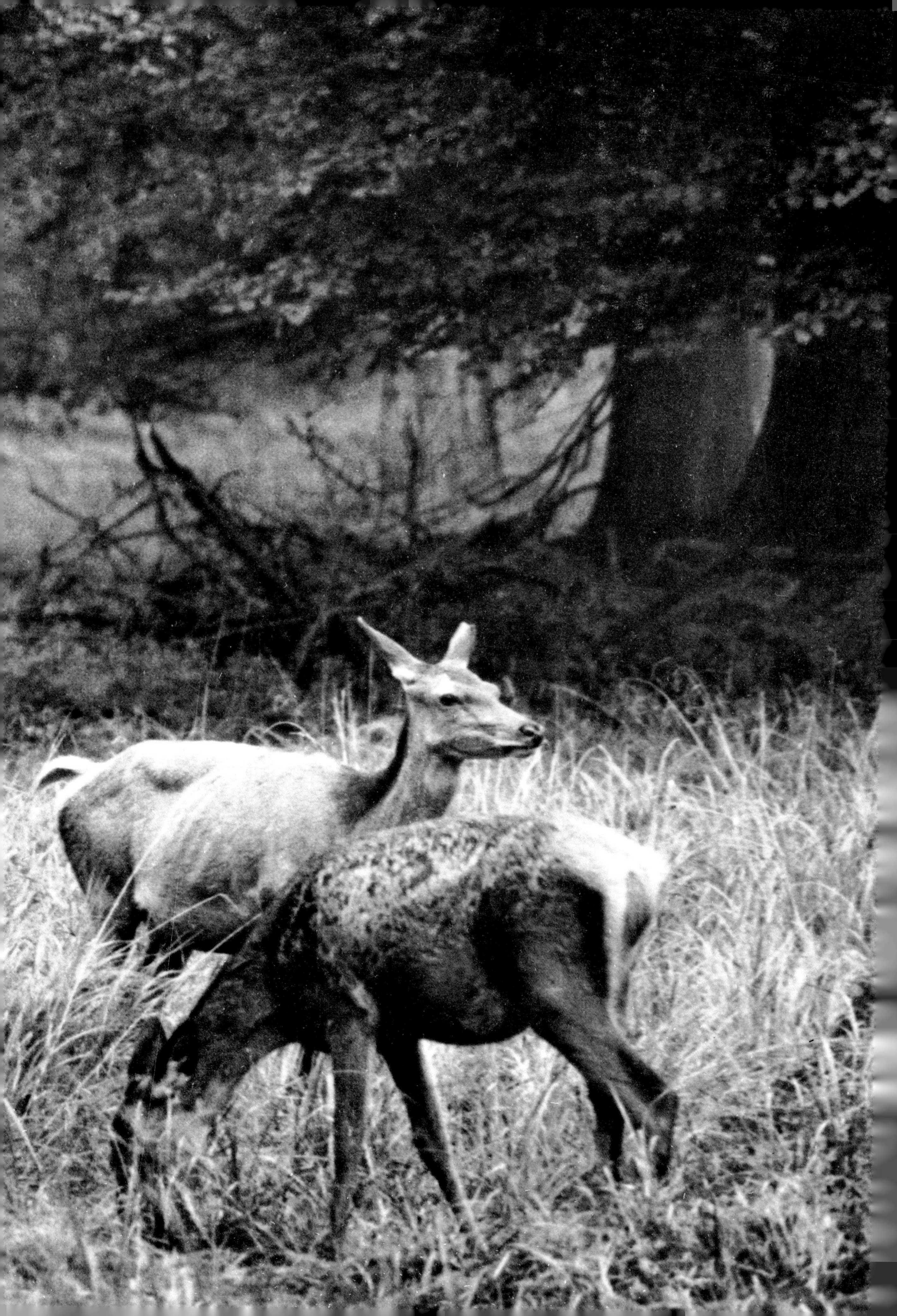

Size of the subject imaged on the negative in a 35 mm camera (negative format 24 mm × 36 mm) in relation to the focal length of the lens employed, the angular field and the practical result (Leitz)

Focal lengths in mm	Angular field for infinity/diagonal	Magnification in comparison with f=50 mm	At this distance (in metres) a man standing erect is photographed to full size of the negative
21	92	0·42 ×	1·1
28	76	0·56 ×	1·4
35	64	0·70 ×	1·8
50	45	1·0 ×	2·5
65	36	1·3 ×	3·3
90	27	1·8 ×	4·5
100	25	2·0 ×	5·0
135	18	2·7 ×	6·8
180	14	3·6 ×	9·0
200	12	4·0 ×	10·0
250	10	5·0 ×	12·5
280	8·5	5·6 ×	14
400	6	8·0 ×	20
560	4·5	11·2 ×	28
800	3	16·0 ×	40

Focal length

The focal length is defined as the distance from the plane in which the lens forms an image of a very distant object to the optical centre of the lens. For any particular lens this distance is constant; it is expressed in millimetres and is engraved on the mount; it is generally denoted by the letter f (not to be confused with the f-number or relative aperture of the lens). As already stated, the focal length of a standard lens is about equal to the diagonal of the negative. If the focal length is increased, the image formed by the lens becomes larger in the same proportion, but the angle of view decreases.

Diaphragm

The diaphragm (adjustable stop) is essentially a plate with a hole, of variable size, mounted inside the lens assembly, generally at the centre of the system. Its function is to vary the aperture and thus regulate the amount of light entering the camera through the lens. In modern cameras the diaphragm is usually of the iris type, in which the hole is formed by a set of thin concentric metal blades whose movements are controlled by means of a ring on the lens mount. The ring is provided with a scale indicating the f-number, i.e. the numerical expression of the relative aperture of the lens at its various stops; the f-number is equal to the focal length divided by the effective diameter of the lens opening: for example, f 8 (or f/8 or f 1:8). On passing from one stop to the next, e.g. from f 8 to f 5·6, the amount of light admitted through the lens is approximately doubled, so that the exposure time is halved. On some modern lenses the real aperture, determined by photometric measurement ('T', signifying transmission), is marked alongside the geometric aperture and relative aperture of the diaphragm. Besides functioning as a 'light gate', the diaphragm improves optical performance by reducing the aberrations, increasing the angular field and, most important, increasing the depth field.

Depth of field

When a particular object is sharply in focus, other objects closer or farther away will not appear equally sharp on the film. But the decline in sharpness within a certain zone extending behind and in front of the focal distance is only slight, so that all objects within that zone–which is called the depth of field of the lens–are imaged with acceptable sharpness.

The extent of the depth of field depends on several factors: focal length of the lens, the f-number used, the distance of the focusing plane and the sharpness required. The depth of field is particularly important in colour photography. Present-day colour films are still relatively slow; therefore a large aperture (low f-number) has to be employed, so that the available depth of field is relatively small.

Sensitivity or speed of the film

To obtain correct exposure times, it is necessary to know the 'speed' of the sensitized material (the photographic emulsion). The relative speed of the emulsion is indicated on the package in which the film is sold. The system of speed figures now most widely used is the ASA system. There are also other systems, notably the DIN system. To compare the figures in the various speed systems it is necessary to consult a comparative table.

Colour sensitivity

The colour sensitivity denotes the relative response of the photographic emulsion to different colours, i.e. to light of different wavelengths. For black-and-white negative materials this sensitivity, which is not equal for the different wavelengths, extends approximately from 200 to 500 nanometres. Theoretically, a colour emulsion should be equally sensitive to all wavelengths of the spectrum.

Grain

If a black-and-white negative, after development, is examined under a microscope, the image formed in the emulsion is seen to be made up of irregularly shaped black grains of silver. The fineness and sharpness of the image depend on the graininess of the photographic material, which in turn determines the

Table for comparison of speed of films as expressed in different systems

ASA/B.S.	DIN	SCHEINER
10	11	22
12	12	23
16	13	24
20	14	25
25	15	26
32	16	27
40	17	28
50	18	29
64	19	30
80	20	31
100	21	32
125	22	33
160	23	34
200	24	35
250	25	36
320	26	37
400	27	38
500	28	39
650	29	40
800	30	41
1.000	31	42
1.250	32	43
1.600	33	44
2.000	34	45
2.500	35	46

ASA : American Standard Association
B.S. : British Standards Institution
DIN : Deutsche Industrie Normen (German)
SCHEINER: As defined by Scheiner

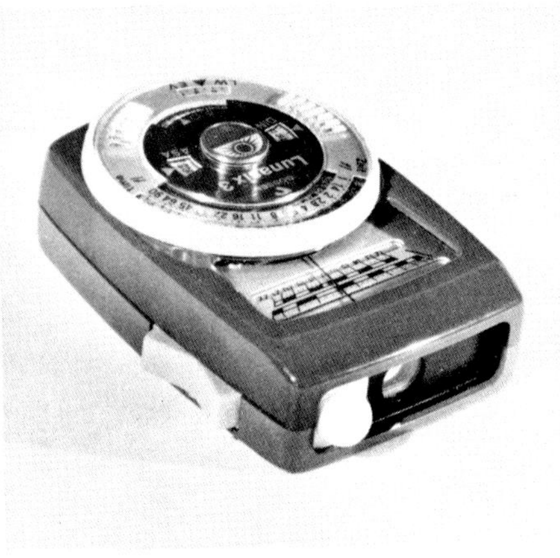

Lunasix exposure meter. This highly sensitive instrument, which gives readings even in extremely poor light, is designed for the measurement of reflected light or of incident light and for use with film speeds ranging from 6 to 12,000 ASA.

resolving power of the emulsion. In principle, a colour image is less grainy than a black-and-white one, but because of the thickness of the colour-sensitive layers the resolving power of colour-negative materials is relatively low.

Hyperfocal distance

This is an important concept. It denotes the distance from the camera to the 'near limit' of the depth of field when the lens is focused on infinity. If the lens is focused on the hyperfocal distance, the depth of field extends from half the hyperfocal distance to infinity.

This depth of field is quite large for a standard lens or a low-powered telephoto lens, so that you can get shots of an animal 'on the run' without your having to make last-minute focusing adjustments. The hyperfocal distance varies with the diaphragm stop (f-number) and the required definition. It is often indicated on the lens mount. But even if it is not, it can easily be calculated from the following formula:

$$\frac{\text{focal length} \times \text{sharpness}}{\text{lens aperture}}$$

For a small picture format the sharpness tolerance, or circle of confusion, should be at least 1/2000 of the focal length.

Magnification

The magnification or magnifying power of a telephoto lens depends on the focal length of the lens and on the distance between the camera and the object to be photographed. For practical purposes the magnifying power is calculated with reference to the normal focal length of the camera, i.e. when fitted with a standard lens. For the 35 mm camera the standard lens has a focal length of about 50 mm; a lens with a focal length of 400 mm will have a magnification of 400 : 50 = 8.

The accompanying table gives recommended shutter speeds for photographing a subject moving at right angles to the direction in which the lens of the camera is pointing. If the direction of movement is approximately at 45 degrees, these speeds can be halved. For movement in line with the lens direction, about one-third of the speeds in the table will give a properly sharp image on the negative.

Recommended minimum shutter speeds for photographing a moving object

Speed of movement of the subject in metres/second	Distance of the subject from the camera			
	5 m	25 m	50 m	100 m
0·25	1/100	1/25	1/10	1/5
1	1/300	1/100	1/50	1/25
5	1/1500	1/800	1/200	1/100
10	1/2000	1/1000	1/300	1/200

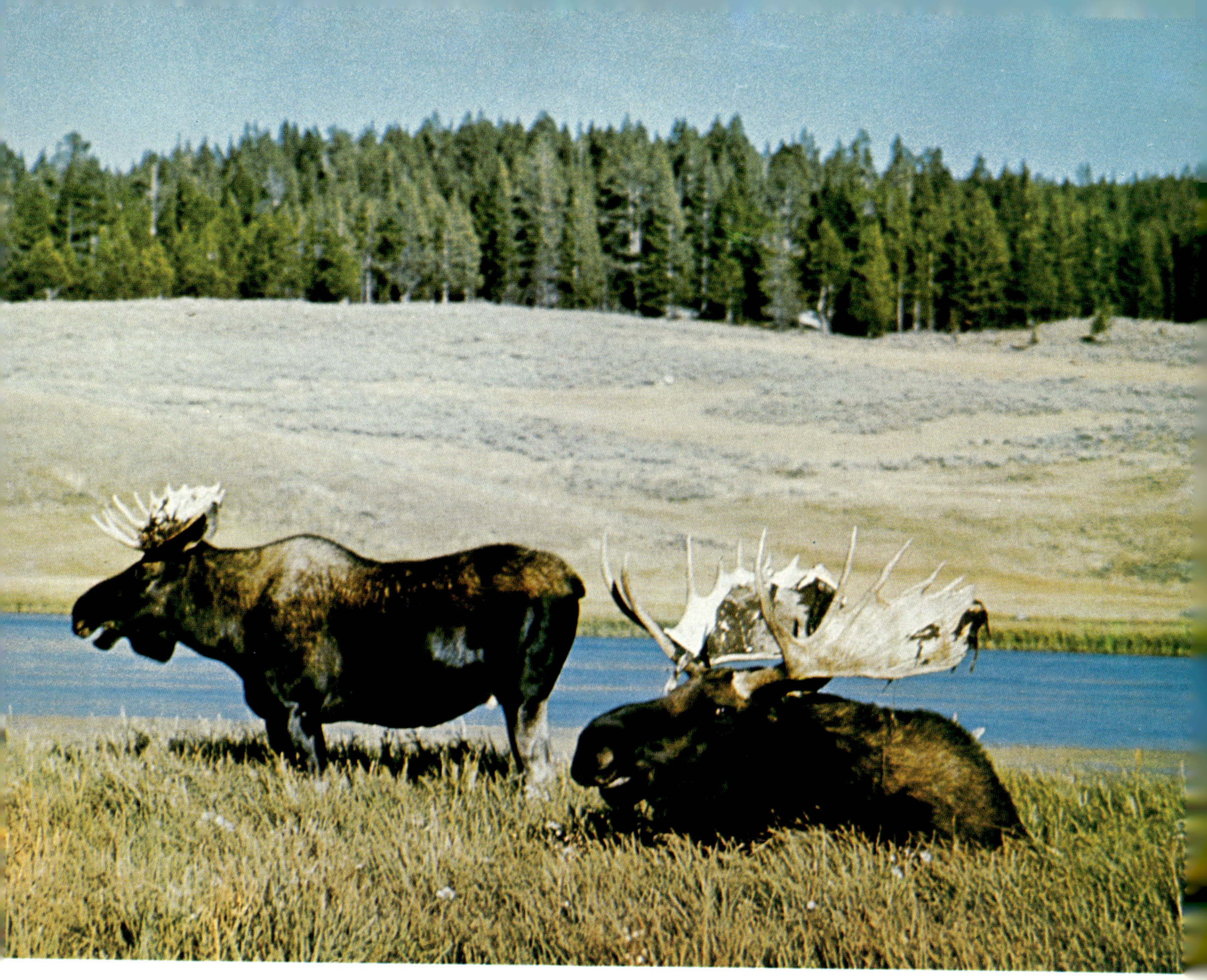

The elk (*Alces alces*), or moose as it is called in America, an enormous animal both in height and weight, lives in the forest regions of the far north of Europe and America. It has a preference for territory where swamps and lakes abound. Although it is a shy creature, a female accompanied by a young animal will attack an intruder, even a man, if it feels threatened. It can deliver vigorous kicks with its powerful front legs. The photograph shows two males in the process of 'renewing' their antlers from which the protective covering of skin is peeling off.

Equipment: 6 cm × 6 cm reflex camera with 500 mm telephoto lens; speed 1/125 sec.; aperture f 8.

The above considerations relate to the case where the object to be photographed is at infinity. But if we can sufficiently increase the extension of the camera, i.e. bring the lens farther outward, and at the same time go closer to that object, the image formed in the camera will become larger. When the object is situated at a distance equal to twice the focal length, image and object will be of equal size.

It should be noted that for the same magnification of the image on the negative the depth of field will be similar, whatever focal length employed (assuming equal image quality to be required and identical circle of confusion).

Exposure

The exposure time is the time necessary for the light which enters the camera through the lens to act on the sensitized material long enough to produce an adequate photographic image. It depends on the diaphragm stop employed, the sensitivity (speed) of the film, the illumination of the subject and the movement (if any) of the latter. The latitude, or range of exposure, of any particular film material is the difference in exposure time between over-exposure and under-exposure. Very slow films and colour films have little latitude, generally equivalent to not more than about one diaphragm stop, whereas fast films have much greater latitude.

A very simple hide consisting merely of a piece of cloth to conceal the photographer from the bird or animal.

Right: A black-headed gull (*Larus ridibundus*) photographed on a lake, where it nests in colonies. In winter it loses most of the characteristic black feathers on its head, which turns white, except for two small black spots behind and in front of the eye. Equipment: 6 cm × 6 cm reflex camera; speed 1/250 sec.; aperture f 8; film Ilford HP4.

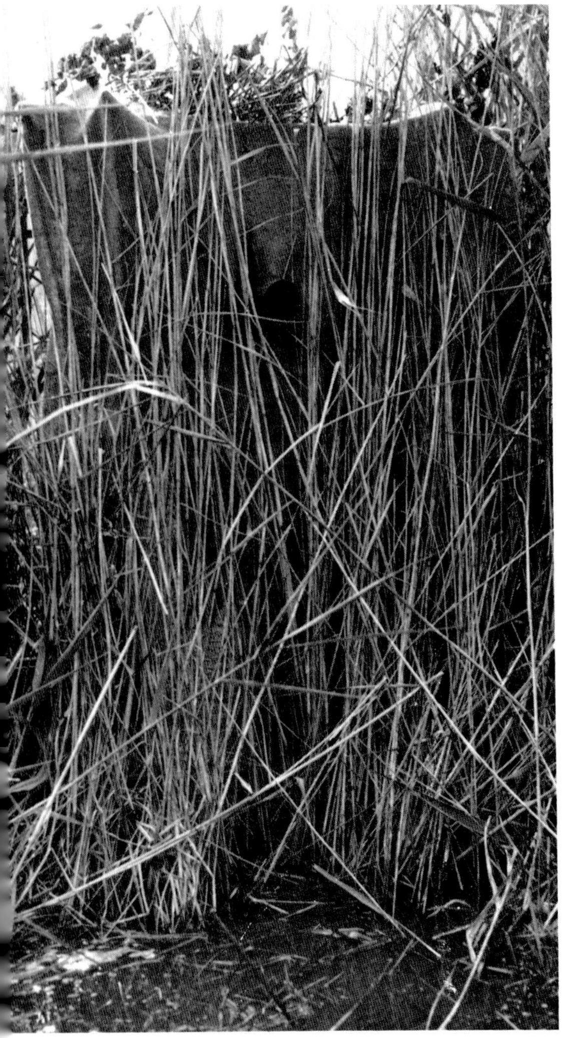

Colour temperature

Colour temperature is expressed in kelvins (K) and is a measure of the 'colour quality' of a light source. It corresponds to the temperature to which a 'black body' has to be raised to emit light having the same colour as that from the source in question. Colour temperature measurements are applicable to sources which have a continuous spectrum, such as sunlight or the light from an incandescent lamp. For discharge lamps (fluorescent lighting) the colour temperature is only an approximation and bears no relation to the actual temperature of the source. The colour temperature of average daylight (a mixture of sunlight and skylight) is between 5500 and 6000 K; photoflood lamps: 3400 K; ordinary incandescent lamps: 2900 K.

Colour temperature meter

This is an appliance for measuring the colour temperature of a light source. It comprises two photocells side by side, one of which is sensitive to blue and the other to red radiation, which give an indication of the colour temperature and enable the colour quality of the light source to be suitably chosen or to be adjusted by means of special filters. In some types of meter there is only one photocell, to which light is alternately admitted through a red and a blue filter.

Lens coating

Coating consists of depositing a thin layer of calcium fluoride or magnesium fluoride on the surface of the lens by condensation from a vapour. A coated (or bloomed) lens has one or more of its air/glass surfaces coated in this way. The effect is to reduce the amount of light lost by reflection. As a result the transmission efficiency, which may be as little as 50 per cent for an uncoated lens system, can be increased to 80 per cent.

Apochromatic lens

An apochromat is a lens which has been corrected for chromatic aberration. In a simple lens such aberration occurs because light of different colours falls in different planes of focus. More particularly, the apochromatic lens has been corrected for the three primary colours of the spectrum; an achromatic lens is corrected for two colours only.

Flash photography

Flash equipment produces a brief illumination of high intensity for still photography. There are two types in present-day use: the flash bulb and the electronic flash.

The flash bulb, which is fired electrically by means of a battery-powered capacitor circuit, consists of a glass envelope containing a wire filament covered with a primer of explosive paste and surrounded by a loose mass of fine aluminium wire in an atmosphere of oxygen. Ultra-small bulbs have a zirconium wire filling. The duration of the flash ranges from 1/125 to 1/500 second.

The electronic flash is produced by an electric discharge between two electrodes in a glass tube filled with an inert gas (such as xenon). The electric energy for the discharge is stored in a capacitor (condenser) charged from a direct-current source such as an accumulator, dry cells or rectified mains current. The duration of the flash ranges from 1/500 to 1/5000 second and even less in various types of equipment. Because of its very short duration, electronic

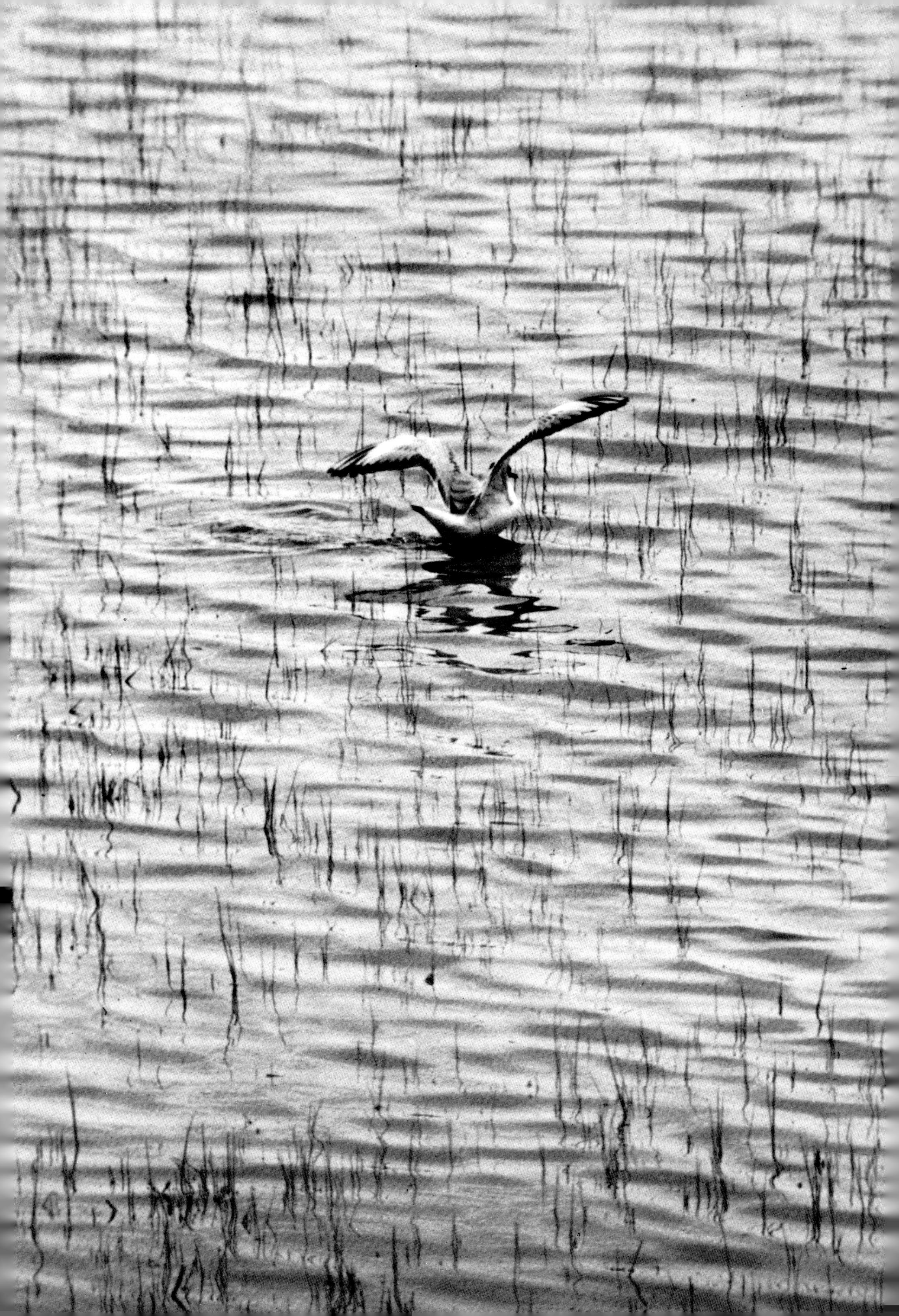

flash is highly suitable for 'freezing' fast-moving objects in high-speed photography.

White light

White light, as is generally known, is composed of a series of colours corresponding to radiations of different wavelengths increasing from one end of the spectrum to the other. These wavelengths are mixed in particular proportions to produce the 'whiteness' of the light. Any disturbance in the balance of this mixture will produce a perception of colour. Light of any one specific wavelength has a specific distinctive colour (monochromatic light). The wavelength of light is expressed in nanometres (nm). One nanometre is one millionth of a millimetre.

A 'coloured' object does not in fact possess colour as an inherent property. Its colour depends on the light that it receives, absorbs and reflects

Photosniper

Marey's 'photographic rifle', invented in the 1880s, has been mentioned earlier on. In its modern form the telephoto camera, mounted on a butt rather like that of a rifle and suitably fitted up for wildlife photography, is a very useful piece of equipment for the stalking of animals in the field, for behaviour research and for the 'dynamic' study of animal movements. It abolishes, as it were, the 40 or 50 yards which is the closest that a shy and wily animal, unaccustomed to man, will generally allow us to approach.

The principle of such a specialized photographic device, sometimes known by such names as 'photosniper', is very simple, so that the wildlife photographer can design and perhaps even construct his own. The models commercially

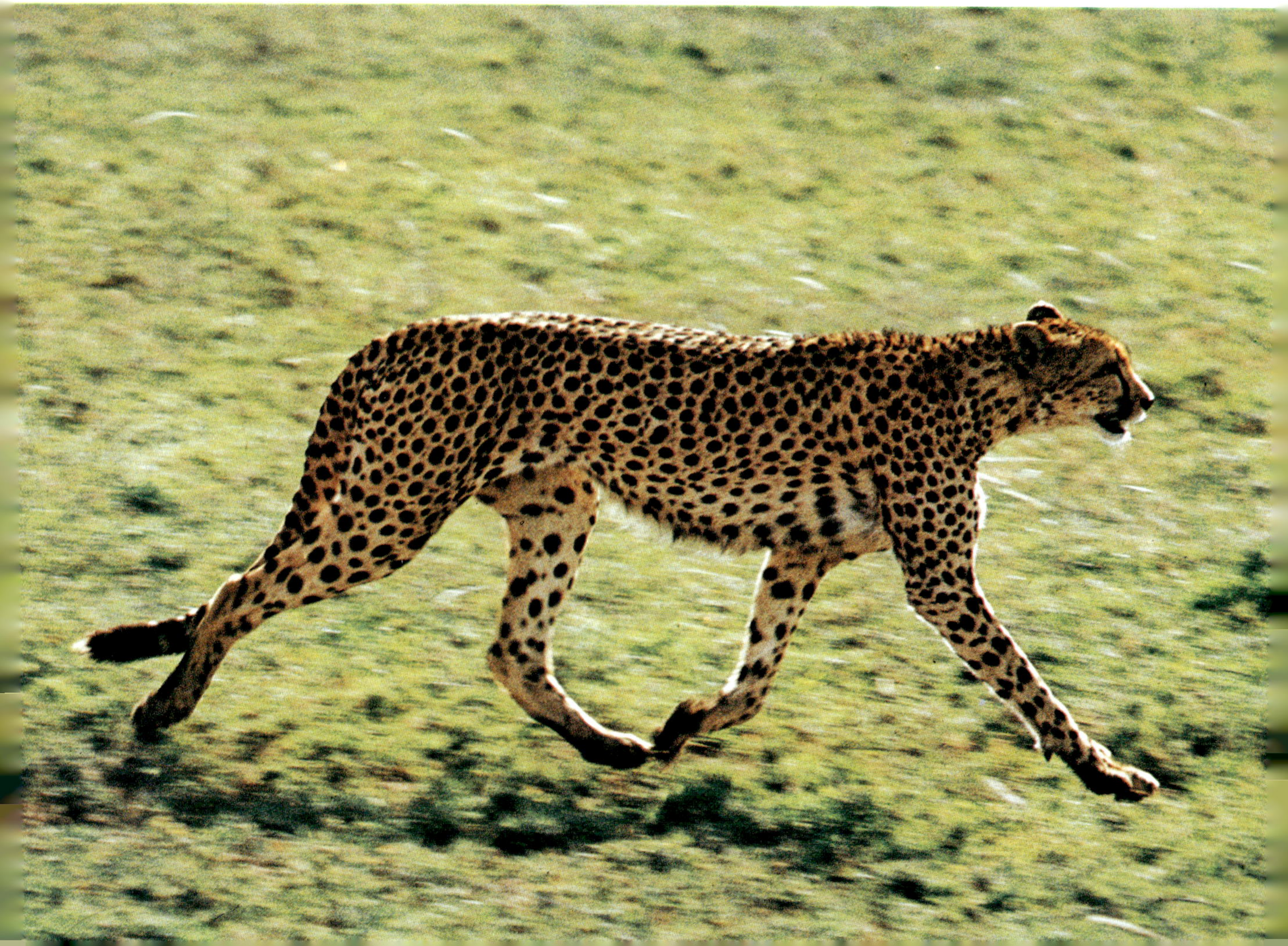

The cheetah (*Acinonyx jubatus*) holds the speed record of the mammal world. It can run at over 60 mph and used to be trained as a hunting animal by the ancient Egyptians and other peoples of the Middle East. It has the retractable claws common to the whole of the cat family and its silhouette is characteristically that of a running animal, comparable in some ways to the hare. Equipment: Photosniper; speed 1/250 sec.; aperture f 5·6.

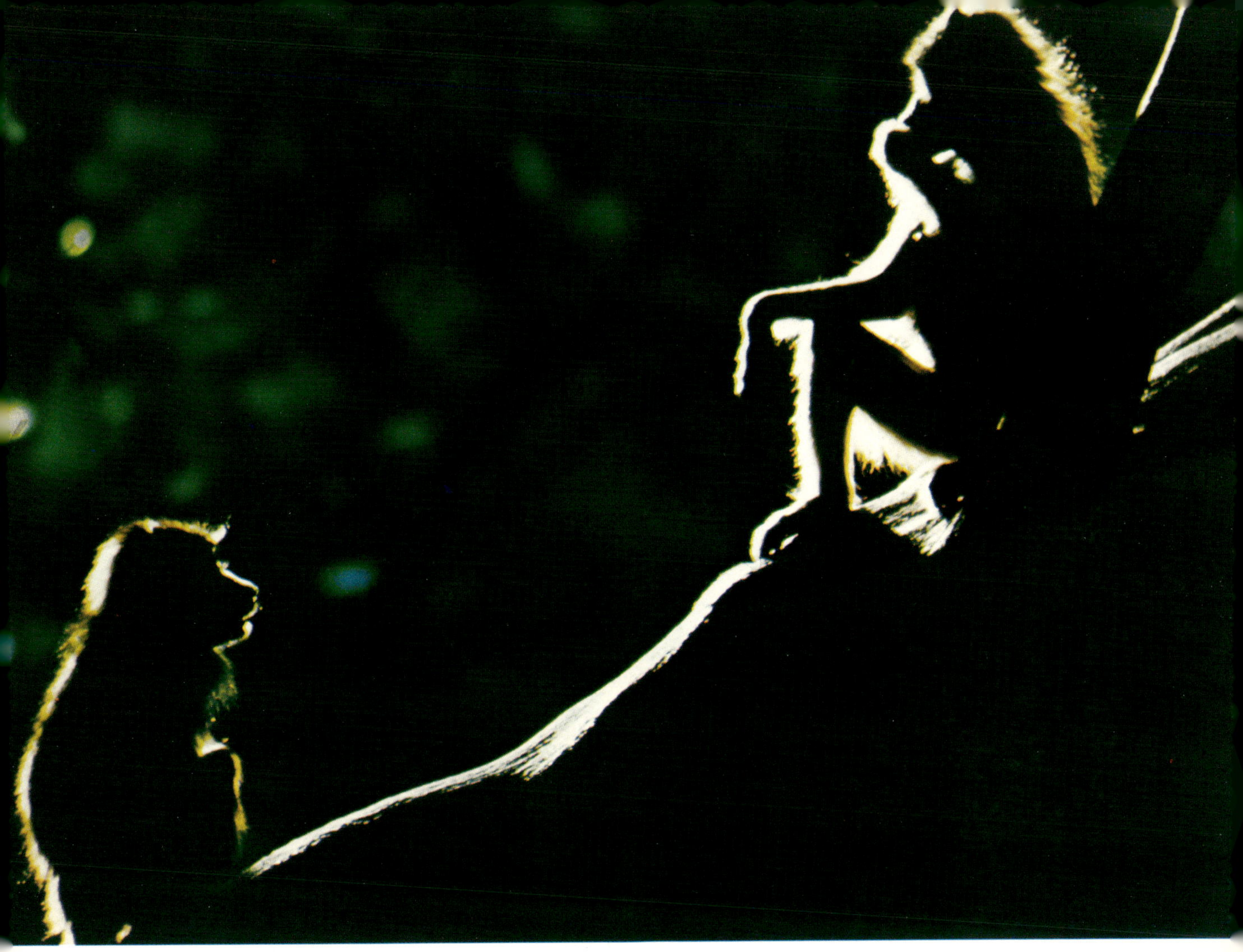

available at the present time generally give good results, though they sometimes require certain modifications. Indeed, the ideal model has yet to be invented, as it has not proved possible so far to mass-produce a universal instrument that can really satisfy all wildlife photographers with their different tastes and characters.

Around 1950 Jean Dragesco reinvented the photographic rifle first conceived by Marey. He used a doublet lens of 440 mm focal length, without a reflex camera body, but equipped with an auxiliary viewfinder for sighting on the subject. We ourselves have designed, built, modified and greatly lightened many models of camera for this purpose. As a result of the experience gained, we have established some significant rules for the design of such an instrument which has to be, above all, practical and convenient. Its essential features are as follows:

–a lens with a focal length of 400 mm;
–a sliding component for rapid focusing;
–a butt which supports the lens and rests against the photographer's shoulder;
–a 35 mm miniature camera (24 mm × 36 mm format);
–an electric motor.

With these basic data it is possible to achieve all combinations and refinements to suit the individual personality and requirements of the user.

There are various reasons for selecting a focal length of 400 mm–although there are lenses of 300, 400, 500, 600 and 1000 mm to choose from. The 400 mm lens has approximately the same magnification (× 8) as ordinary field-glasses. It is also just about the maximum with which it is possible to get pictures without blurring them due to unavoidable camera shake (minimum shutter speed 1/125

The choice of illumination is of major importance with regard to the composition and aesthetic value of a picture. With back light, as in this photograph of two baboons (*Papio papio*) in a tree, it is possible to emphasize a gesture or an intention by suitably bringing out the significant masses. Equipment: Focal length 135 mm; speed 1/250 sec.; aperture f 5·6; film Kodachrome II.

The photographic rifle invented by E.-J. Marey (1882).

Below it are shown models of birds in flight based on photographs obtained with Marey's rifle.

Opposite, above: Modern version of the photographic rifle comprising a Nikon camera with electric motor drive and 400 mm lens with special focusing attachment to enable small subjects at a distance of 10 ft to be photographed. The butt, which can swivel to permit rapid loading of the camera, contains the batteries which supply the motor with current. The shutter release is actuated by means of a micro-switch.

Opposite, below: Hasselblad camera equipped with electric motor, 70-shot magazine, Zeiss 500 mm telephoto lens (f 8) and exposure meter in the viewfinder. Beside the camera is shown the butt attachment for converting it into a 'photosniper' or 'photographic rifle'.

second). Finally, it is just about the limit above which atmospheric turbulence makes it difficult to obtain a large number of shots in succession.

The second important feature in this arrangement is the sliding device for focusing. This should be of high-precision construction and function very smoothly. It should provide an extension of at least about 10 cm (for this focal length of 400 mm), for it is often necessary to be able to photograph a small animal, or a detail of an animal, at a distance of less than about 9 feet without having to fit extra attachments such as adapter rings or extension tubes, as this would take too much time and make too much noise so close to the subject.

Except if the lens is mounted on a cine camera, the screw-type focusing ring is not suitable. With this device, quick accurate focusing is difficult, and it is awkward to manipulate if there is to be no risk of blurring the picture due to camera shake.

The butt may be of metal, wood or plastic. Wood is the most agreeable material to handle under severe climatic conditions (metal will stick to the skin in very cold weather; plastic tends to be brittle). It should be so designed that it enables the lens to be supported in a steady position with one hand (which hand also does the focusing) and should comprise a mechanical or electrical shutter release system actuated by the other hand, which also ensures stability by keeping the butt pressed against the photographer's shoulder.

The camera should be of the reflex type. Tests which we performed with a rangefinder camera were invariably disappointing.

Cameras equipped with motor-operated controls offer significant advantages. The batteries for powering the motor can conveniently be accommodated in the

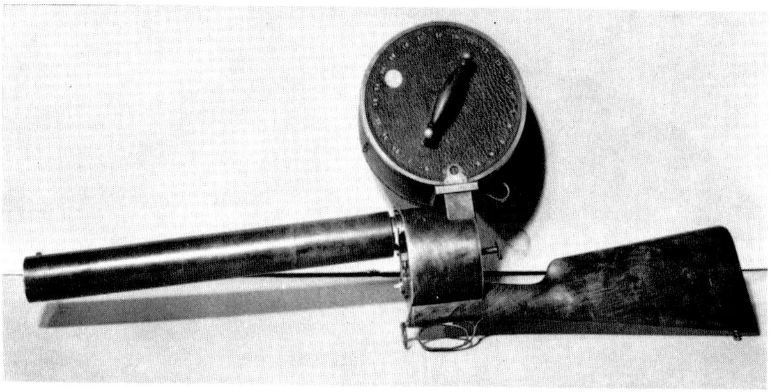

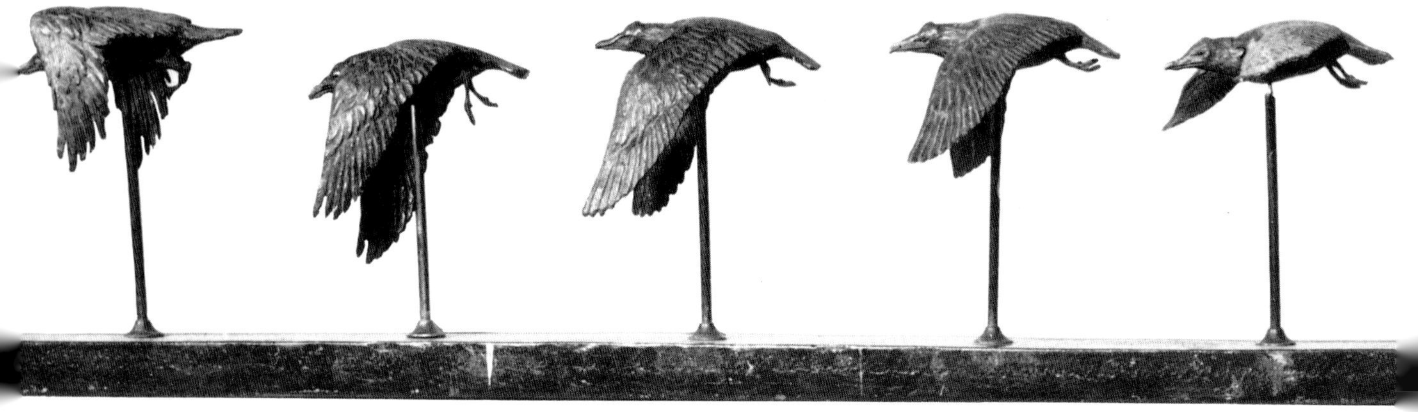

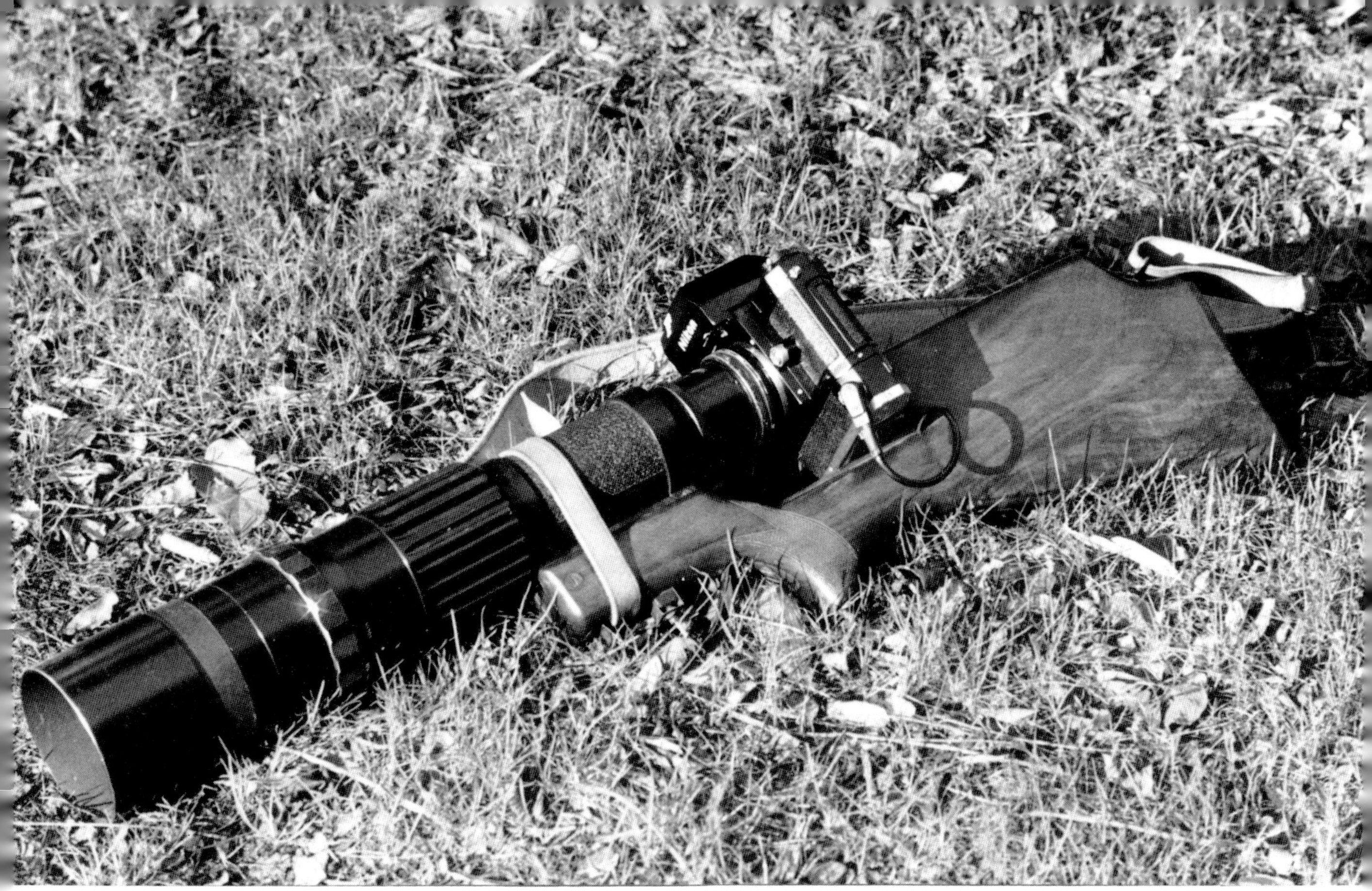

butt, and the shutter release device is a small electric switch which is very simple to install.

The motor enables the user to be ready at any time without ever having to take his eye off the viewfinder and without his hand having to interrupt the continuous focusing adjustment. Besides, to follow a running animal or a bird in flight, it may be desirable to take shots at a rate of up to three or four per second, i.e. something intermediate between conventional still photography and cinematography. We believe that the wildlife photographer's ideal instrument of the future will probably be a form of cine camera which can take sequences of shots at a rate of fifty or one hundred frames per second, from which pictures of a quality equal to that of the best still pictures can be selected.

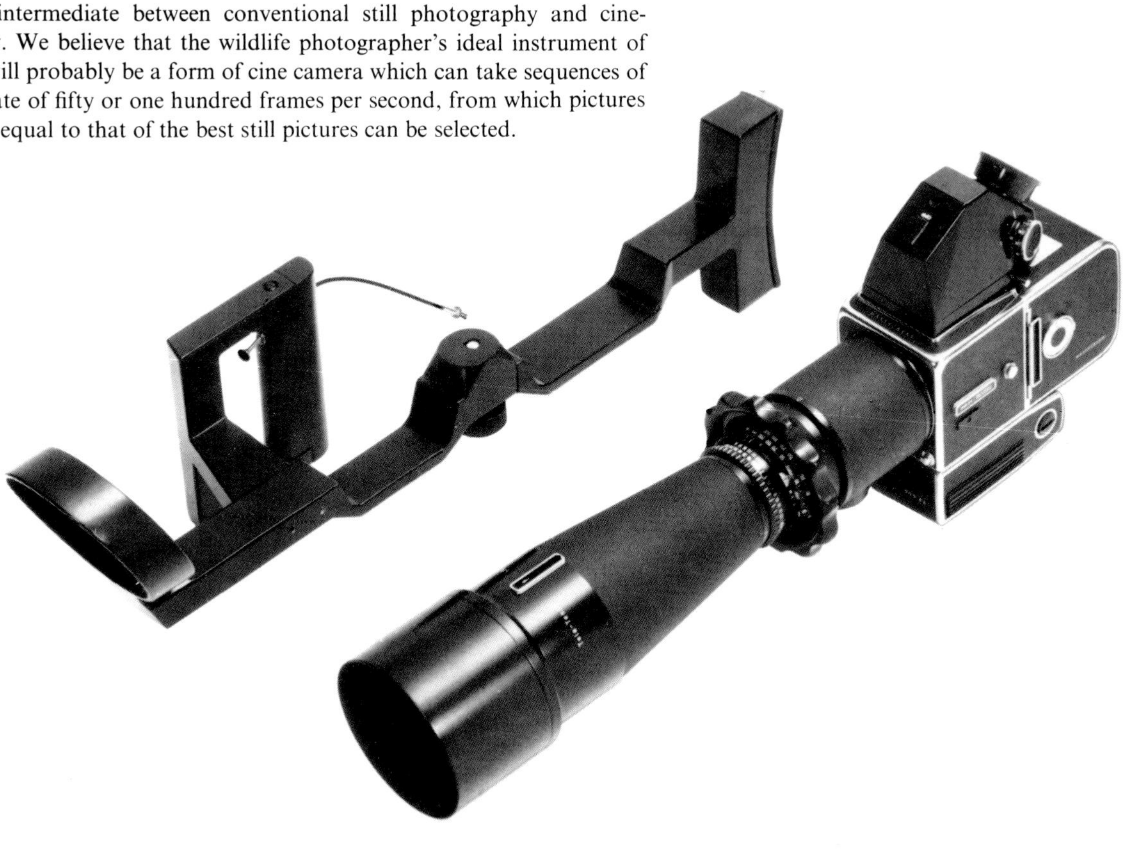

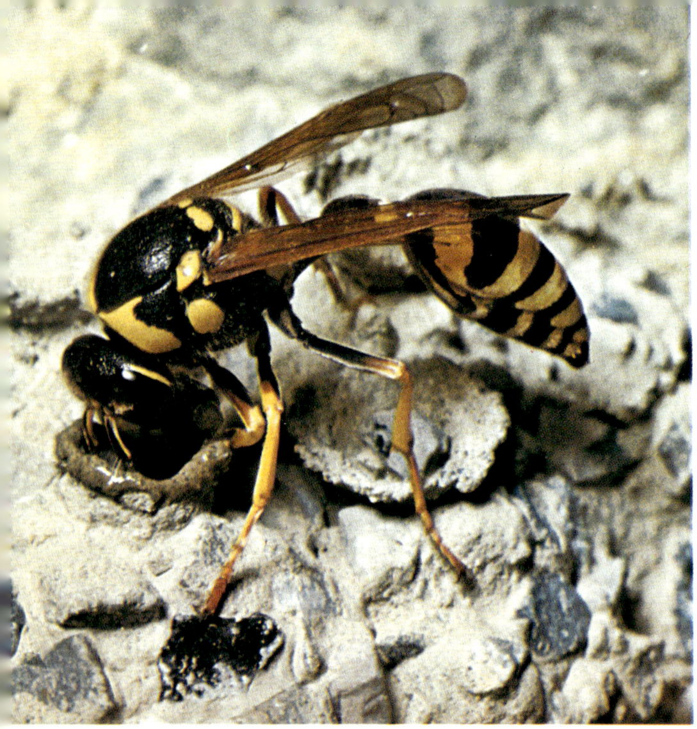
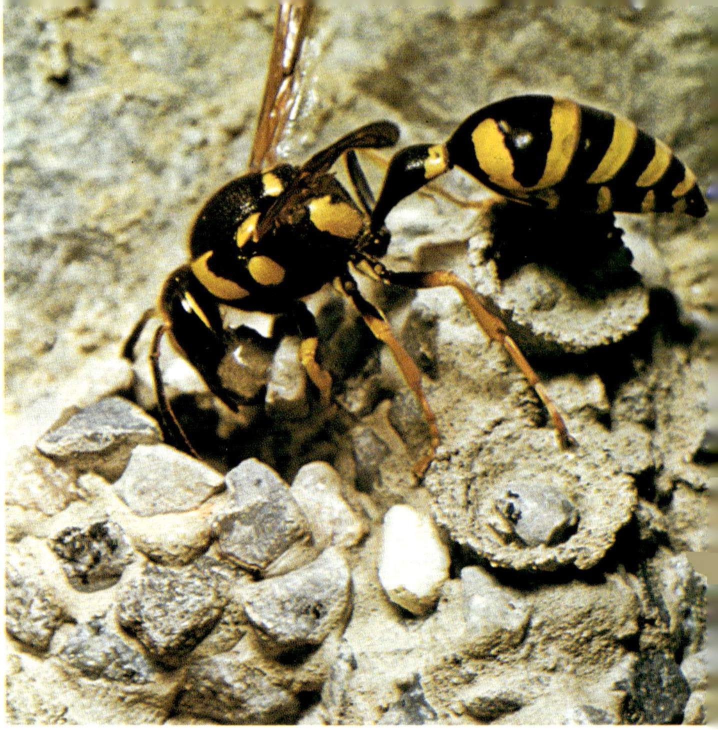
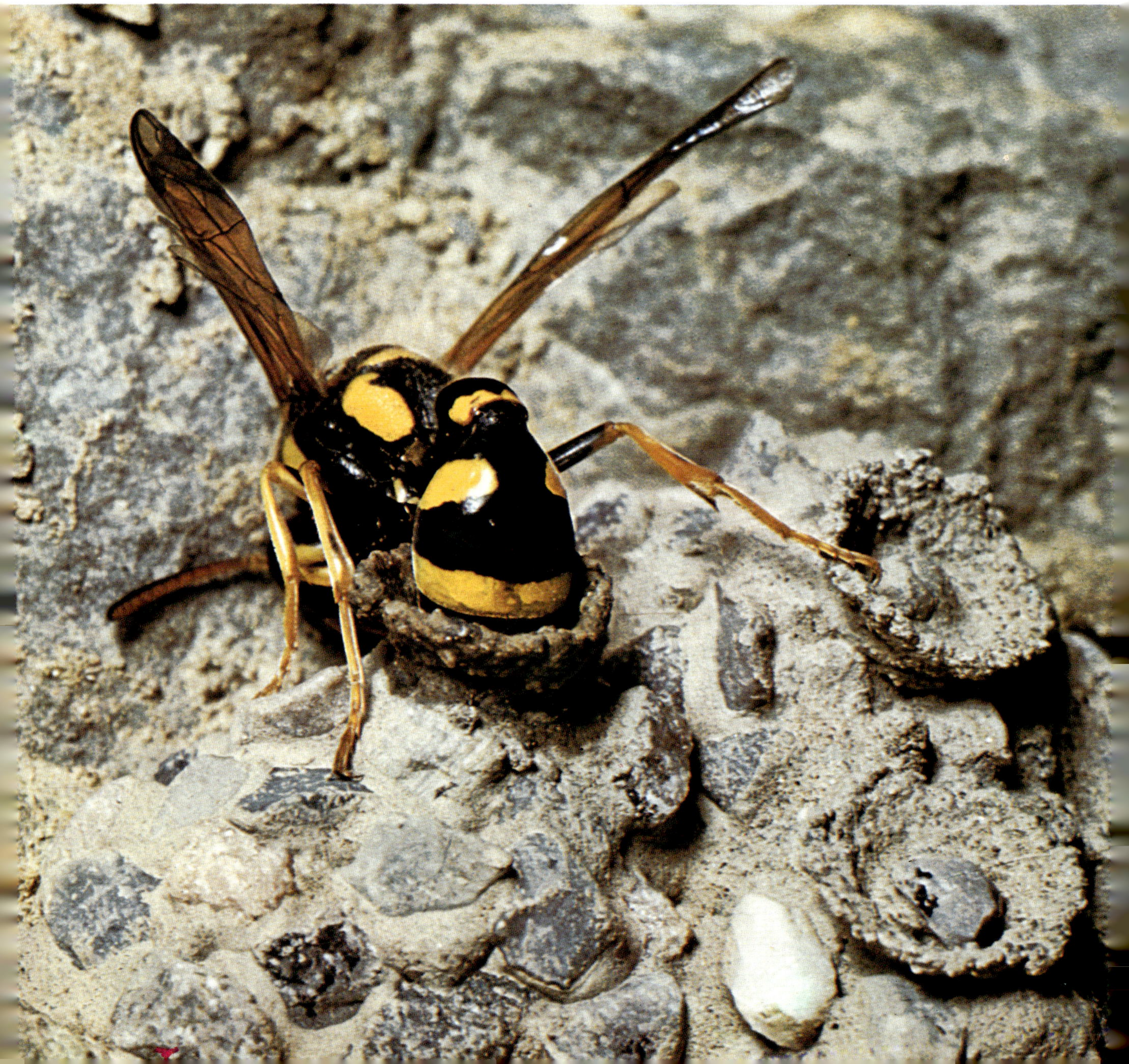

Wasps of the family *Eumenidae* include insects with curious habits, such as the species *Eumenes arbustorum* illustrated here. The eggs are laid in a nest constructed of small stones bonded together with a kind of cement which the wasps make themselves. In these 'concrete' cells the wasps deposit caterpillars which they have captured and paralysed with a sting and which will serve as food for the larvae.
Above left: The wasp brings a blob of cement for building its third nesting cell (the other two, completed and sealed, are visible on the right in the photograph).

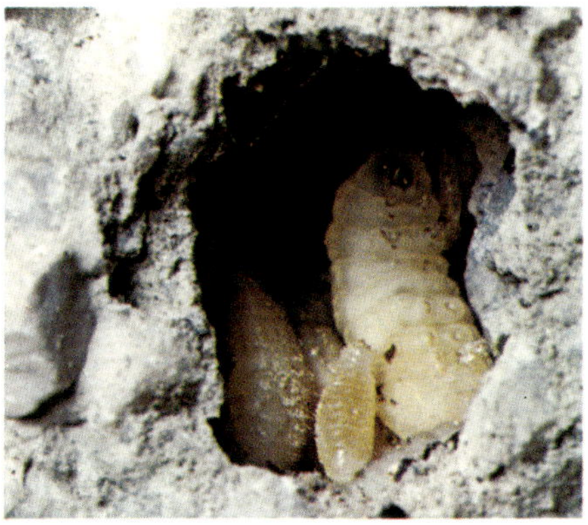

Above right: The wasp finishing the third cell by providing it with a funnel-shaped rim.
Below: The wasp is seen laying its eggs in the cell while the rim is drying and setting. The other two cells, already sealed, are clearly seen on the right.
The photograph on this page shows the interior of an opened cell, with an egg, a wasp larva and its food supply of caterpillars.
Equipment: 35 mm reflex camera with Luminar macro lens; electronic flash; film Kodachrome II.

The diagram on the right shows an exposure meter of a modern reflex camera. Instead of an external measuring instrument, it consists of elements built into the mirror which receive all the light through the lens (Topcon).

Attachments and accessories

Interchangeable camera bodies and film magazines are just a part of the photographer's equipment. But these and other attachments and accessories are important in that their proper use can often determine the success of a quick shot. With their aid the technical possibilities of the equipment can be extended and difficult subjects tackled, thereby opening up new and varied fields of photographic achievement.

Exposure meters

The built-in through-the-lens meter installed behind the lens (or in the reflex viewfinder) becomes a 'must' as soon as you wish to apply special techniques such as telephotography, macrophotography and photomicrography. Such metering is essential also in cinematography, where the succession of sequences does not tolerate a variation in exposure time.

But it is necessary to know the limitations of a separate exposure meter. For example, it is not reasonable to expect an ordinary meter with an angular field of about 60 degrees correctly to measure the exposure time for photographing a white bird perched in a green tree at a distance of 50 or 60 yards. Some exposure meters have a variable field, so that they can be used for exposure measurement at a distance, but they require an awkward additional manipulation just when you are about to get your shot.

Modern exposure meters of the cadmium sulphide (CdS) type are highly sensitive and accurate. Such a meter comprises a CdS cell which changes its electrical resistance according to the amount of light falling on it. The current for the metering circuit is supplied by a small mercury battery.

If your camera is not already equipped with a good built-in meter, as many modern 35 mm cameras are, it is essential to get a suitable meter and mount if convenient on the camera body.

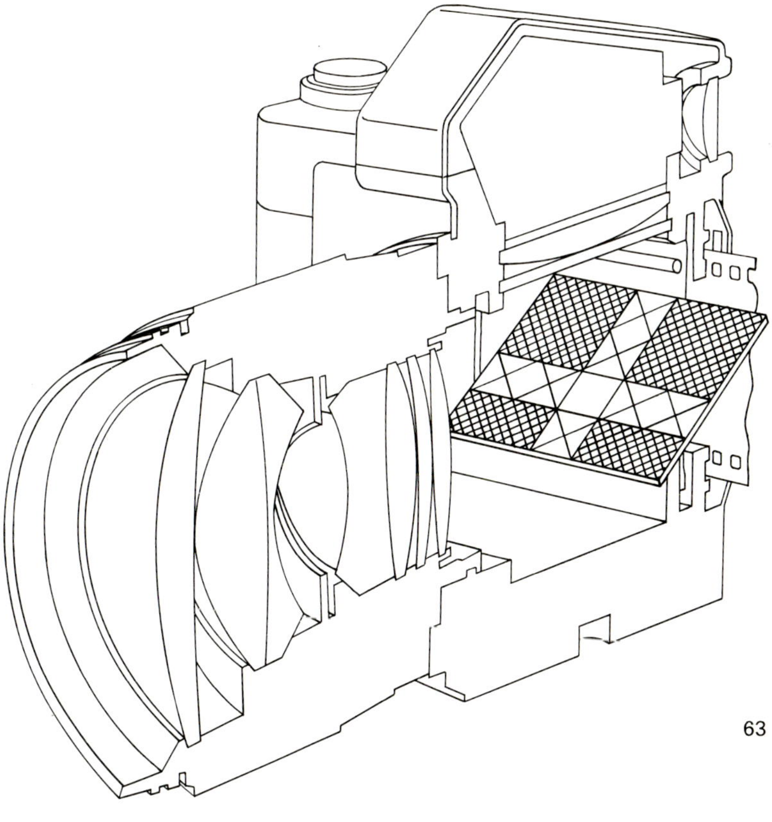

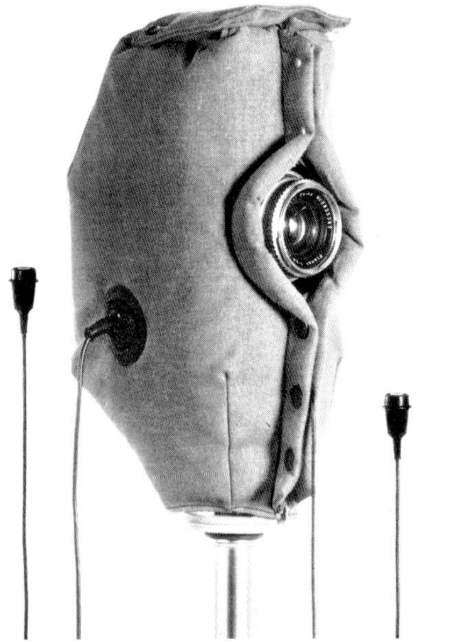

Waterproof and soundproof jacket ('blimp') of green-grey cotton fabric for Hasselblad 500 EL camera.

Soundproofing

In nature a metallic sound is quite out of character. The continuous whirring of the mechanism of a cine camera or the clicking of the shutter of a still camera, especially a reflex camera, is often liable to put the animal to flight or at least startle it.

It is therefore advisable to use all appropriate means to eliminate the noise made by the shutter release mechanism or sharp metallic sounds or at least to reduce the pitch of the sound if you cannot get rid of it entirely. To do this, the camera is enclosed in a sound-proof housing (called a 'blimp'), which may take the form of a jacket of sound-absorbing material (such as foamed nylon, rubber, polystyrene, felt, etc.), with suitable openings for access to the main controls. It is made by cutting pieces of such material to the appropriate size and assembling them with the aid of special glue or adhesive fabric. Besides sound-proofing, it is desirable to eliminate reflections from shiny metal parts of the camera and its tripod or stand, as these flashes of light may also arouse the animals' suspicion.

Stand

The camera stand, usually in the form of a tripod, is an indispensable item of equipment. For cinematography it is essential to use a stand with a panoramic top that can move very smoothly and precisely. With a 'photosniper' you may have to work under conditions of poor light or you may have to spend long hours waiting in a 'hide'. It is therefore important to choose the stand for your camera with great care. We favour the wooden stand, which is light, flexible, capable of absorbing vibrations or jolts, unaffected by sea-water and non-reflecting. Metal fittings on the stand (its top, locking screw, etc.) should not be brightly reflective. If necessary, they should be coated with a special dull-black varnish. The stand should be at least 12 inches high.

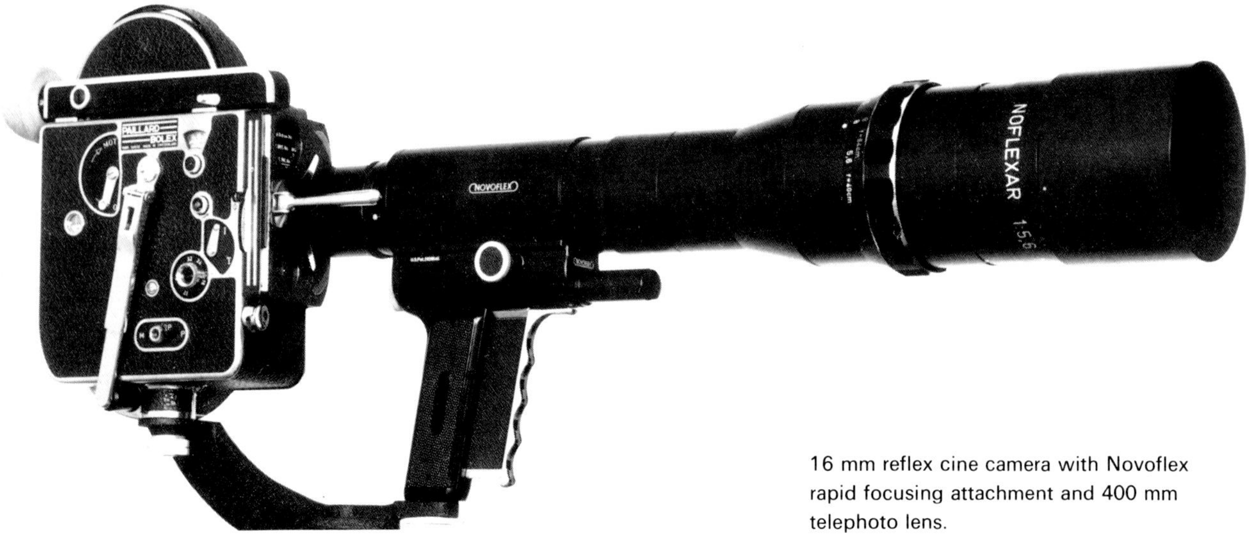

16 mm reflex cine camera with Novoflex rapid focusing attachment and 400 mm telephoto lens.

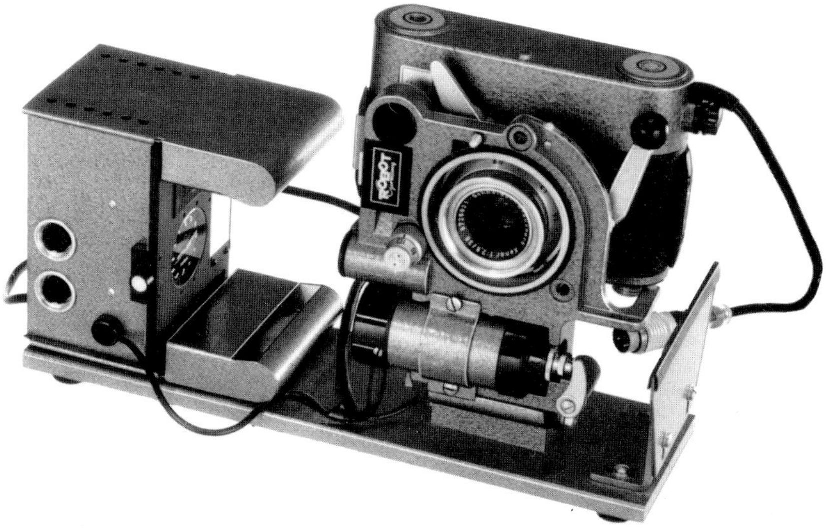

Fully automatic camera with all-electric control and time-switching device for taking successive shots at predetermined intervals.

Below: 6 cm × 6 cm reflex camera with electric motor and radio control unit (range: nearly 2 miles).

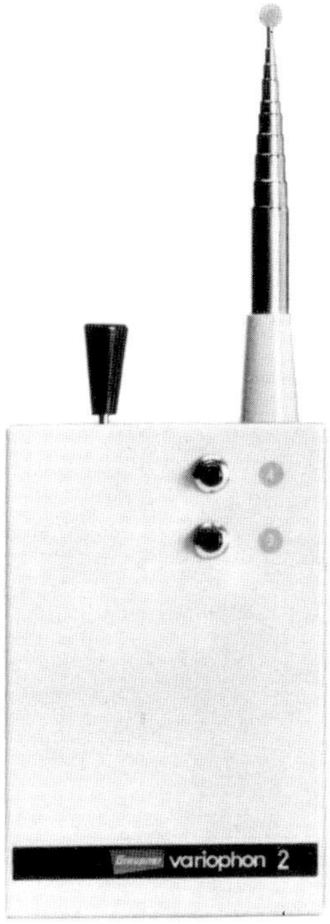

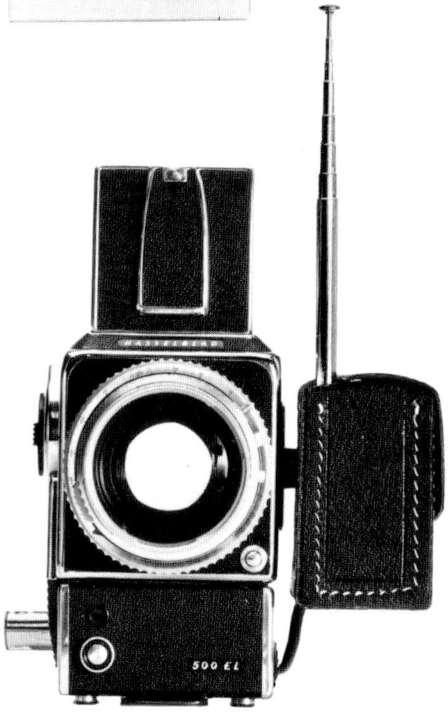

Remote control

This technique calls for long hours, sometimes days, of meticulous preparation and rehearsal. It consists of actuating the shutter release of the camera – which should be securely fixed and concealed in a strategic position – from some considerable distance by mechanical or electrical means or by radio control. The photographer, who takes up his position a hundred or more yards away, observes through field-glasses the arrival of the subject within the picture area and focusing range of the camera.

Remote control is employed mainly in circumstances where the terrain itself presents unusual problems (difficult accessibility) or the animal or bird to be photographed is particularly shy or dangerous. The results obtained in this way are often disappointing, for it is difficult to judge from a distance whether the subject's behaviour at a particular instant is really of interest, so that there is considerable risk of releasing the shutter too soon or too late. Besides, there is the ever-present risk of being let down by the controlling equipment itself, which is never perfectly reliable, no matter which system is used. On one occasion, with radio control, we found the whole film wound onto its take-up spool, although we had in fact released the shutter only once – or so we thought. Somehow the electric motor in the camera, presumably responding to some unknown frequency, had 'gone berserk' and wound up the whole film.

Obviously, it is essential to fit the remote-controlled camera with a properly adapted electric motor drive for film transport, as it is impracticable to go up to the camera to wind on the film after each shot. Such action could frighten away the animal or bird and would certainly give away the whereabouts of the camera.

Transport

For transporting photographic equipment in the field, especially in conditions where it will be exposed to humidity, dust or wind-driven sand, it is necessary to provide sealed lightweight boxes lined with foamed plastic in which cameras will be safe from jolts and corrosive attack.

However, since you may always want to get out your camera quickly for some impromptu shot, it is essential that the box or container should be of such design that it can be opened quickly and silently, that the equipment is readily accessible and that the cameras are always kept loaded with film in readiness for action.

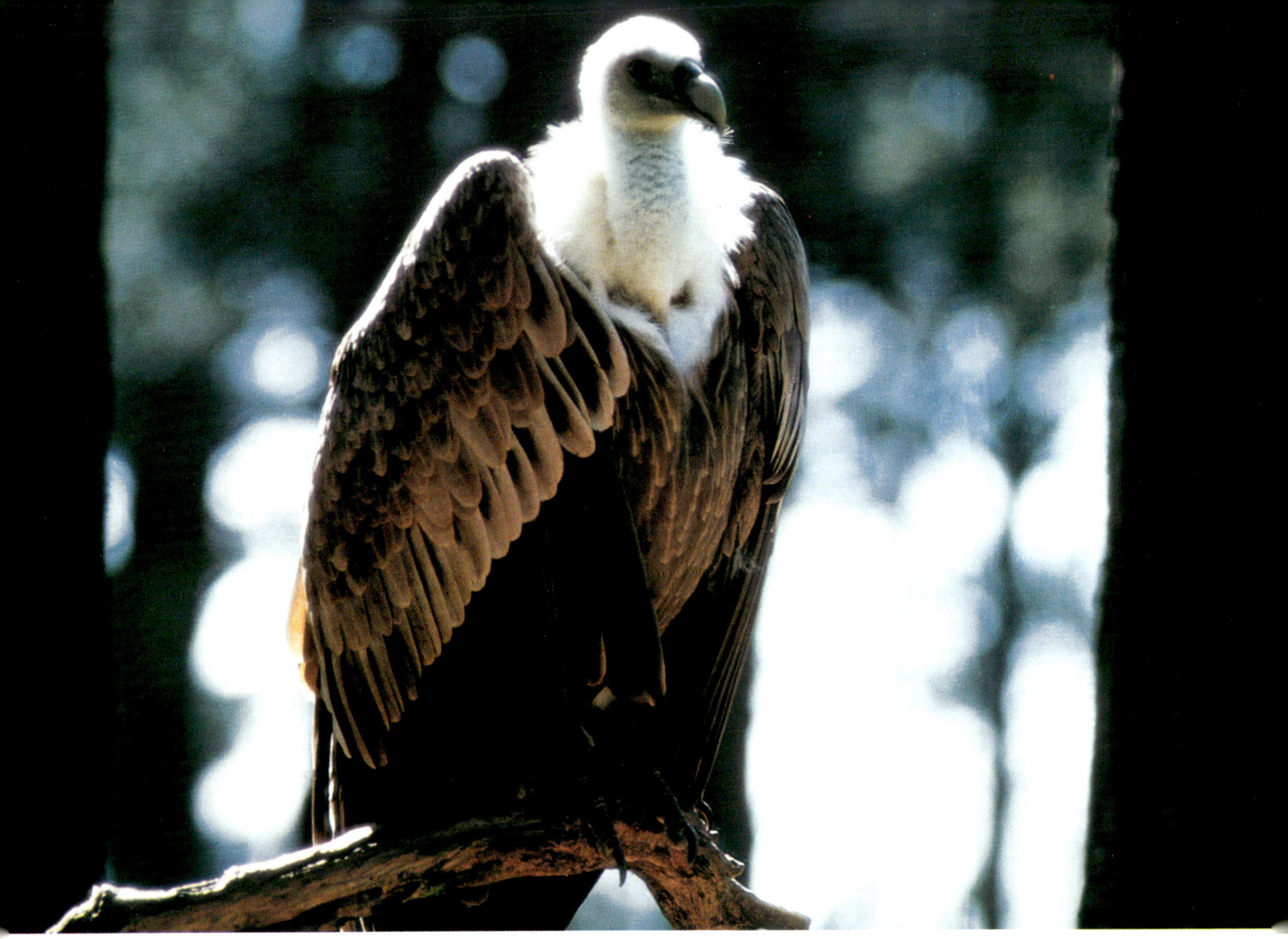

Not very long ago the griffon vulture (*Gyps fulvus*) used to be hunted for its feathers, which were used for decoration on ceremonial garments. This large bird of prey has become very rare in France, where only a few couples remain in the Pyrenees. This photograph was taken in a zoo with back light.

Light-tight bag (changing bag)

Though not indispensable, this can be a very useful piece of equipment. It has a zip fastener and two holes through which you insert your arms to open your camera and a film with which you can load it. The bag is also a very convenient standby in an emergency when a film becomes jammed in the camera. It enables you to open the camera and release the film without fogging it to broad daylight.

We have refrained from mentioning the lens hood and filters as accessories. In fact, the lens hood is to be regarded as an integral part of the lens in that it can improve its performance, while the correct use of filters is closely associated with camera technique and a knowledge of the type of film you are using.

Films

A well known press photographer remarked not so very long ago: 'Whenever I have to take a colour photograph, I close my eyes when I press the release button.' These words express a real or affected lack of interest in getting colour pictures. But that man belongs to a bygone school of photography. To think and see in colour are the characteristics of the modern generation of photographers.

We ourselves have always held black-and-white photography in high esteem, as it makes constant demands on the photographer to achieve correct illumination and harmonizing of masses and tonal values. The thrill of getting a good picture as a reward for skilled work done in the silence of the darkroom forms, as it were, the extension to the successful camera work that preceded it.

Although colour photography originated as far back as the last century, it is still only in its infancy. Physically and chemically the process still leaves much to be desired, and it gives only an approximate rendering of the true colours.

Because of the complexity of the process, the amateur – and many professionals too – rely on the services of large commercial laboratories for processing their exposed films.

Colour film processing has thus become an industry, not a craft; as soon as the film is out of the photographer's hands, he ceases to have any control over the quality of the result. This is certainly to be regretted, for we still believe that the interpretation of a 'moment' captured from nature owes more to art than to technology.

The choice of film is a matter of taste and also of technical necessity. This choice must be made – as has already been pointed out in the discussion of cameras – before starting out on a photographic expedition in the field; for it is very awkward, once you are on the scene of your photographic activities and about to start getting your pictures, to have to change the film in your camera. This could spoil everything.

Even as recently as about twelve years ago certain colour photographs were impossible because the emulsions of the films available then were too slow. But no wildlife photographer can afford to ignore the possibilities offered by the new generation of colour films for photography early in the morning or late in the evening – periods of great activity in the animal world.

The sensitized material is the interpreter of the light to which it is exposed in

The fulmar (*Fulmarus glacialis*) is a species of petrel which is found chiefly in arctic latitudes, though it occasionally comes as far south as the English Channel. It is a very powerful flier which can remain aloft for days on end, gliding with wings outspread or swooping lower over the waves. It comes ashore only for nesting.
Equipment: 35 mm camera with lens of 250 mm focal length.

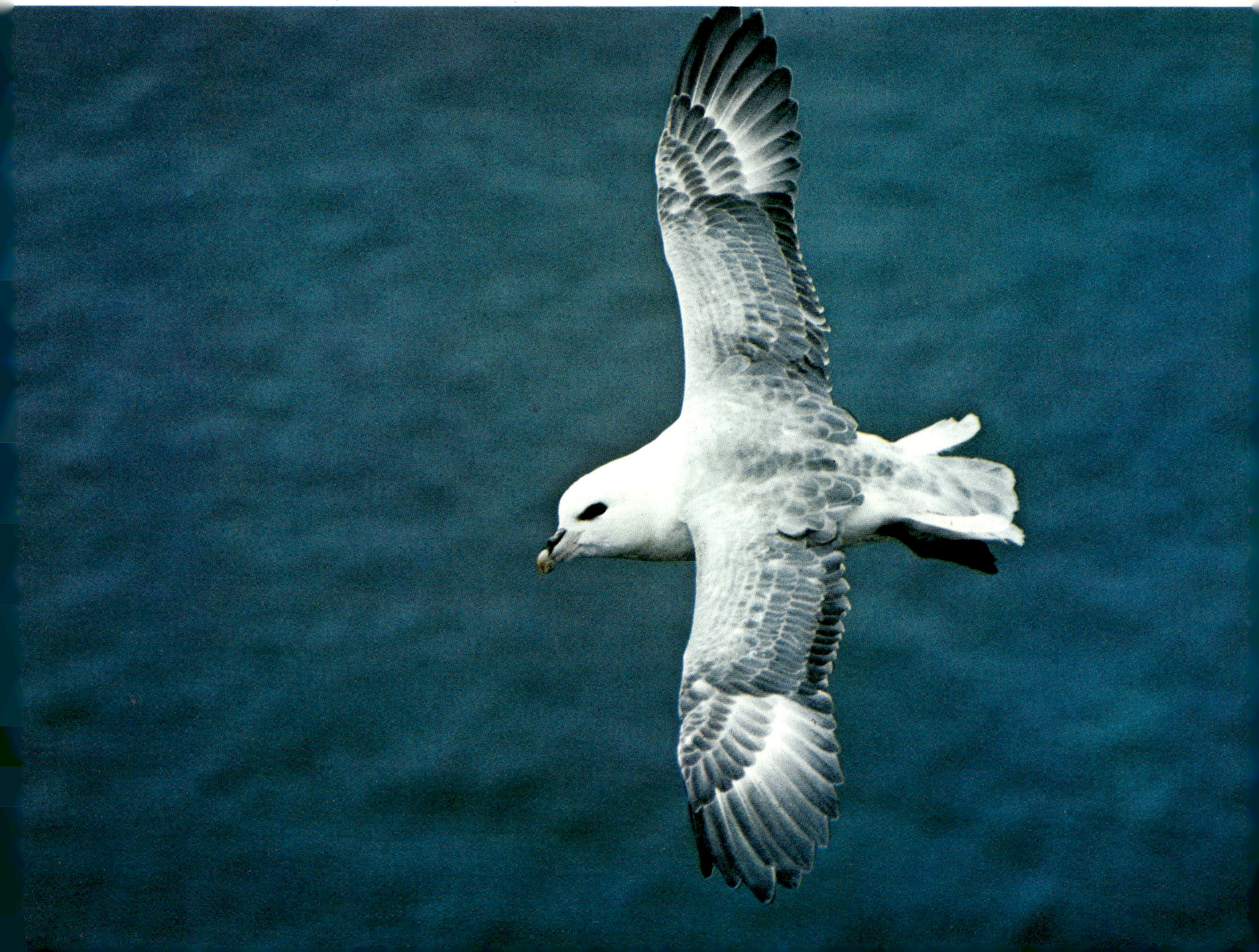

The curlew (*Numenius arquata*) is a very suspicious bird which takes to flight as soon as it is disturbed, uttering the characteristic cry from which it derives its name. After a short flight it alights and tries to lure the intruder away from its territory. To surprise a curlew on its nest requires elaborate precautions.
Equipment: Photosniper with 400 mm focal length (bird in flight); the nesting bird was photographed with a 35 mm camera and 250 mm lens from a light portable hide.

the camera, and it is necessary for the photographer to know something about its general characteristics, which it shares with any other photographic emulsion, whether colour or black-and-white: sensitivity or speed, contrast or gamma, grain, resolving power and colour sensitivity.

Apart from colour sensitivity (which you can modify by means of filters), all these characteristics are closely interrelated and interdependent. A film with a speed of 400 ASA, for example, i.e. a fast film in terms of amateur photography, will have a rather coarse grain and relatively low contrast. The grain size of the emulsion increases with its sensitivity, so that a fast emulsion will have a coarser grain than a slow one.

The grain of a photographic emulsion, as has already been explained, is due to the lumps of silver which form the image in the negative. A fast emulsion will generally also have a lower resolving power, and the graininess of the developed negative can be very noticeable. But one should not be dogmatic and attach excessive importance to this above all other considerations, as sometimes used to be done in the earlier days of photography, when technical perfection was often rated higher than artistic merit. Although the grain may appear very

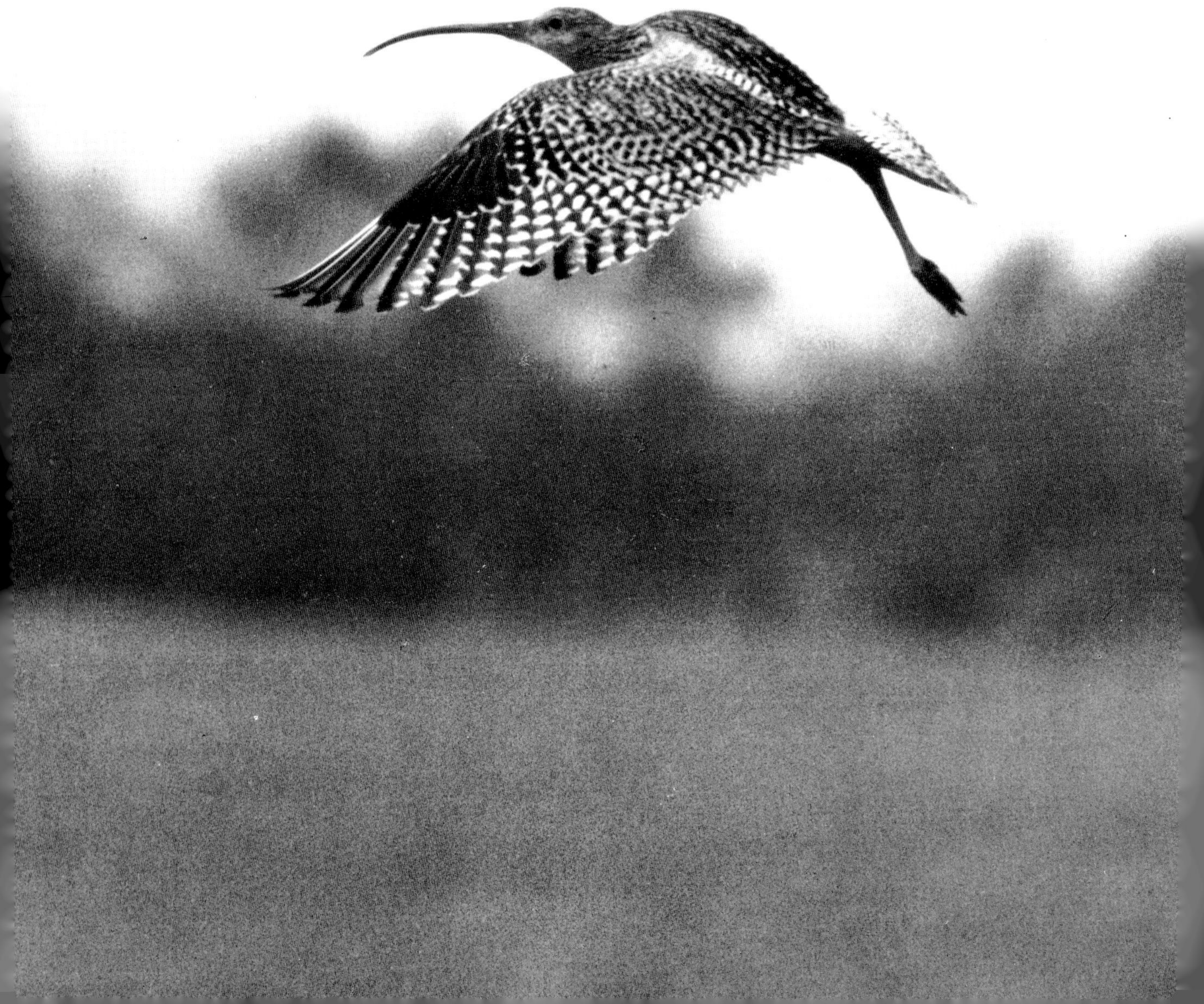

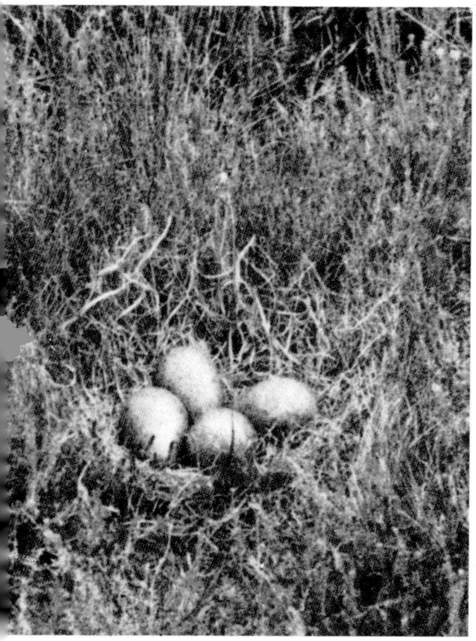

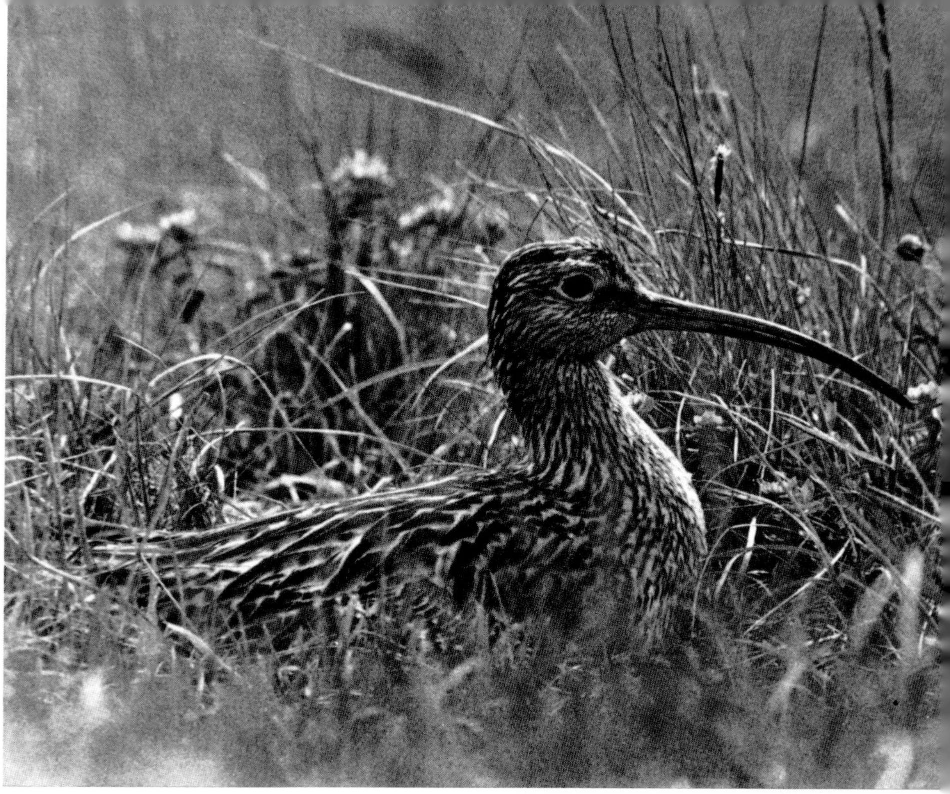

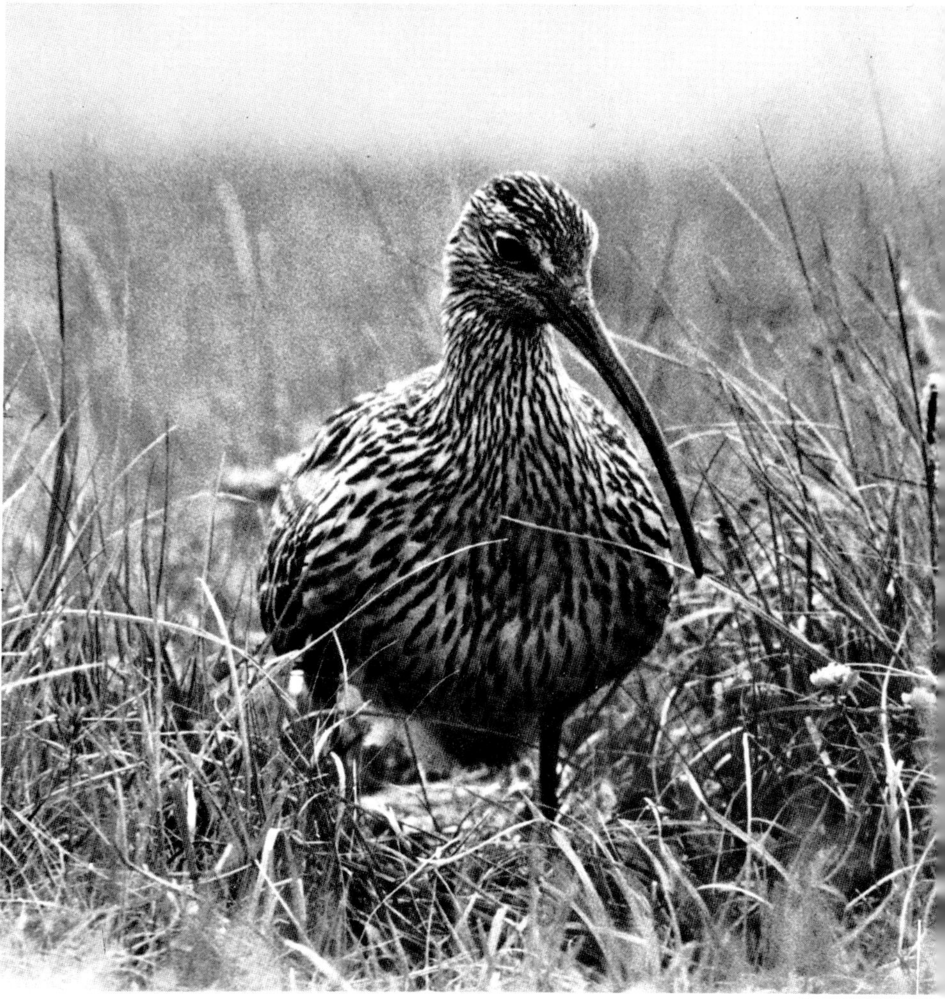

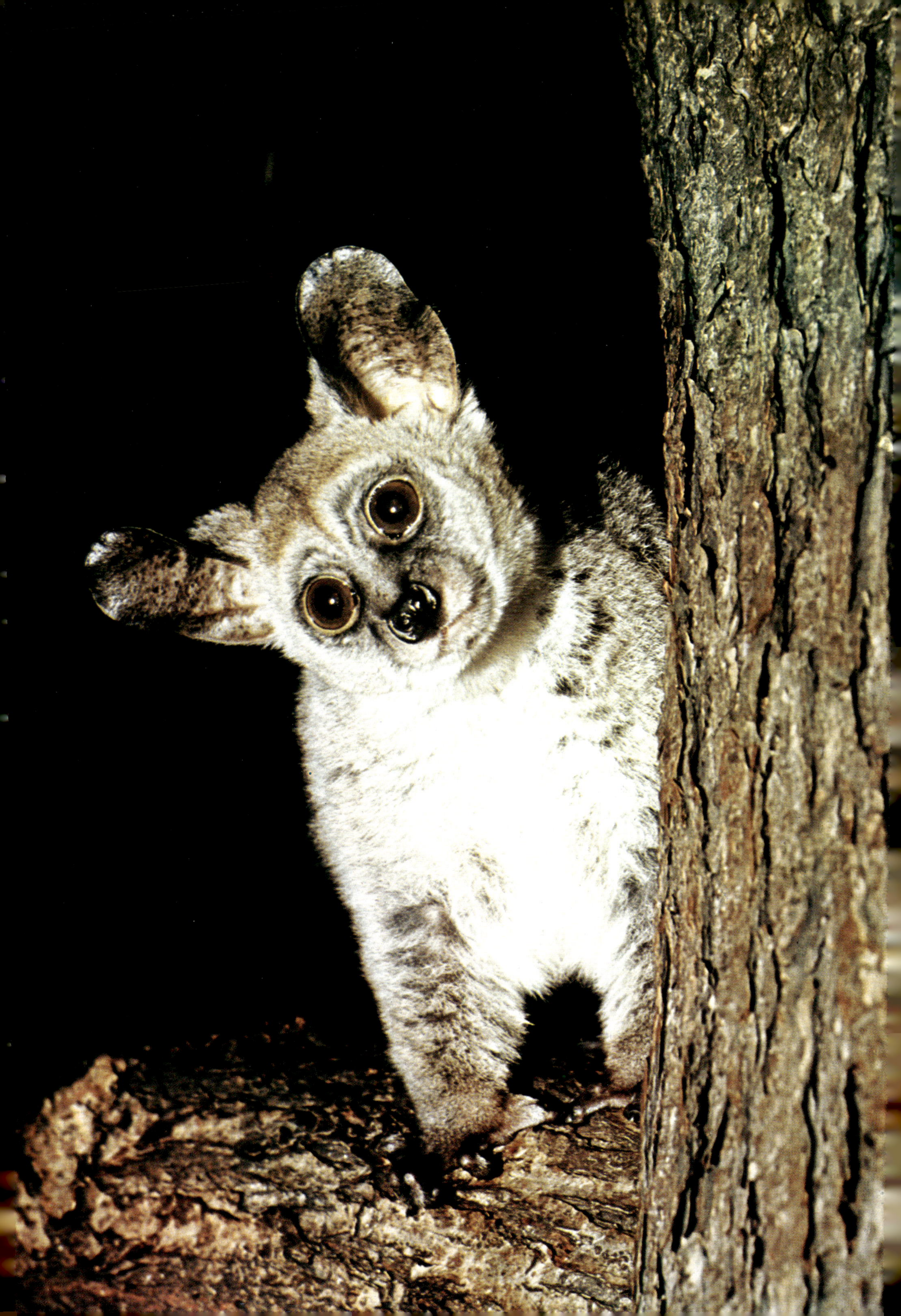

The galagos or bush babies are lemurian creatures of the family *Lorisidae* and are found in Africa, where they live in trees. During the hours of daylight they sleep in groups in the treetops and become active at dusk, showing great agility in leaping from branch to branch and tree to tree. The species depicted in the accompanying photograph is the large galago (*Galago crassicaudata*). Equipment: 'Photographic trap' (camera triggered by the creature itself), 90 mm focal length; magnesium flash.

The horseshoe bat (*Rhinolophus ferrum-equinum*) derives its name from the characteristic appendages on its face. When asleep in the daytime it wraps its wings around its body and hangs head downwards. Equipment: 35 mm camera, 50 mm focal length, with extra extension; electronic flash.

distinctly in the enlarged picture, this does not necessarily constitute a serious blemish or diminish its value.

For technical or scientific photography it will generally be preferable to use a slow film with relatively high contrast and fine grain in order to record the maximum amount of detail.

In colour photography we come up against very similar problems, but there is an additional factor to consider: the colour temperature, which is a measure of 'colour quality' of the light source to be used for the film chosen. For example, a film intended for use in daylight (colour temperature about 5500 K) should be used only for outdoor photography or with special blue lamps or with electronic flash equipment. In general, the manufacturers of such film recommend that it should not be used out of doors before about 8 am or after about 6 pm (in temperate geographical latitudes, that is). We personally consider that such recommendations can best be ignored. It is quite true that some lack of colour balance will then occur. But such lack of balance exists in nature, too: at dawn and at sunset there is a predominance of red radiation. There is no valid reason to use a different film just because it is 7.45 instead of 8 o'clock in the morning. It is basically a question of interpretation, and the sense of judgment that the photographer acquires from the results he obtains will be his best guide.

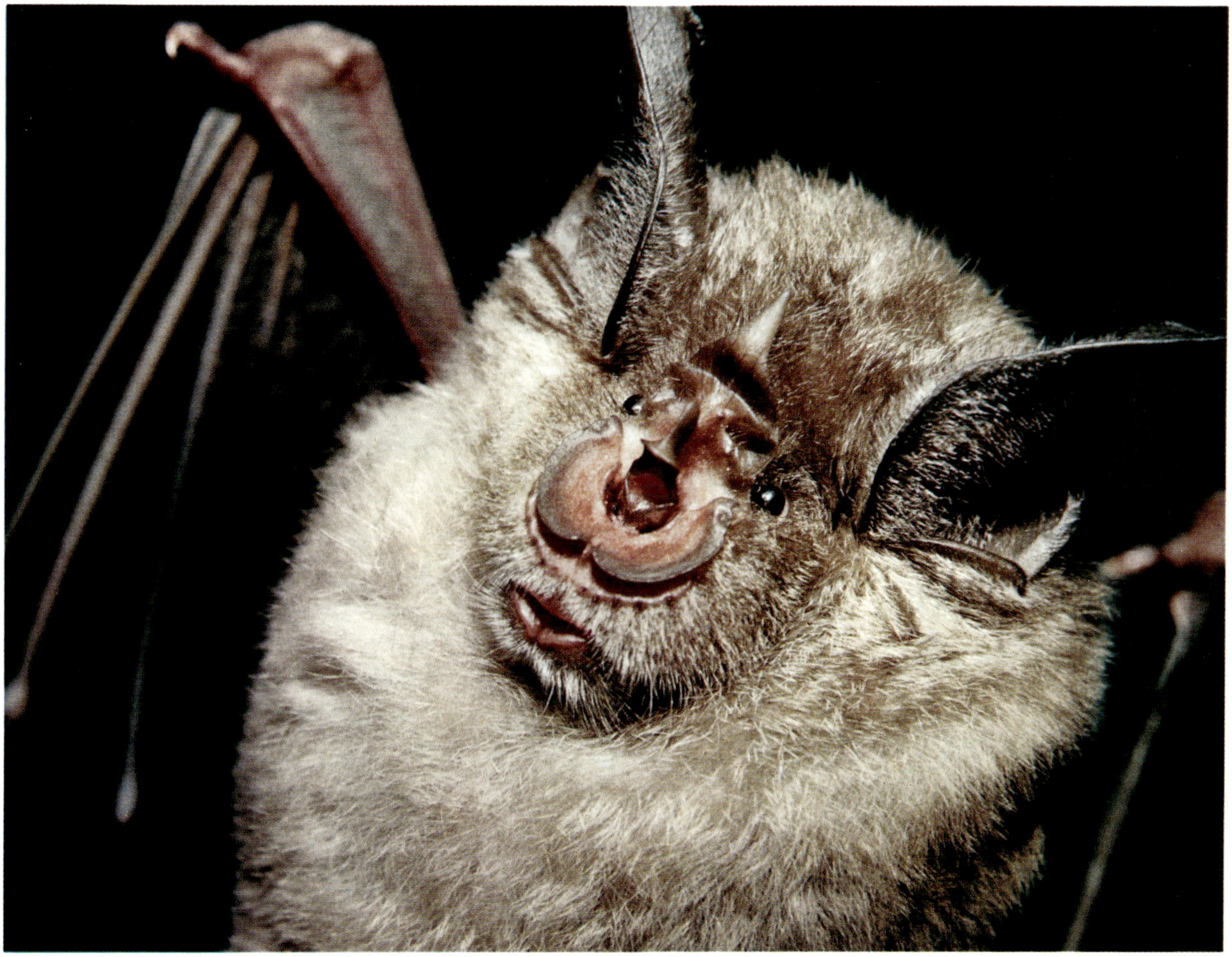

Cinematography indeed adopted colour long ago, as it is easier to produce colour in a film or transparency for projection than in a print on paper.

Choice and speed of emulsions

Films for still photography and for cinematography can be classified into three main groups:

1. Black-and-white films which are intended to give negative images which in turn are printed, usually enlarged, in black-and-white on photographic paper.
2. Reversal colour films, i.e. producing a positive image directly on the film, intended more particularly for transparencies (colour slides) and amateur cinematography. Such pictures, processed commercially in a laboratory, can be used for making good enlarged colour prints on paper. There are two main types of such film: for daylight and for artificial light.
3. Negative colour films, which are used mainly in professional cinematography and also in amateur still photography. It is the process of the future for still photography generally, as it enables enlargements to be made direct either on black-and-white or on colour printing paper and can also be used for obtaining positive transparencies. As yet, however, this type of film is still little used for serious work because of the difficulty of obtaining prints which represent correctly evaluated colours in the negative.

The type of film and its speed are always indicated on the package in which it is sold. The speed, which is determined with reference to the so-called density threshold, is now almost universally expressed in ASA units (American), B.S. (British) or DIN units (German), occasionally still also in Scheiner degrees. The ASA and B.S. scales are linear, e.g. a film with a speed of 100 ASA or B.S. (21 DIN) is twice as fast as one with a speed of 50 ASA or B.S. (18 DIN).

It is not possible to lay down hard-and-fast rules about the use of films. The circumstances in which a picture has to be taken (moving or stationary subject), the conditions of illumination (daylight, artificial light or flash) and the contrast value of the scene, are determining factors in giving preference to one type of film or another.

The photographer who does not do his own developing has little scope for controlling the sensitometric qualities of his films; and the speed of each type of film will undoubtedly be his best guide for judging its range of application and understanding the limits within which it can suitably be used.

The slow black-and-white film (25 to 40 ASA) with its fine grain and high resolving power is preferable in all cases where the subject requires faithful reproduction of the maximum amount of detail. However, the lack of speed of such materials confines their usefulness to very bright conditions or to subjects where slow shutter speeds can be employed.

Medium-speed film (50 to 125 ASA) is true all-purpose photographic material. It is adaptable to all indoor and outdoor work under normal lighting conditions, its grain is inconspicuous and its wide contrast range (gradation) allows accurate reproduction of all the colours and tonal values of the subjects to be photographed, whether these be animals, plants, inanimate objects or landscapes.

High-speed (250 to 500 ASA) film and very high-speed (800 to 1600 ASA) film are fairly extensively used for photographing rapidly moving subjects. For the wildlife photographer, who has to accept the often unfavourable lighting conditions as they happen to be at the time when the animals are most active, e.g. in the early morning or at dusk, and who has to operate under all circumstances (rain, mist, dense forest), fast film often holds the key to success. Pronounced graininess and low gradation can partly be corrected by extended and

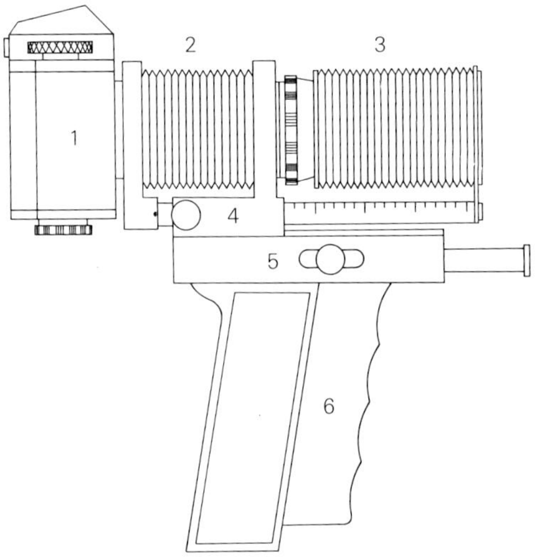

Rapid focusing bellows device for macrophotography or for adaptation to telephoto lens or long-focus lens (Novoflex).
1 reflex camera
2 bellows
3 folding lens hood
4 knob for adjusting extension
5 locking knob
6 focusing handle

Colour films in current use

BRAND	ASA speed	Reversal film	Negative	TYPE OF LIGHT: Daylight	Artificial	Universal	TYPE OF PACKAGING: Roll film	35 mm cassette	16 mm	Super 8	8 mm
Agfacolor CT 18	50	☐		☐			☐	☐			
Agfacolor CK 20	50	☐			☐		☐	☐			
Agfacolor CN S	80		☐			☐	☐	☐			
Agfacolor CK 17	40	☐			☐				☐	☐	☐
Agfacolor CT 135	16	☐		☐					☐		☐
Anscochrome 64	64	☐		☐			☐	☐			
Anscochrome 100	100	☐		☐				☐	☐		
Anscochrome T100	100	☐			☐			☐			
Anscochrome D500	500	☐		☐				☐			
Anscochrome 200	200	☐		☐				☐	☐		
Ektachrome X	64	☐		☐			☐	☐			
Ektachrome HS	160	☐		☐			☐	☐			
Ektachrome HS B	125	☐			☐		☐	☐	☐		
Ferraniacolor Dia 28	50	☐		☐			☐	☐			
Ferraniacolor MC	25	☐		☐			☐	☐	☐		☐
Ferraniacolor MC	40	☐			☐		☐	☐	☐	☐	☐
Ferraniacolor NM	64		☐			☐	☐	☐			
Fujicolor	100		☐			☐	☐	☐			
Fujichrome	25	☐		☐				☐			
Gevachrome N	50	☐							☐		
Gevachrome HS	160	☐							☐		
Kodachrome II	25	☐		☐				☐	☐		☐
Kodachrome II A	40	☐			☐			☐	☐	☐	☐
Kodachrome X	64	☐		☐				☐			
Kodacolor X	64		☐			☐	☐	☐			
Perutzcolor C 18	50	☐		☐				☐			
Perutzchrome	25									☐	

Ektachrome Infrared (20 exp. 135): speed varies around 100 ASA.

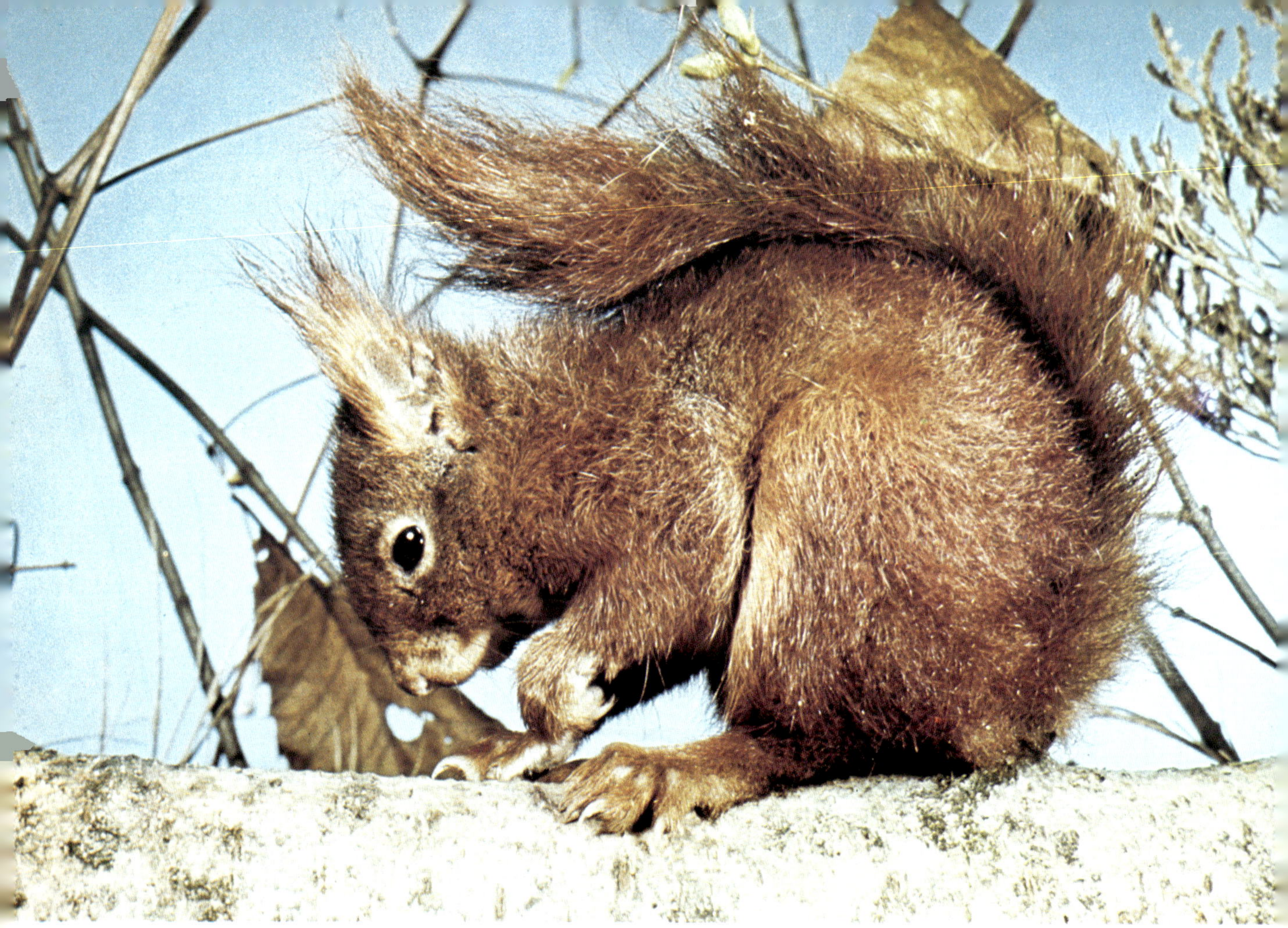

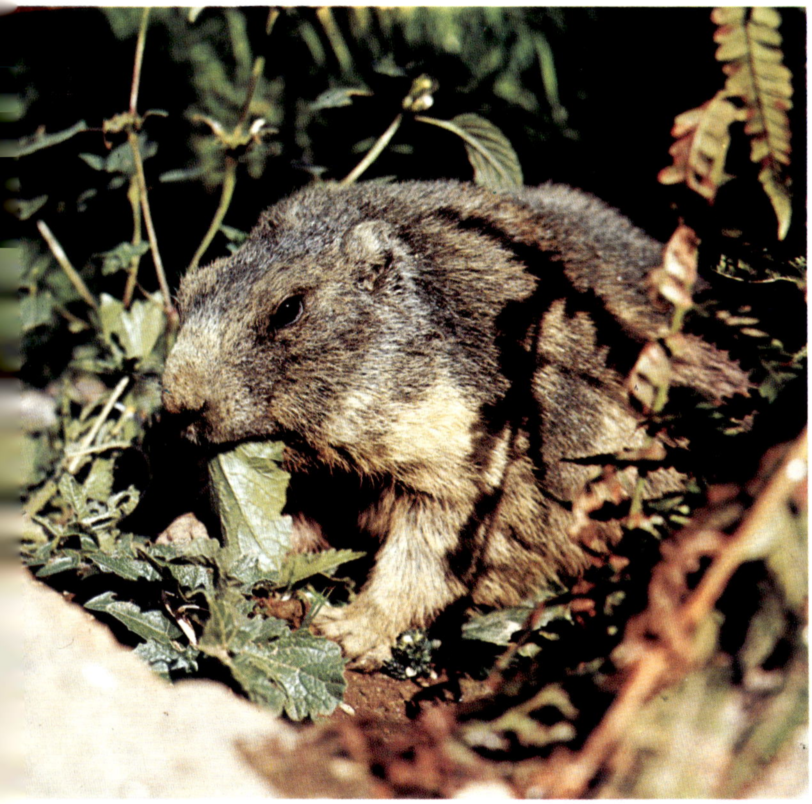

The red squirrel (*Sciurus sciurus*) is a graceful little creature, easily recognizable by its bushy tail which it keeps raised forward over its body and its reddish brown coat. It is a highly agile tree dweller which can make huge leaps from branch to branch. It climbs even the highest and thinnest branches in quest of the pine seeds that are its principal food.

The marmot (*Marmota marmota*) lives in colonies on mountainsides, preferably on open ground, but is also found among rocks.

The ermine or stoat (*Mustela herminea*) is recognizable by the black tip on its tail at all seasons. The rest of its coat is mainly white in winter and brown in summer. Moulting takes place in spring and in autumn.

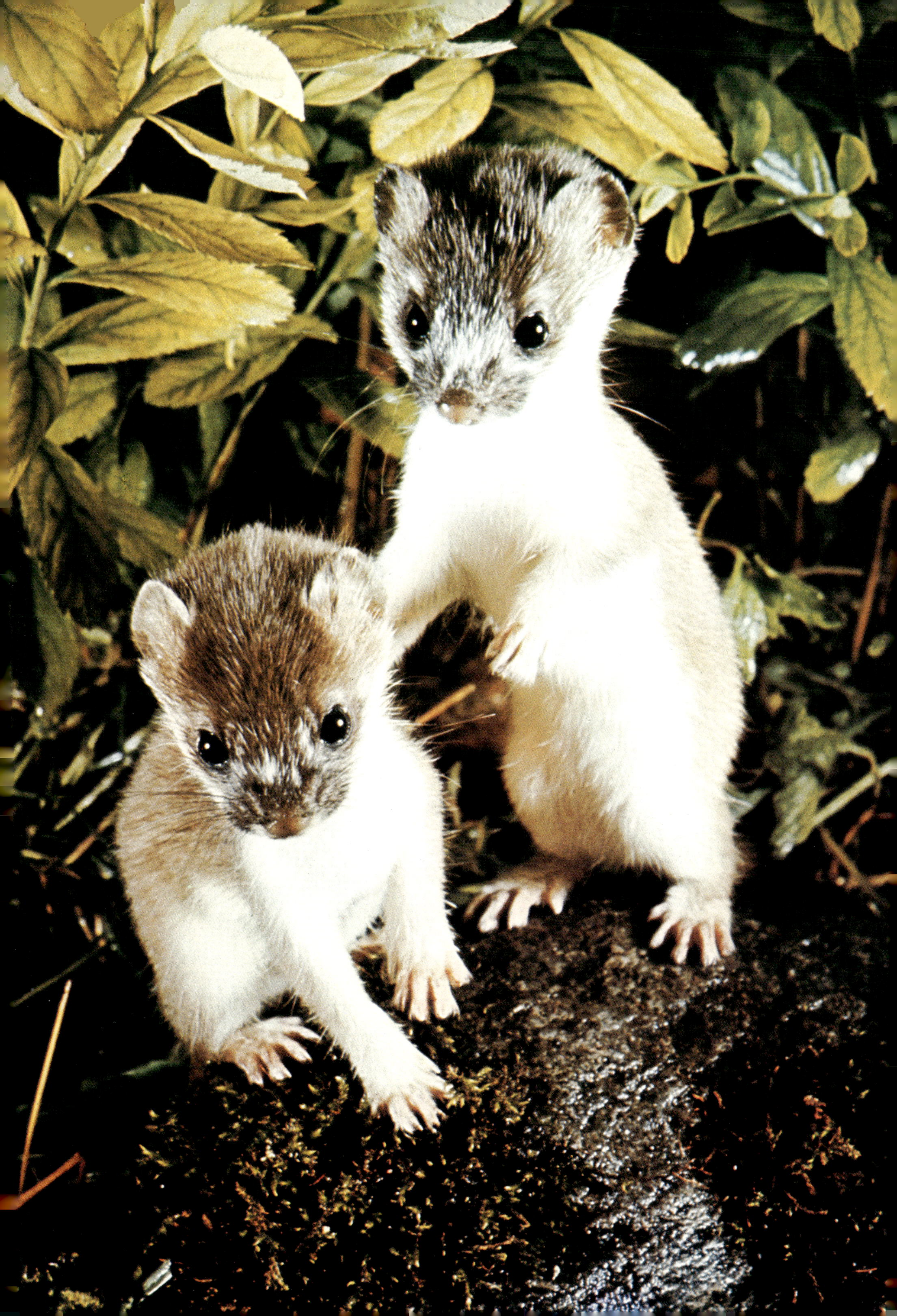

concentrated development so as to capture some rare and fleeting scene. For medium-format photography—$2\frac{1}{4}$ square or larger—some photographers regard such fast film as essential to the success of most of their pictures. In many cases the linear enlargement, with such formats, is no more than three or four times, so that graininess need not be objectionable. There is no doubt that these films improve the chances of securing good 'dynamic' pictures. Also, the short exposures they require enable satisfactory hand-held shots to be obtained, not requiring a stand or tripod for the camera, and the lens can be stopped down to give considerable depth of field.

Exposure

With any kind of film the all-important condition for making good enlargements from sharp and detailed negatives is the determination of the correct exposure

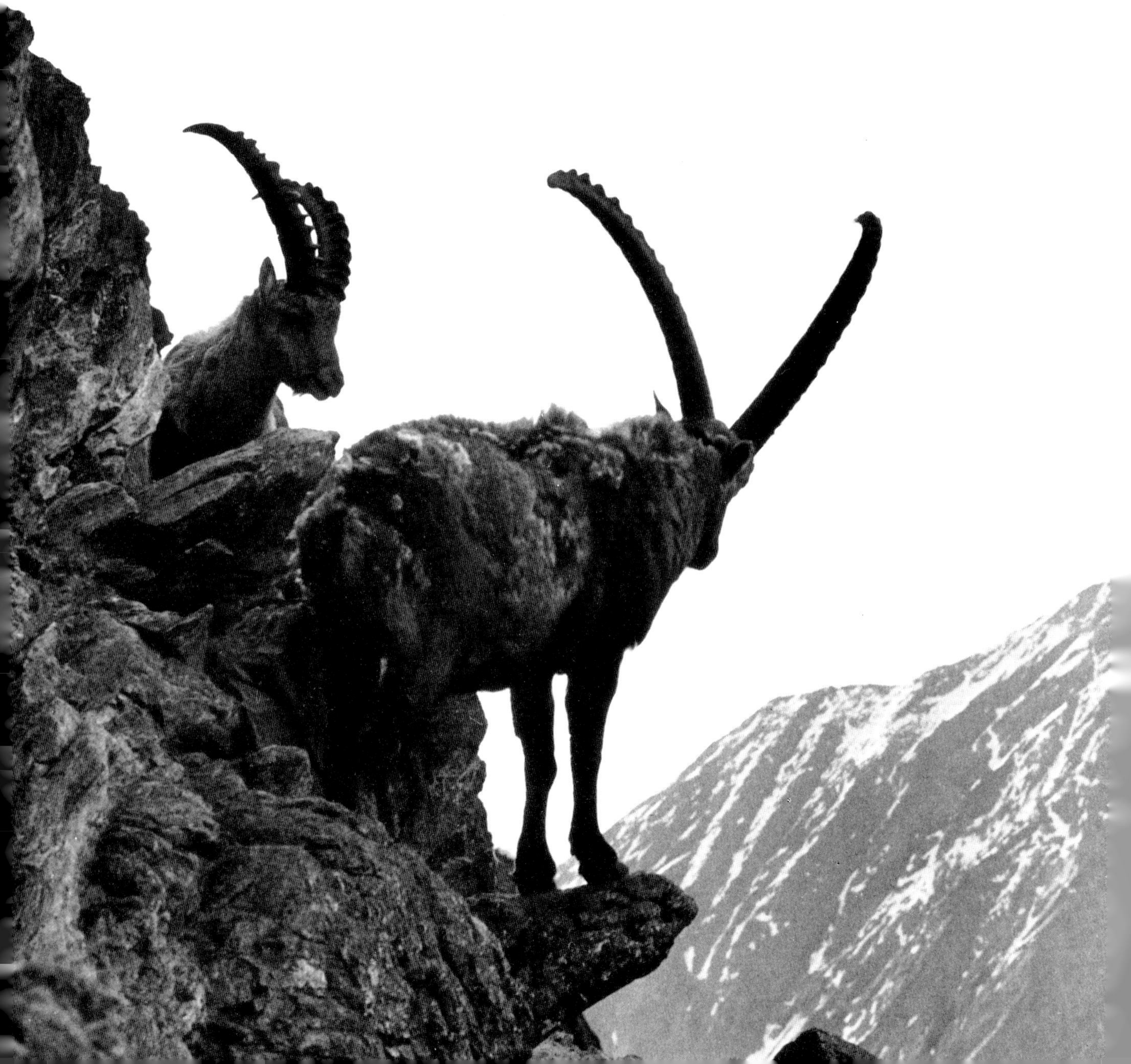

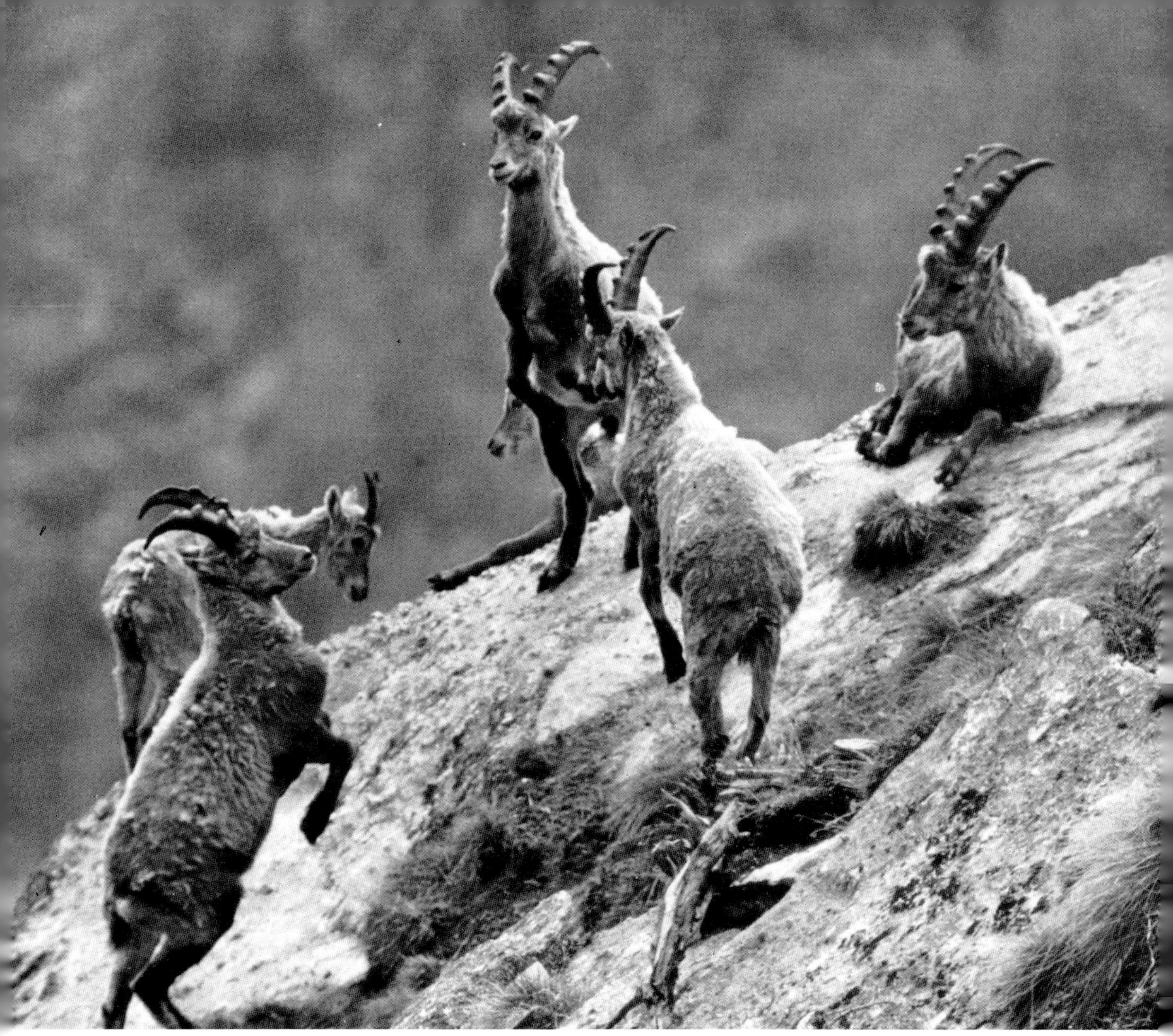

time. If you do not have a good exposure meter at your disposal, the next best thing is to seek guidance from the instructions that film manufacturers issue with their films. These indicate practical exposure times for various diaphragm settings and are suitable for various typical subjects and weather conditions. You should memorize the following rule of thumb, which, though admittedly not very accurate, has the advantage of convenience and may save you the trouble of bad guesswork: 'In bright sunshine, at f 16, use an exposure time equal to the ASA speed of the film.' For instance, for a film whose speed is 125 ASA, give an exposure of 1/125 second at f 16; for a 60 ASA film the exposure time should be 1/60 second at f 16. If there is hazy sunshine, increase the diaphragm setting by one stop and double the exposure time, e.g. for 125 ASA film these become f 11 and 1/60 second respectively. If the sky is overcast, these values should again be doubled, i.e. for 125 ASA: f 8 and 1/30 sec.

The ibex (*Capra ibex*), a wild goat of the Alps and Apennines, looks rather clumsy, but its movements are very elegant. On the left a pair of older males survey the females and younger animals from a high vantage point. In the photograph above, young males are seen engaged in a mock fight which is more like an acrobatic dance.
Equipment: 35 mm camera, photosniper mounting, with 400 mm telephoto lens.

The fallow deer, a smaller animal than the stag, is extensively bred in deer parks. The males of this species of deer (*Dama dama*) have antlers with wide flattened ends (called palms) from which the tines project. The colouring of the coat ranges from reddish brown spotted with white, to black at one end of the scale and completely white at the other. Equipment: Photosniper with 400 mm focal length; speed 1/250 sec.; aperture f 8; film high-speed Ektachrome. (The upper photograph on the right was taken at daybreak at 1/10 sec., the camera being mounted on a stand.)

Stick to one make or type of film

Whatever film speed you decide to work with, it is advisable to cut down the number of types of film you use. All the leading brands have very much the same qualities (and the same shortcomings) and it is preferable to know one particular type of film 'intimately' and take full advantage of all its possibilities rather than to change continually from one type to another with the object of getting supposedly better results.

For both black-and-white and colour photography it is sufficient to use, and be really familiar with, two types of very fast film and two medium-speed films. This range of film is adequate to deal with almost any subject in wildlife and nature photography.

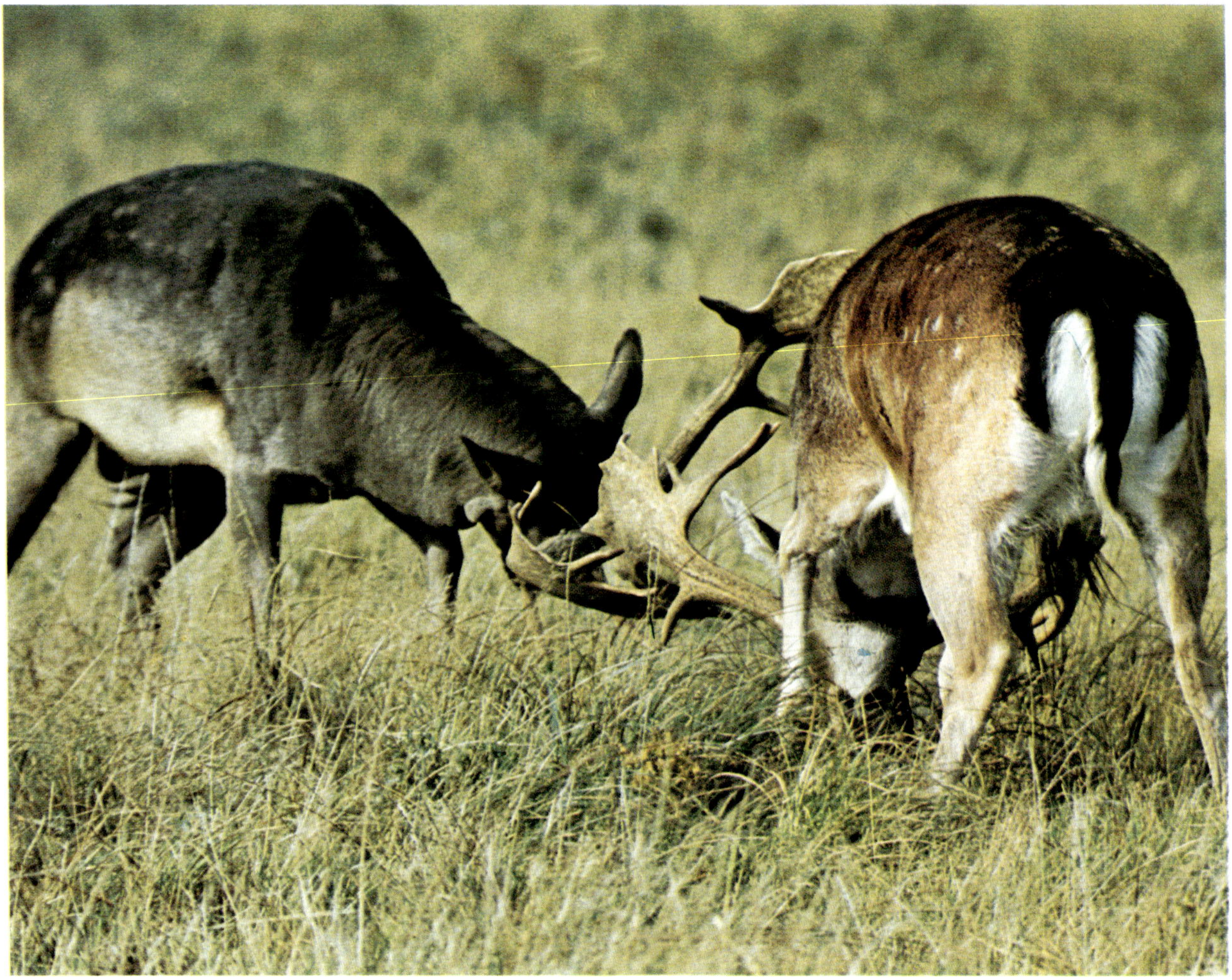

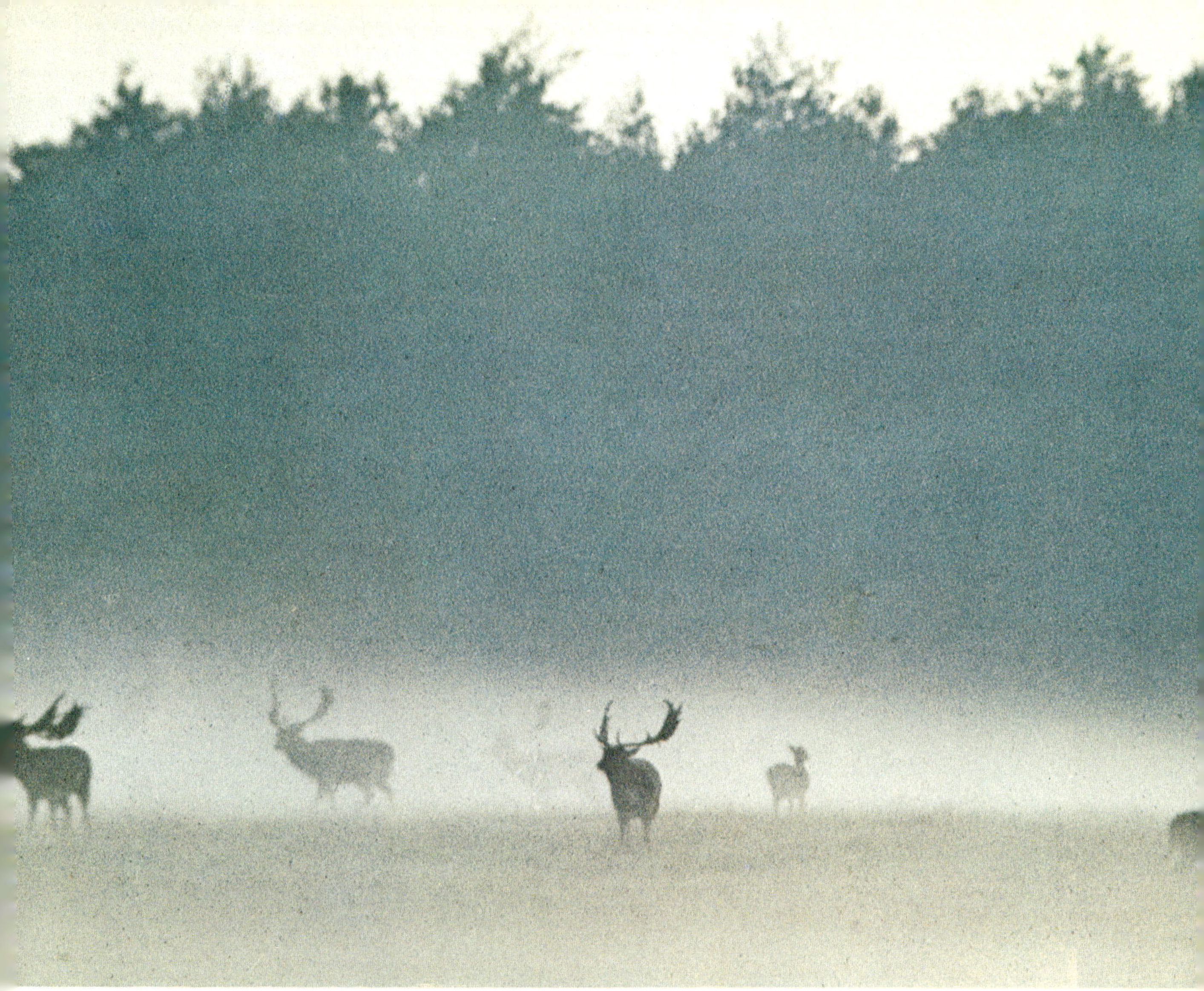

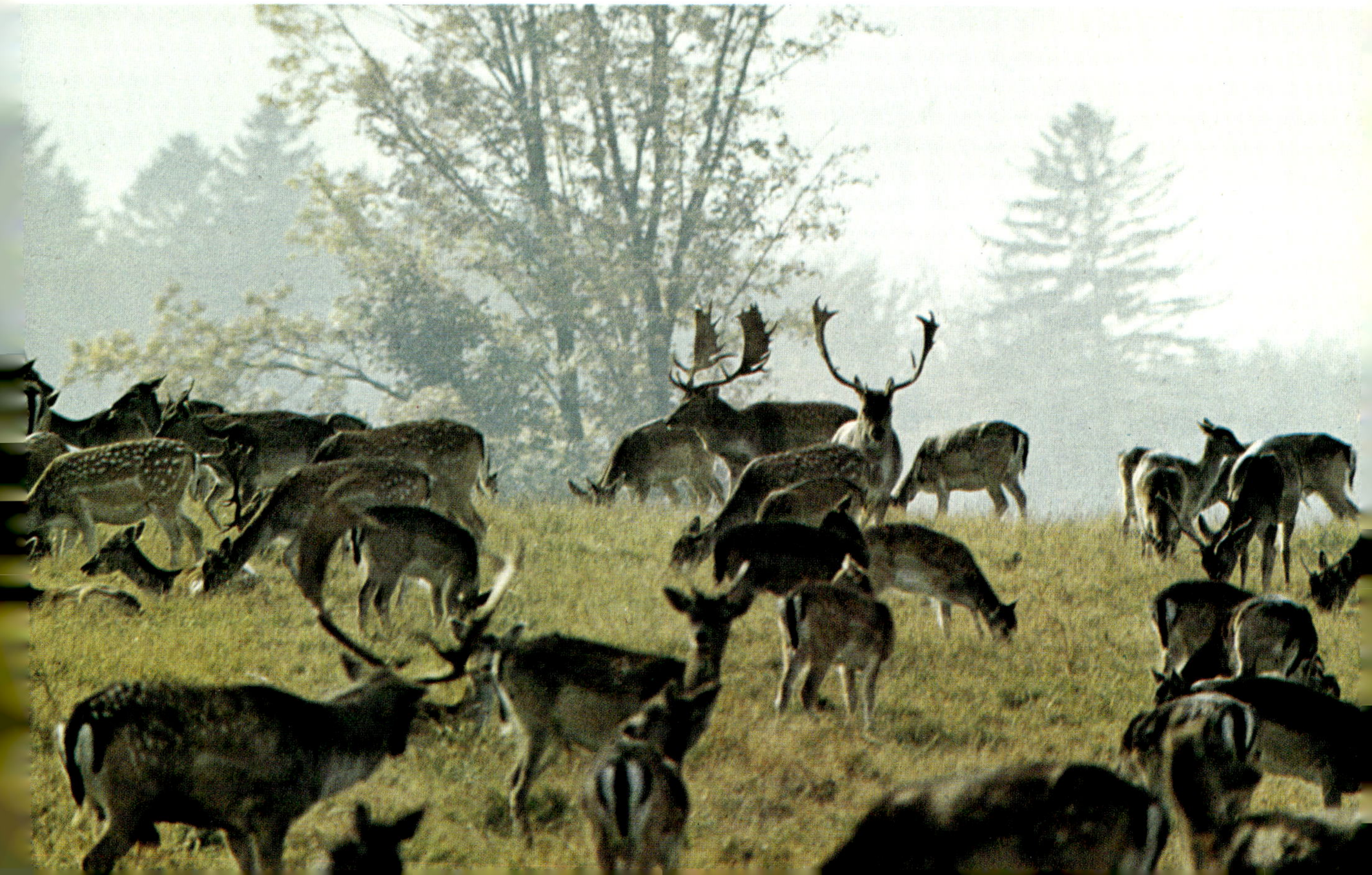

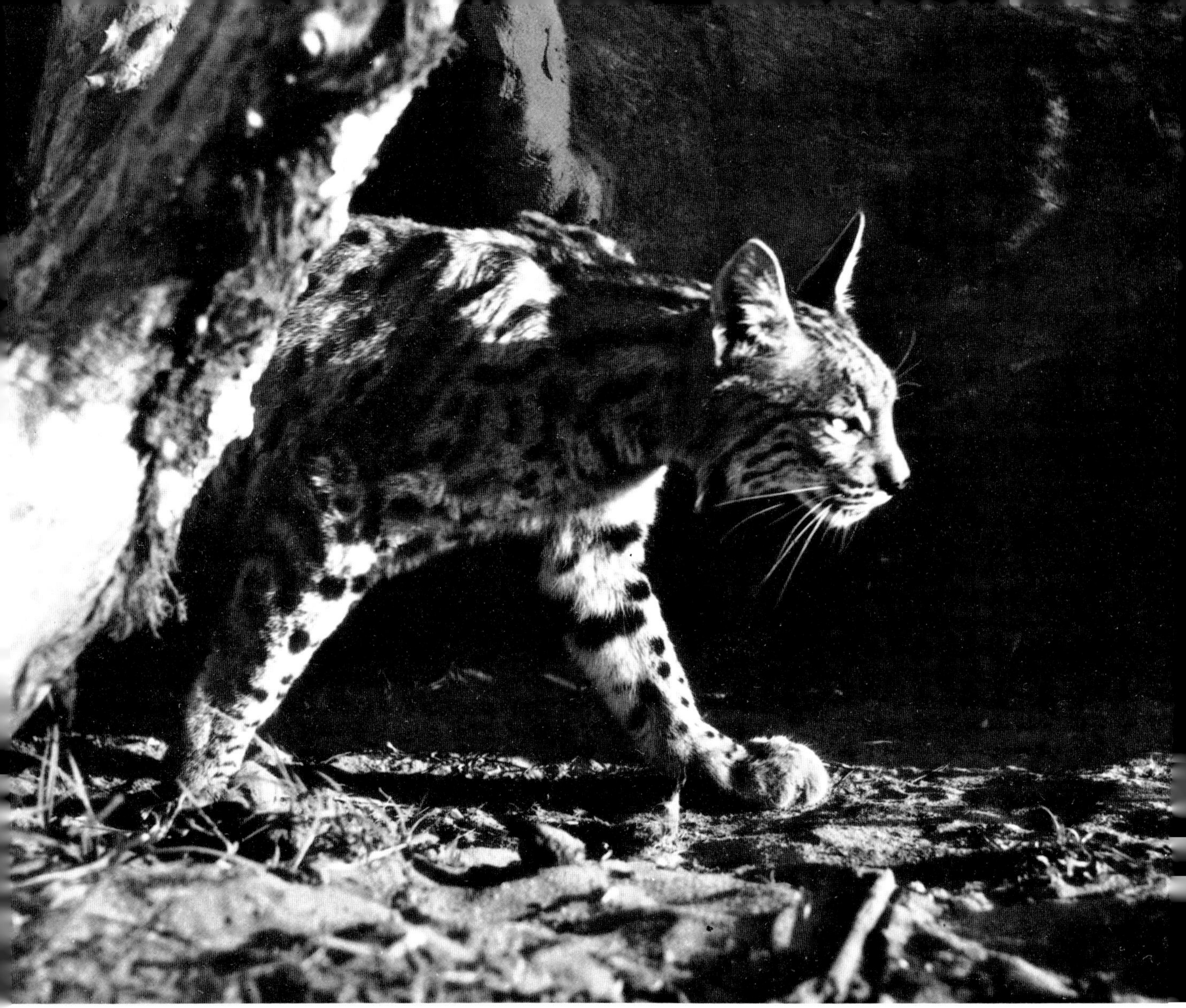

The lynx (*Lynx pardellus*) is a rare animal, very shy and secretive in its way of life and its habitat. In Europe they are to be found in the wild state only in parts of Spain and in the Pyrenees. This lynx was photographed in a nature reserve in Spain.

Some day we shall no doubt have to extend our knowledge of sensitive materials to include the latest technical information on the properties and performance of magnetic video recording tape. Perhaps this technique of the future will make up for the shortcomings in the sensitivity of present-day photographic emulsions.

Another important recommendation: always take a good supply of film with you when you go abroad, so that you will not run out of film in a country where your particular type may be unobtainable. Even when you go only on a short journey, make a point of taking along more spools of film than may appear necessary. There is nothing more frustrating than to see exceptional wildlife scenes and to have to stand by helplessly with an empty camera.

Finally, take good care of your exposed films: do not subject them to sharp knocks and bumps; keep them properly stored in closed containers which protect them from dust, heat and humidity. A desiccant may be placed in the bottom of the container or box as an additional precaution against moisture.

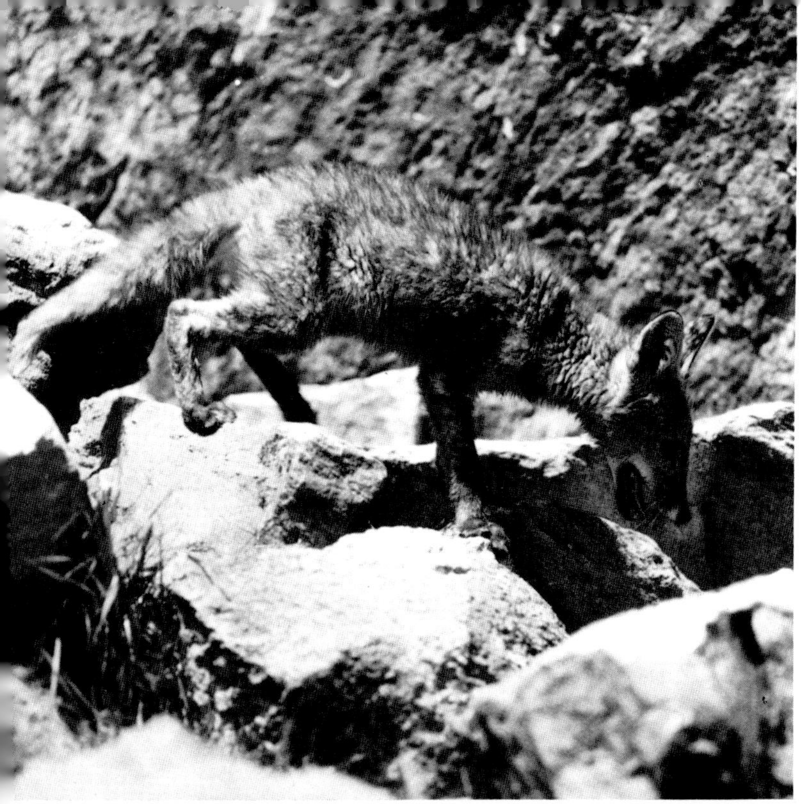

The fox (*Vulpes vulpes*) and the wild boar (*Sus scrofa*) are two interesting subjects for the wildlife photographer because they call for a quick reaction on his part when he comes across one of these animals in a chance encounter.
Equipment: 35 mm reflex camera, using a 135 mm lens focused on the hyperfocal distance, for photographing the fox; the boar was photographed with a 400 mm lens, the photographer concealed under camouflage netting at the edge of the woods.

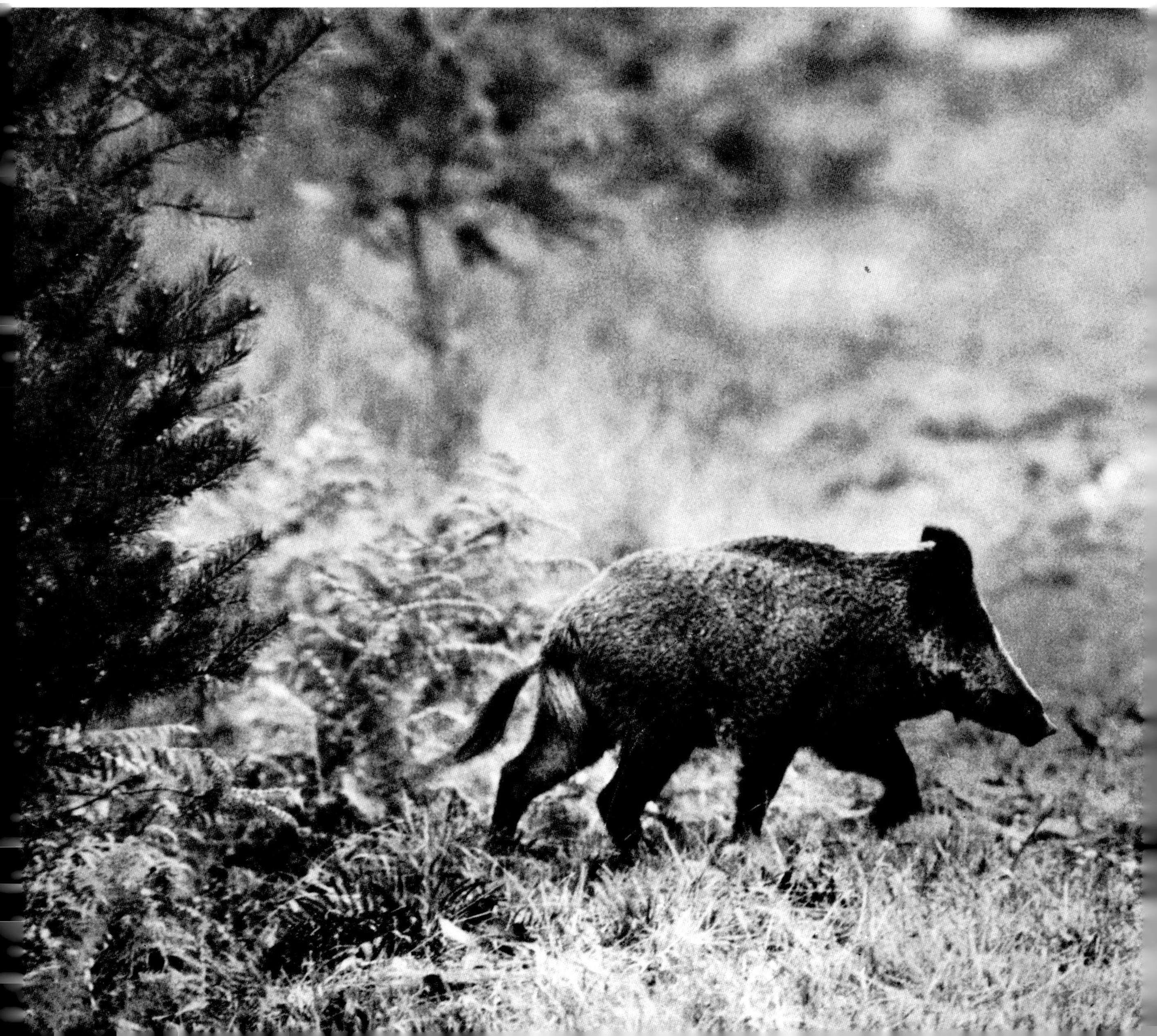

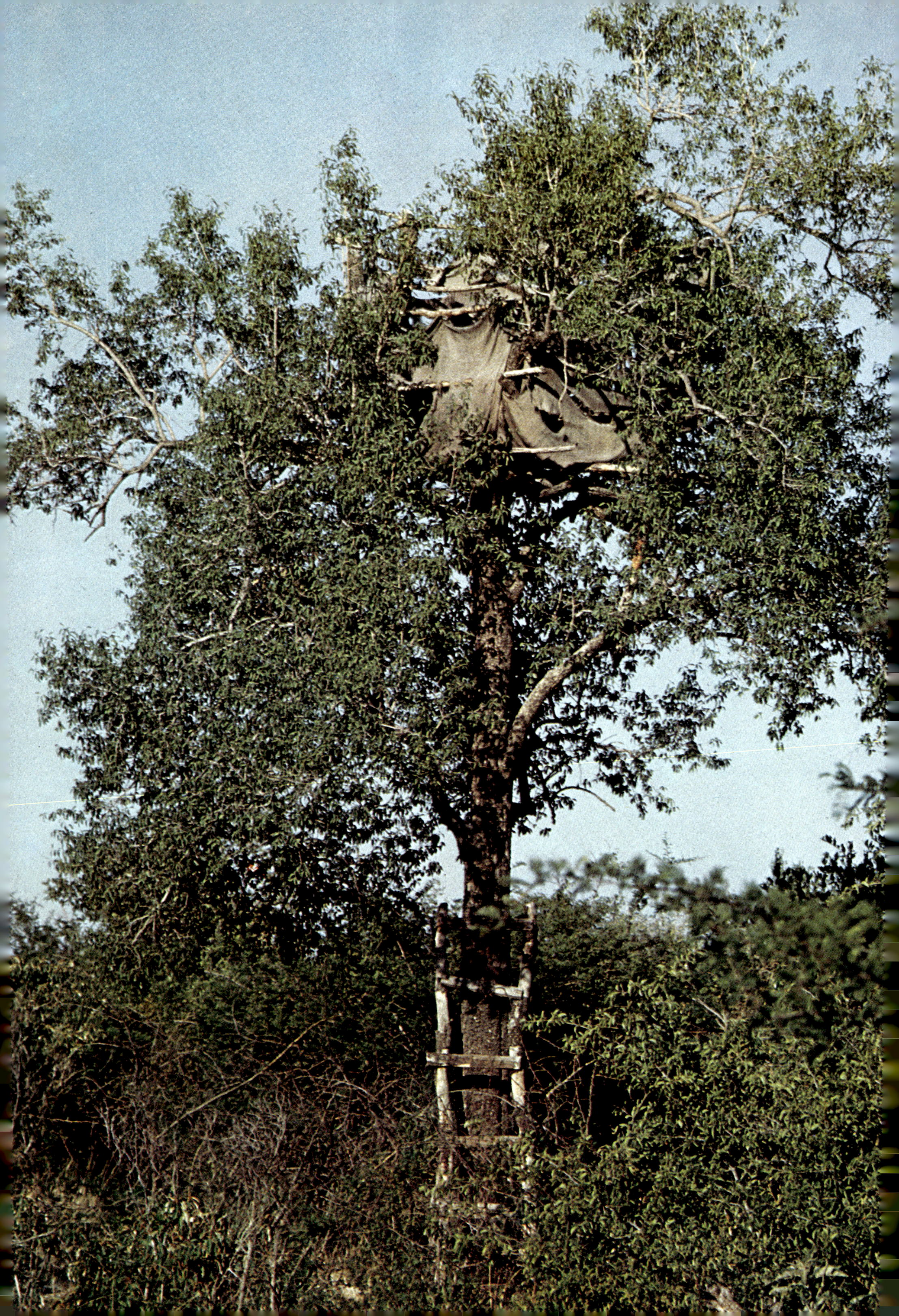

outdoor and indoor photographic techniques

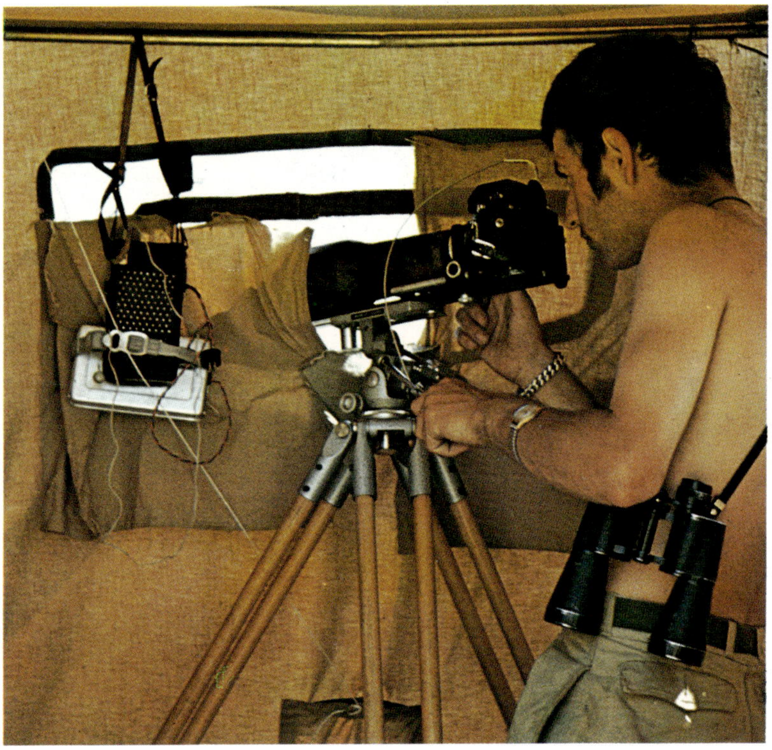

Tree-top hide constructed from materials found in the vicinity and neutral-coloured hessian fabric.

Right: The interior of a comfortable tent-type hide in which the photographer can stand erect and use a variety of equipment: radio transmitter/receiver, very long-focus telephoto lens with double extension, strong tripod to ensure good camera stability, etc.

The larger animals and birds occupy very extensive areas of terrain as their natural living space. Birds, in particular, cover immense distances in flight. And yet, to observe their most interesting behaviour patterns, it is necessary to study them in their own ecological surroundings.

A great many wildlife photographers are fascinated by the challenge of getting pictures of these creatures in their natural environment. It is a sport–often a solitary one–for which there are many possible techniques, all of which, however, are derived from two main principles, one static, the other dynamic: photographing from a hide, and stalking in the open.

The means and equipment demanded by the two methods (techniques, cameras, camouflage) are very different; in addition, they require different personal qualities and a different attitude of mind on the photographer's part. The choice of method will therefore in part depend on your own personality. ▹

The hide

Where practicable, this method gives by far the best results, not only from the technical point of view – since pictures with the maximum of definition and detail can be obtained in this way, because you can use a firmly mounted large-format camera loaded with medium-speed (and therefore relatively fine-grained) film – but also in that it does not disturb the animal and thus enables it to be photographed in its natural environment and activities.

To build a hide, you must first reconnoitre the terrain very carefully in order to choose a suitable location close to a point where a certain animal will pass or to a bird's nest. Depending on circumstances, you can make use of natural concealment or construct a suitably camouflaged artificial shelter, commonly known as a 'hide'.

To determine the correct location of your hide you certainly cannot rely on book knowledge alone. You must also have the naturalist's knowledge and ability to judge the terrain. After a prolonged inspection through field-glasses, it should be possible to decide with reasonable accuracy just where the hide should be erected.

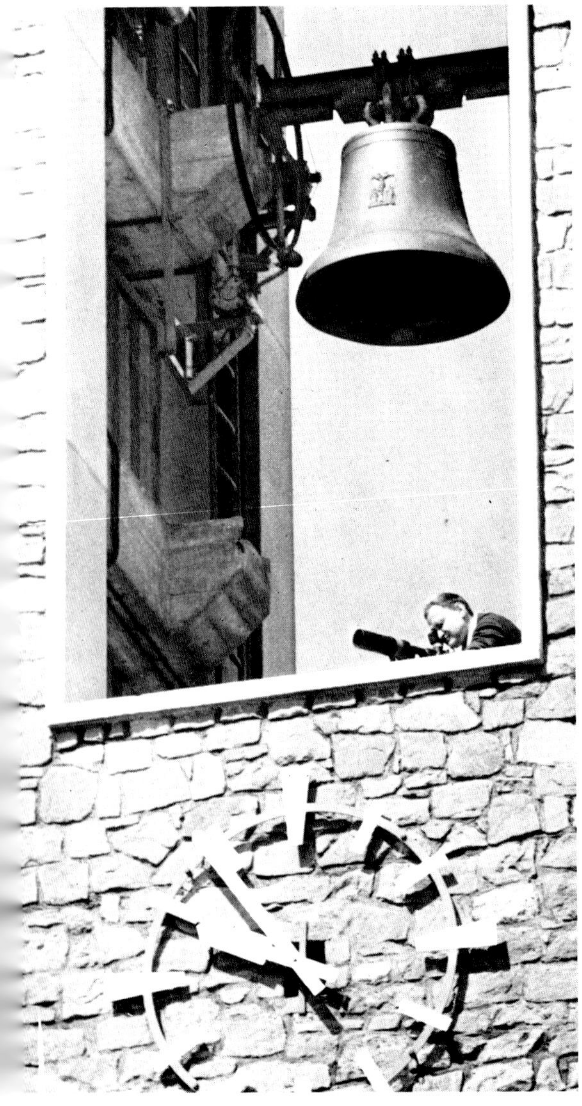

Precautions must be taken to ensure that the animal or bird to be photographed is not disturbed or frightened away by the presence of the camera or the operator. He in turn must spare a thought for the risks he may be running, e.g. from being close to a dangerous animal or from having to install his hide in a precarious position or on treacherous ground.

It is also necessary to consider that the direction and intensity of the light (flat illumination or backlighting) will vary in the course of the day. So the hide will have to be oriented according to the prevailing illumination at the time when the animal to be photographed is likely to be most active.

Also, you should not overlook the importance of wind, which can transmit sounds (even tiny ones), and scent, which may betray your presence to the animal over long distances.

The hide to conceal the photographer and his equipment (or only the latter, if remote control is to be used) may be constructed from materials found ready to hand in the vicinity (branches, reeds, etc.). But the use of this method, which is usually prohibited in wildlife sanctuaries anyway, is on the decline because of the destruction it causes to the natural habitat. Alternatively, the hide may take the form of a tent or portable larger shelter brought to the site by the photographer(s). Sometimes the hide is quite a large structure assembled from ready-made (prefabricated) components and intended to accommodate several observers, sometimes for long periods of time.

Another possibility is to make use of existing natural objects for concealment. Thus a tree can be an excellent hiding place, though admittedly a bit unsteady for photography. Other possibilities are: fire-watching towers, shelters used by sportsmen for hunting or shooting, or even an old stone wall. All such places of concealment already form part of the scenery and therefore have the advantage of not arousing the suspicion of the animal or bird that knows every detail of its territory.

Some photographers prefer a spacious tent, which, although it is a conspicuous feature, is comparatively comfortable for long and sometimes irksome vigils. Others, preferring to travel light, use a small tent, less conspicuous and more effective.

For photographing animals which are not fierce but whose curiosity sometimes makes them over-bold, a screen formed merely by a piece of linen cloth stretched between two stakes in the ground may provide sufficient concealment and protection for the photographer. However, it is important not to have the sun behind you, otherwise your shadow will appear on the screen and frighten the animal.

This last-mentioned point is indeed relevant to any type of photographic hide involving the use of textile fabric in its construction. The drawback of tents made from densely-woven canvas-type materials of the usual kind is that, although they are very useful in keeping out rain, they tend to become intolerably hot in warm weather unless they are well ventilated. The part of the tent facing the subject to be photographed may, for that purpose, be provided with an aperture covered by several thicknesses of folded fabric netting to ensure good ventilation and allow comfortable observation. In any case it is essential to form vertical openings on all sides of the tent to enable you to be constantly on the look-out in all directions. You may always be taken by surprise: a suspicious animal or bird will often circle round the hide a number of times, drawing closer and closer, before returning to its lair or nest. And, anyway, there is little you can do other than keep constant watch: you certainly should not have a transistor radio switched on, and if you pass the time reading an exciting detective story, you will run the risk of missing your best opportunities. If you are a smoker, you must suppress your craving, however much of a sacrifice that may be.

Left: The belfry of a church provides a useful ready-made platform for photographing storks' nests.

Below: A semi-rigid commercially available tent intended for use in hunting or shooting, here suitably adapted for wildlife photography and camouflaged with local vegetation.

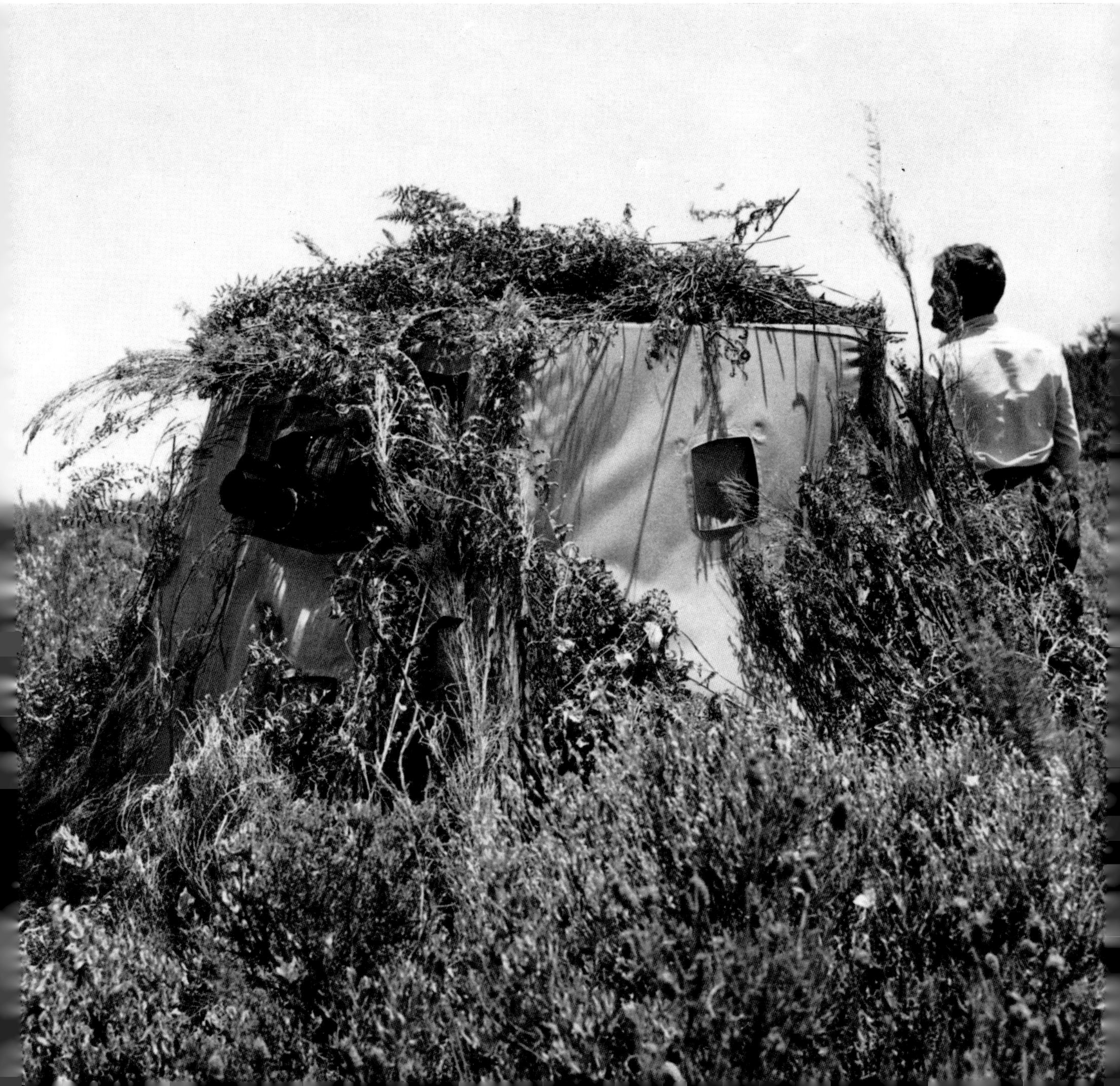

Right: A moorhen (*Galinula chloropus*) near its nest, photographed from a hide installed on a boat.

Below: Three shots of a red-throated diver (*Gavia stellata*) taking off from the water. It would not have been possible to get these pictures without the use of a camera with an electric motor for rapid film transport, enabling the operator to take three shots per second while keeping his eye on the viewfinder.
Equipment: Electric-powered Nikon camera, photosniper mounting; speed 1/250 sec.; aperture f 8; film high-speed Ektachrome.

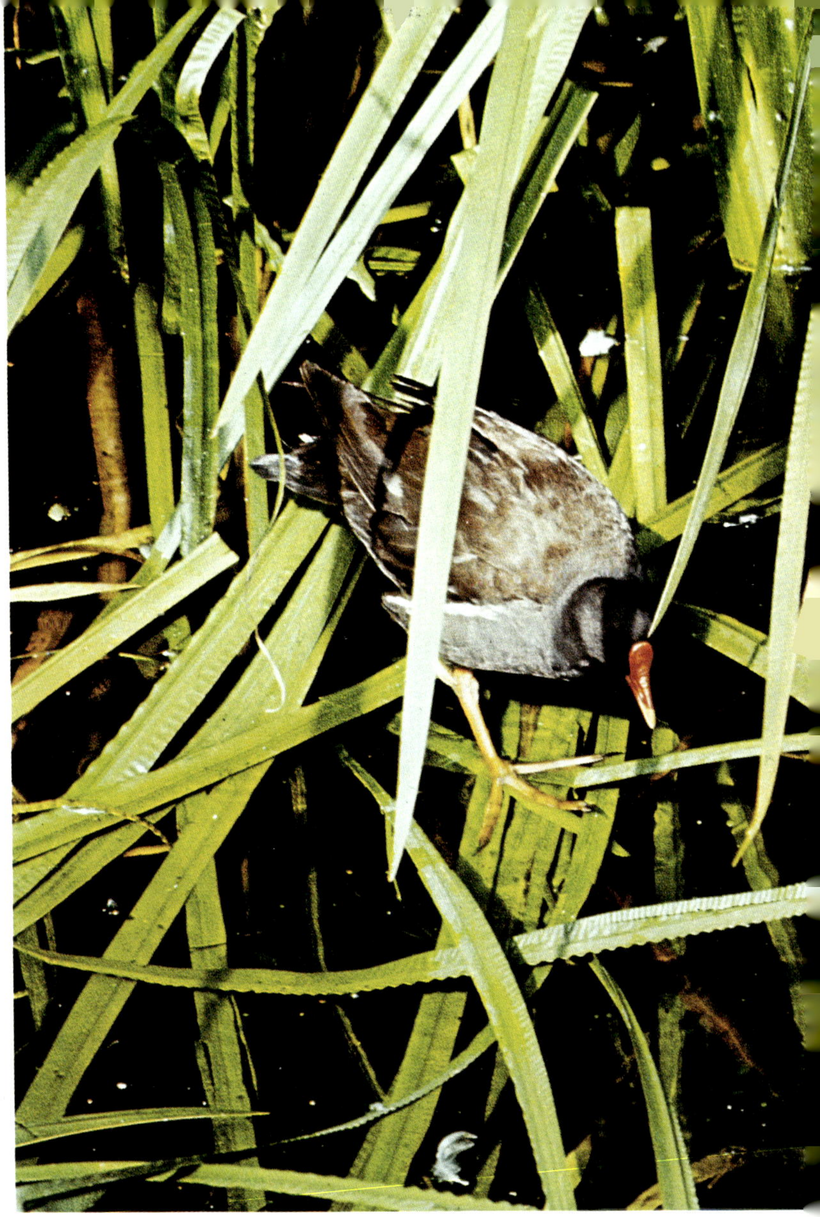

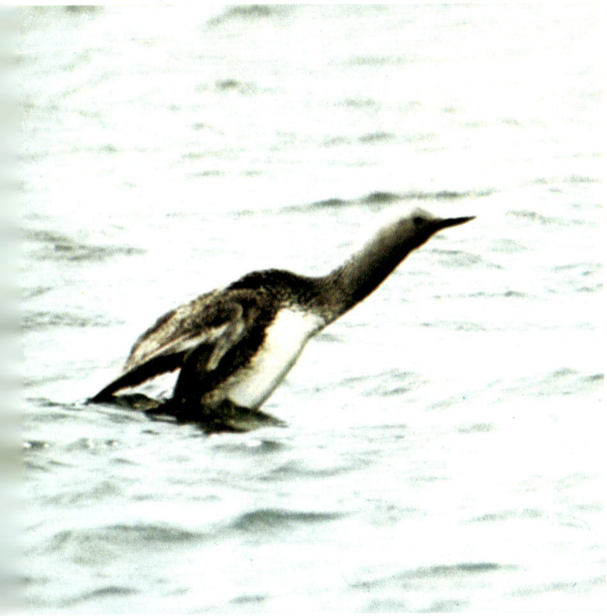

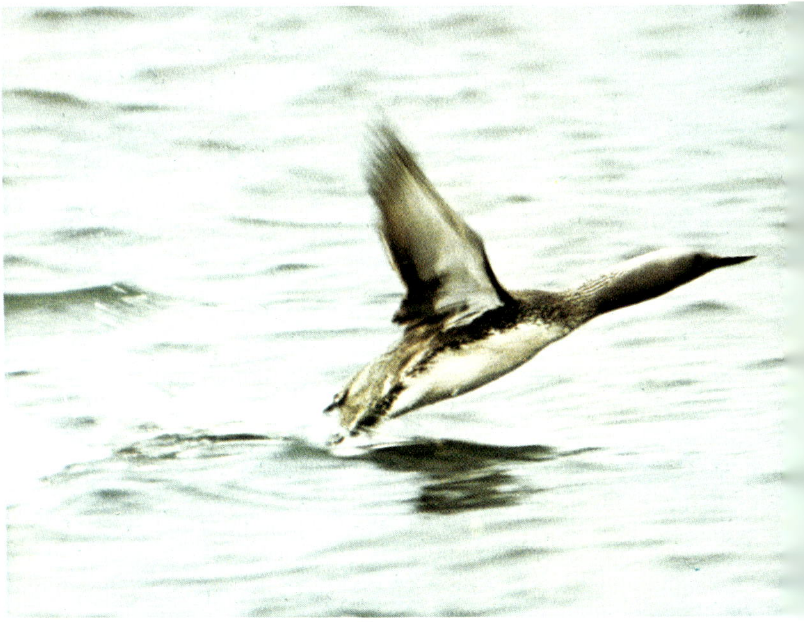

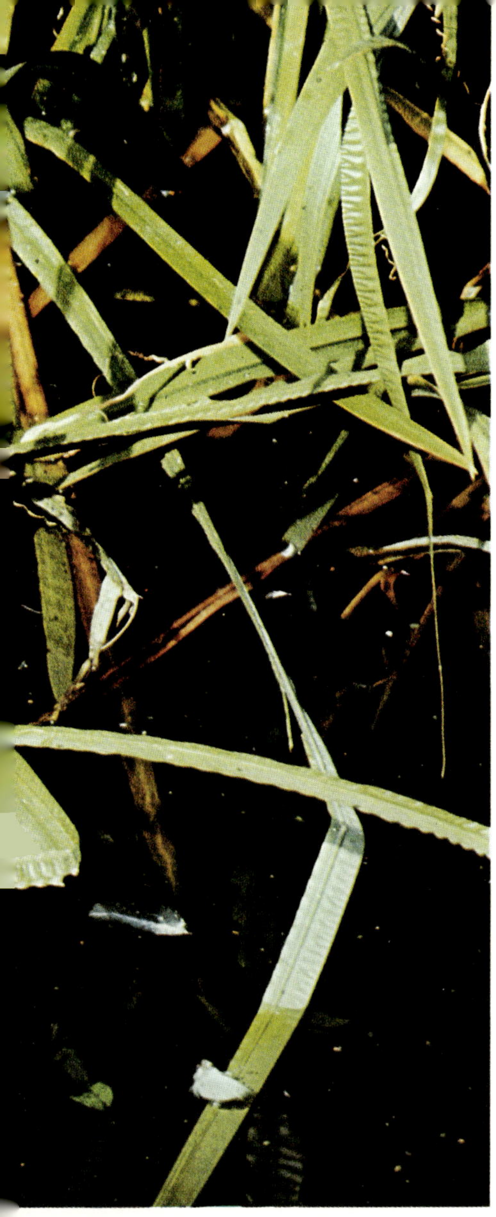

It is essential to let the animal grow accustomed to the presence of a 'foreign object' in its territory. In addition to light portable shelters which are suitable for vigils lasting only a few hours or perhaps a day or two at most, you may have occasion to use a larger and more permanent hide where circumstances require it, e.g. a big hut or indeed an observation tower assembled from logs lashed together or from prefabricated components such as metal tubes with bolted connections. An observation tower, which should be surmounted by a suitable hide, has the advantage of providing a view from above, which is essential for obtaining good photographic shots of a nest in an elevated position or of mammals (which are generally rather indifferent to what is happening overhead and will therefore pursue their natural behaviour undisturbed). Depending on the 'personality' of the animal or bird with which you have to deal, this sort of structure should be erected with considerable care so as not to disturb the creature's normal pattern of behaviour.

One method is to build your tower very quickly, in an hour or two, the component parts having been carefully prepared beforehand far away from the intended location. Alternatively, it may be assembled in imperceptible stages, gradually becoming an integral feature of the landscape: each day a piece is added to the structure, and building operations will thus continue for days, perhaps for even more than a week.

Such tall structures must be strong enough to resist wind forces and be very firmly fixed to the ground, for the slightest movement at the top will be transmitted to the whole tower, startling the animal and perhaps scaring it away. They are more particularly intended for the photographing of rare species or obtaining pictures of the animal's whole behaviour pattern (nesting region, hunting territory, etc.).

Since all the shots will have to be taken from one position, i.e. with one and the same camera angle, the location of the permanent hide should be planned with care, for it is hardly possible to alter it afterwards. Also, the hide should be reasonably comfortable, as the photographer may have to spend a day or two in it waiting for something to happen.

One of the great advantages of the permanent hide, whether installed at ground level or at the top of a tower, is that the photographer can use heavy equipment of quite conventional design. Cameras for any desired picture format

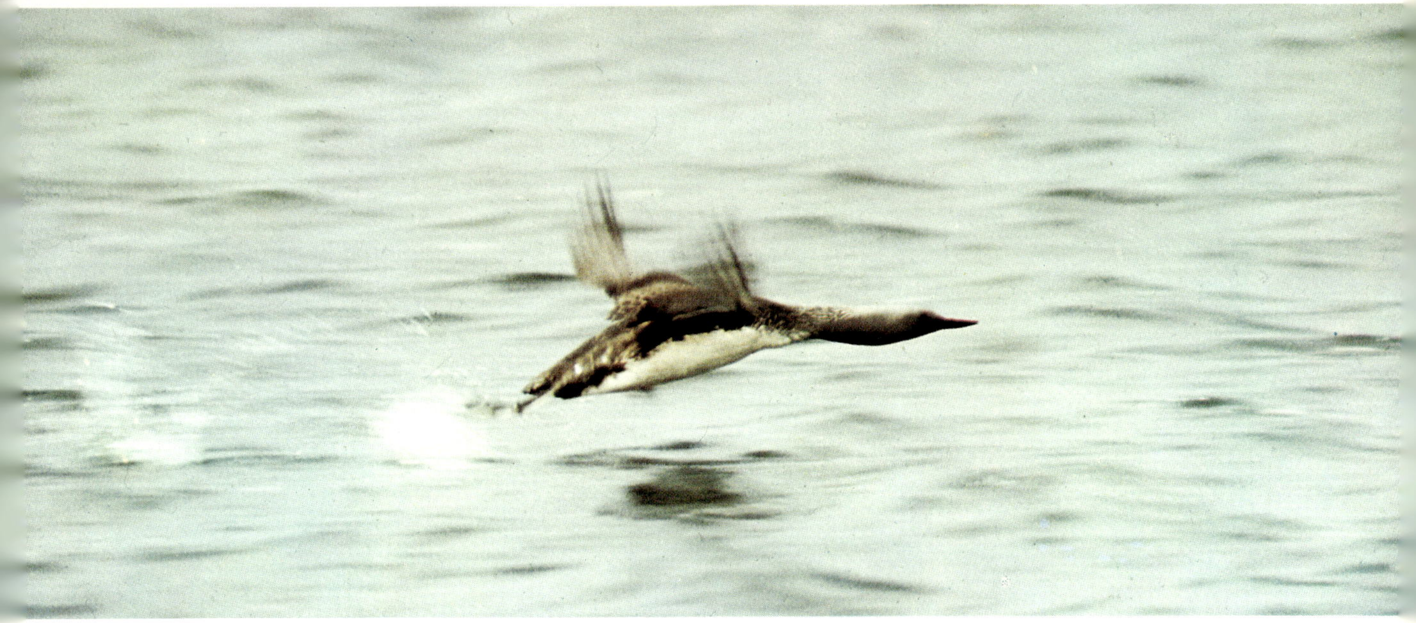

The tower illustrated below was constructed from light alloy tubes manufactured for industrial purposes. It is surmounted by a hide providing a view in all directions and is secured by steel guy ropes. Ladders give convenient access to the hide, which is perched 35 feet above ground level.
The pictures of nesting storks were obtained from the top of a tower of this type. In this case the hide was large enough to enable relatively heavy equipment comprising cameras of different sizes to be employed.
Equipment: 6 cm × 6 cm and 35 mm cameras, photosniper, focal lengths 80, 200, 400 and 600 mm.

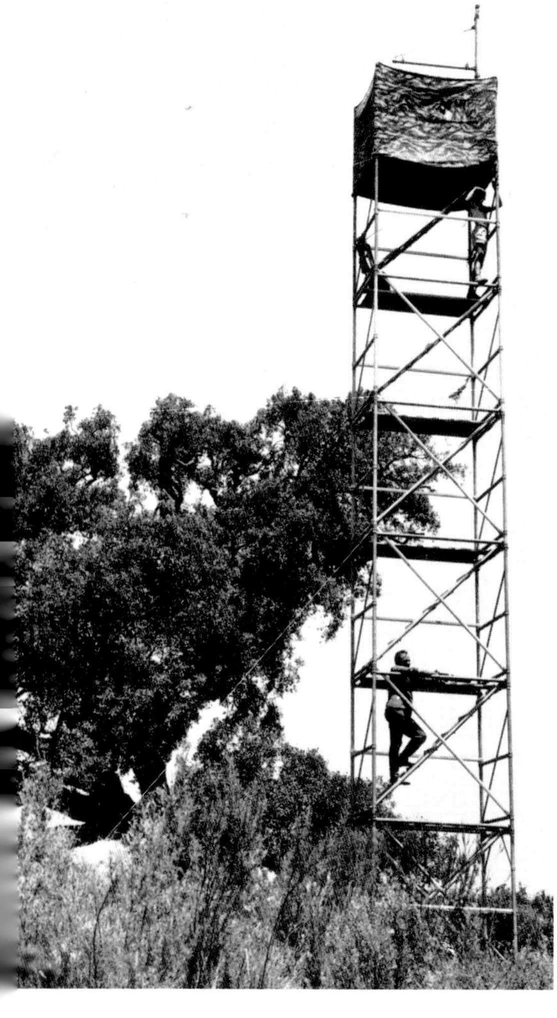

can be employed, almost invariably with telephoto lenses, if the hide is installed at some considerable distance from the subject to be photographed.

The telephoto lens sticking out of the hide may be covered with a sleeve to prevent reflections. Precautions may also be necessary to suppress reflections from metal components used in the construction of the hide itself; but the actual colour of the hide does not matter very much. Although we have on occasion used blue or red camping tents for concealment, we have never noticed the animals to be particularly sensitive to these alien blobs of colour in their landscape. But such tents have the drawback that walkers and other people who happen to be in the vicinity are likely to be attracted to them from a sense of curiosity – and this is obviously something to be avoided at all costs if you do not want some gaping tourist to appear in your field of vision at the critical moment, just when you are about to get a good shot.

Another possibility to be reckoned with is that the wind, an ever-present hazard, will turn your hide into a permanent scarecrow because some rope or piece of canvas which has not been securely fastened will start flapping.

And here is another piece of advice that may save you much fruitless waiting: never go alone into a hide. Eyes are watching you. Although animals and birds cannot count (this is fairly certain), they are nevertheless sensitive to comings and goings and they remain very suspicious of that other 'animal' which has

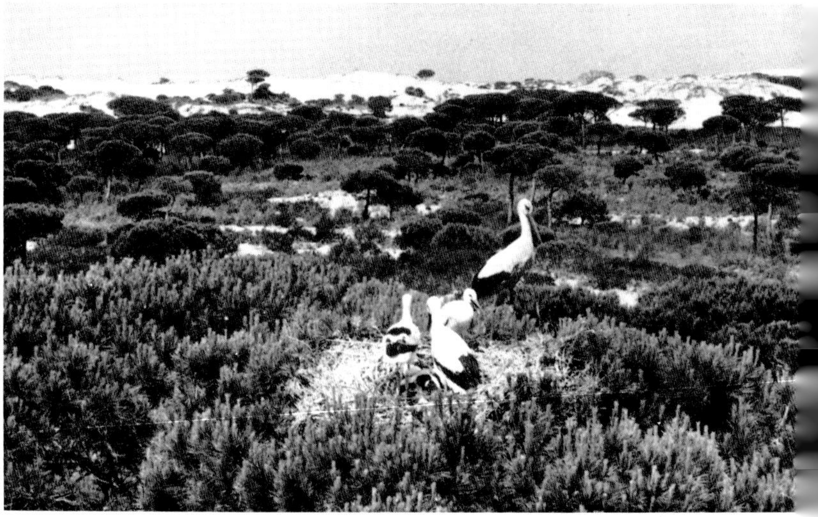

come into their territory and will not go away. So approach the hide in a group, quite openly (but not making too much noise); the photographer can then slip unobtrusively into the hide before his companions depart.

On the borderline of the two methods – working from a hide and stalking – is the practice of using a motor vehicle as a mobile hide. It has the advantage of being a familiar feature to many species and will therefore not scare them off. Another useful means of conveyance is the boat, propelled along quietly and discreetly, surmounted by a tent or hide constructed of reeds and branches, which is excellent for watching and photographing species which live on or beside the water.

Stalking

The British, with a long tradition as excellent wildlife photographers, often used large-format cameras fitted with short-focus lenses, which made it necessary to get close to the animals. To accustom the latter to the presence of the hide, they would advance it a few yards closer to the subject each day. This procedure

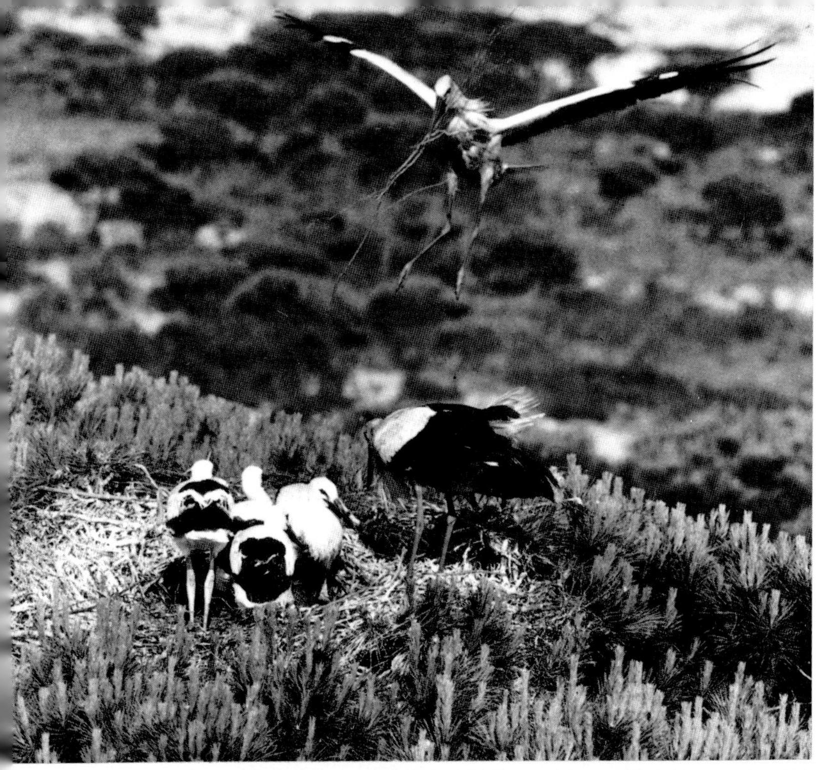

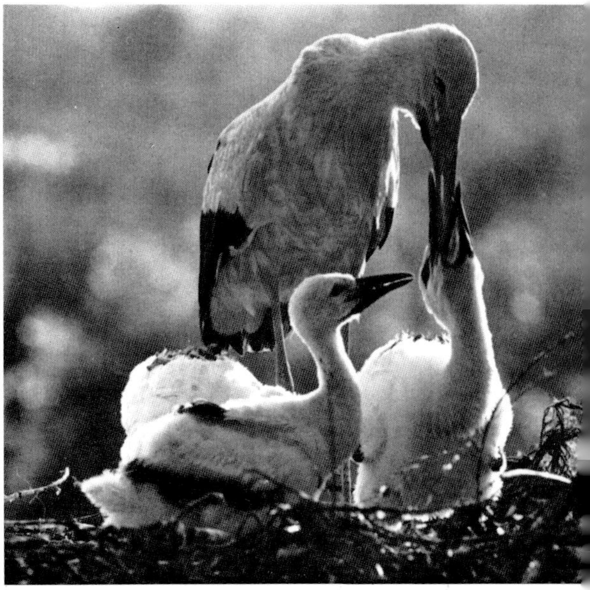

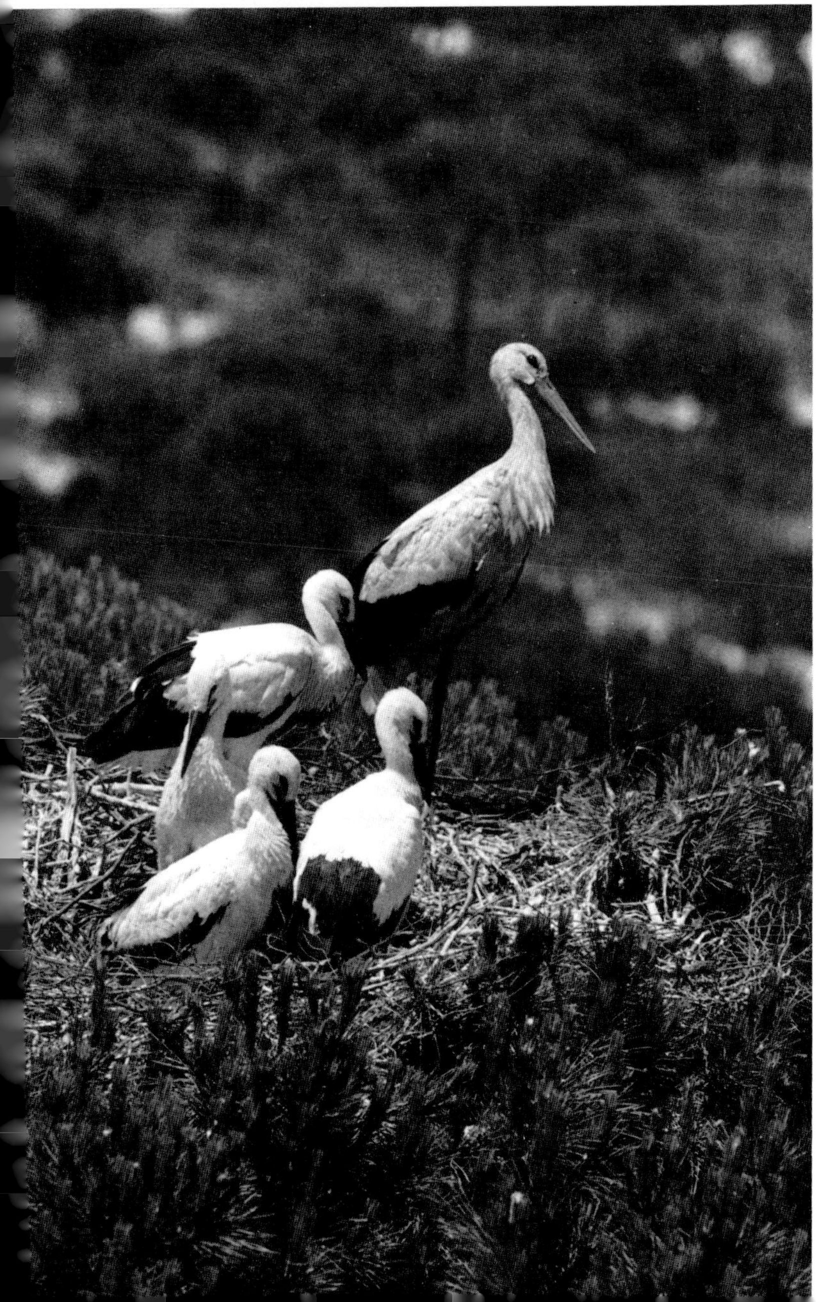

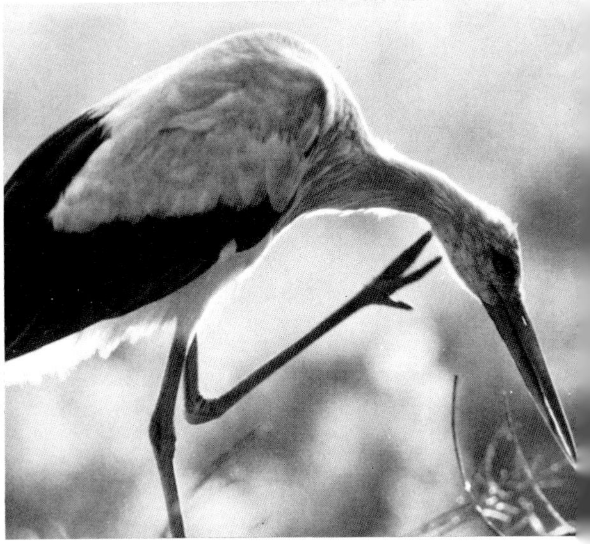

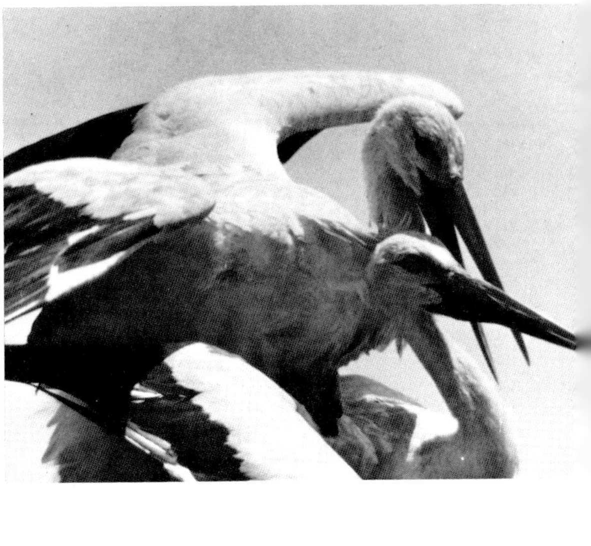

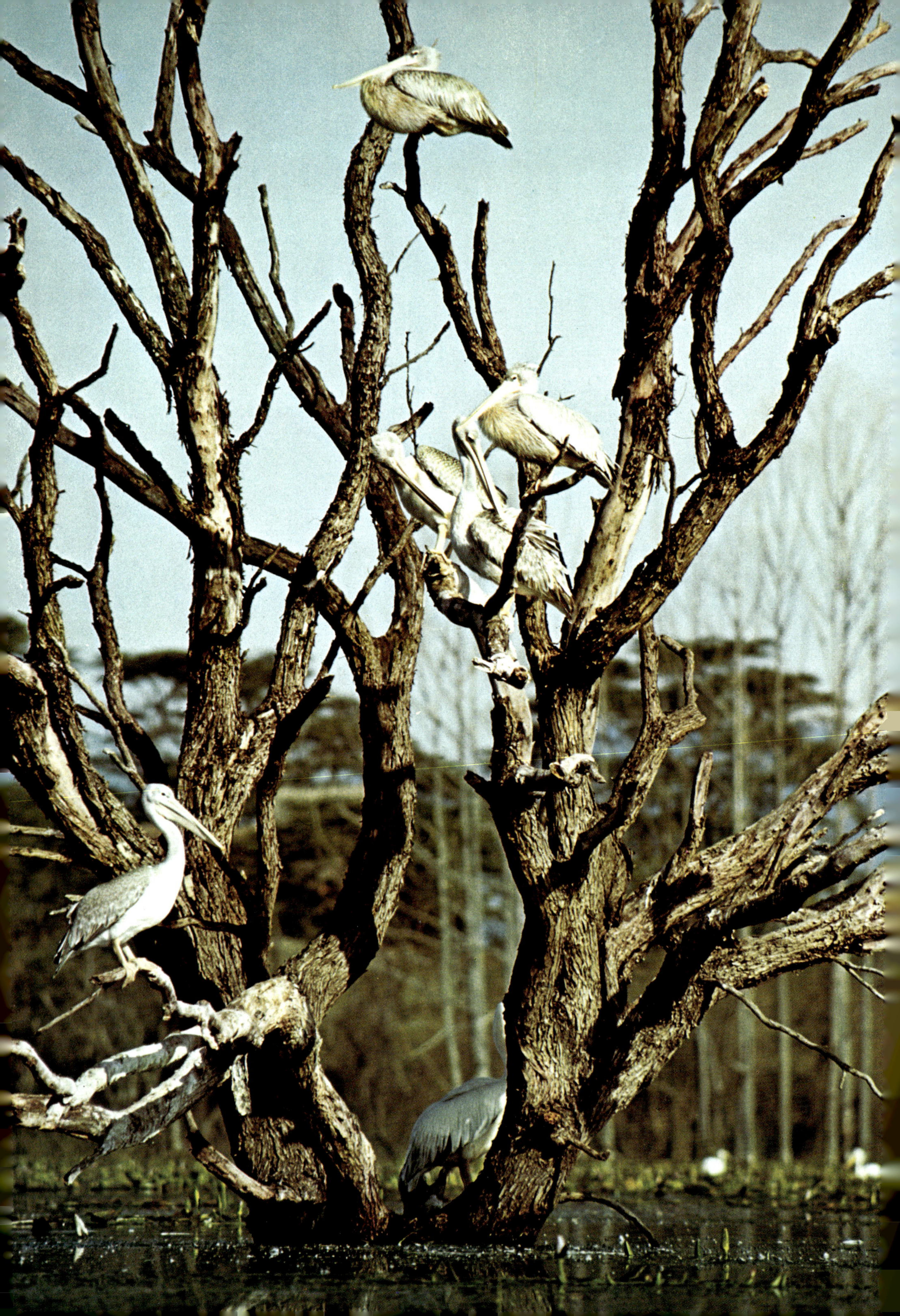

might take anything up to ten or twelve days before a single picture could be obtained. Nowadays few wildlife photographers are prepared to spend so much time on getting a few pictures. For this reason, and also for the study of highly mobile species (e.g. migratory birds or animals), or because of the low density of a particular species in a vast territory, it is necessary to adopt a different, simpler and also mobile technique: stalking. The pictures obtained by this method are, generally speaking, not of such high technical quality as those obtained from a hide, but what they lose in definition is largely compensated for by the dynamic quality they derive from capturing a fleeting instant of reality.

The wildlife photographer who sets out to stalk his subjects should have the right kind of equipment – light and compact – and possess great skill in handling his 'photosniper' and in using his telephoto lenses. The latter should be focused on the hyperfocal distance (in which case the depth of field extends from half this distance to infinity) and ready for quick action, for it is the animal or bird that must be taken by surprise by the photographer, not the other way round.

Obviously, for the photographer, stalking requires an entirely different attitude of mind from working in a hide: passive waiting is replaced by vigorous physical effort, extreme caution and sustained attention. You have to be cunning in order to outwit certain species with their very highly developed senses. For example, the sense of sight in birds is about six times sharper than human sight; some mammals can detect smell about five times more acutely than man is able to. For animals accustomed to a peaceful and silent world, in which any alien intrusion is immediately detected, the photographer's behaviour is at least as important as the camouflage of himself and his equipment. Bright metallic parts of the camera and lens (chromium plating on the body, focusing ring, etc.)

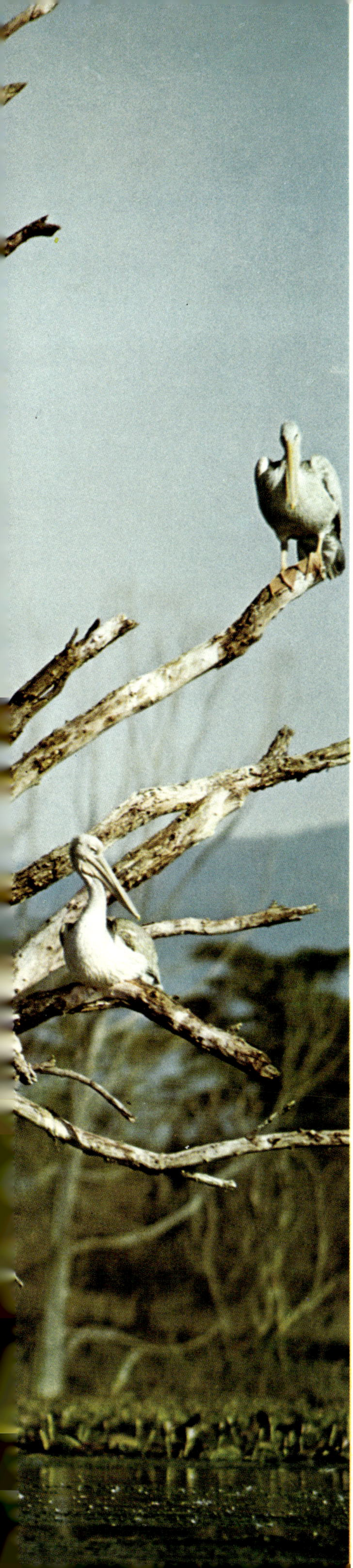

White pelicans (*Pelecanus onocrotalus*) perched on a half-submerged tree in an African lake.
Equipment: 35 mm reflex camera, 200 mm telephoto lens, photosniper mounting; photographed from a camouflaged boat.

Below: An immature night heron (*Nycticorax nycticorax*).

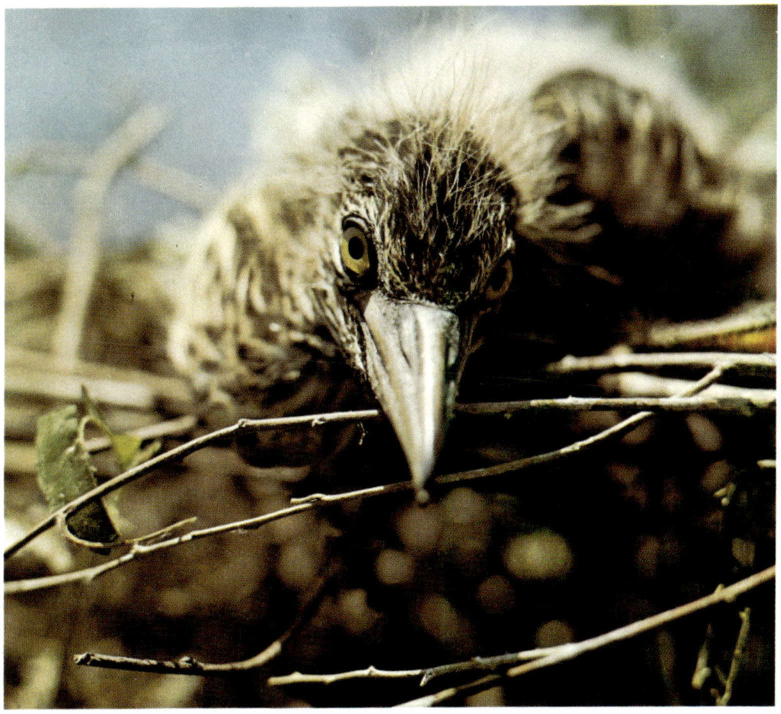

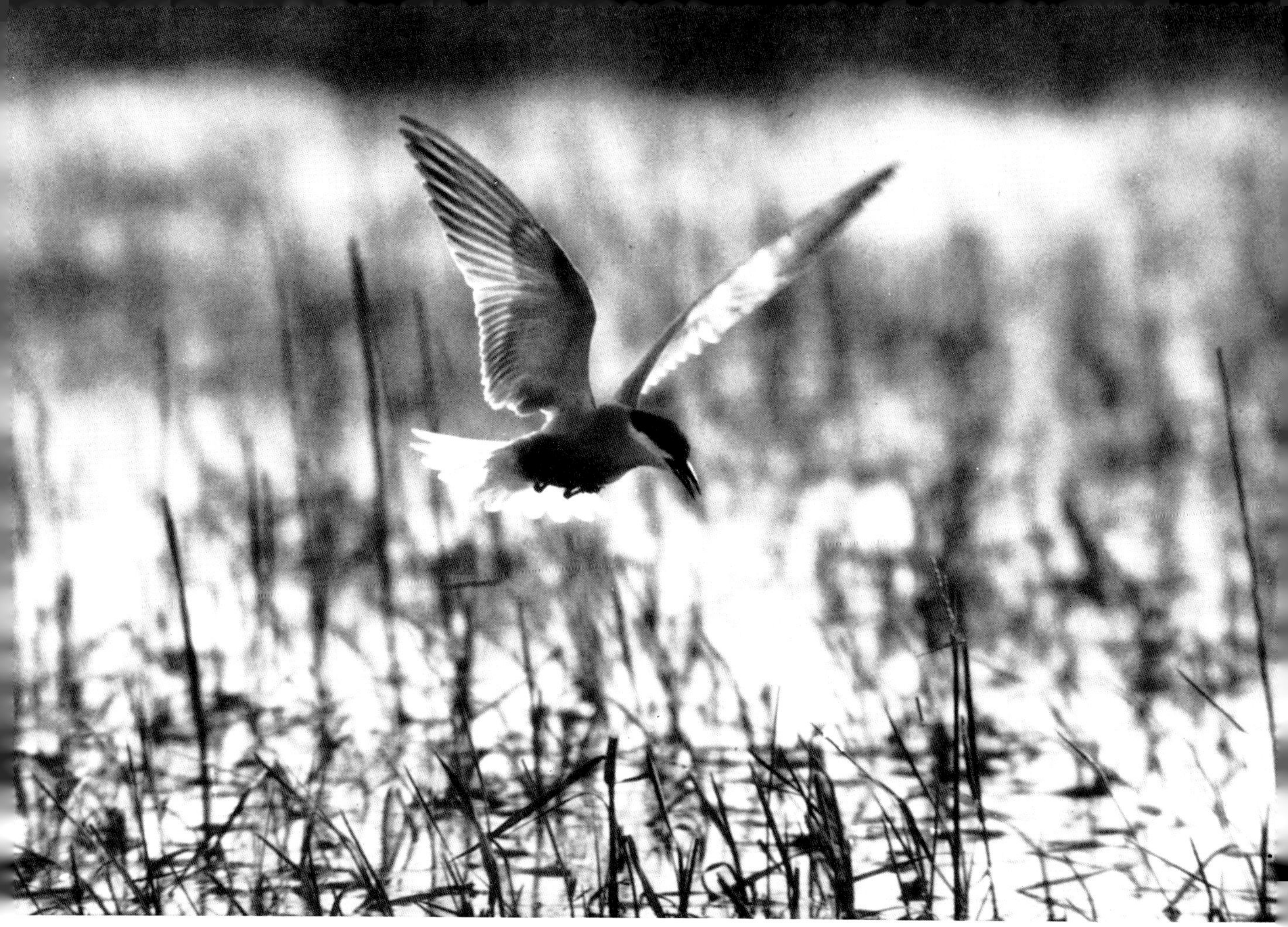

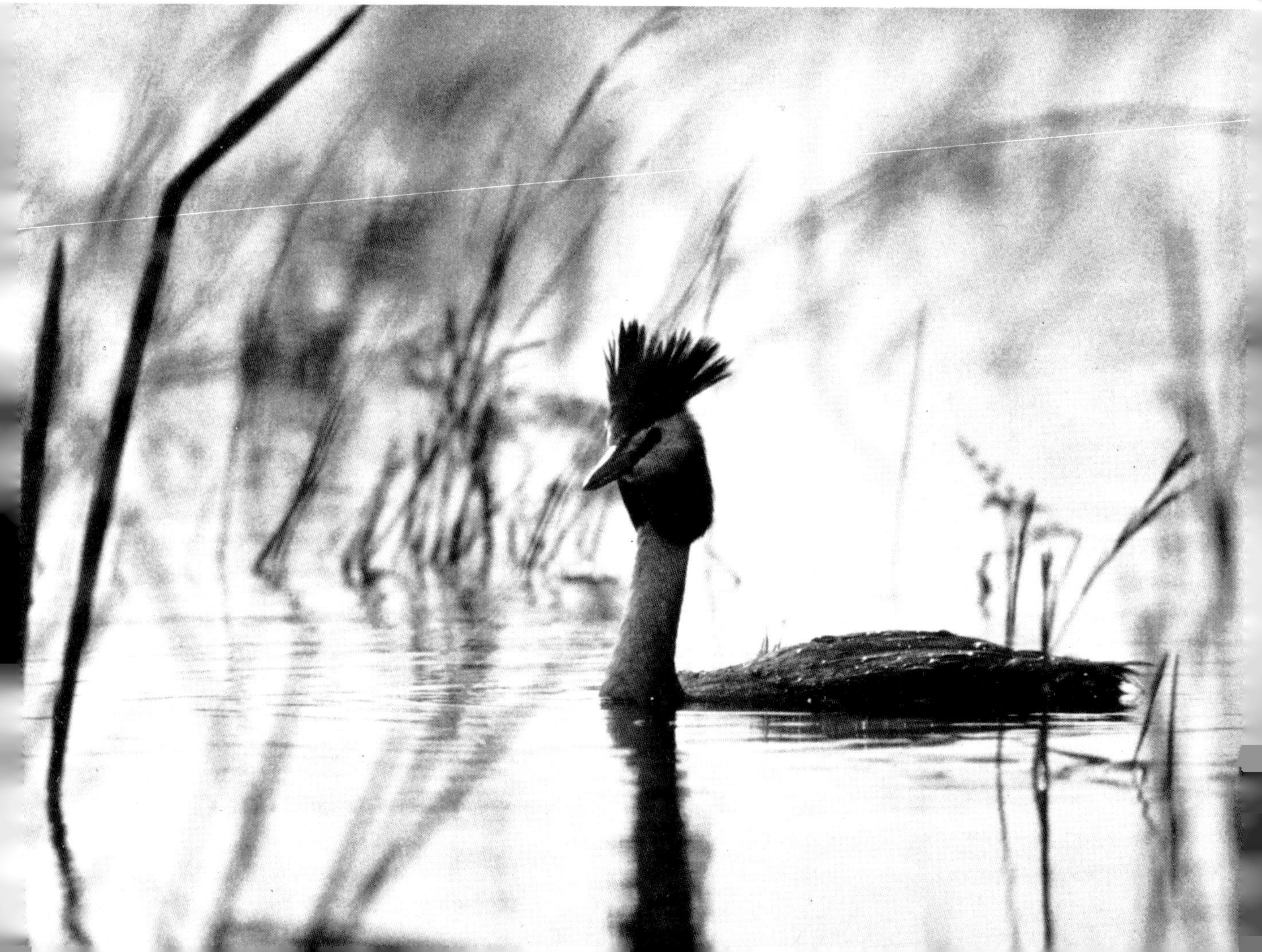

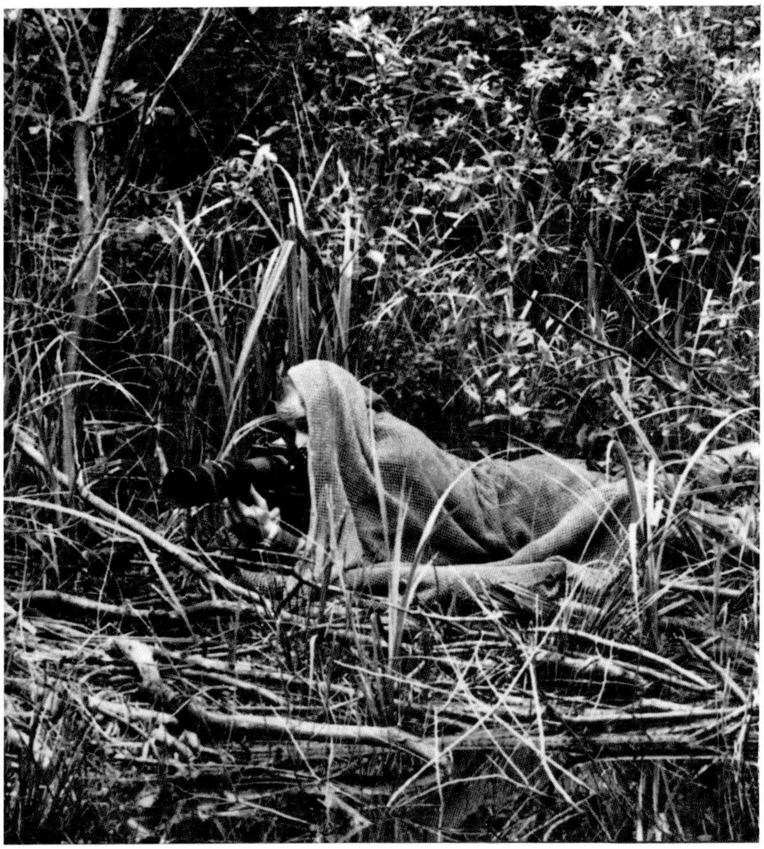

Left-hand page: A tern (*Chlidonias hybrida*) photographed against back light with a photosniper using a lens of 600 mm focal length.

The great crested grebe (*Podiceps cristatus*) presents an elegant silhouette which harmonizes pleasingly with the aquatic scenery.

On this page, above: Photographer concealed under camouflage net. Below: Camouflaged unsinkable fibreglass boat propelled by an absolutely silent electric motor.

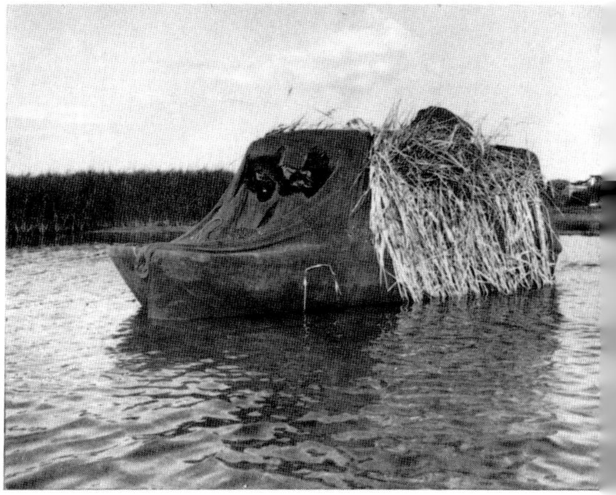

should be suitably treated to minimize reflection. It is also absolutely essential to avoid any metallic clicks or clanks caused by fasteners, straps, cases and camera accessories.

You should wear practical clothes to allow you to move freely and noiselessly (waterproof materials and corduroy tend to be very 'noisy'). Since the clothing must, in a sense, take the place of the hide, it should be serviceable, without unnecessary accessories and appendages. You should wear boots made of a soft material, or canvas shoes. The colour of your clothing is less important than is generally supposed, for it is probable that the eyesight of animals and birds is different from ours and that they do not see colour values as we do. However, for reasons already referred to in connection with tents (attracting people prompted by curiosity), it is preferable to choose a neutral colour and to cover one's face and hands so as not to interrupt the uniformity of the get-up.

You should stalk your subject silently, unerringly and cautiously. After thoroughly scrutinizing the territory through field-glasses and having ascertained the direction from which the wind is blowing, you must also consider what the conditions of illumination of the subject are likely to be at the end of the stalking approach, i.e. at the instant when you get your shot (or so you hope). Remember, too, that the shortest way to your subject is not always a straight line, and you should know how to take advantage of every fold and undulation of the ground.

Although this kind of wildlife photography requires fewer preparations than those involved in building a hide or shelter, the camera you use for this work should possess special qualities and form part of a set of equipment that is almost tailor-made to suit your individual needs. Above all, as a result of thorough training your camera must become your dependable and faithful servant.

The puffin (*Fratercula artica*) uses the webs of its feet as aids in guiding its flight. Here a puffin is shown coming in to land.
Equipment: 35 mm camera, photosniper mounting, 400 mm focal length.

Below: Gannets (*Sula bassana*) parading their plumage. Greetings and 'ceremonial' behaviour patterns play an important part in the lives of these birds.
Equipment: 35 mm reflex camera with 1200 mm telephoto lens, on a tripod; film high-speed Ektachrome.

Right: Kittiwakes (*Rissa tridactyla*) nesting on a cliff face.
Equipment: 6 cm × 6 cm reflex camera with 500 mm Zeiss lens; aperture f 8.

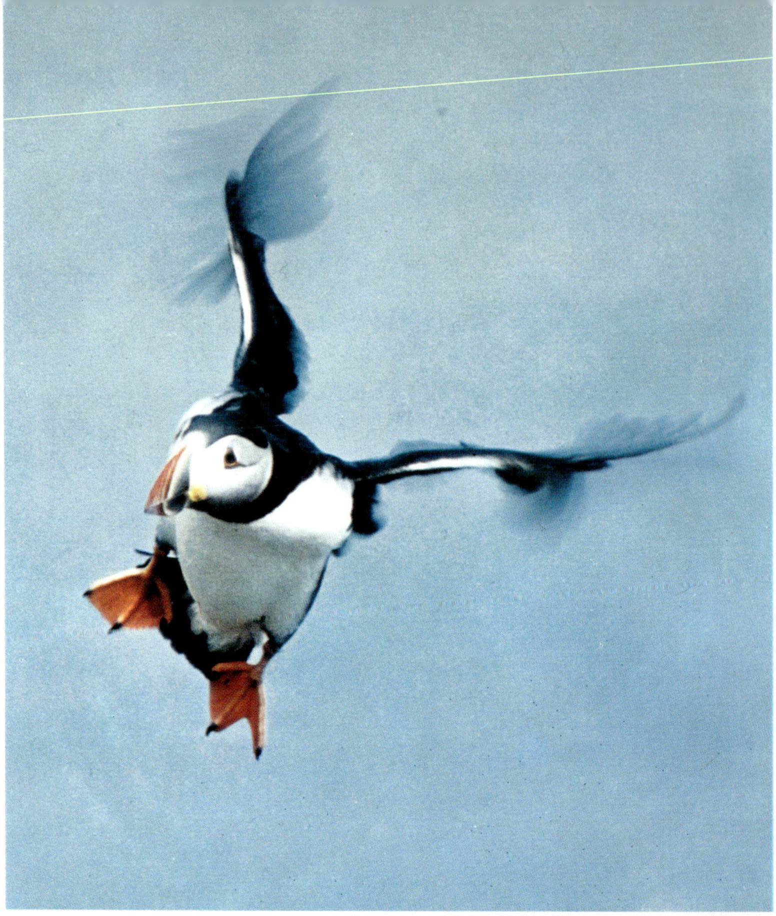

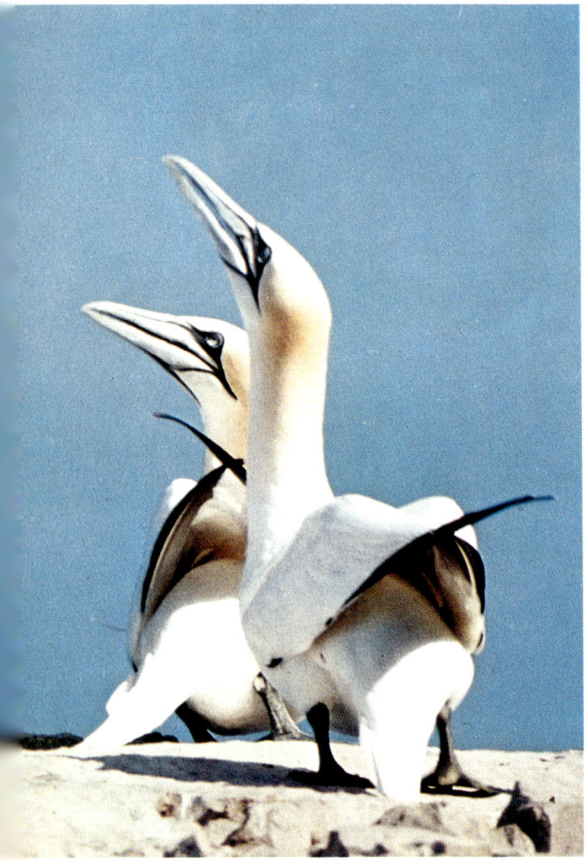

Wildlife stalking is something you can do anywhere, at any time of the year. For this you can make use of various stratagems for concealment–'melting away' into the surroundings.

The early practitioners of this technique sometimes went to great lengths to camouflage themselves, e.g. as hollow trees, bushes, etc. which they moved along with them. Sometimes they even concealed themselves in the skins of animals such as cows or bison (veritable mobile 'hides' indeed!) to outwit the suspicious subject of their attentions. When at last they got near enough to the creature, they were so exhausted in mind and body after their ordeal that the pictures they obtained were often disappointing–to say nothing of the risk that such a photographer, dressed up in his animal skin, might run if he happened to come within gunshot range of a novice out hunting or come face to face with some enraged large real animal!

There is, however, no reason why you should not make use of 'local materials' such as reeds, furze or small branches for camouflage, transforming yourself into a crawling bush or perhaps even a floating island.

The humble bicycle can be an excellent aid in stalking your subject, provided that you cover both yourself and your machine with a camouflage net reaching to the ground. You can see quite clearly through the meshes; it certainly will not be suffocatingly hot under the net; and the whole contraption will look like nothing on earth–which is probably the best way to avoid frightening the animal or bird in which you are interested. The bicycle also provides a good means of moving about quickly and quietly in all sorts of terrain.

Having chosen strong and reliable equipment, you must also remember to carry enough film with you and bear in mind that many things can crop up at the last minute to rob a fine long stalking operation of its deserved success: for example, a battery may be defective, or the shutter may fail to function. Also, you must allow for disagreeable eventualities: a sudden change in the weather, an aggressive animal or losing your bearings in unknown territory.

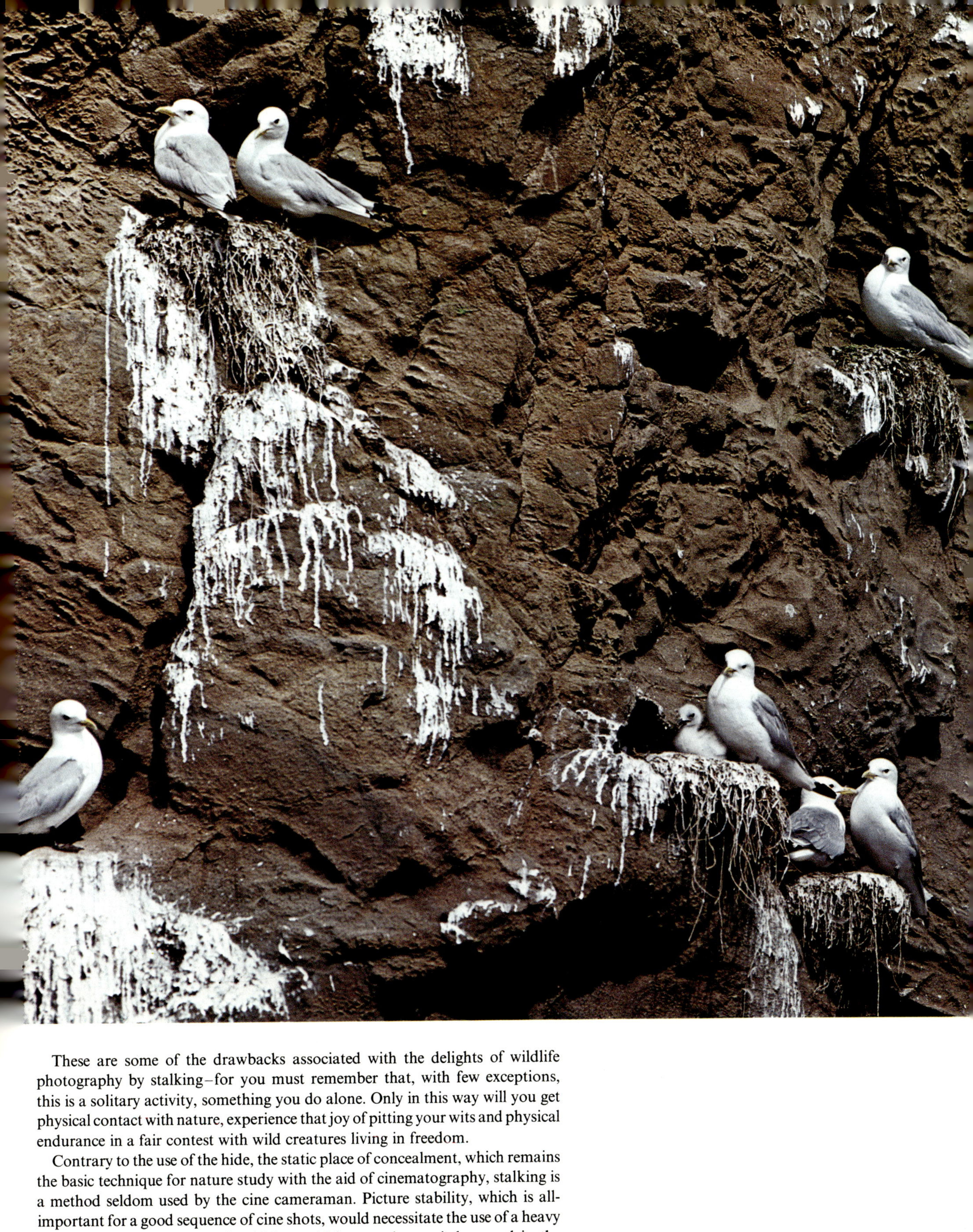

These are some of the drawbacks associated with the delights of wildlife photography by stalking–for you must remember that, with few exceptions, this is a solitary activity, something you do alone. Only in this way will you get physical contact with nature, experience that joy of pitting your wits and physical endurance in a fair contest with wild creatures living in freedom.

Contrary to the use of the hide, the static place of concealment, which remains the basic technique for nature study with the aid of cinematography, stalking is a method seldom used by the cine cameraman. Picture stability, which is all-important for a good sequence of cine shots, would necessitate the use of a heavy tripod or cumbersome stand, which would have to be carried around in the field. However, a cine camera mounted on a shoulder tripod is sometimes

Bladder-wrack (*Fucus vesiculosus*), a seaweed, photographed at low tide. Such photographs which fill in the background of a particular animal's habitat can be very useful to the naturalist.
Equipment: Hasselblad 6 cm × 6 cm camera with 80 mm focal length.

Right: An octopus (*Octopus vulgaris*) photographed swimming in an aquarium. The photographer had to wait patiently for a long time to get this picture. The creature's arms covered with suckers and its head and one of its eyes are clearly visible.
Equipment: 6 cm × 6 cm camera, 120 mm focal length; electronic flash.

successfully used for filming birds in flight or fast-running animals, provided that the camera is run at a high enough speed – at least sixty-four frames per second. The camera, fitted with a sports-type viewfinder, is sound-insulated and is loaded with high-speed film.

Underwater photography

Sea covers three-quarters of the surface of the globe and yet the underwater world has scarcely been explored by man.

The photographic techniques employed for penetrating this mysterious world and studying marine life in its natural environment are highly specialized and belong more to the domain of the professional than of the amateur. All the same, we feel that a description of the essentials should not be omitted from this book. In this relatively new field the diving enthusiast who also happens to have an enthusiasm for photography will find plenty of scope to satisfy his taste for getting pictures of unusual places and creatures.

On account of the vastness of the field of exploration that it opens up, underwater wildlife photography is essentially based on stalking. It is difficult to imagine the amateur photographer comfortably installed in some kind of underwater hide, patiently waiting for some obliging fish or crustacean to swim before his lens.

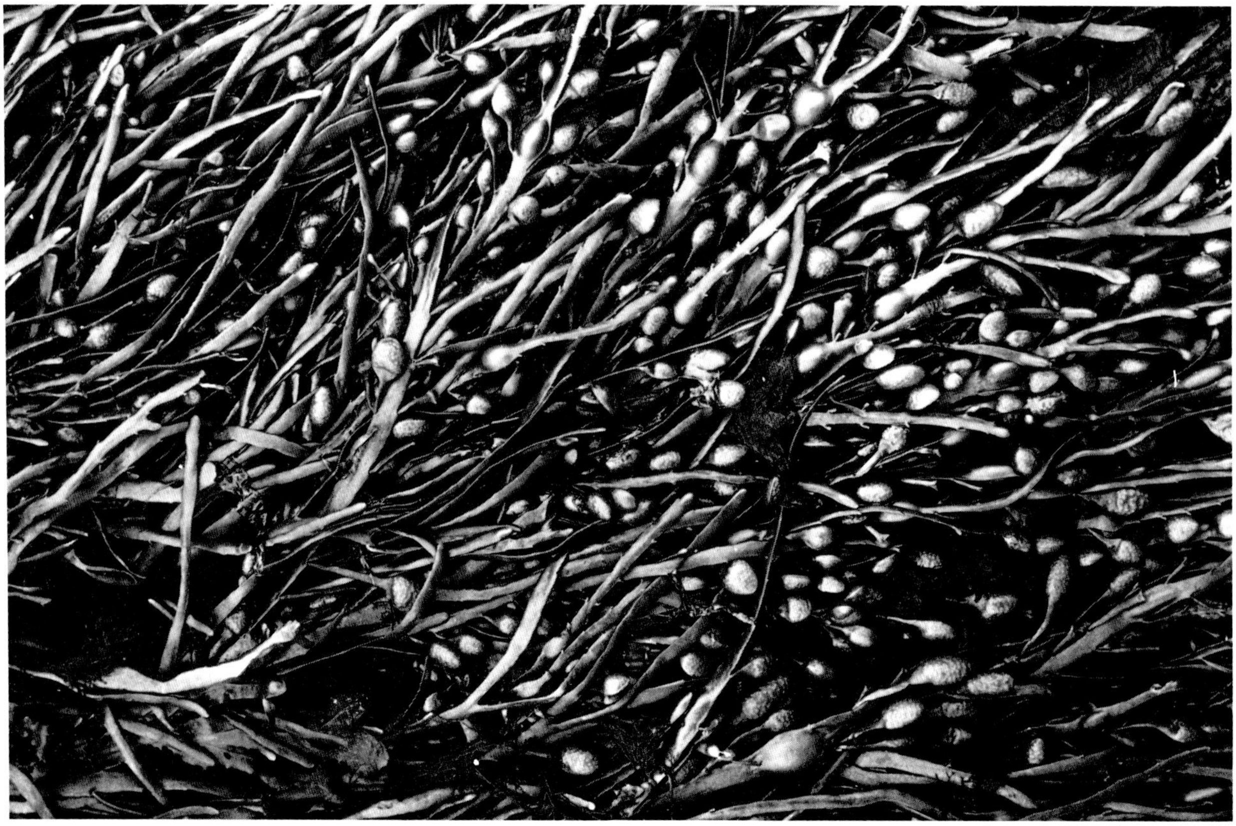

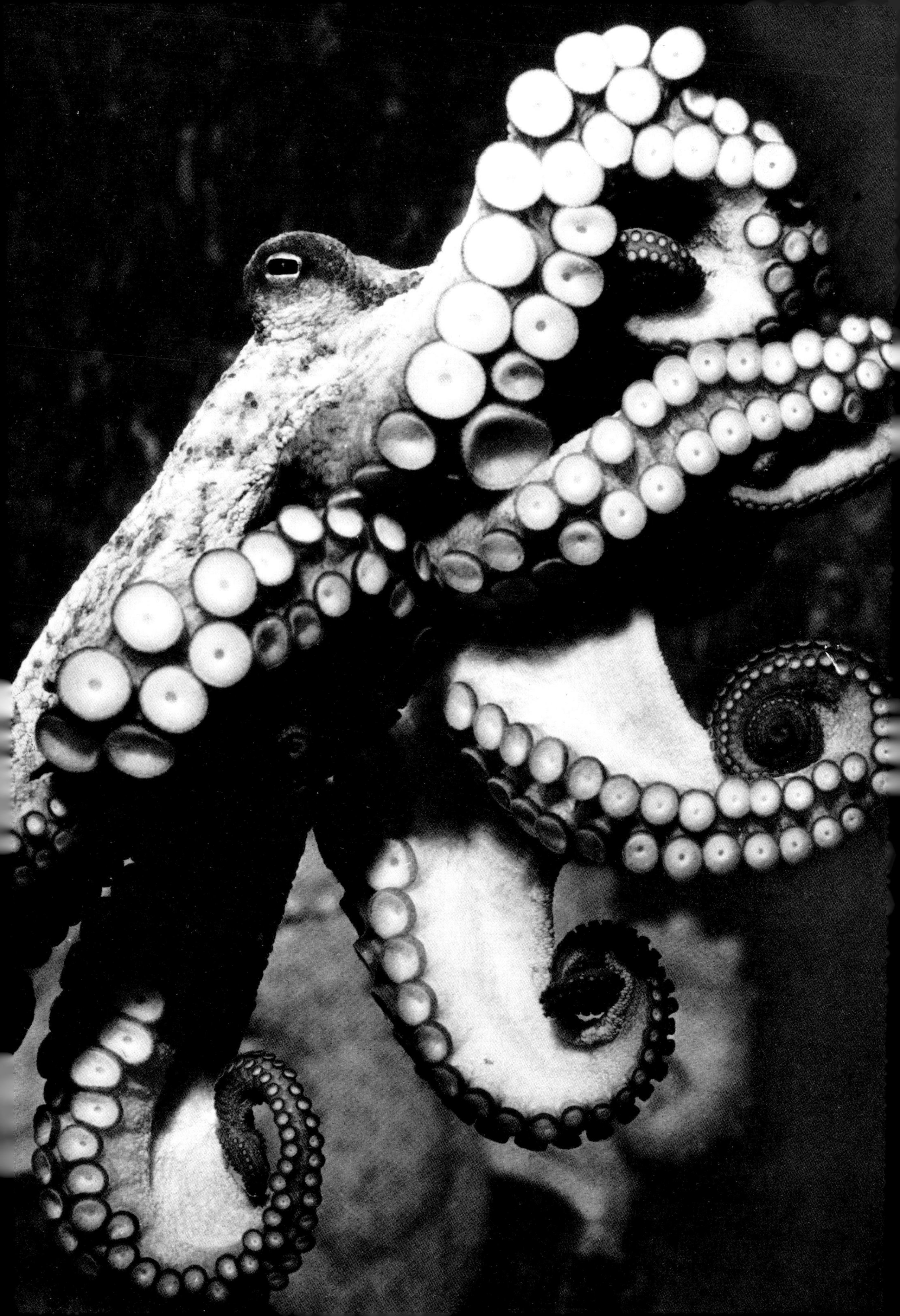

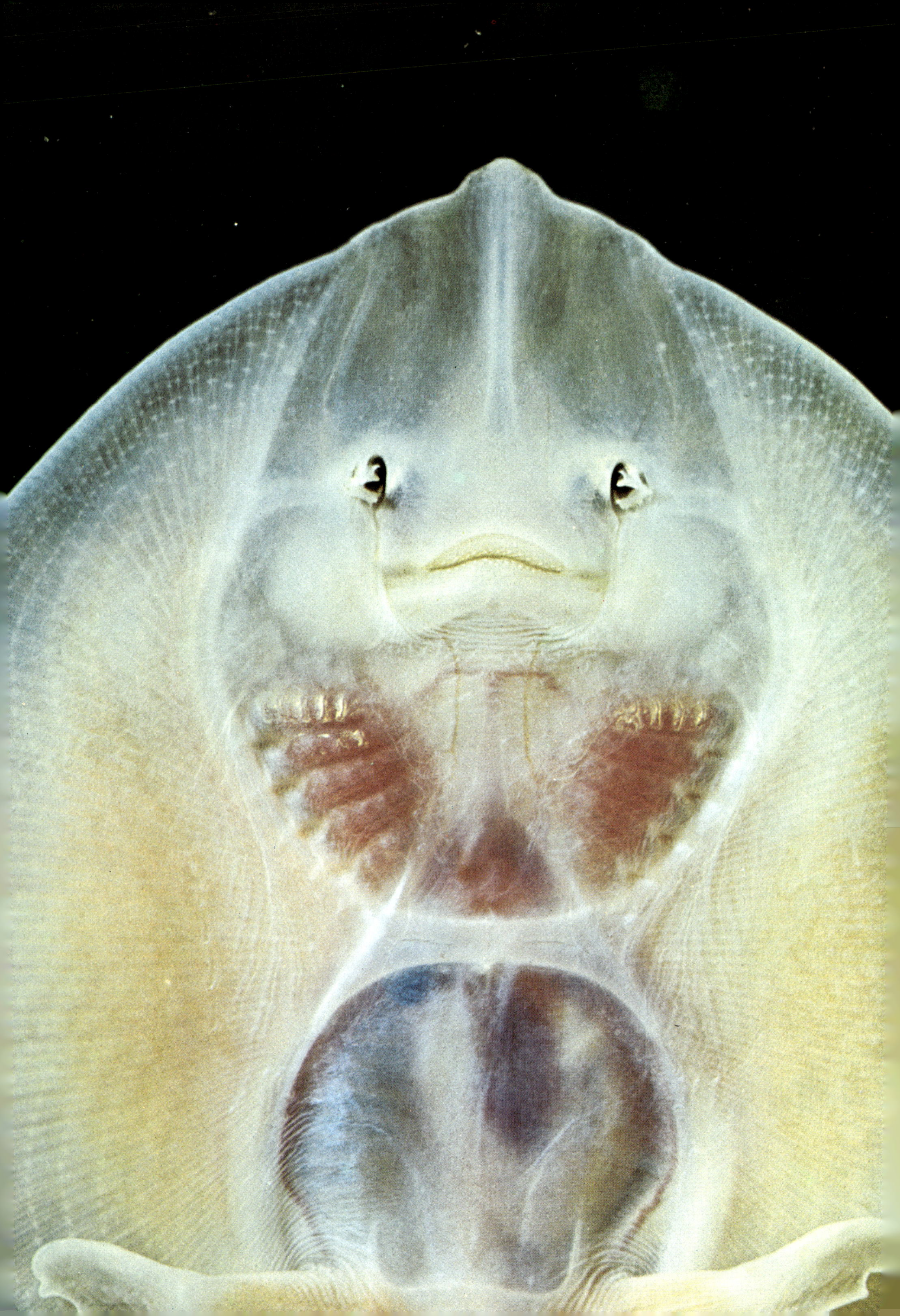

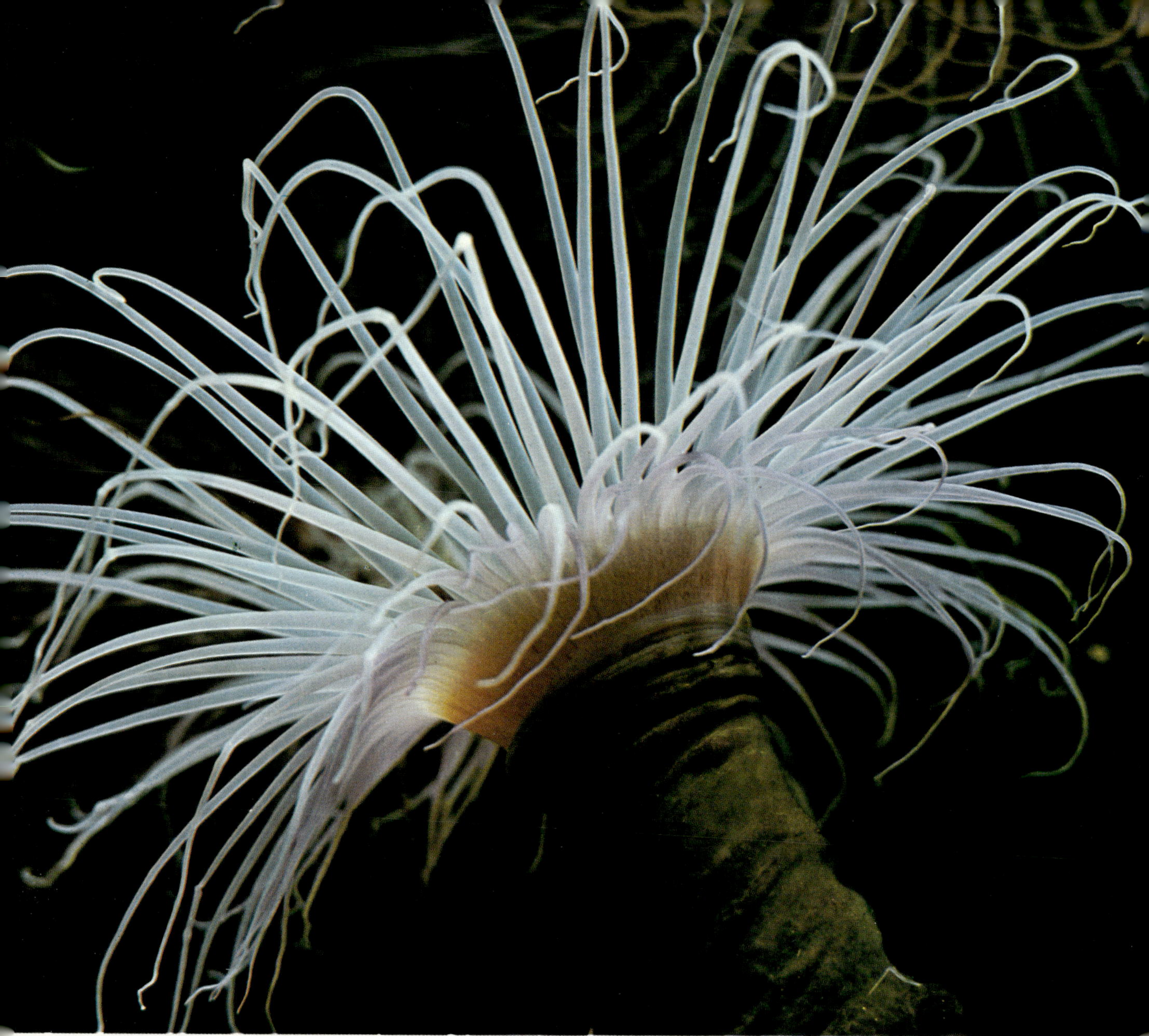

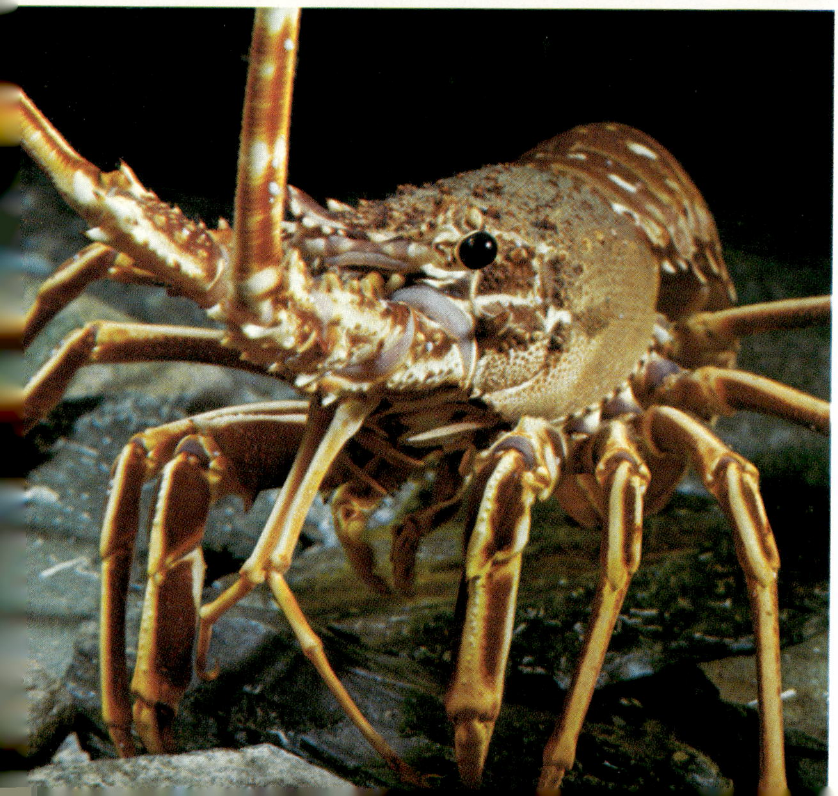

The undersea world offers inexhaustible possibilities to the photographer in search of new subjects. The picture on the left shows an underside view of a skate or ray (*Raja clavata*). The fish's mouth, gill slits and nostrils are clearly seen.

Above: A sea anemone (*Cerianthus membranaceus*) spreading its stinging tentacles.

Below: Spiny lobster, or crayfish (*Palinurus vulgaris*). The creature's eight legs and other appendages are displayed.

There are at least three main possibilities in choosing one's photographic equipment:

1. You can use a camera of the conventional type, reflex or otherwise, equipped with a normal-focus or short-focus lens and enclosed in a waterproof housing. The latter may be in the form of a flexible bag provided with a window, an opening through which to insert the camera, and a rubber glove attachment by means of which the underwater photographer manipulates the controls. The advantage of this type of housing is that it is 'universal' in the sense that it can accommodate various types of camera. It cannot, however, be used at depths exceeding about 30 feet.

2. Some makes of still camera and cine camera can be fitted with rigid (pressure-resistant) housings which can be used at considerable depths (at least 300 feet). Such housings may be specifically designed for one particular type of camera, but there are general-purpose housings that can be tailored to suit various cameras. The camera controls are operated from outside the housing by means of a suitable coupling mechanism, or electrically.

3. Finally, there are cameras designed specifically for underwater photography. Their bodies are constructed of pressure- and corrosion-resistant materials; the controls are operated through watertight glands.

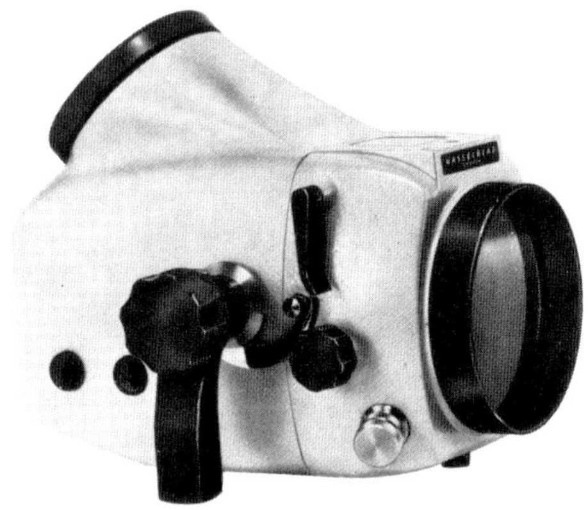

Above: Watertight housing for underwater photography (Hasselblad).

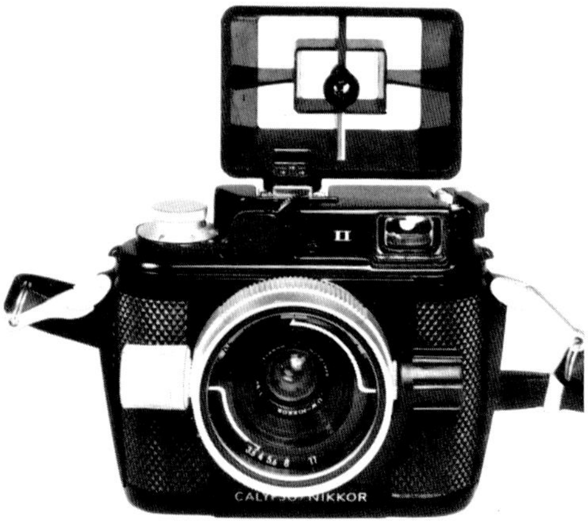

Below: Calypso Nikkor camera, of watertight construction, which can be used under water and is also useful for photography on land under adverse climatic conditions (rain, wind-driven sand).

For photography at or just below the surface of the water the camera can be placed lens-downward in a simple submersion mask. Under the right conditions quite attractive pictures can be obtained in this way. With a flexible housing, operating at depths not exceeding about 15 feet, the techniques of underwater photography are quite simple. Since the photographer's movements and also those of his subjects tend to be slower than on land because of the density of the water, the shutter speeds employed generally need not exceed 1/125 or 1/250 second for a film such as Kodachrome II (25 ASA). If the water is clear, the diaphragm setting will be almost the same as above water, and if you confine your photography to the hours of daylight when the light falls more or less vertically into the water (roughly between 10 am and 4 pm), you can get pictures to a depth of 15 feet without the predominantly blue or green tint that affects all underwater photographs taken at greater depths.

A cloudless sky may, however, cause some excess of blue colour in the underwater picture. You can eliminate this by using a red or magenta filter.

Below 15 feet it is absolutely essential, for colour photography anyway, to use an independent source of illumination: flash for still photography, an incandescent or quartz-iodine lamp for cine. Black-and-white pictures, however, can be obtained without artificial lighting down to depths of at least 90 feet.

Because of the refraction of the light rays in water, the apparent distance of objects under water is about three-quarters of the actual distance, so that they appear larger than they really are. This being so, it may be a good idea to train yourself beforehand in accurately judging underwater distances in a swimming pool. Probably the best solution, however, is to fit the camera lens as well as the diver's facemask with correction lenses which provide a normal angle of vision.

The presence of millions of particles in suspension causes diffusion of the light and thus reduces transparency, so that it is generally not possible to take long-range shots under water. It is therefore preferable to use short-focus lenses and get close-ups.

To obtain pictures of veritable underwater landscapes is quite exceptional. If you content yourself with going after subjects close to the surface in dives of short duration, lasting about a minute or so, you can manage with very simple equipment: facemask, snorkel tube, and fins to increase your swimming power.

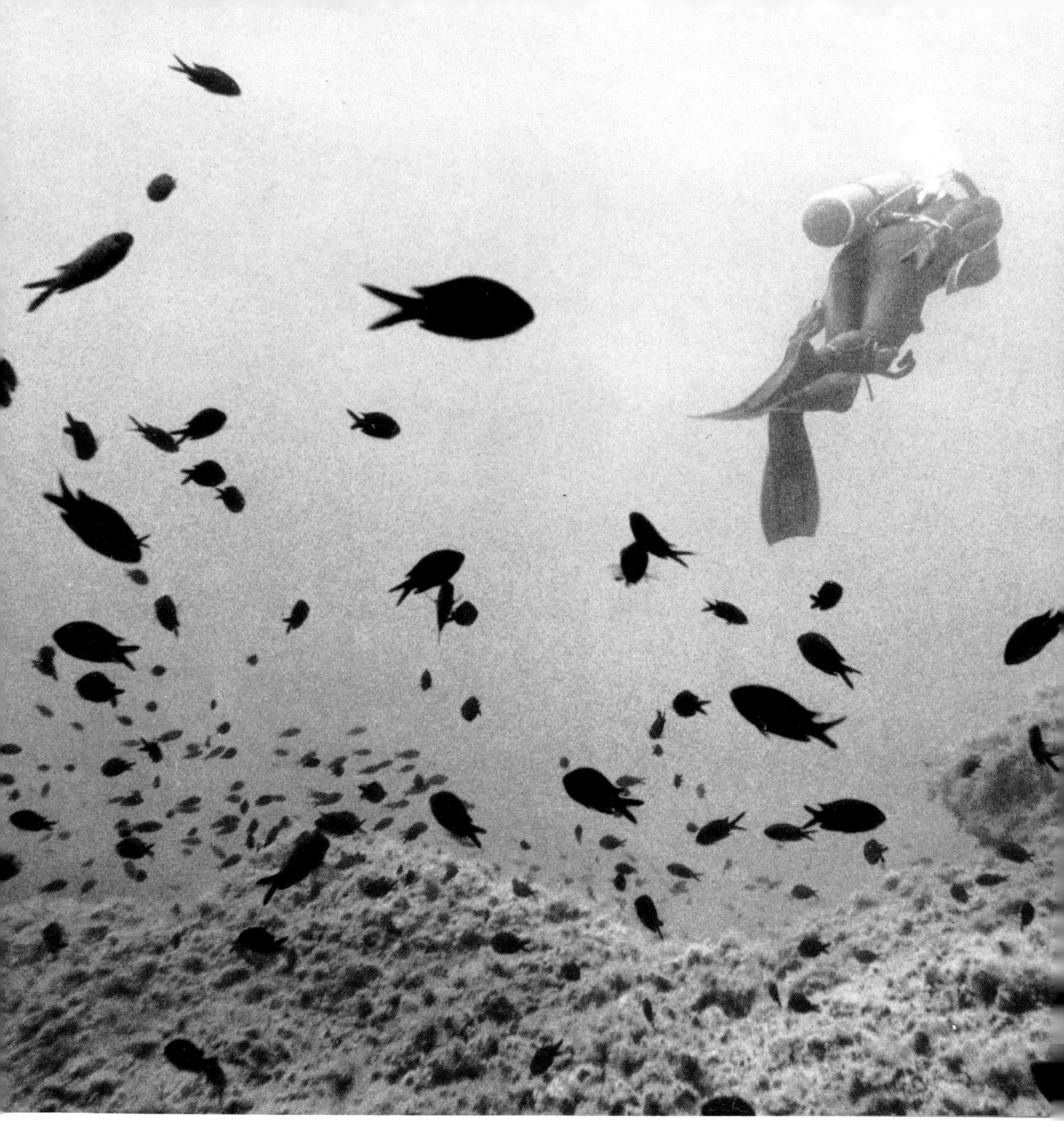

With aqualung equipment comprising a supply of compressed air in cylinders it is possible to work at greater depths and spend a longer time there (thirty to sixty minutes), but this requires thorough training which can be properly acquired only at a diving school. On no account should the underwater photographer operate alone.

Underwater 'landscape' photography is difficult because the water's lack of transparency makes long-distance shots virtually impossible.

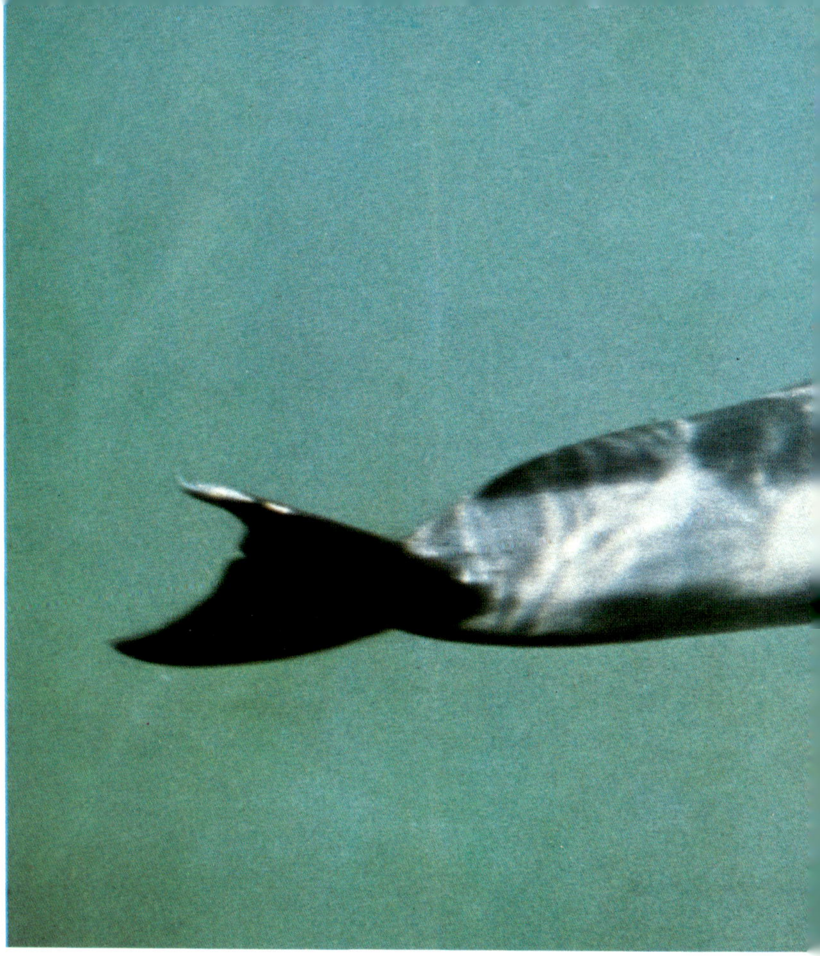

These three underwater photographs were taken in a very large tank.
Above: Dolphin (*Lagenorhynchus obliquidens*) photographed just below the surface of the water, where the sunlight provides adequate illumination.

Below, left: Beluga or white whale (*Delphinapterus leucas*); the animal's blow-hole through which it takes in air for breathing is clearly seen on top of its head.

Below, right: A turtle (*Caretta caretta*) using its flattened legs as efficient means of underwater propulsion.

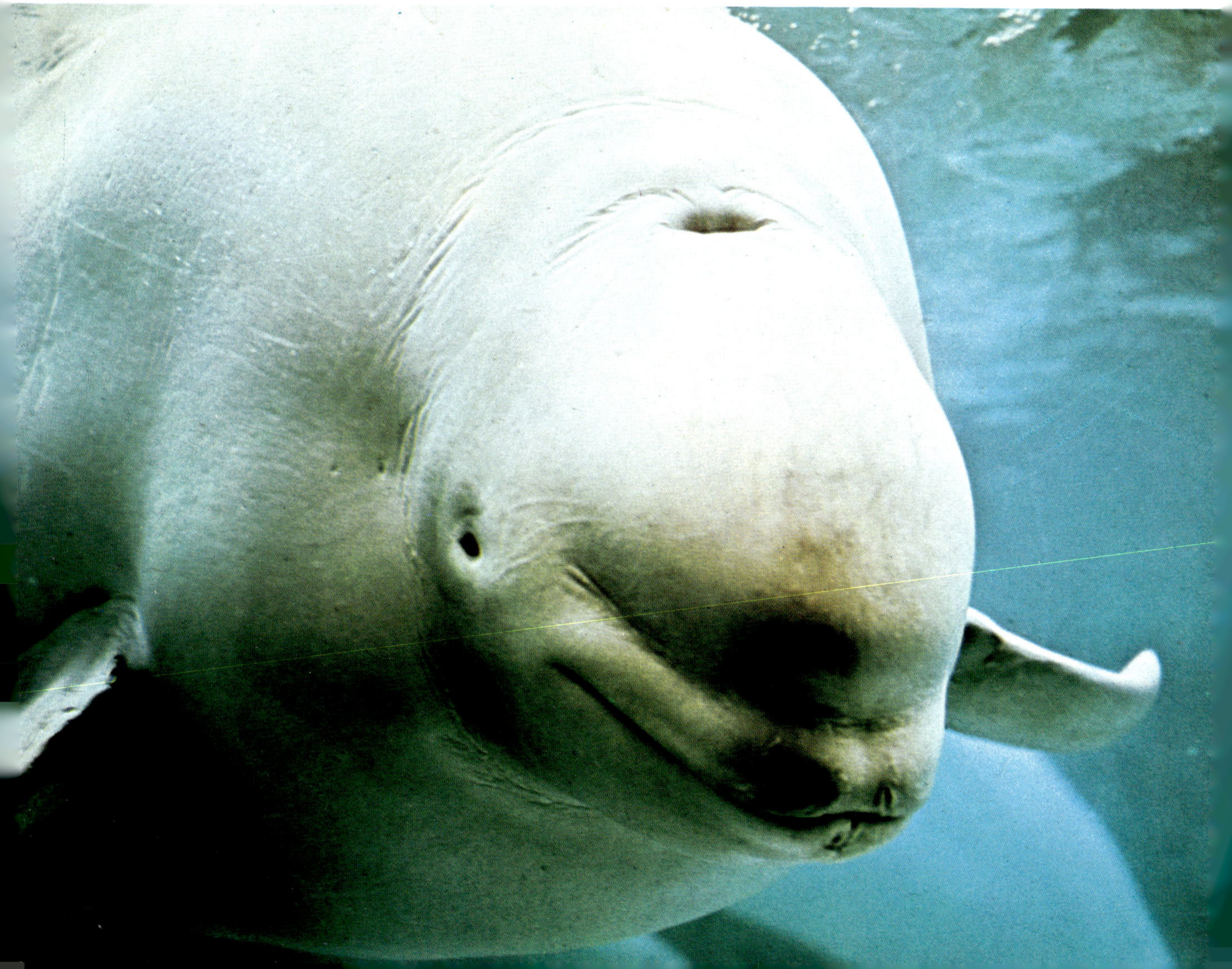

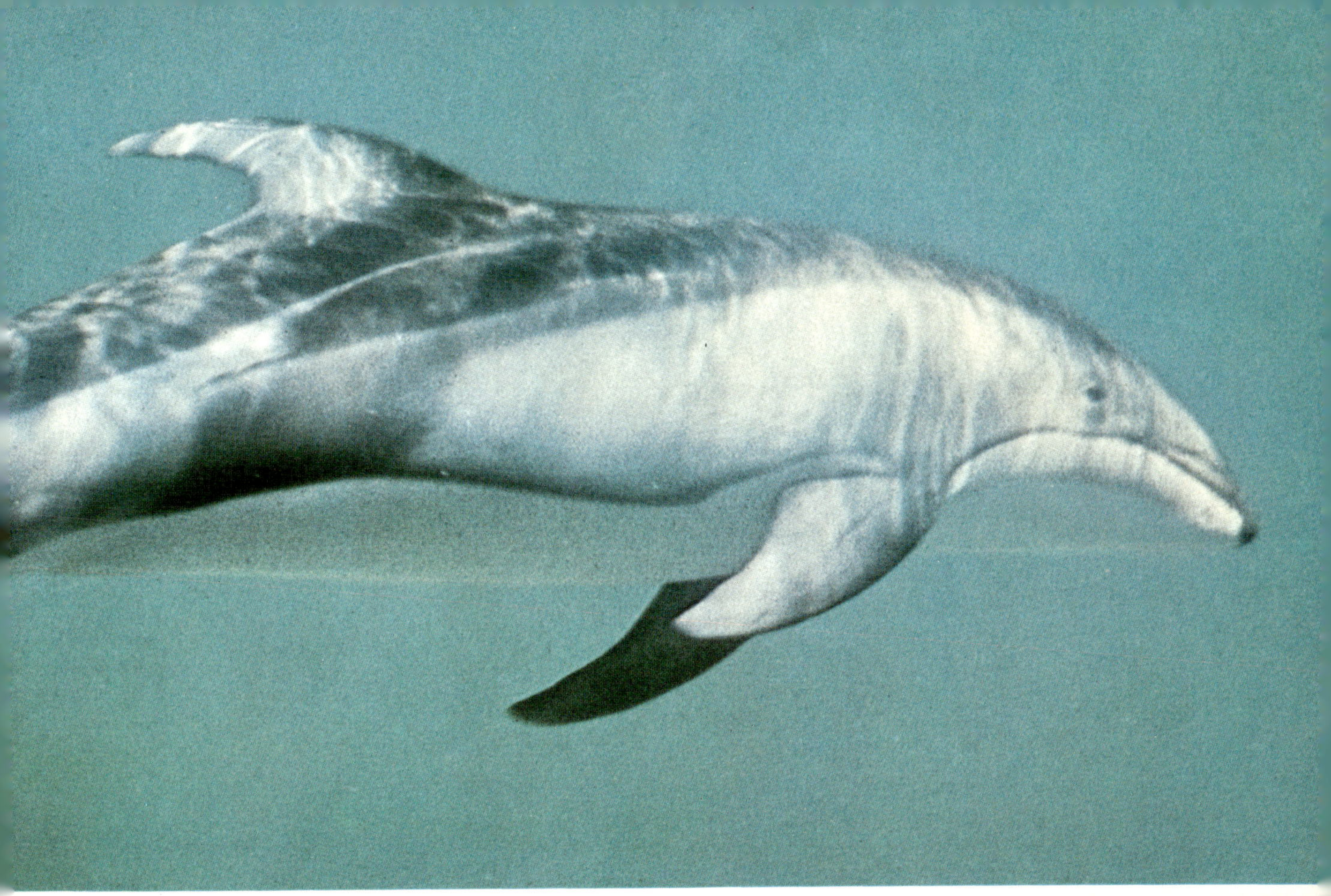

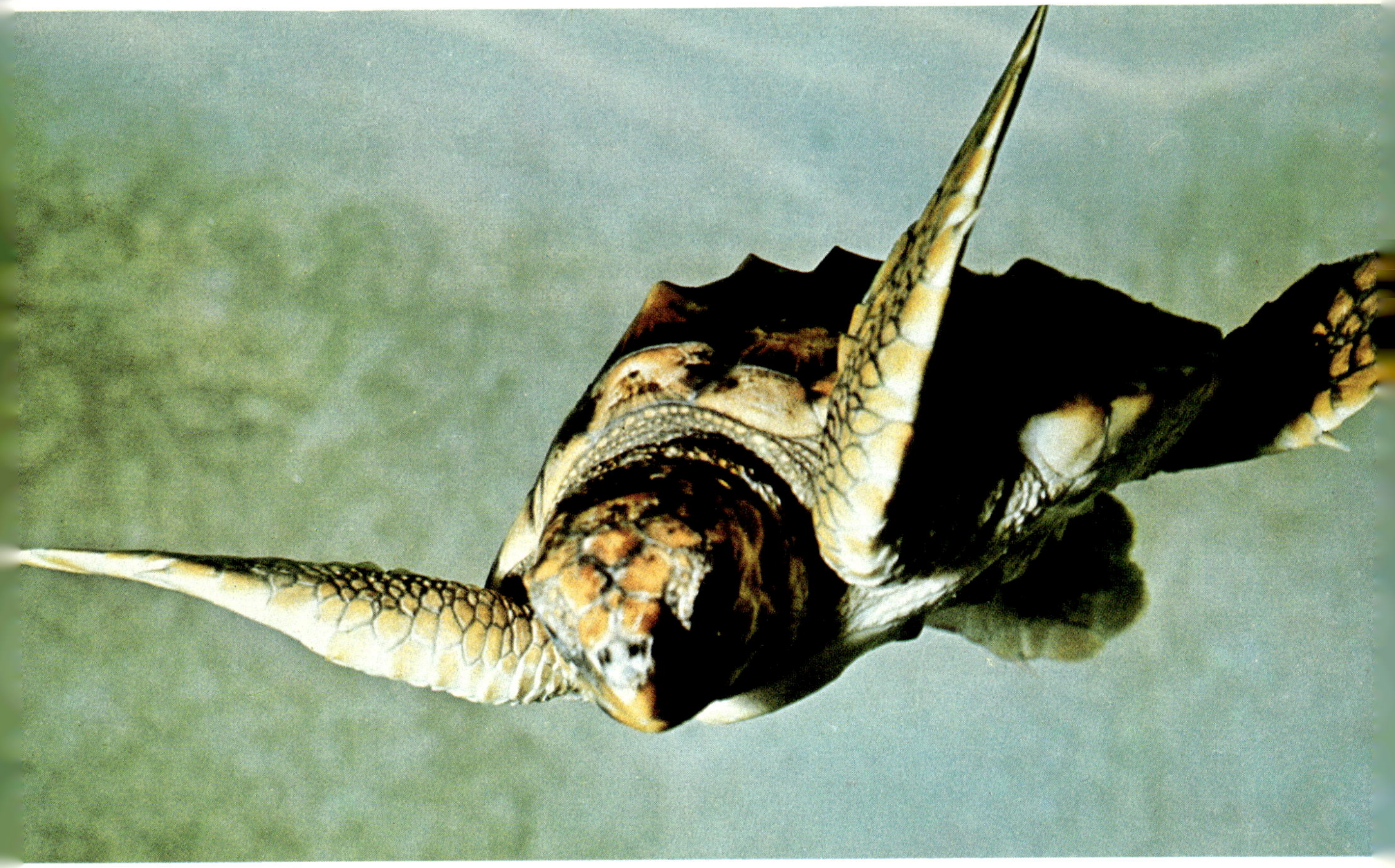

Diagram of a universal stand for photomicrography and macrophotography, suitable for attachment to any size of camera (Leitz).

1 body
2 reflex mirror lever
3 ground-glass screen
4 reflex chamber 9 cm × 12 cm
5 sliding rail
6 set-screw for locking to rail
7 bellows
8 shutter
9 baffle for photomicrography
10 fine adjustment
11 double-column support
12 base

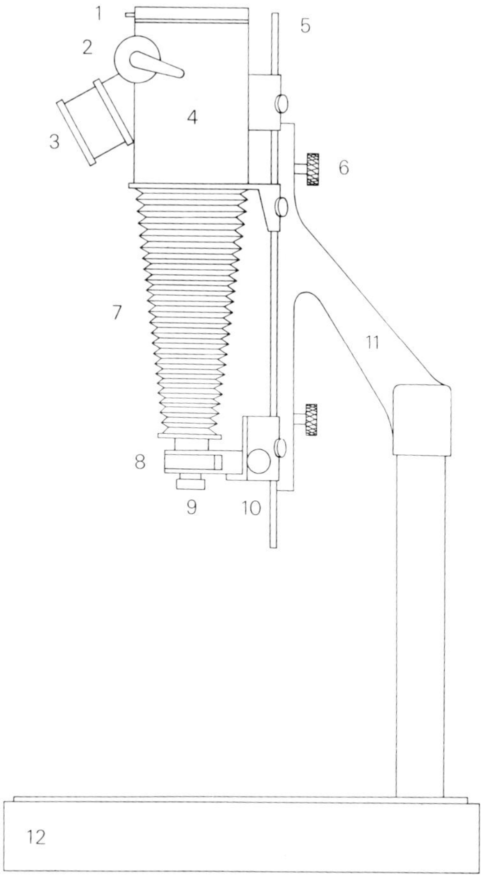

Three different systems for altering the extension of a camera

EXTENSION TUBES

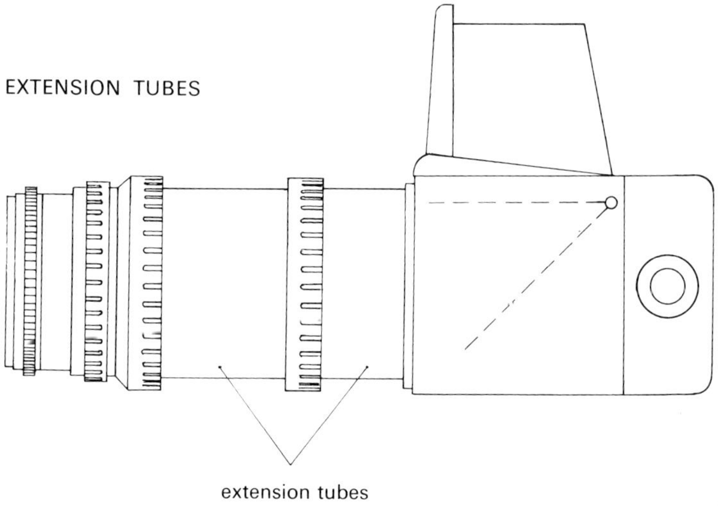

BELLOWS

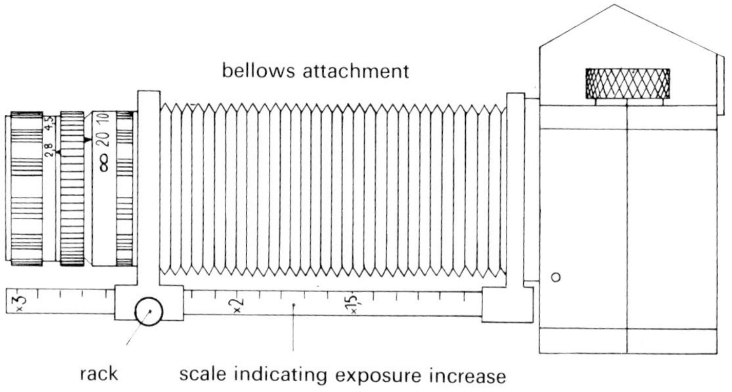

ADAPTER RINGS

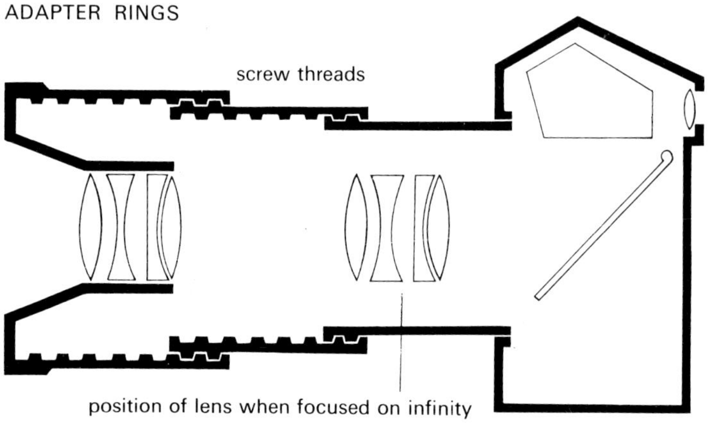

Photography in the laboratory

To us wildlife photography is synonymous with research in a wide sense: ecological, biological, graphical, technical; and for this reason we consider that no sector of the animal kingdom deserves to be left unexplored and unrecorded photographically simply because of supposed boundaries–imprecise ones at that–between so-called 'free' nature and nature existing in the artificial confinement of a game preserve, a park or indeed the small garden of a house in town. And if we accept that no such boundaries legitimately exist, then the photographic depiction of animals studied in the laboratory also comes within our province.

We must not neglect the possibilities offered by the new techniques of observing and exploring the world around us and condemn them simply because physical contact with 'nature' appears to be momentarily interrupted. From the knowledge gained as a result of such investigations we may tomorrow be able better to understand the behaviour of the animal and its relations with its environment. Provided that we never try to conceal, either intentionally or by omission, the conditions under which any particular picture was obtained, then with indoor photography of living creatures in a laboratory environment a new world of activity will open up to those who combine a taste for reasoned research with the qualities of a naturalist and a fair amount of skill with their hands.

This kind of photography cannot be carried on by improvisation. You have to let the animal become accustomed to privileged living conditions, which should resemble its natural habitat as closely as possible as a result of a judicious choice of its components: earth, rocks, bushes, etc. in perfect logical harmony.

At the time of actually taking the photographs the terrarium, vivarium or aquarium should be shut off from daylight, which is variable and difficult to control. Instead, an artificial light source should be utilized, which is independent of weather conditions and the time of day and whose intensity and even its colour temperature can be controlled at will.

The main drawback of artificial light is the heat it produces. This may be harmful to animal life. The intense heat given off by most floodlights should be moderated by means of special heat-absorbing filters or by powerful and well-directed ventilation.

If the presence of the photographer near the animal is not absolutely essential, it is preferable to use automatic systems for releasing the camera shutter at the appropriate time. They operate with precision and are essential to the study of certain species whose reactions are unpredictable (insects in flight) or very rapid (small tropical birds). These release systems are quite easy to construct with the aid of electrical contacts or mechanically actuated relays concealed in the scenery.

Another method of automatic release is by means of invisible infrared light beams and photocells sensitive only to this radiation. This method is especially suitable for studying the behaviour of nocturnal creatures. The system simply consists of a number of spotlights directed at a photocell which actuates a high-precision relay; this in turn operates the source of light or the camera shutter giving a 1/1000 second exposure. This relatively inexpensive equipment can be constructed by any amateur with a little skill in electronics. It can even be made self-contained by providing it with a 6- or 12-volt electricity supply from batteries, so that it can be taken out of doors for fieldwork. The scope for applying this technique is considerable. It enables the camera to be focused and the picture to be composed with great precision so as to comprise a small selected area. Being automatic and self-contained, it enables the photographer to withdraw to a distance, which can be advantageous when photographing shy or dangerous animals. Any camera, whatever its size, can be adapted for this method of photography. All that is needed are some attachments such as extension tubes

Exposure time corrections for macrophotography

Distances expressed in focal lengths and valid for any lens. The distance D is measured from the object to be photographed to the plane of the film.

Scale of reproduction	Distance D	Exposure correction factor
1 : 10	12·1 f	1·21
1 : 5	7·2 f	1·44
1 : 4	6·25 f	1·56
1 : 3	5·33 f	1·77
1 : 2	4·5 f	2·25
1 : 1·8	4·36 f	2·4
1 : 1·4	4·11 f	2·9
1 : 1	4 f	4
1·4 : 1	4·11 f	5·7
1·8 : 1	4·36 f	7·8
2 : 1	4·5 f	9
3 : 1	5·33 f	16
4 : 1	6·25 f	25
5 : 1	7·2 f	36
10 : 1	12·1 f	121

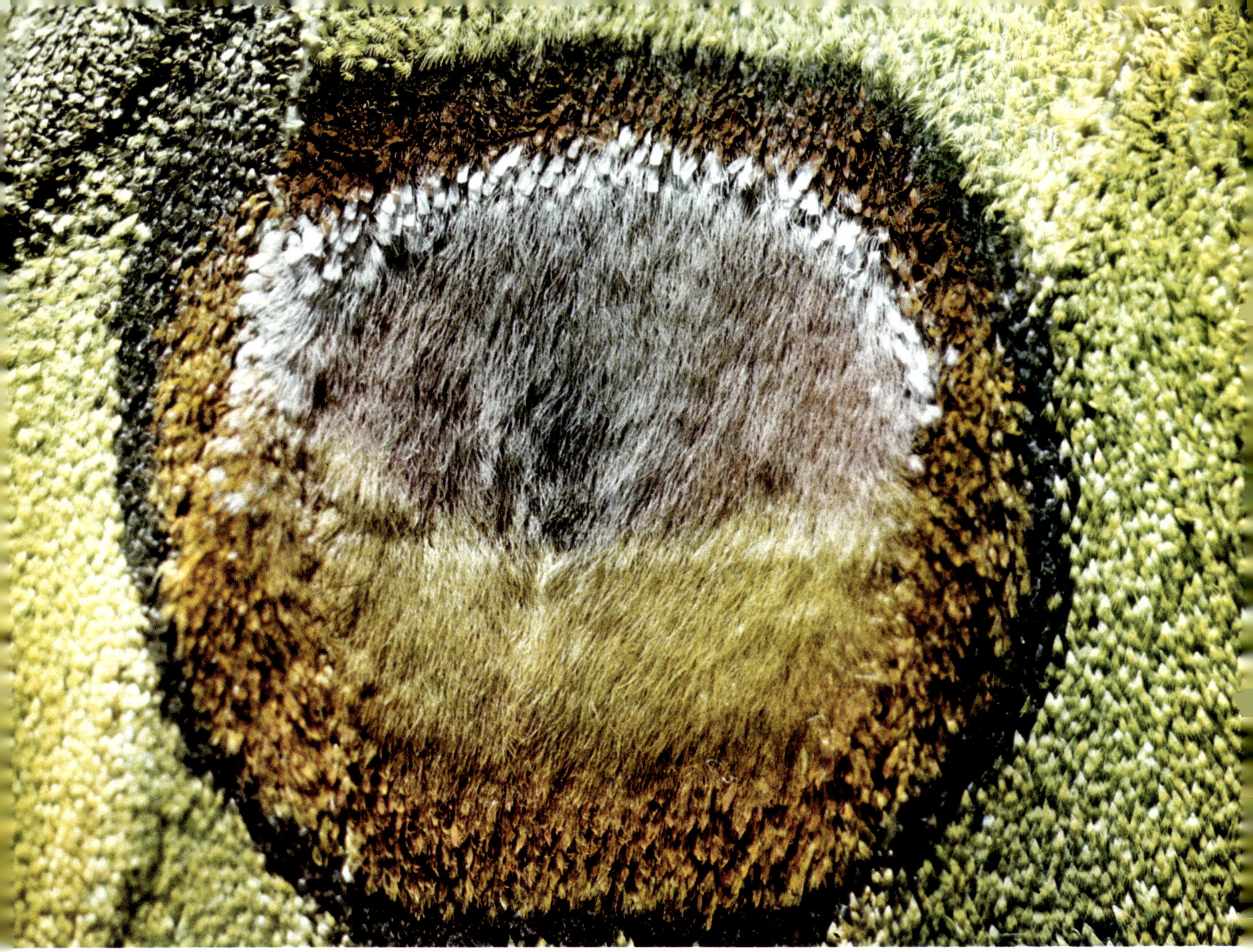

Macrophotograph of a detail of a butterfly's wing: the 'eye spot' is actually 5 mm in diameter.
Equipment: 35 mm reflex camera with Micro Summar lens, 42 mm focal length, fitted with an adapter ring; film Kodachrome II.

Right: This insect is a species of alderfly (*Sialis flavilatera*) belonging to the order of the *Neuroptera*, which also includes the familiar pale green lacewing flies. The photograph below shows a batch of the alderfly's eggs, each terminating in a tiny neck or spout (the micropyle). The eggs are laid in these compact masses of as many as a thousand. The larvae that emerge from them undergo all stages of their evolution in the water of ponds or lakes.
Equipment: 35 mm reflex camera with Micro Nikkor lens; electronic flash.

or bellows and, if repeated shots are required, the addition of an electric motor for film transport.

Macrophotography

This technique of taking life-size or larger-than-life photographs is more often done indoors than in the field on account of the difficulties inherent in its functional principle (very small depth of field, low brightness, disturbance by wind in outdoor situations). It can be used with nearly all types of camera and adds greatly to the joys of exploration and discovery.

Macrophotography produces magnified pictures, revealing details often invisible to the naked eye and which, when presented 'out of context', appear in a novel form. The familiar 'puzzle pictures' consisting of extreme close-ups of sometimes quite ordinary objects are based on this principle. The limits of what constitutes macrophotography are somewhat ill-defined. Its characteristic feature is that it is concerned with small objects far closer to the lens than is possible with a camera not provided with special attachments for the purpose. On the other hand, its pictures are not such high magnifications as those obtained in photomicrography, which is generally considered to begin at a magnification of about 10 times.

At the other end of the scale, macrophotography can be said to begin where the unaided human eye reaches its limit of close-up perception, i.e. at a distance of about 30 cm. To see details at shorter distances, the eye requires optical aids such as a magnifying glass. Ordinary camera lenses cannot focus down to distances less than about 50 cm. To obtain close-ups at shorter range it is necessary to modify the optical features of the lens by means of suitable attachments.

Any kind of camera can be adapted to macro work, but it is preferable to use a single-lens reflex camera because the very small depth of field associated with the magnification of the image requires very accurate focusing. Such focusing is difficult to achieve by any other method. Also, with a reflex camera, there is no parallax in composing the picture, and the image/object ratio can be varied continuously without having to refer to a table for calculating the depth of field and magnification.

Unless you have equipment specially designed for this type of work, macrophotography involves changing the extension of the camera (i.e. the lens-to-film distance) or the focal length of the lens.

A supplementary lens alters the focal length of the standard lens, but has the drawback of introducing aberrations into the lens system and thus impairs its optical quality. Hence only relatively low-powered lenses can be used for the purpose. On the other hand, the supplementary lens has the advantage that it does not greatly alter the exposure time as required by the standard lens. On a zoom lens it is in fact essential to fit a supplementary lens if the advantages of the zoom action are to be retained in macrophotography.

Extension tubes or bellows provide a reliable and accurate means of magnifying the image, but they involve a fairly considerable increase in exposure times.

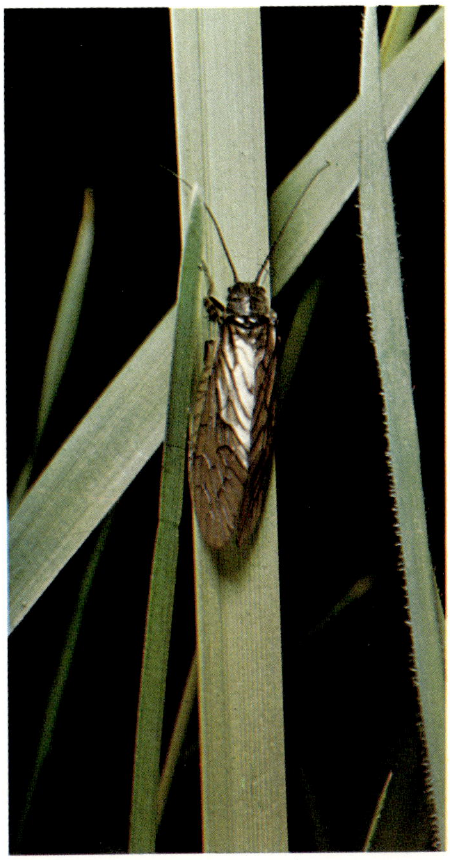

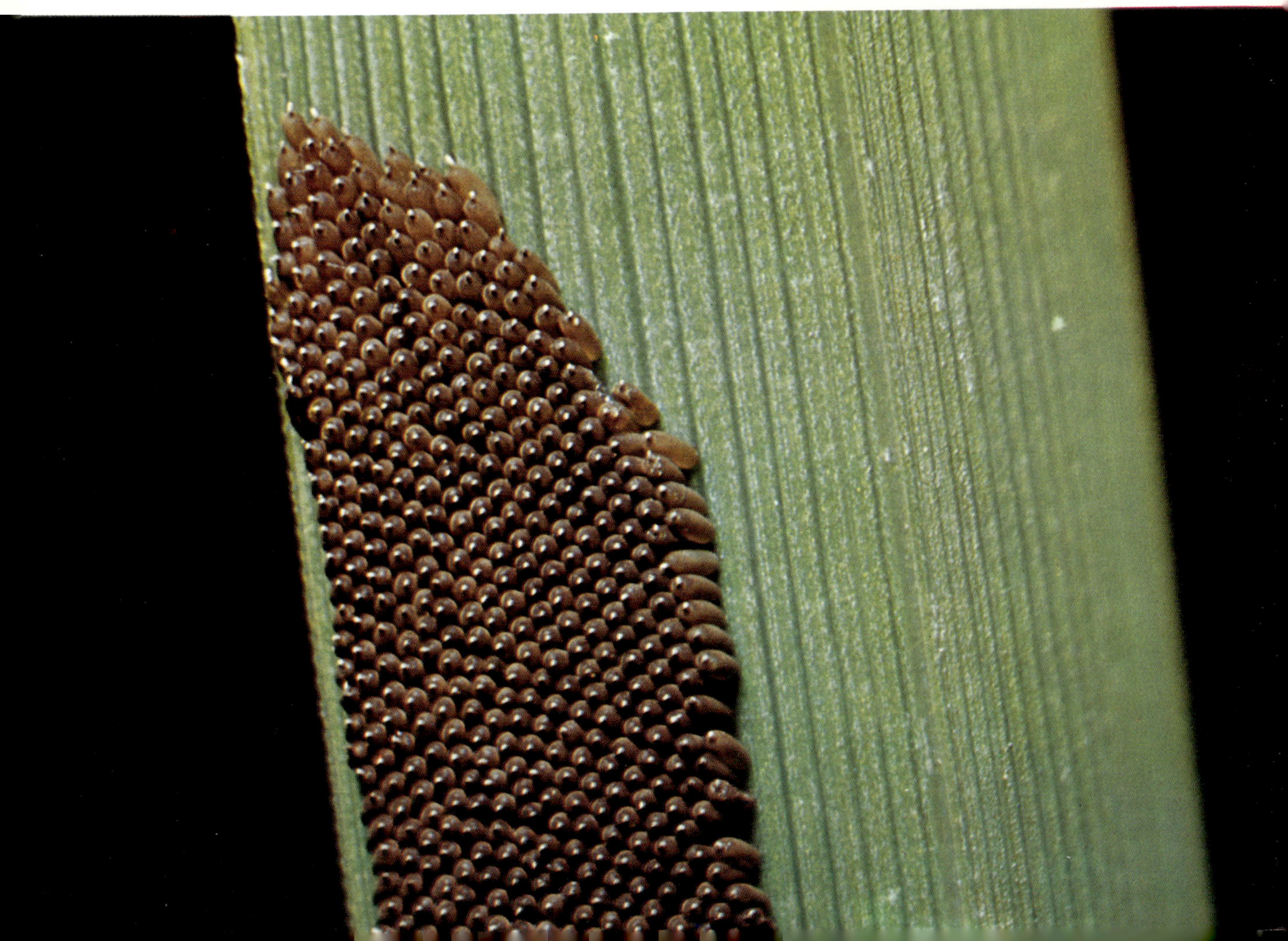

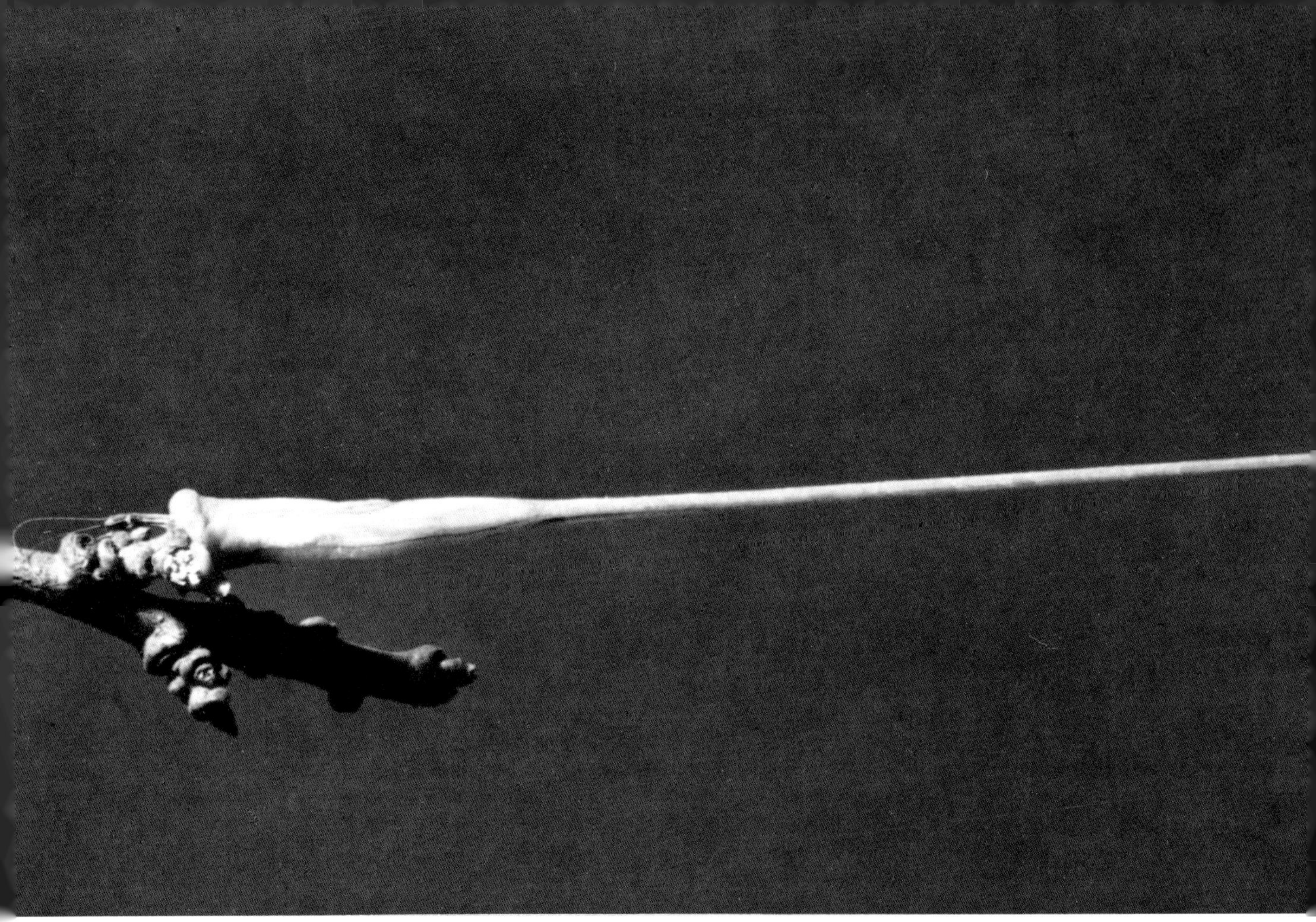

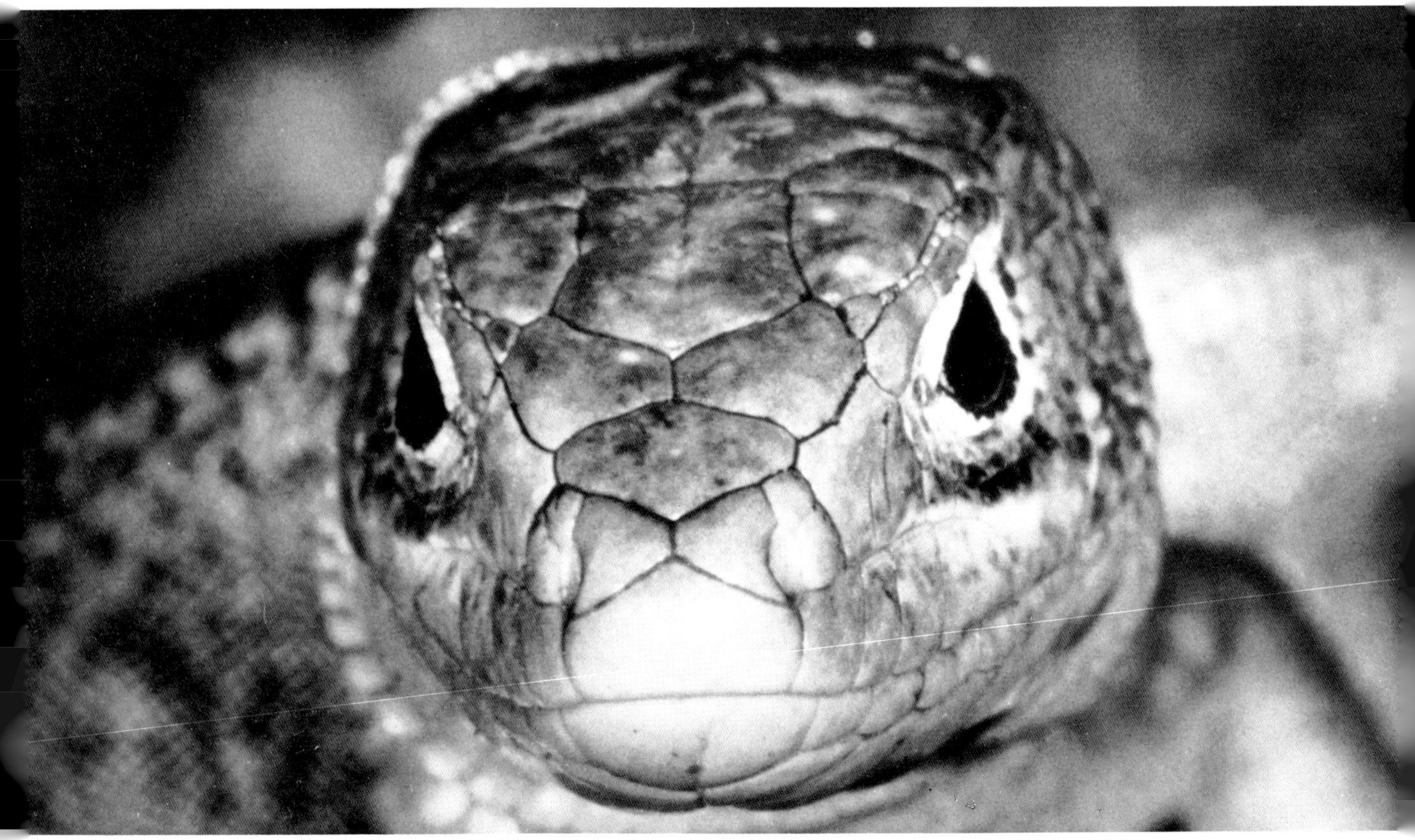

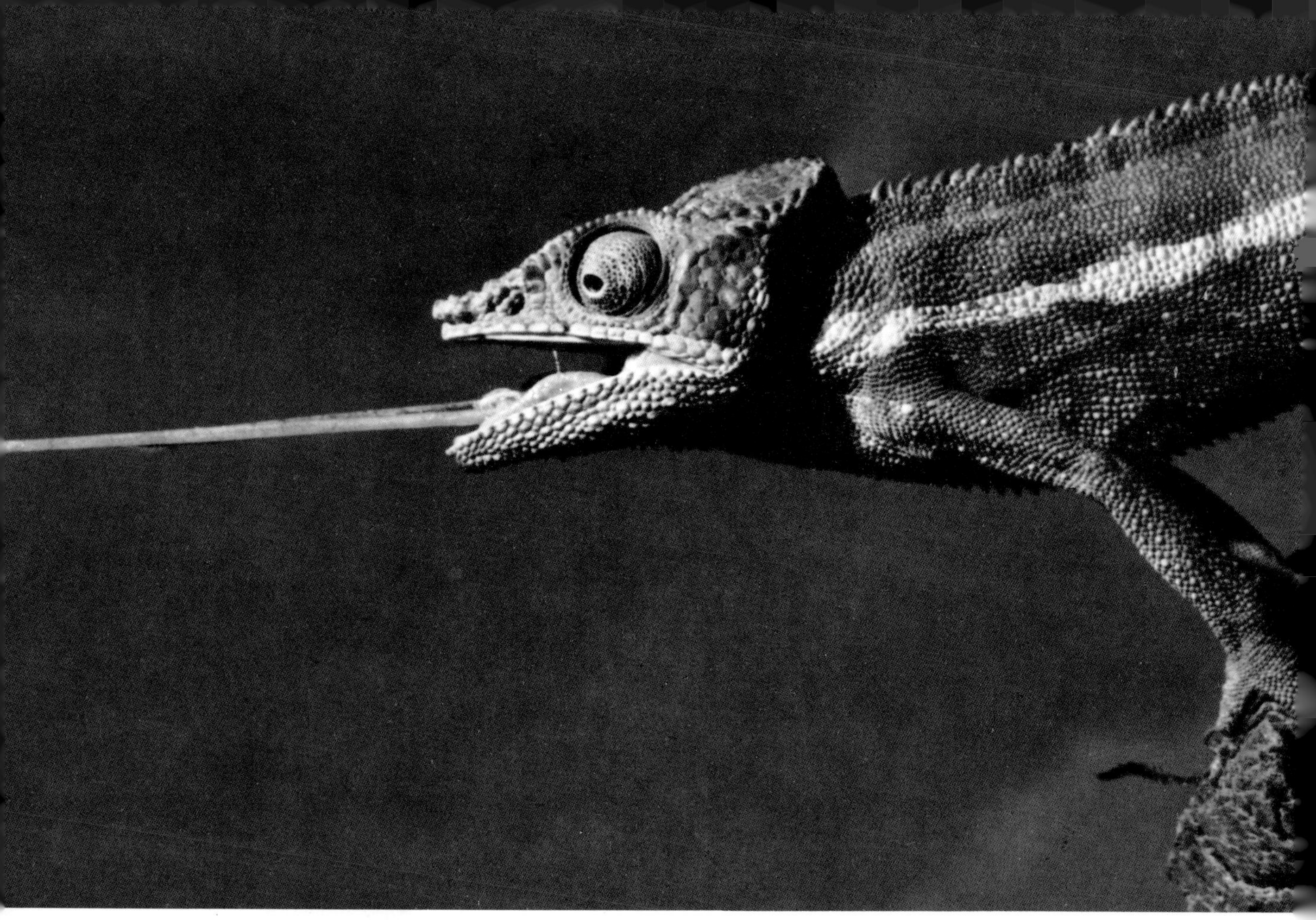

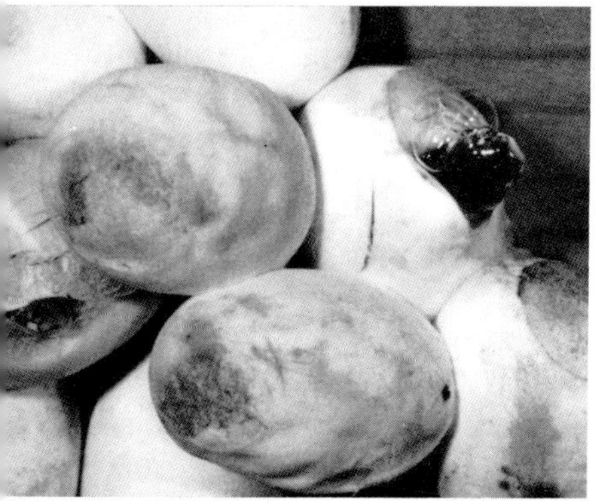

Reptiles can be very interesting subjects for the photographer.
Above: Chameleon (*Chamæleo chamæleo*) with extended tongue, photographed at 1/1000 sec. The tongue, which can shoot out to a distance of up to 12 inches, i.e. equal to the animal's body length, terminates in a kind of suction pad which seizes the prey (a fly or other insect) and whips it back into the chameleon's mouth.
Left: Front view of the head of a lizard (*Lacerta viridis*).
Below: The grass snake (*Natrix natrix*) with forked tongue extended. The small photograph above it shows the snake's eggs hatching out.

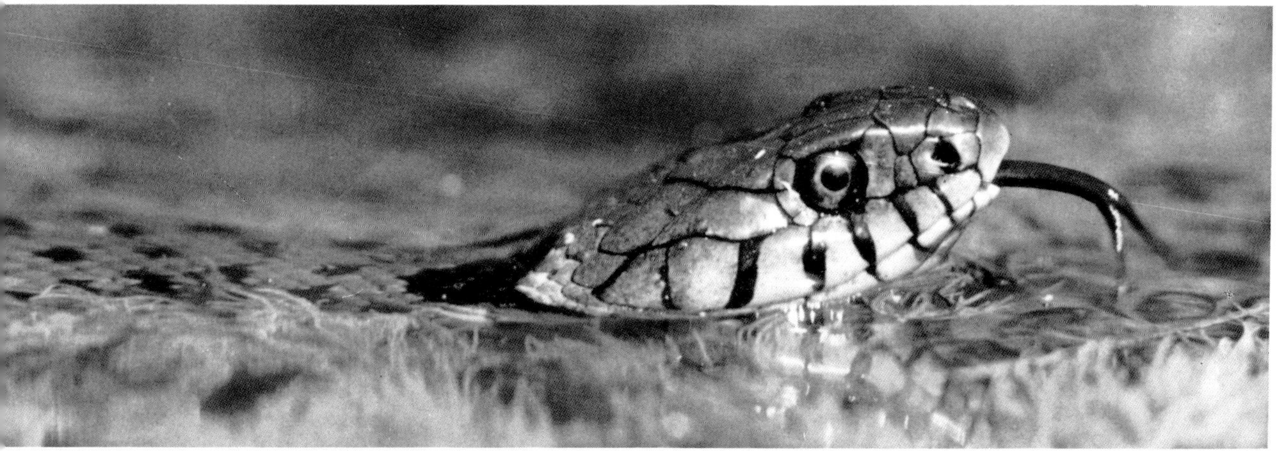

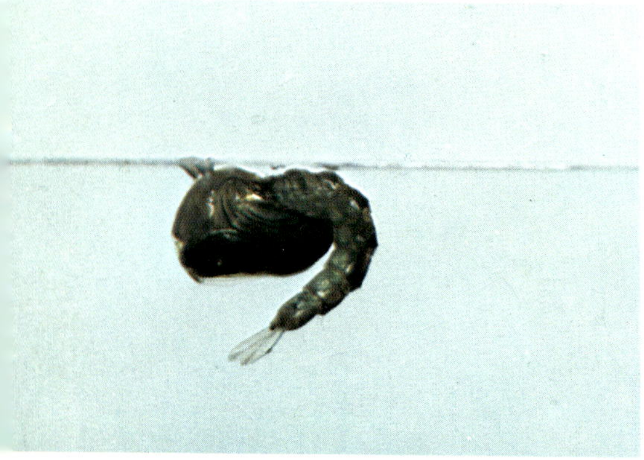
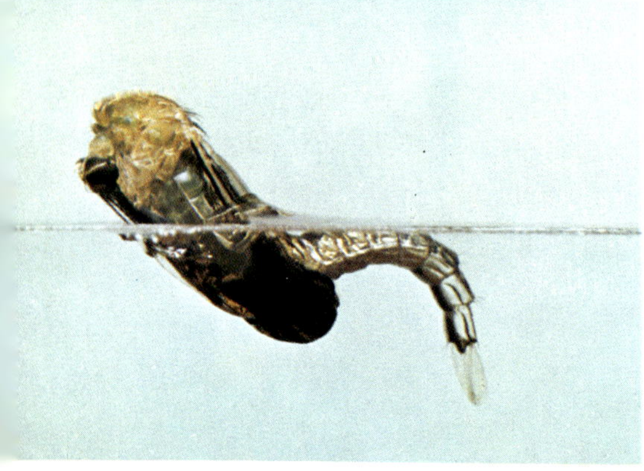
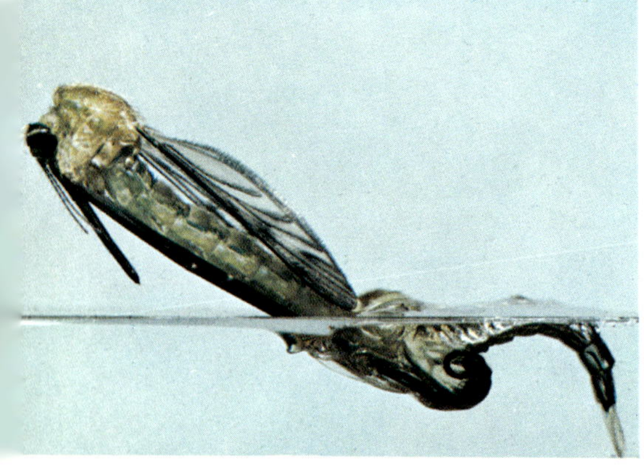
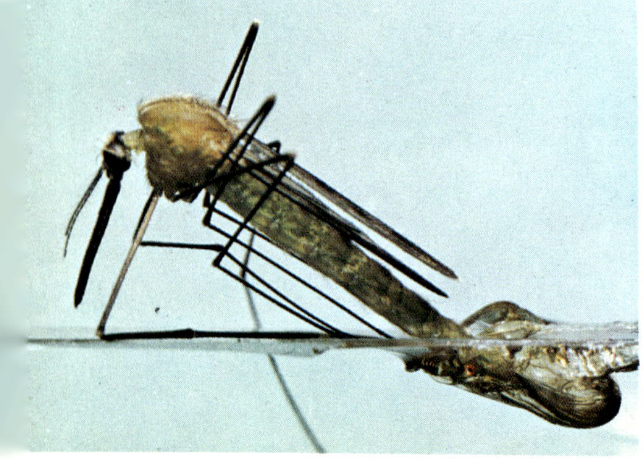

Some large-format cameras are equipped with double or triple extension systems. The lenses used in such cameras are designed for normal photography, i.e. they are focusable on infinity, but by the interposition of suitable adapter rings or tubes they can be used to photograph objects at only a few centimetres' distance. The longer exposures required in such circumstances are usually engraved on the lens mounting.

Special short-focus macro lenses are designed for this class of photography. They provide the best solution for difficult work, but have to be specifically suited to the camera and have no diaphragm presetting system.

Macrophotography requires the use of a powerful and concentrated source of light. Flash bulbs or electronic flash are ideal for the purpose because the intense illumination of very short duration enables the lens to be stopped down to very small apertures, thereby increasing the depth of field. Besides, movement of the subject or the camera during exposure at such short distances, which is liable seriously to impair the picture, has virtually no effect with flash photography, since the exposures are so extremely short.

For cinematographic macro work special high-intensity narrow-beam lamps fed by a low-voltage power source should be used for lighting the subject to be filmed. These self-contained lighting systems can be taken out into the field, where they can be used for night photography or as a supplementary light source in the daytime.

In macrophotography, image brightness is closely bound up with magnification and rapidly falls off with increased camera extension.

The best method of determining the correct exposure time in macrophotography is by means of through-the-lens metering. If your camera is not equipped with such an exposure meter, you should consult a suitable exposure table or you may use the following simple formula:

$$C=(F+T)^2/F^2$$

where C is the exposure coefficient and T the additional extension (bellows or tube).

Example: $C=(50+30)^2/50^2=2{\cdot}56$

Calculating the correct exposure time is especially important if the background to the subject must enter into the composition of the picture. Since the illumination intensity varies proportionally to the square of the distance, it is advisable to ensure proper distribution of the illumination over the whole subject area, otherwise the background may come out too dark.

Photomicrography

Photomicrography is the technique of obtaining photographs of very small objects with the aid of a camera and microscope.

To observe the teeming microscopic life in a single drop of pond water is an absorbing pursuit; but the microscope is a complex instrument, and its effective use will, for the present, remain confined to a limited number of experts possessing a sound knowledge of optics and biology.

The animal life observed under the microscope is incredibly rich and varied, and the contests that are sometimes fought in a space of one square inch are characterized by the same sort of violence that we observe in the fighting of animals in our own everyday world that is visible to the naked eye.

Professional photomicrography generally makes use of elaborate equipment and special techniques. For amateur purposes the camera used with the microscope can be of conventional type, with or without a reflex viewfinder. Within limits, quite interesting and worthwhile results are obtainable even with a simple microscope. The camera, which should preferably have a lens with a focal length of 75 or 80 mm, is placed over the eyepiece of the microscope and is focused on infinity, the diaphragm being set at a large aperture (low f-number). The microscope should first be focused visually in the ordinary way. A number of tests should be carried out to determine the correct exposure time if the camera is not equipped with a through-the-lens meter.

Some miniature cameras can be fitted with adapters, so that the camera, minus its lens, can be fixed onto the end of the draw tube of a microscope, no external support being needed. For serious scientific work the microscope should be of good optical quality, with adequate resolving power. Microscopy and the preparation of specimens involve specialized and complex techniques which are outside the scope of this book.

Macrophotography, both outdoors and in the laboratory, as well as photomicrography are techniques also extensively used in cinematography. Special books dealing with the subject should be consulted.

The larvae of the mosquito (*Anopheles maculipennis*) live and develop in the water of swamps and ditches, but breathe air through a tube which has to be protruded periodically above the surface of the water. The four photographs show successive stages of the emergence of the adult insect. To obtain pictures like these it is essential to understand the insect's life history and know the right moment to take the photographs. Equipment: 35 mm reflex camera with 135 mm lens and bellows.

Below: Photomicrograph of spirogyra, a freshwater alga with characteristic ribbon-like chloroplasts (structures in the plant cell which contain the green pigment named chlorophyll). The picture was obtained with a reflex camera with built-in exposure meter; illumination by incandescent lamp; film Kodachrome IIA.

Slow-motion cinematography

Slow motion can be of great value for the analysis of rapid movement. Some amateur cine cameras can expose the film at speeds of up to 64 frames per second, so that slow motion in the ratio of about 1:4 is obtained when the film is projected at the normal speed of 18 or 24 frames per second. Special high-speed cameras can shoot film at 500 frames per second; with projection at the normal speed, each second of the original scene filmed will thus last twenty seconds on the screen. Very high-speed cameras, operating at between 3000 and 10,000 frames per second, are also available as battery-powered portable equipment capable of being taken into the field. However, the equipment is rather heavy and the emulsions are of relatively low sensitivity, so that very high illumination intensities are needed, and their resolving power is rather poor. These factors conspire to place very high-speed cinematography (extreme slow motion) beyond the reach of most amateurs.

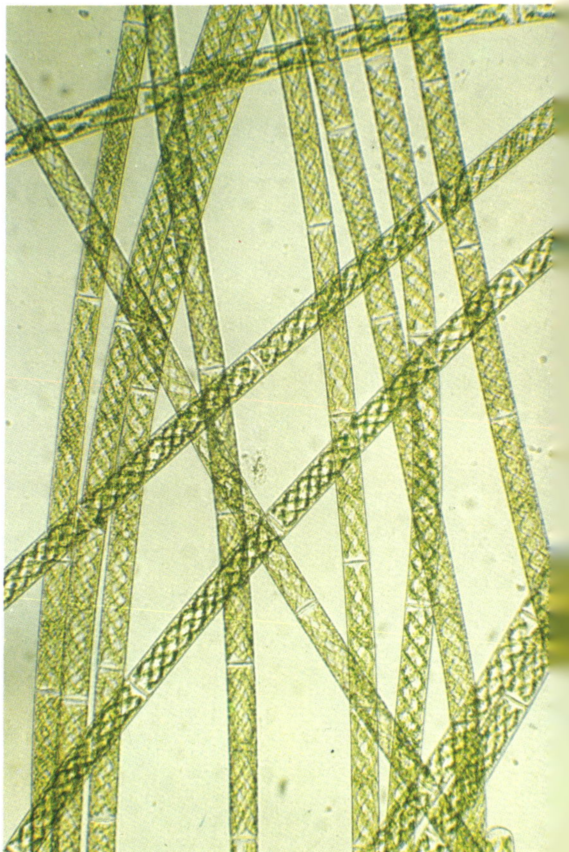

Time-lapse cinematography

This is the opposite of slow motion. When the individual frames are exposed at long intervals of time between successive shots and the film is projected at normal speed, the motion will appear accelerated. The movements of certain animals and the growth of plants can be 'made visible' in this way. If cine film is exposed at a rate of, say, one frame every twenty seconds, the resulting film will show the motion speeded up about 500 times.

The equipment needed for this technique is relatively simple. It can be augmented by a fairly advanced degree of automation, so as to relieve the photographer of the need to attend to the equipment at frequent intervals. Preparation of the shots requires some precautions and careful study of the phenomena to be revealed by the film.

First of all, it is necessary to determine the interval of time between successive frame exposures to give a suitable speed-up of the movement. For purposes of biological study this interval usually ranges from 1 frame per second to 1 frame every 15 minutes for a film sequence intended to give 30 to 60 seconds' viewing time on the screen. If a bud in the process of opening is filmed at 1 frame every 120 seconds for 48 hours, the resulting film will take 1 minute to run through the projector. For making films of this kind it is essential to connect the shutter release on the camera to a mechanical or electrical system (time switch and relay, for example) to ensure that the shutter will be reliably actuated at accurately regular intervals. To obtain adequate picture stability on the screen, the camera should be mounted on a firm stand which will not be affected by vibrations. Also, a controlled source of artificial lighting should be used, preferably of a kind that will generate the least possible amount of heat (electronic flash, or a lamp which lights up only just before the exposure of a frame). Similar techniques are used for making certain types of animated cartoons.

Sound recording

The hunter of wildlife sounds is a peaceable naturalist, too. Although the equipment he uses is very different from that of the photographer in quest of wildlife pictures, his methods of research, approach and camouflage follow the same principles.

The tape recorder remains the basic instrument for sound recording in the

Directional characteristics of microphones

Omnidirectional

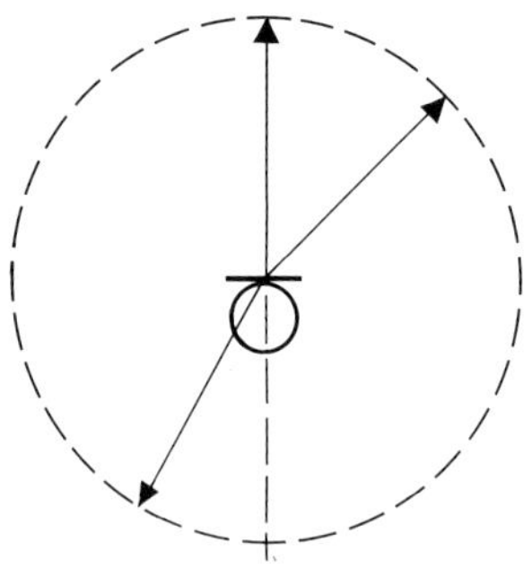

Cardioid

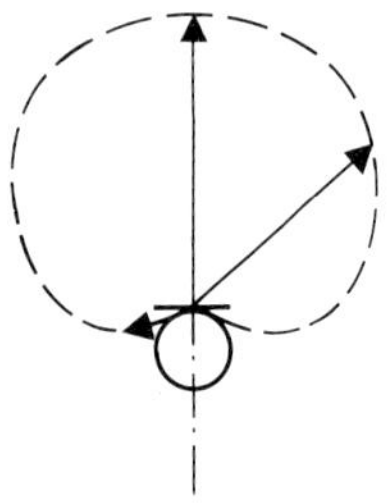

Super-cardioid

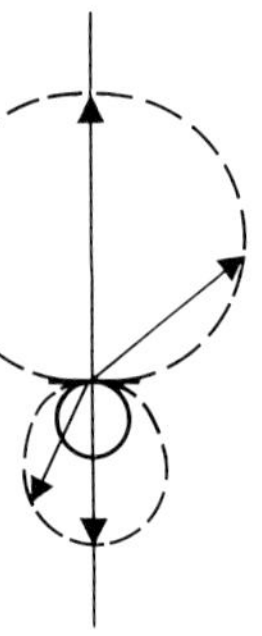

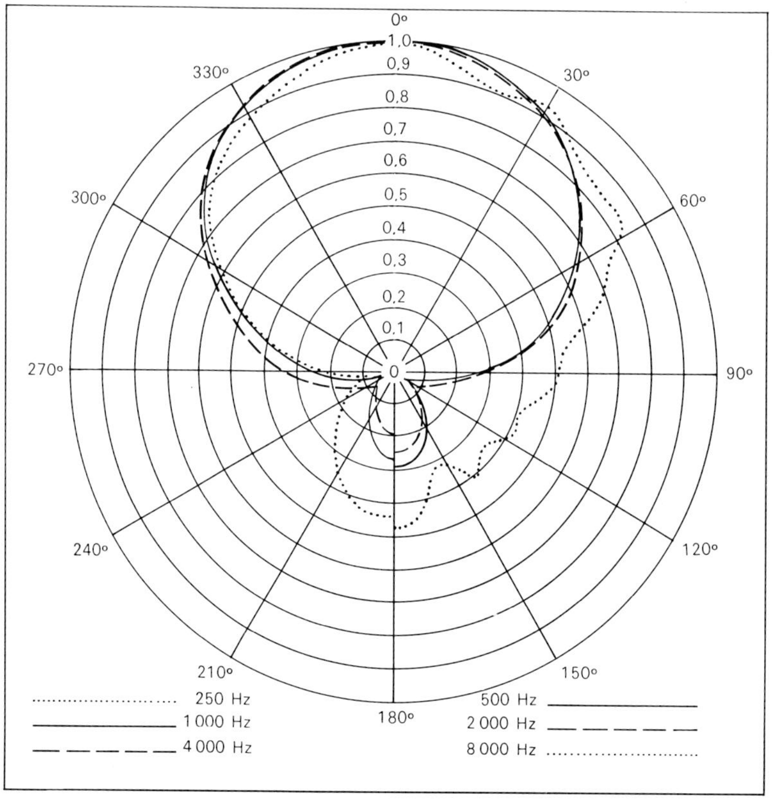

Directional response pattern of a super-cardioid microphone (Sennheiser)

field, and it is easy to use, even by the not-so-skilled, because of its simple controls. It has become a standard adjunct to the still camera or cine camera in nature study: bird calls, animal 'languages', sounds made in mating ceremonies, the observer's own comments or notes, etc.

The main characteristics of sound are its pitch or frequency (number of vibrations per second), its amplitude (loudness intensity, usually expressed in decibels) and its timbre or tone quality (which depends on the shape of the vibrations). Modern technology enables the mechanical energy of the sound waves to be converted into electrical energy, which in turn can be amplified and recorded in various ways, more particularly magnetically on coated tape in a tape recorder. The tape, coated with a ferromagnetic compound, is wound at uniform speed from one spool to another. It passes a recording head which is magnetized by a current varying in step with the sounds, which are thus recorded as varying degrees of magnetization along the tape. To play back the recording, the tape travels past a playback head, in which corresponding electrical signals are induced which are fed to an amplifier and loudspeaker. On some machines the same head does both jobs: recording and playback.

The electronic amplifying unit usually serves both for recording and playing back. In recording, the amplifying unit varies the strength of the incoming signal from the microphone to the correct recording level at the head. For playback, the amplifier boosts the weak signal from the tape to make it powerful enough to drive the loudspeaker.

Standard tape recording speeds most extensively used for amateur work are 4·25, 9·5 and 19 cm per second ($1\frac{7}{8}$, $3\frac{3}{4}$ and $7\frac{1}{2}$ inches per second). For high-fidelity recordings higher speeds are used–38 and 76 cm per second (15 and 30 inches per second)–which enable a wider range of frequencies to be recorded and reproduced.

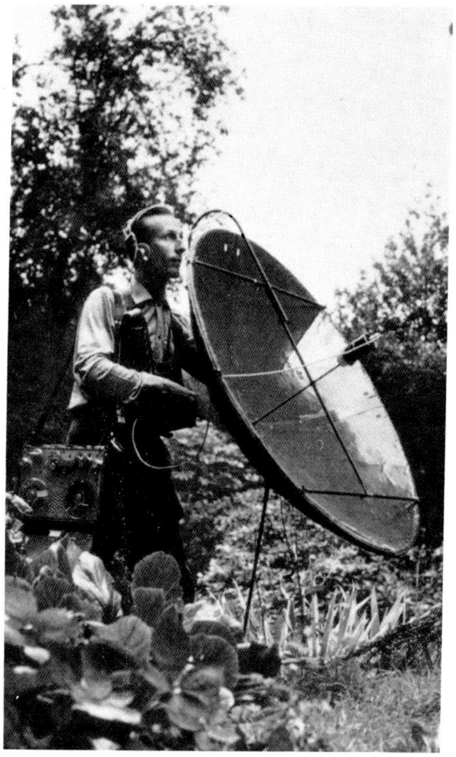

For sound recordings of birds and animals it is necessary to use robust and highly sensitive microphones and good tape recorders.
Above: Recording bird calls with a microphone installed at the focus of a parabolic reflector.
Below, left: Nagra 4 tape recorder using $\frac{1}{4}$ inch magnetic tape, with sound-and-picture synchronizing equipment.
Below, right: Nagra NS miniature high-fidelity tape recorder.

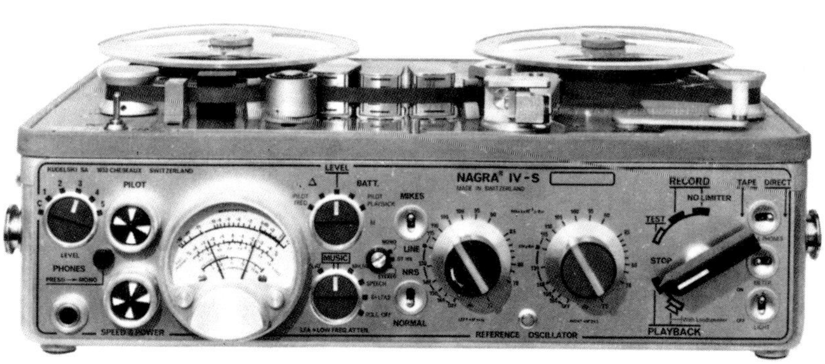

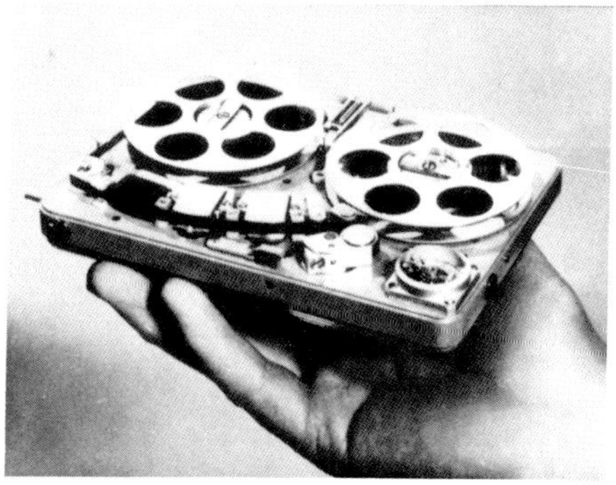

Like the camera manufacturers, the makers of tape recording equipment are not much interested in the kind of problems that naturalists encounter in their attempts to obtain sound recordings of animals or birds. This class of users of such equipment will therefore have to make certain modifications or additions in their requirements. For field use the tape recorder must of course be battery-powered (dry cells or rechargeable accumulators).

The most important single item of sound recording equipment is the microphone–comparable in some respects to the lens of a camera. But the microphone, however sophisticated it may be, does not possess magic powers any more than the lens does. The best way to obtain good sound recordings is to get close enough to your animal or bird. For fieldwork it is necessary to use a directional microphone, i.e. one designed to pick up sounds coming from the direction in which it is aimed and largely excluding sounds coming from other directions. The selectivity of the microphone can be further enhanced by using a parabolic reflector to concentrate the sound, the microphone being mounted at the focus of the reflector. In this way is is possible to eliminate most of the background noise and sounds coming from sources other than the one in which you are interested, so that accurate recordings even at distances of 50 yards and more are possible.

Microphones are of many different types, embodying different electro-acoustic principles. Which particular type can most suitably be chosen will depend on the result you wish to get, the circumstances in which the microphone will be used, and who uses it–for individual preferences of the person who

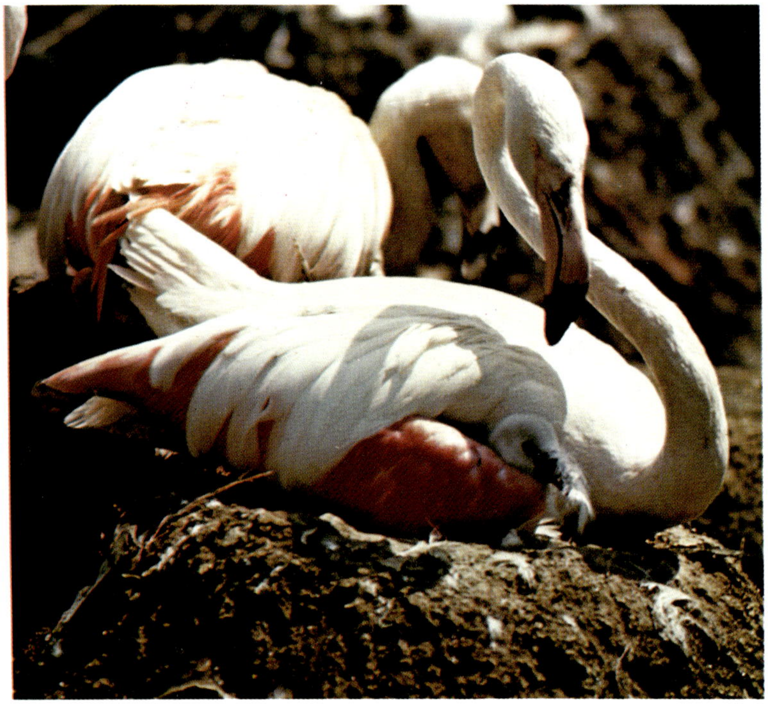

The chick of the greater flamingo (*Phoenicopterus ruber*) is the object of much care and attention from the parent birds, which take it in turns to watch over the chick and protect it from the sun and from predators. The nest should be approached with great caution, because the adults, if frightened, may permanently abandon the eggs or their young.
Equipment: 35 mm reflex camera, lens of 800 mm focal length, on tripod.

Right: Aerial view of a flamingo colony feeding in shallow water, outside the nesting season.
Equipment: 35 mm reflex camera, lens of 250 mm focal length.

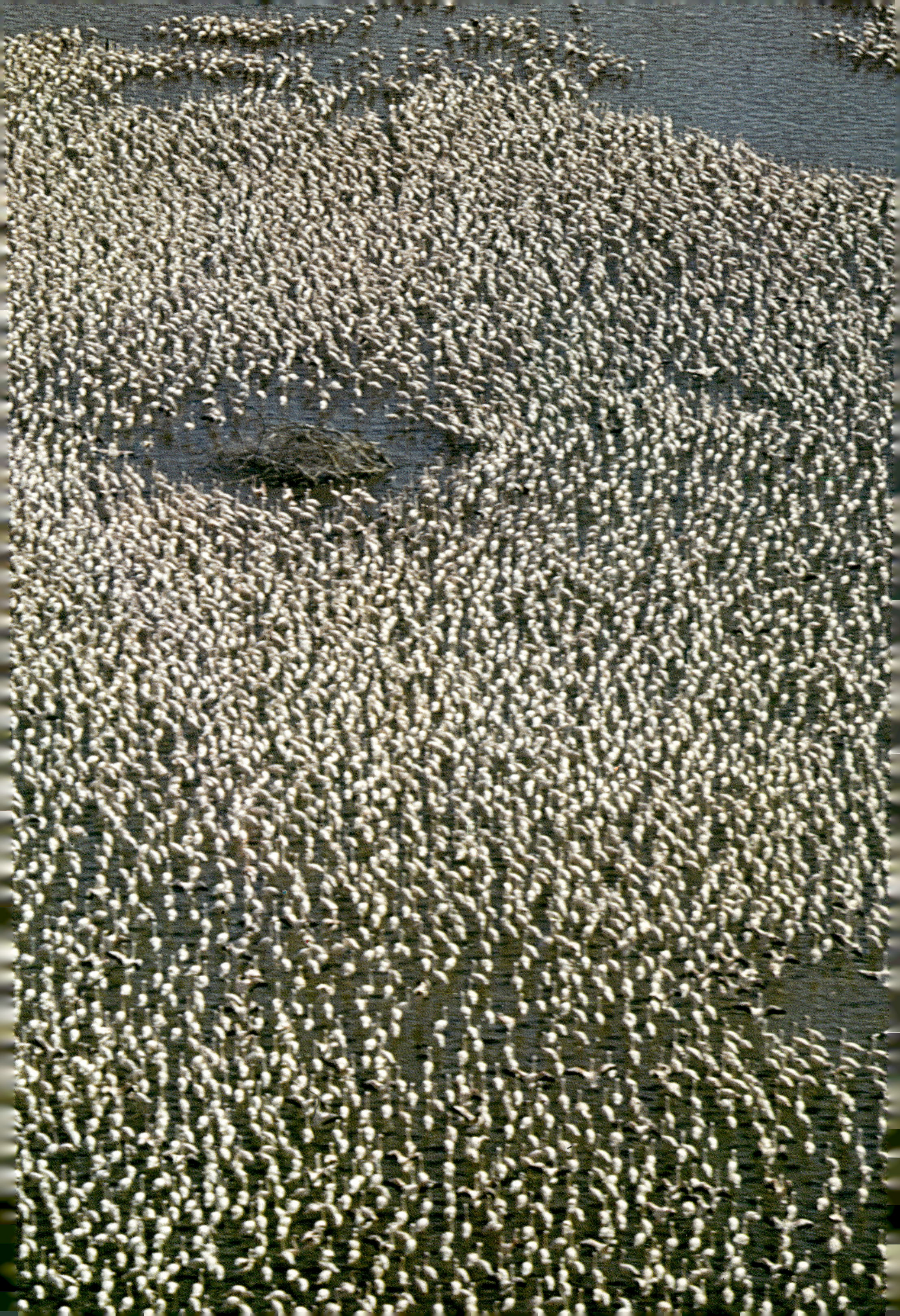

Flamingoes spend hours with their heads under water, filtering the water through their curved bills and agitating the mud with their feet to drive out the small creatures that live in it and on which they feed.
Equipment: 35 mm reflex camera, focal lengths 135 mm and 200 mm; photograph taken from a camouflaged boat.

In the morning or evening, or at other times when agitated by some irrational fear, the flamingoes take to flight: first they appear to run on the surface of the water and then take off with a great flapping of wings.
Equipment: 35 mm camera, photosniper mounting, telephoto lens of 400 mm focal length.

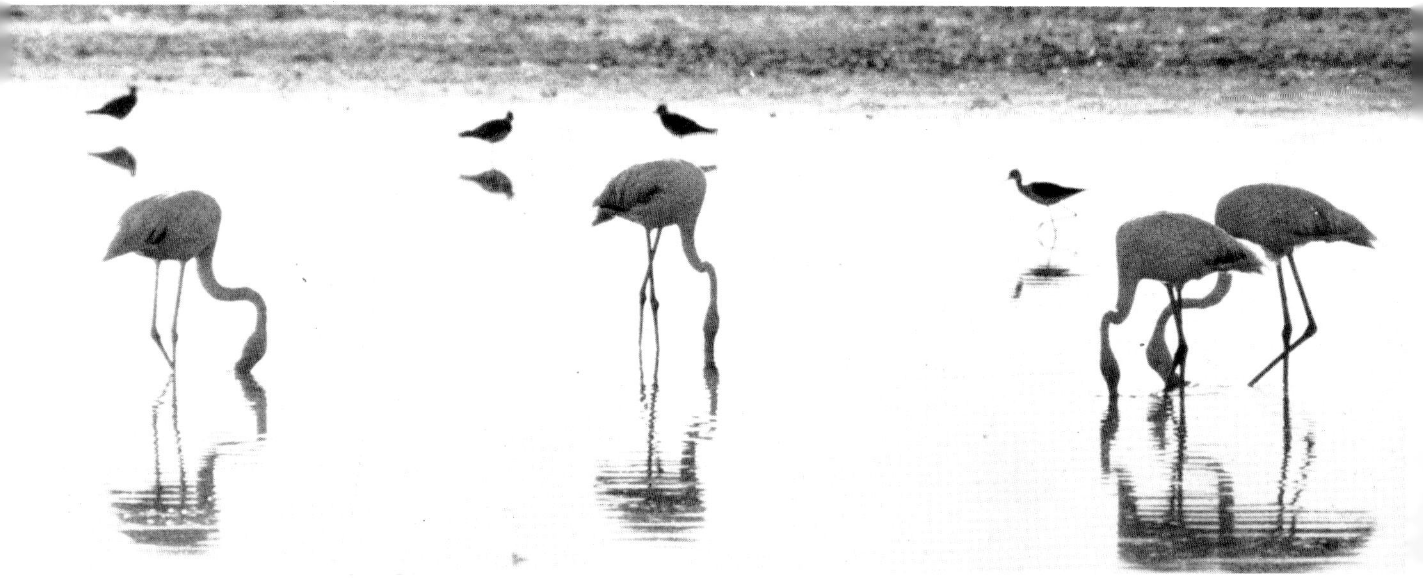

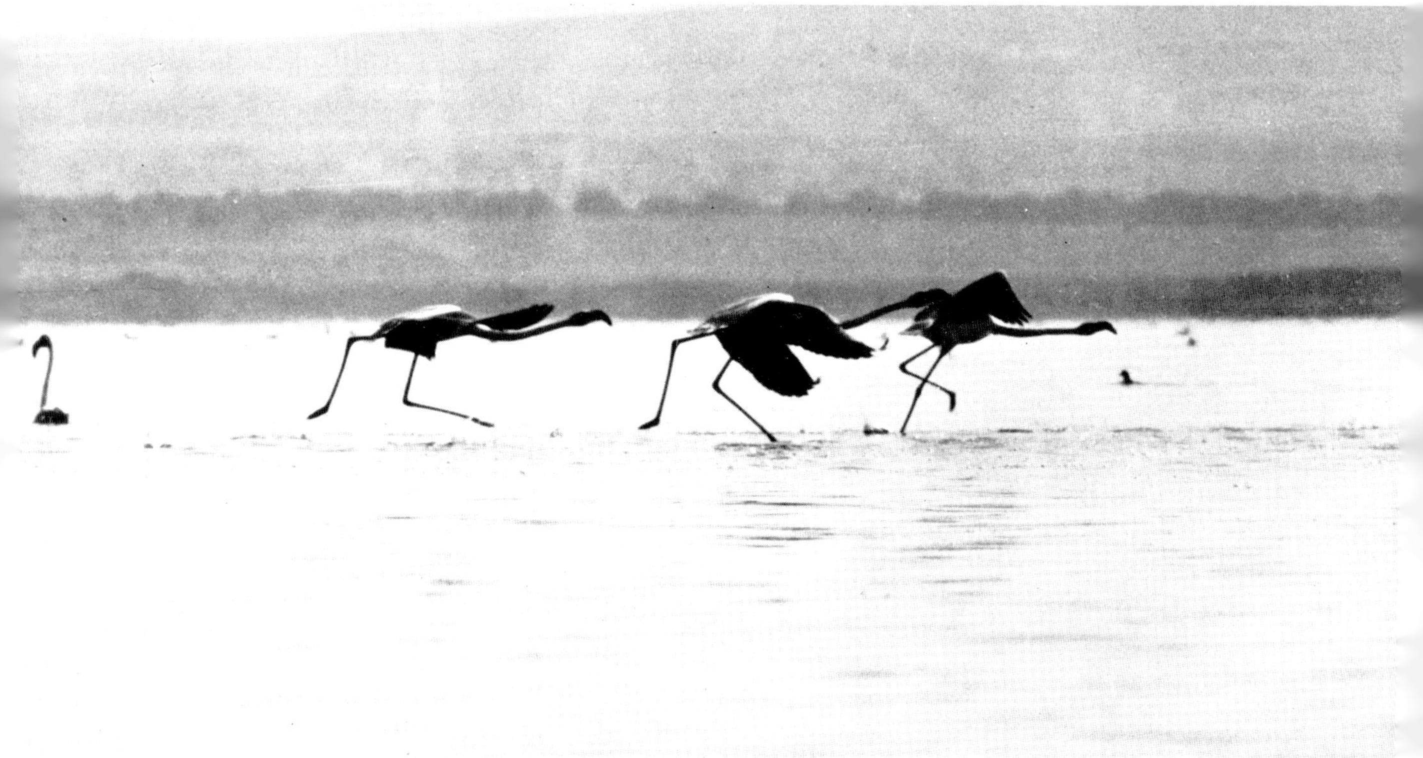

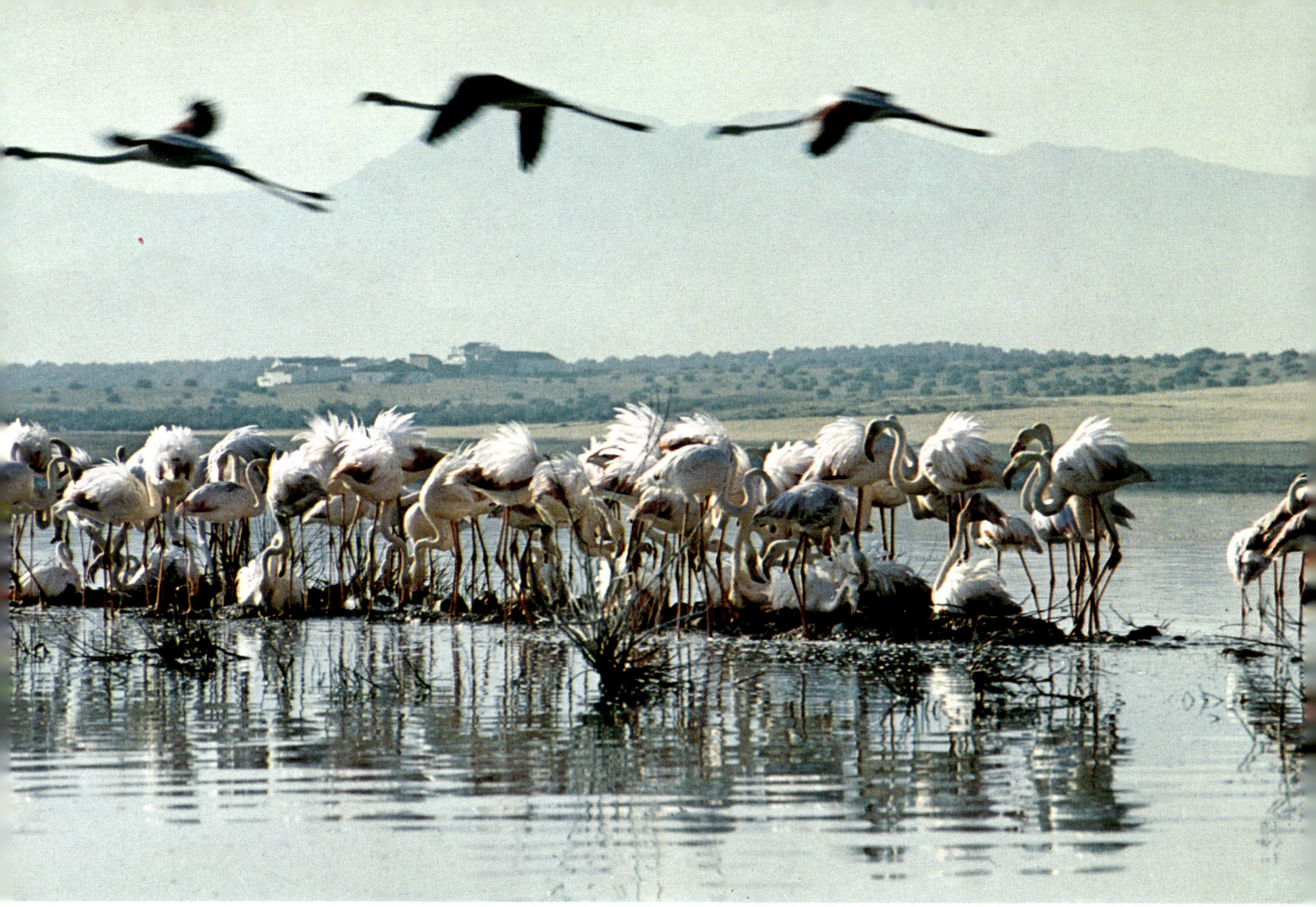

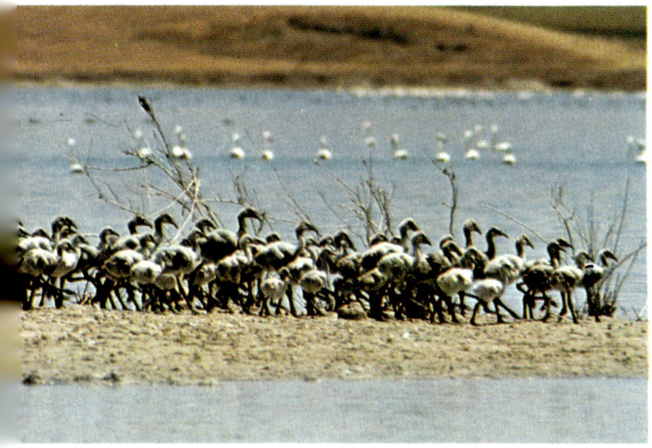

records the sounds are also an important deciding factor. In terms of the sound effects that he strives more particularly to capture and bring out in his recording, he will impress his own personality on the result.

If a suitable electrical or electronic coupling and synchronizing system is used, it is possible to record sound and shoot cine film simultaneously. Close synchronism between film and tape recording is difficult to achieve unless mechanical or electrical coupling of the recorder to the projector is employed. In some cases the two are combined, being driven by a single motor. For really accurate synchronism the magnetic stripe system of sound recording is preferable. In this system the sound is recorded on a narrow magnetic track applied to one margin of the film. Because of editing difficulties this technique is not so suitable for direct recording of the sound while the film is being taken. Simultaneous filming and sound recording will not normally be used in wildlife cinematography, however. There are many difficulties and considerations involved: camera noise, need to bring the microphone close to the animal or bird, risk of disturbing the subject, amount of time at the cameraman's disposal, etc. For these reasons it is usually preferred to obtain the sound recording independently of the film and subsequently to combine the two. This procedure, though not strictly scientific, gives good results if close synchronism between image and sound is not essential.

During the nesting season the adult birds take turns at performing guard duty at the nest and going off to feed, which they do in the company of numerous other flamingoes, with much squabbling and noisy squawking. The first chicks to hatch are in the middle of the colony, but are herded together in a nursery as soon as they can stand on their feet.

A new and very interesting technique in conjunction with wildlife photography consists of using the tape recorder as an 'acoustic trap'. Prerecorded animal or bird calls are emitted in a particular direction and lure the creature, prompted by curiosity, response to a mating call or a desire to defend its territory against an intruder, to within a short distance of the photographer lying in wait, suitably hidden, near his tape recorder.

Present-day high-fidelity recorders using standard tape ($2\frac{1}{2}$ inch) tend to be rather heavy and bulky, which is a reason why they cannot always be used by the wildlife photographer, who has also his other equipment to carry and must preserve adequate mobility in the field. In such circumstances he may prefer to use a cassette recorder. These compact little machines are certainly useful for notes and commentaries. Their quality is generally still inadequate for obtaining good sound recordings of animals or birds, but is being steadily improved. In the not-too-distant future it is likely to become the ideal addition to the still camera or cine camera and may even become a built-in feature of it.

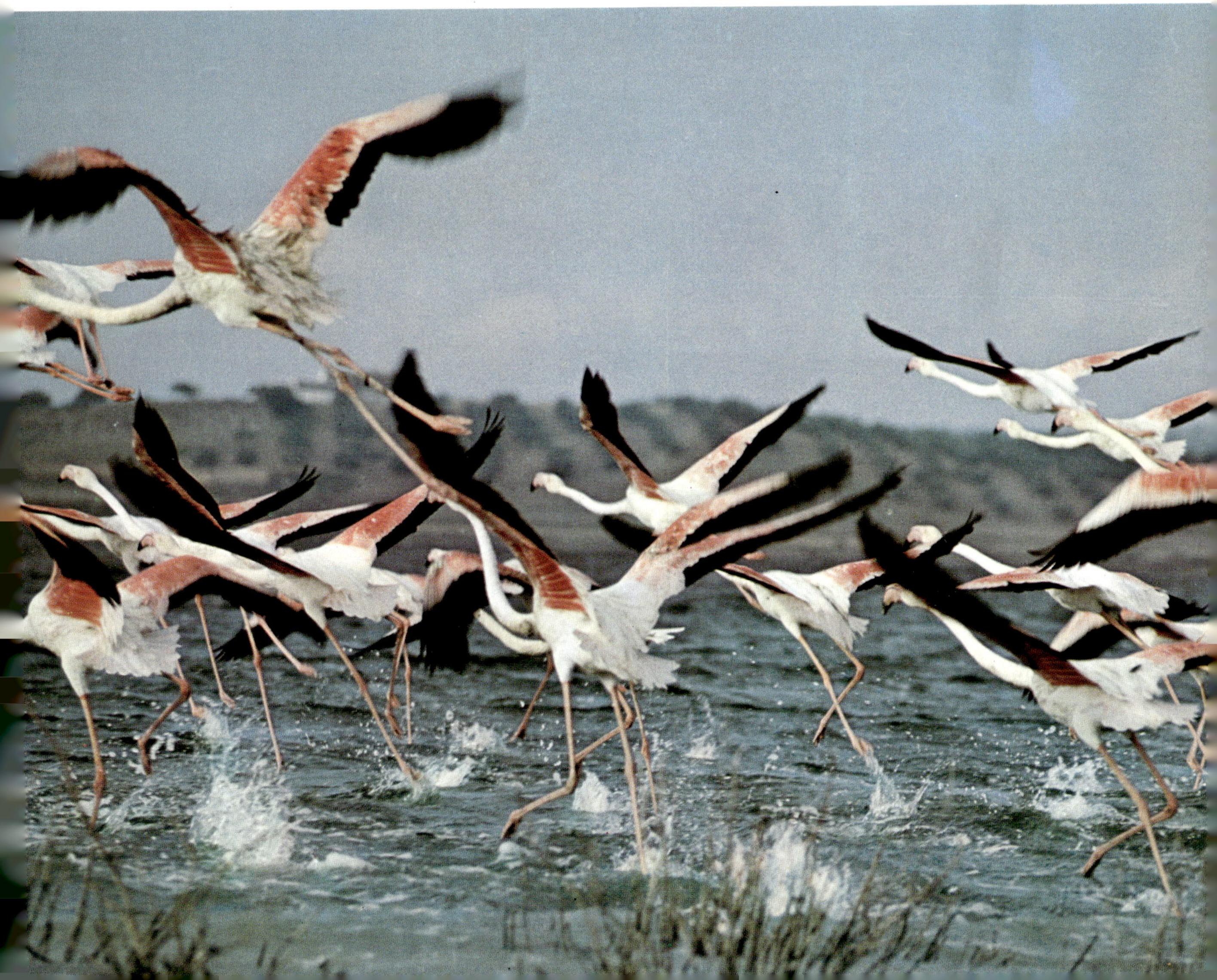

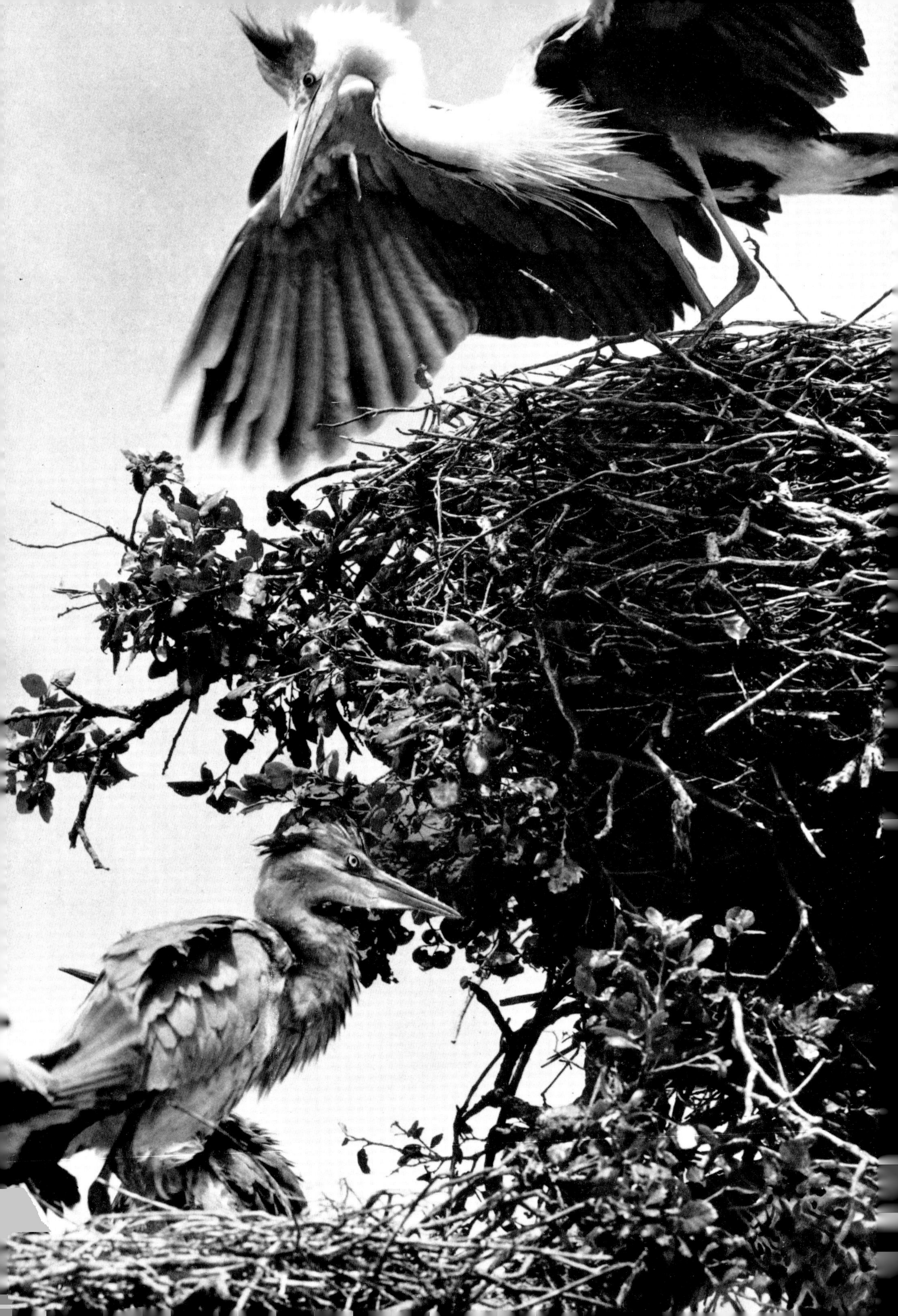

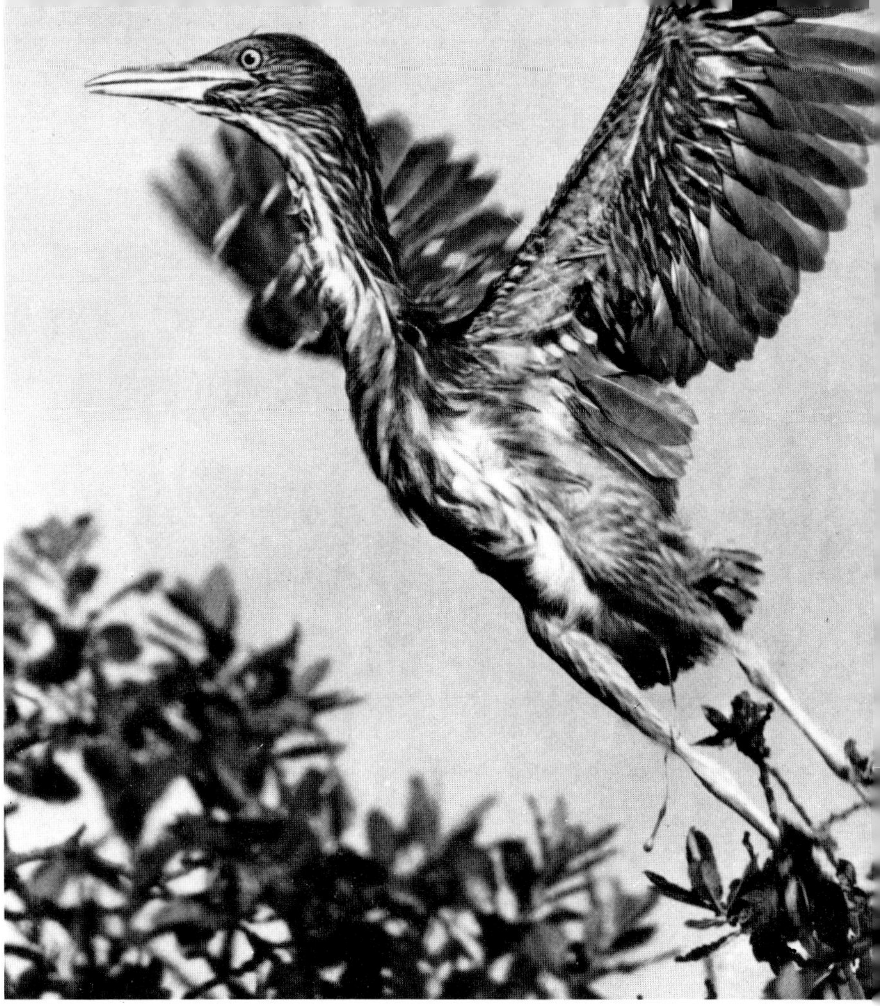

nature in action

Left: A blue-grey heron (*Ardea cinerea*) alights gracefully on its nest at the top of a tree. Lower down, the rather dishevelled-looking quarrelsome young birds sit waiting for their parents' return.
Equipment: 6 cm × 6 cm reflex camera, focal length 250 mm; the photograph was taken from a hide.
Above: A young night heron (*Nycticorax nycticorax*) puts in some flying practice.
Equipment: 35 mm camera, photosniper mounting, focal length 400 mm.

Basing ourselves on experience gained in the field, we shall now attempt to outline the working conditions of the wildlife photographer and his entirely personal approach to his favourite pursuit.

As we have already pointed out, photographic equipment and technical know-how are in themselves not enough to guarantee the success of a shot, and even the most expensive camera is merely an instrument possessing no inherent creative powers of its own.

To overcome a physical obstacle in the terrain, or a tactical difficulty, or to fill a gap in your knowledge, you must be able to draw upon the resources that every naturalist in contact with nature should possess: a thoughtful mind, patience, perseverance and cunning.

A few years ago, in the Dombes marshes, we discovered a crested grebe's nest which was too far out in the water to enable us to get a good picture. At regular

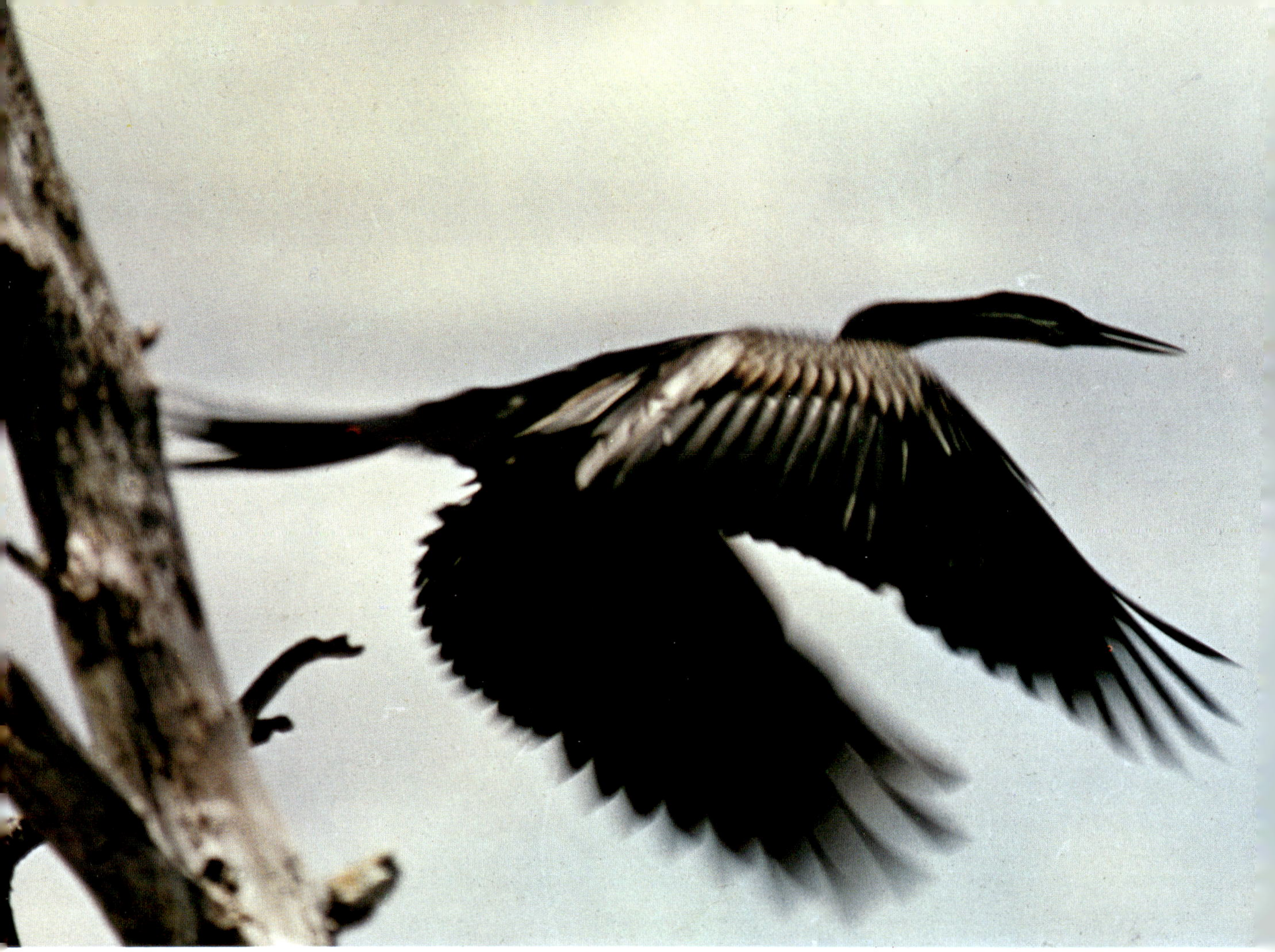

intervals the grebe would leave its floating nest, and the eggs in it, to go in search of food. Taking advantage of one of these absences, we swam out to the nest, tied a thin nylon string to it, and hastened back to the concealment of our hide on the river's bank. Each time the bird flew off to find food, we pulled the nest very gently a short distance towards us by means of the string. In a couple of days the nest, with the grebe sitting on it, was close enough to the hide to let us get good pictures.

At all times man has been the animal's deadliest enemy; and even with the best will in the world it is impossible for the naturalist to re-establish with it the confidence that would be his best ally. To observe, to approach, to photograph or film the animal or bird in its environment, you must use cunning and guile. These terms are meant to suggest the use of 'fair' stratagems, within reasonable limits, to outwit the wild creature. To be successful, they call for logical thinking and tremendous patience.

For stalking aquatic creatures a famous photographer has devised an elaborate system of camouflage, virtually a self-propelled floating hide, calculated to overcome even the most deep-rooted distrust. He wears a lifebelt which keeps him afloat, with the top part of his body out of the water, and frogman's fins for moving smoothly and rapidly through the water. His head is covered by a construction worker's safety helmet surmounted by a transparent plastic umbrella to give him a good view in all directions. All this is covered by a camouflage net. The whole purpose of such camouflage is to look as much as possible like something inoffensive–a pile of floating reeds, perhaps, or a drifting log. The illusion created by this particular get-up was so realistic that

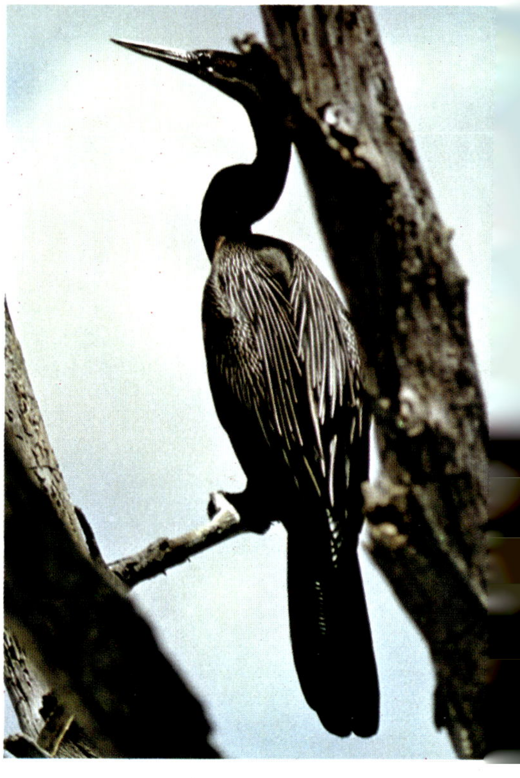

on one occasion an obstinate duck persisted in trying to build its nest on this ideal platform: it clambered on and off the hide, flew round and round it, and, after sticking its head in through the camouflage netting a few times, finally departed with squawks of disgust and rage at finding so delightful a place already occupied by another 'duck'. . .

The art of concealment, of merging with, and melting away into, the scenery of the territory you are exploring, remains the surest way to achieve success. And in passing from the idea to its realization the photographer will place the stamp of his own personality on the whole process of devising and constructing the contraption that will make him as inconspicuous as possible. Any method, any technique is a good one if it is suited to the environment in which it is to be used. You can make use of known and well-tried methods or you can invent new and original schemes of your own.

One summer's day on a North Sea beach we met a slab of rock moving about slowly in the middle of a flock of seabirds. The photographer operating under this mobile hide was wearing an enormous hat from which was draped yards and yards of hessian painted in camouflage colours. The whole fantastic concealment could be rolled up onto the hat when not in use and weighed only a few pounds.

Left: The anhinga or water turkey (*Anhinga anhinga*) has a long snake-like neck adorned with red and black. It feeds on fish and sits watching the water. When fishing, its whole body is submerged, with only the neck and head projecting above the surface.
Below: The giant heron (*Ardea goliath*) is a magnificent African wader whose colouring enables it to merge perfectly with the papyrus plants while it stands quietly in the water on the look-out for fish.
Equipment: Photosniper, 400 mm focal length; photographed from a floating raft covered with a tarpaulin.

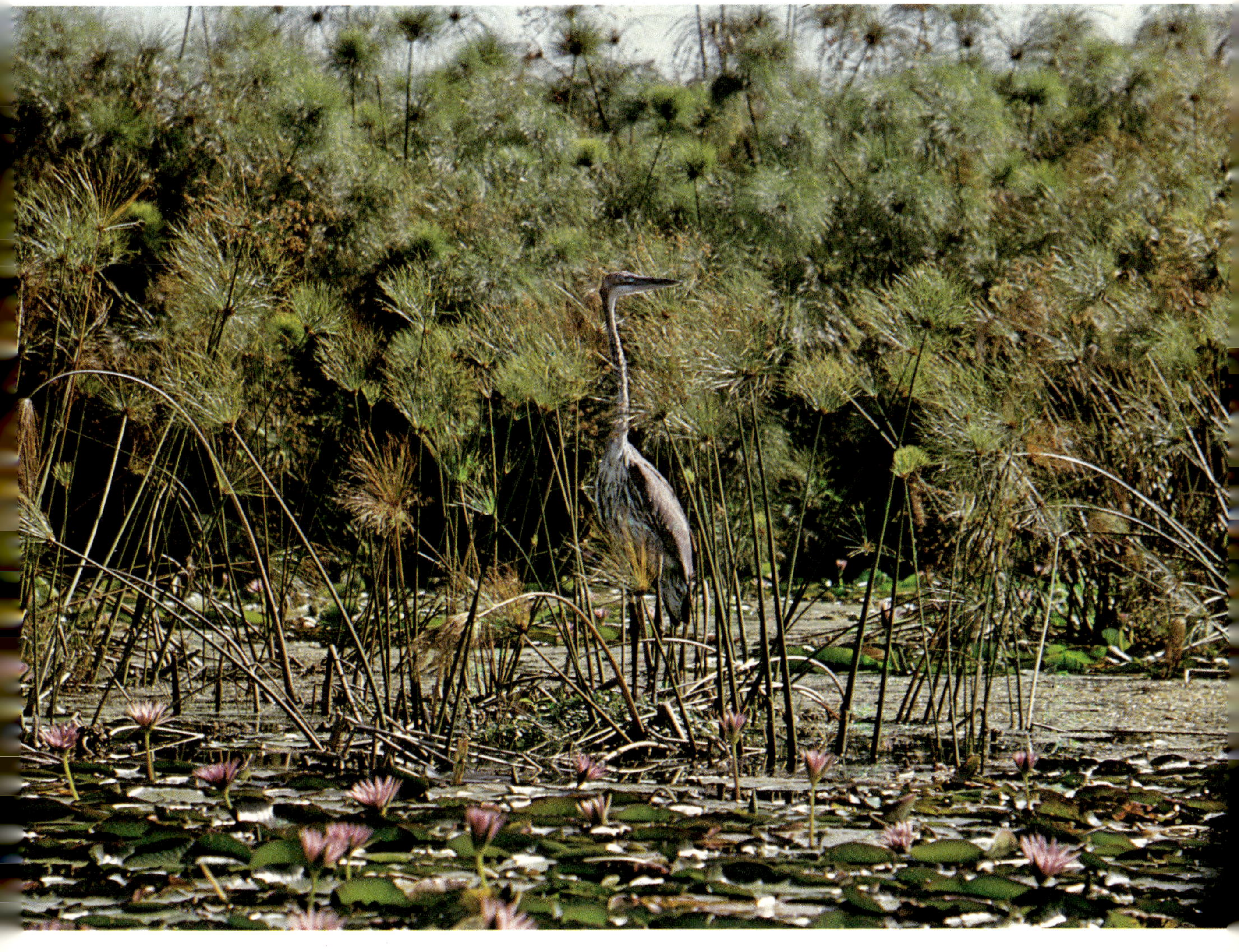

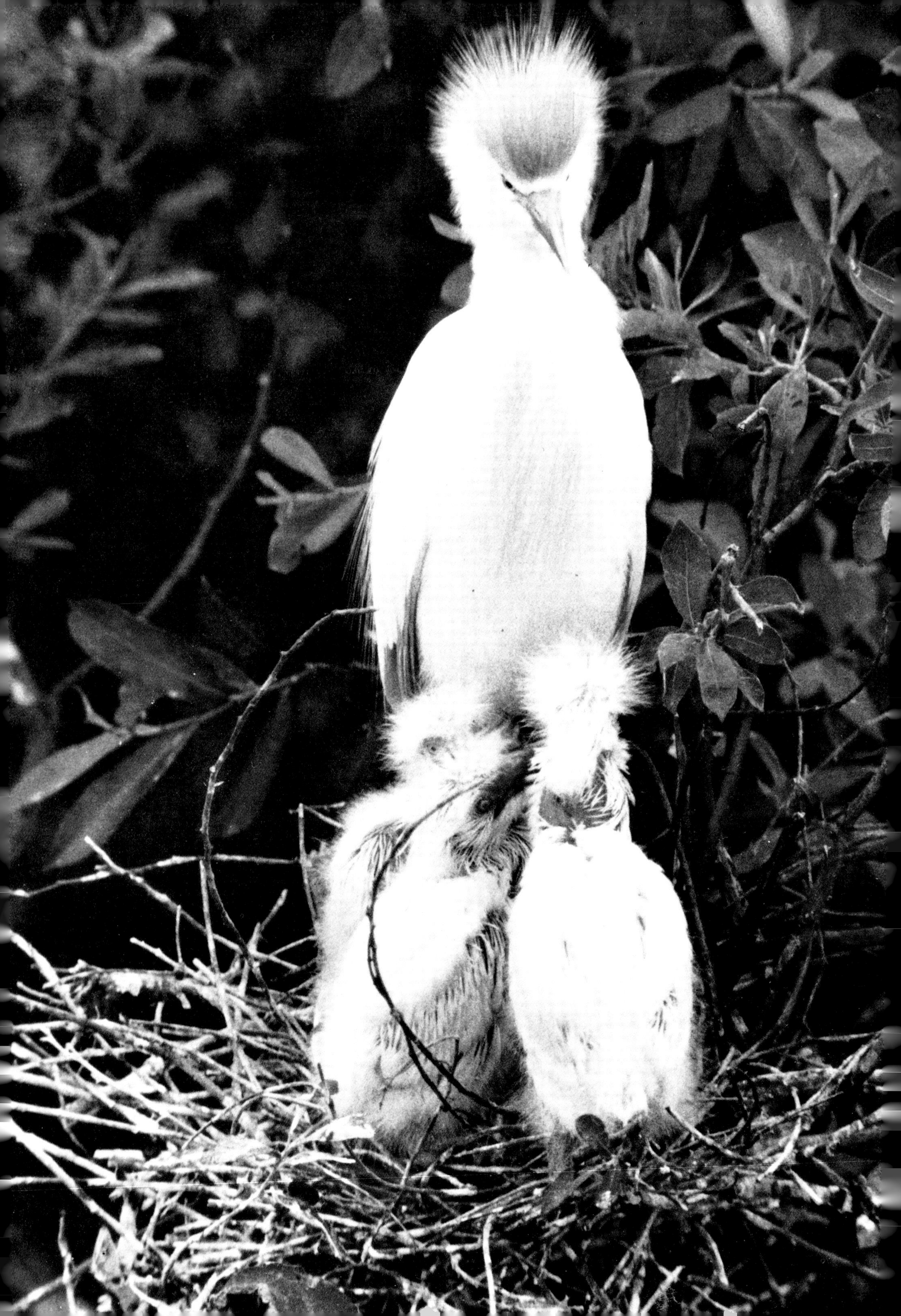

The ibis heron (*Ardeola ibis*) watches jealously over its ever-hungry young, for which it is constantly on the hunt for food. This bird nests in colonies, and it is fairly easy to construct a hide of suitable height from which a large number of interesting shots can be obtained.
Equipment: Hasselblad camera with 250 mm telephoto lens.

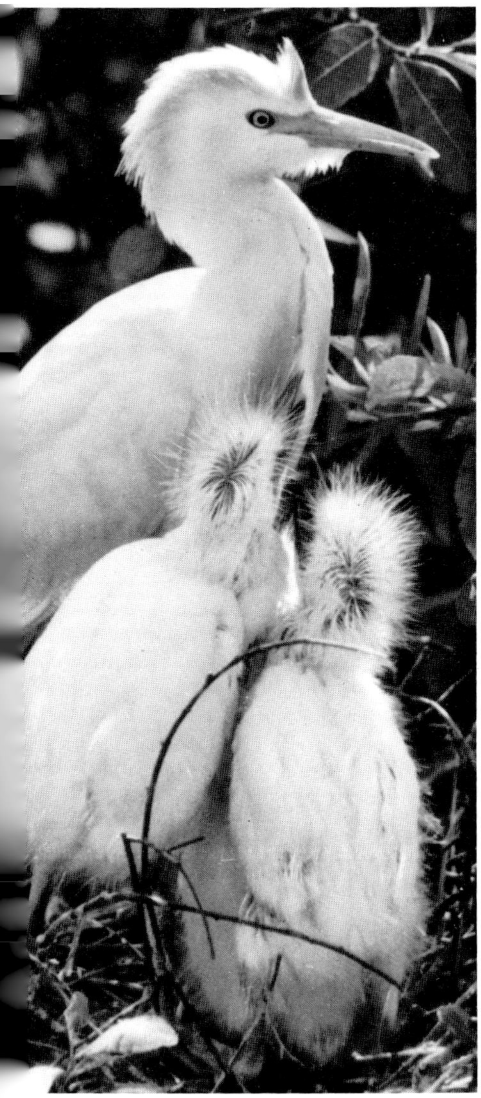

Very shy animals or birds can be photographed by remote control, the shutter being released by the photographer watching from a distance. An alternative method is to arrange a 'photographic trap', i.e. a set-up whereby the animal itself releases the shutter of the hidden camera by some kind of trigger mechanism. With remote control the photographer is still to some extent in command of the situation in that he continuously observes the animal's movements when it has come within camera range. Also, it is a more satisfying technique than the automatic trap because the photographer rctains a sense of involvement and suspense instead of having to wait passively for something to happen, the results of which he cannot influence or indeed judge until the picture has been developed.

First, you must select the most favourable spot frequented by the animal or bird that you wish to photograph. You then get the animal accustomed to a decoy–e.g. a cap, a camera case or even a tin can. After a time, when you perceive that the animal's behaviour is no longer affected by this alien object in its vicinity, you replace it by the camera itself. Next, you withdraw to a 'safe' distance, where you lie quietly in hiding, watching your camera and still in communication with it by means of your remote-operation shutter release system of whatever type. Where only short distances are involved it may be quite suitable to use a pneumatic release. For longer distances an electric system employing relays and electromagnets may be used, provided that the wires are not too complicated to install and can be easily concealed. Where this is not possible or where the distance is too great, radio control may be used. However, if you want to remain involved in an active sense–i.e. observe what is happening and judge the best instant at which to operate the shutter–you cannot withdraw to a distance much exceeding 200 yards, even if you have power field-glasses. The camera should, as a rule, be equipped with an electric motor for film transport.

In a suitably modified form this method can be used for obtaining pictures at close range even of aggressive animals. We once visited an exhibition which included a remarkable series of photographs obtained literally from under the very noses of bulls. The photographer had placed some bait in the middle of the herd. Concealed in the bait was the camera, enclosed in a strong box provided with a window. The camera, thus protected from knocks, was fitted up for remote control (by radio) of the film transport and shutter release movements. It had a wide-angle lens.

The design and construction of such equipment require some ingenuity. It is certainly not possible to use conventional techniques for dealing with a subject of this kind. The remote control principle does, however, involve the use of cxpensive and fragile equipment which cannot be left out in the open for days on end without serious risk of damage or loss. For these reasons the 'photographic trap' may be a preferable alternative. Indeed, this is just about the only possible technique for photographing certain nocturnal animals (foxes, badgers, etc.).

A very simple camera should be used, e.g. a box camera or perhaps even one of those old wooden cameras taking plates. It should be installed close to the path that the creature is known to use on its nightly prowls. Light for taking the photograph is provided by a flash bulb synchronized with the camera shutter. Electronic flash is not suitable for the purpose because it cannot be left charged for hours on end. The flash and shutter are triggered by a piece of nylon thread, or any other arrangement devised for the purpose, which works a switch. This in turn energizes an electromagnet for actuating the shutter release.

Obviously, this system will produce only a single picture each time. Well camouflaged, protected from rain and moisture, the camera and its trap mechanism can be left unattended for long periods waiting for the animal to come. There is no need even to go near it to find out if it has been triggered: through field-glasses you can see whether the flash bulb has been fired.

You may get some surprises: domestic animals such as dogs or cows may walk

The male cock of the rock (*Rupicola rupicola*) is a highly photogenic bird with its vivid colours and fan-shaped crest. This specimen was photographed in a zoo. Equipment: 35 mm reflex camera, 135 mm focal length; electronic flash.

Right: The capercaillie (*Tetrao urogallus*), the largest member of the grouse family in Europe, is here seen displaying its plumage, head thrown back, tail feathers outspread. This bird, though very difficult to approach in normal circumstances, tends to become indifferent to intruders during its mating display, when it may even become bold enough to attack the photographer. Equipment: 35 mm reflex camera, 250 mm focal length.

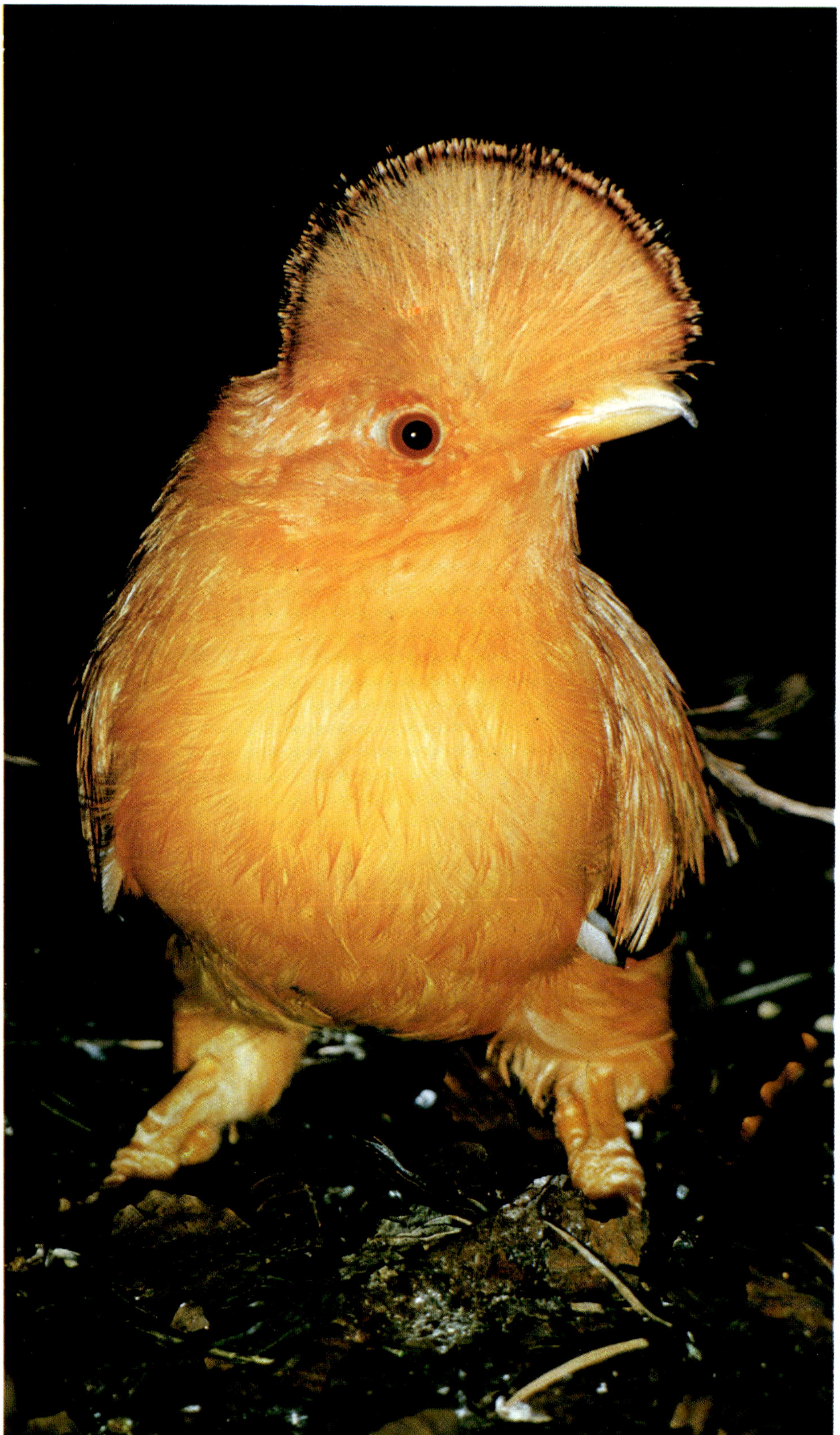

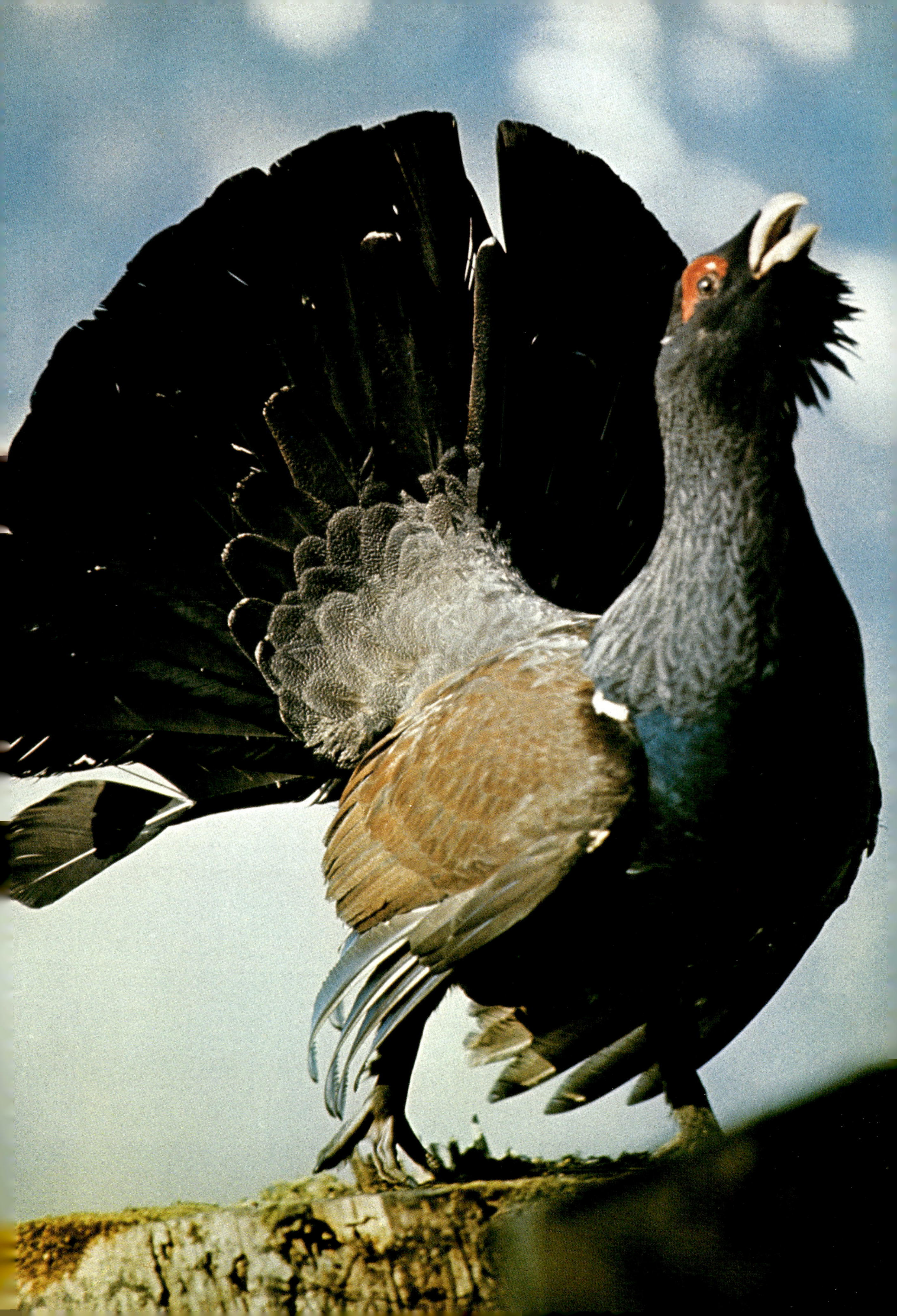

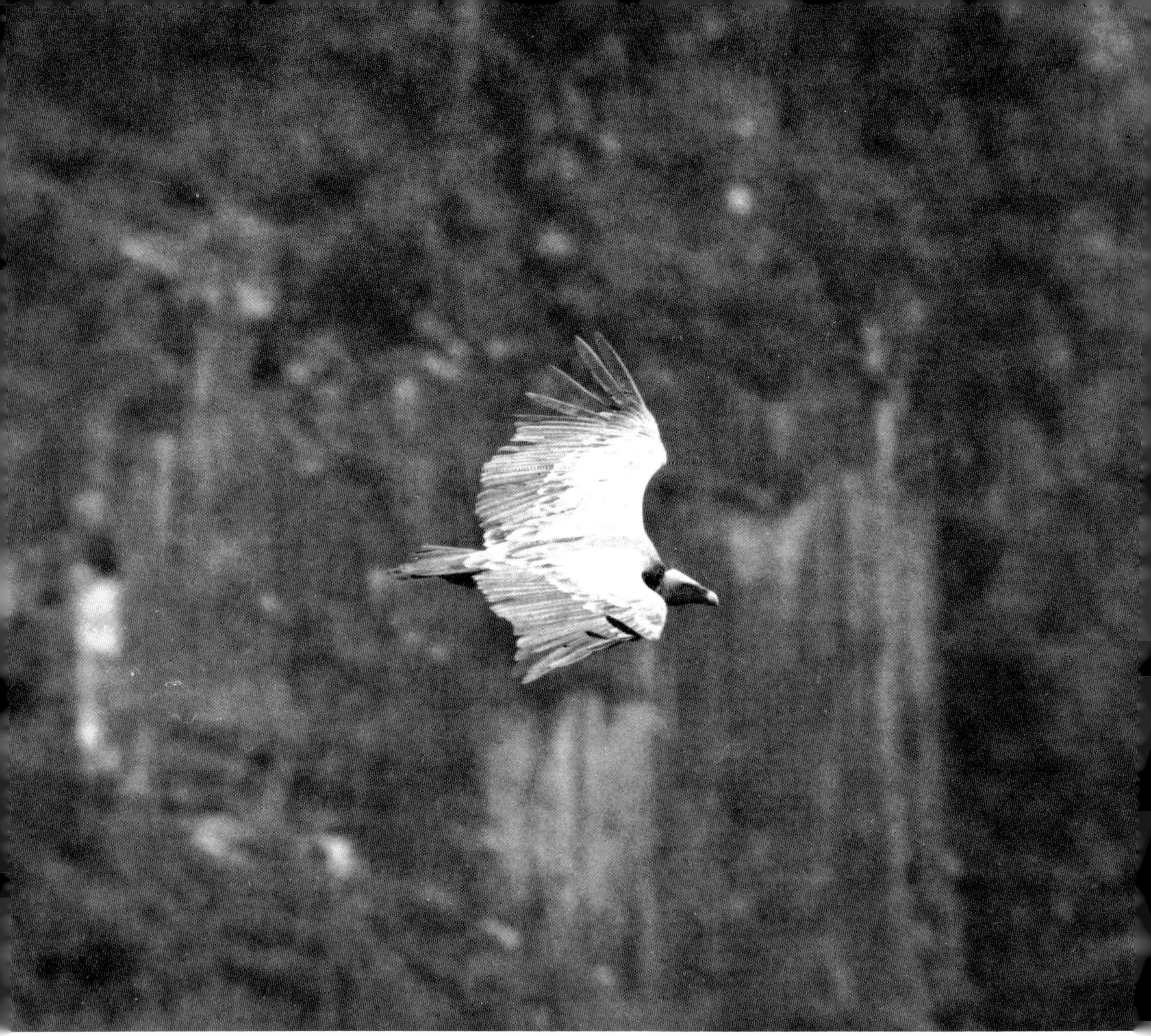

A griffon vulture (*Gyps fulvus*) soars over the valley in search of carrion. Like a skilled glider pilot it can remain aloft for hours with wings motionlessly outspread, utilizing the rising currents of air that develop over the rock masses. It builds its primitive nest on steep and inaccessible rock faces.
Equipment: The photograph was obtained with a photosniper from the top of the rocky wall of the valley.

into the 'trap' so cunningly set for another creature. On one occasion we even found that we had photographed a poacher in the act of setting one of his snares!

To act with patience and circumspection is the first requirement for the naturalist, and this inborn patience can be a good observer's most valuable asset.

To photograph an eagle's nest we once had to spend twenty-one hours almost motionless at the top of an observation tower, waiting for the bird to return to its nest. Before erecting our tower and the hide surmounting it, we had watched the development of the eaglet through field-glasses for three weeks, until we felt certain that the adult bird would not abandon its nest on account of our presence. At the end of the first day of observation, near nightfall, the adult returned to the nest very briefly, just for a few seconds, to feed its young. On the second day, at the same time, it returned again and remained on the nest for quite twenty seconds. It was not until the fifth day that the eagle, satisfied

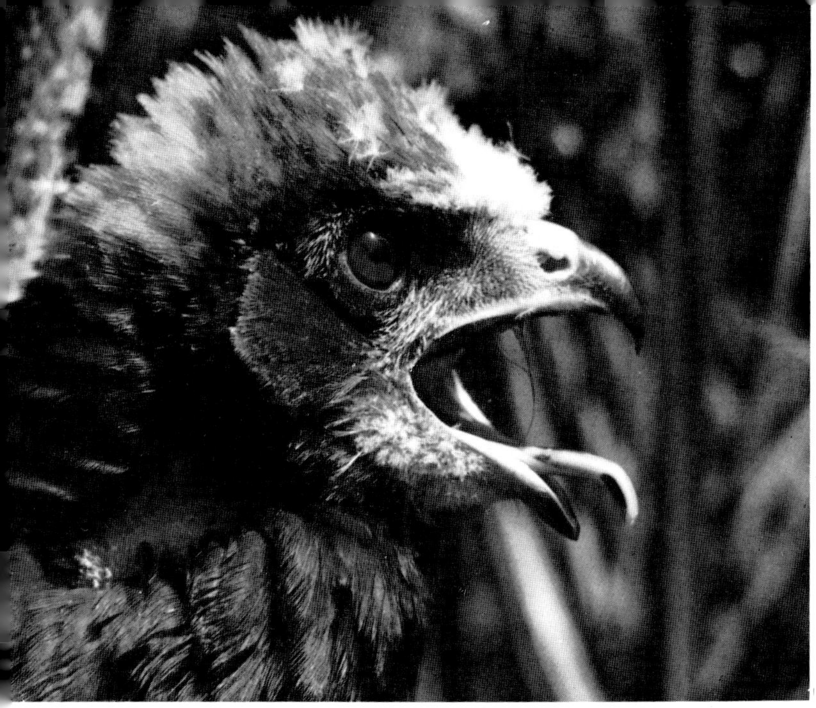

Above: A young marsh harrier (*Circus aeruginosus*) on its nest hidden in the middle of a reed bed. If you happen to discover a marsh harrier's nest, you should carefully replace the reeds and other vegetation in their original position, to protect the nest from predators.
Below: An imperial eagle (*Aquila heliaca*) alights majestically on its nest at the top of a tree. Birds of prey approach their nests by certain fixed routes which are always the same for a given wind direction. The photograph was obtained from a hide with the aid of a photosniper.

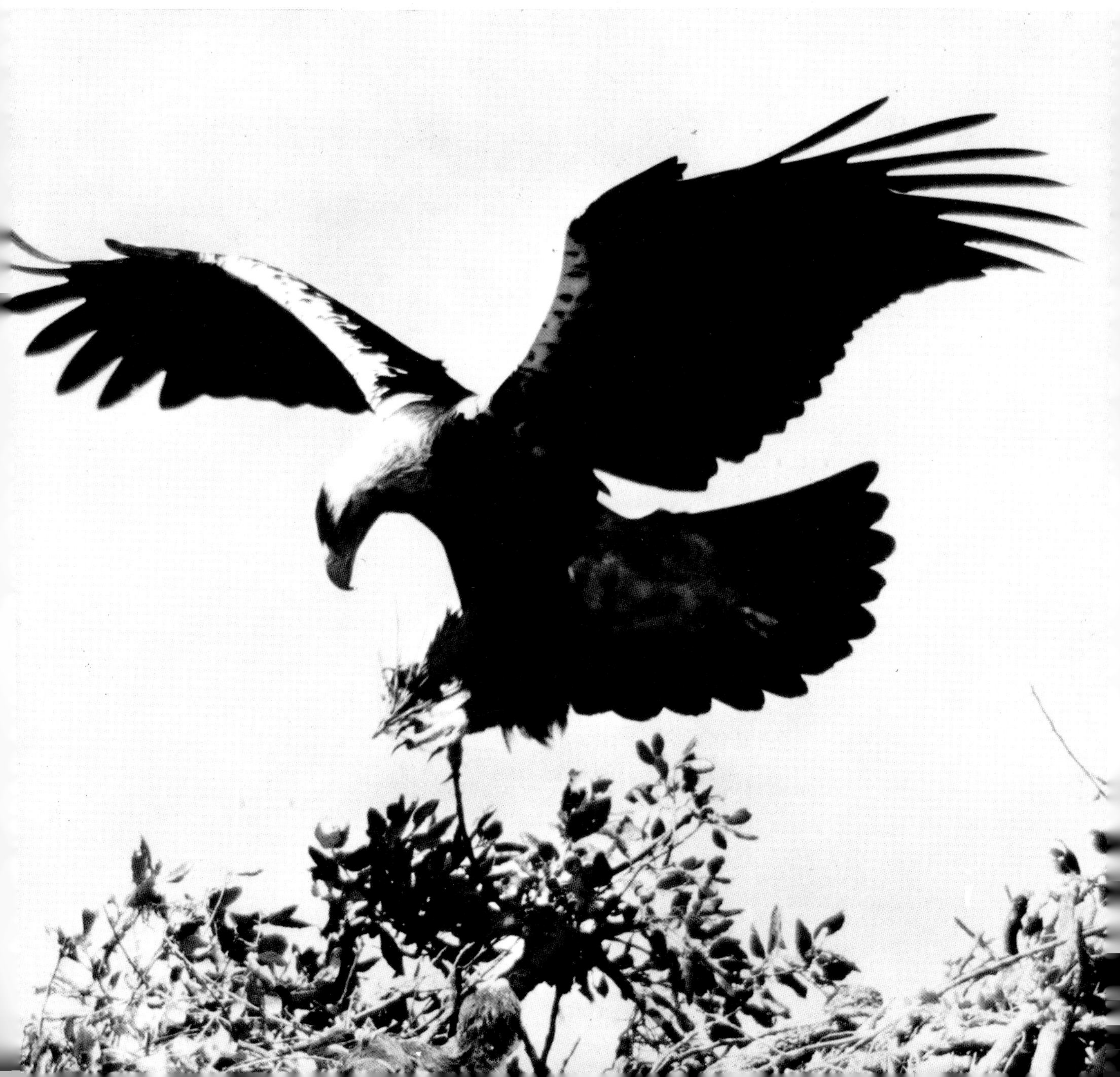

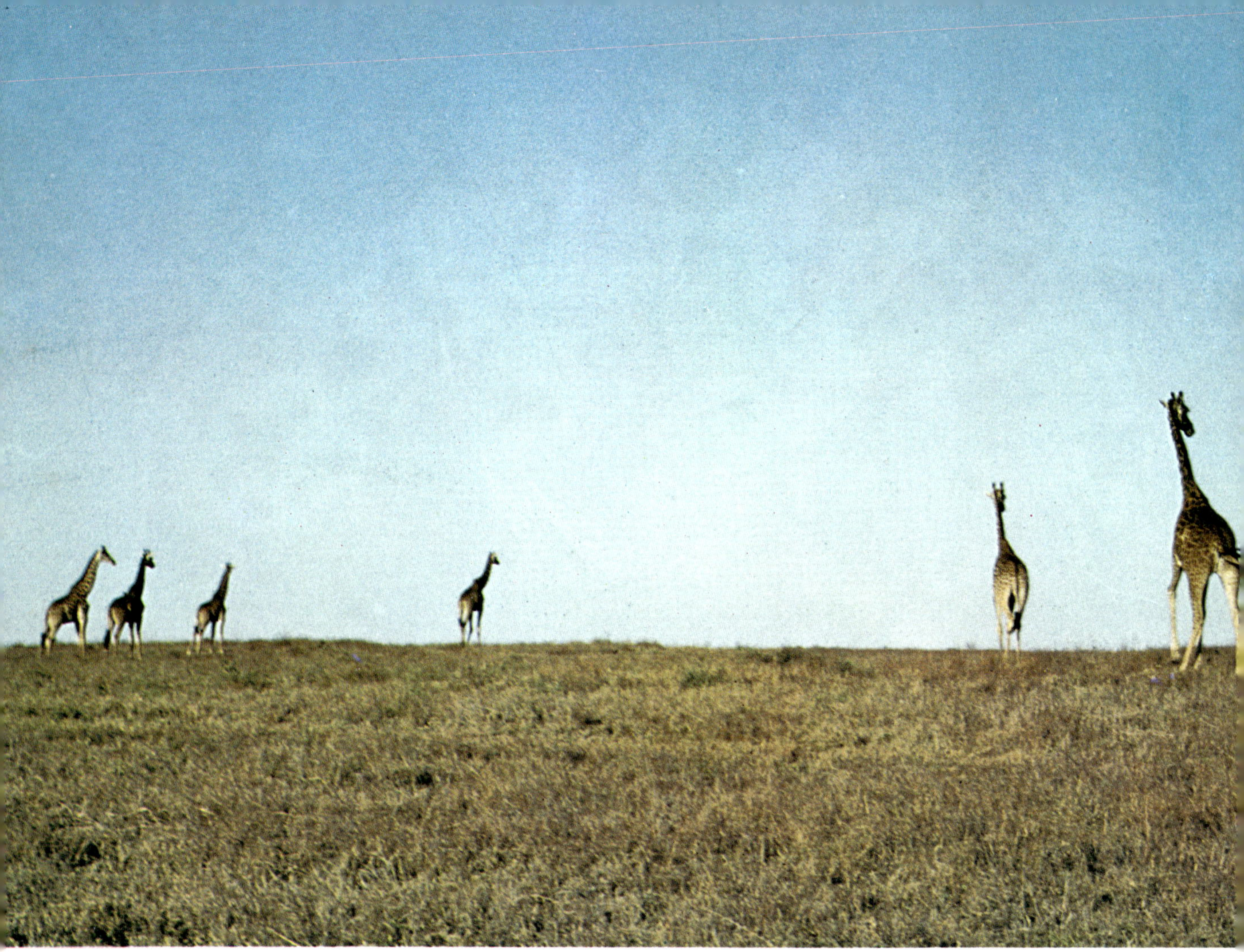

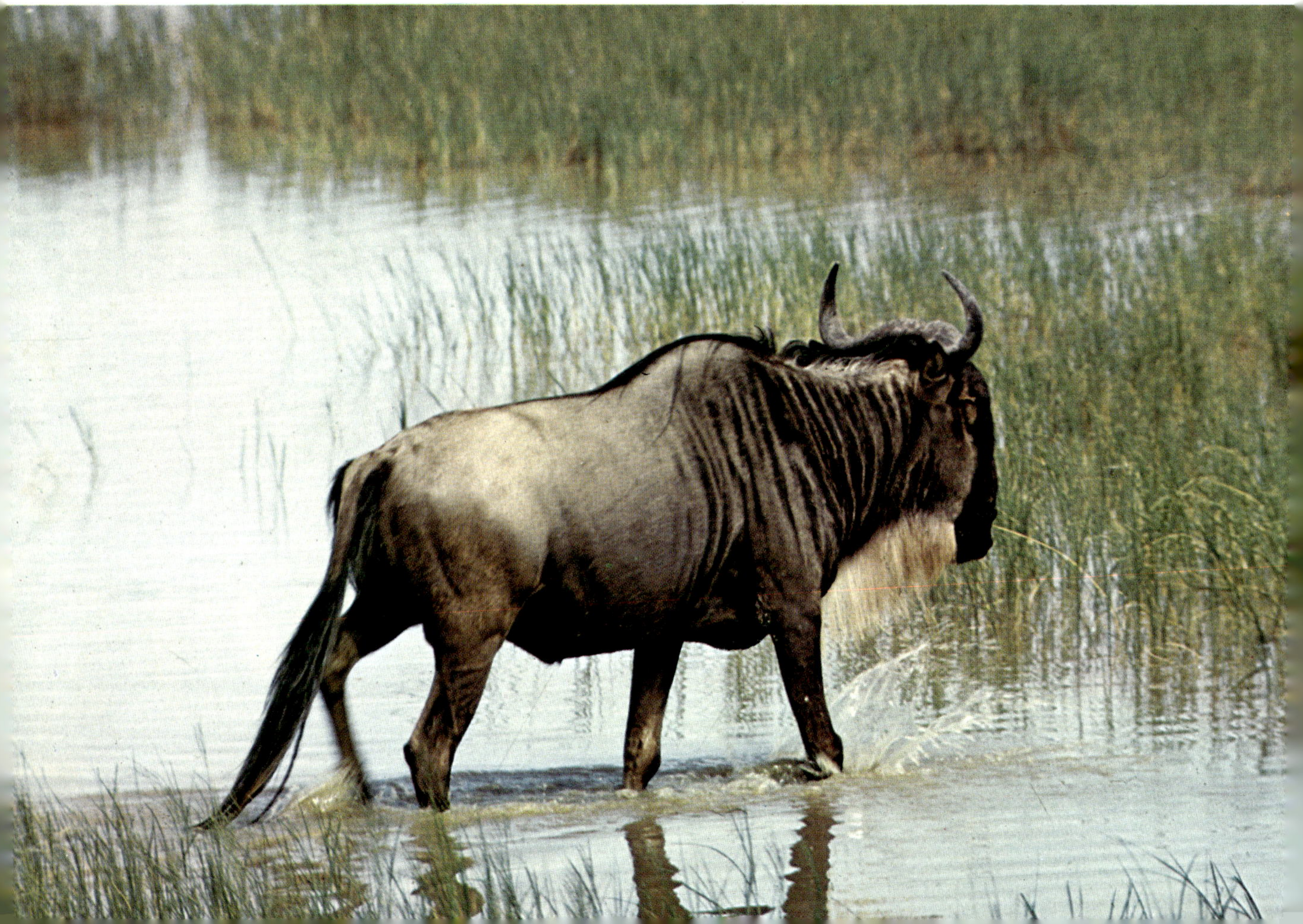

that we–those motionless watchers–had peaceful intentions, returned in the middle of the day, though not without first making a long reconnoitring flight and a series of intermediate stops in its cautious final approach.

Inventions and discoveries all come as the result of experimenting. The old saying 'practice makes perfect' certainly applies to wildlife photography.

To the amateur starting out in this branch of photography the first opportunities for experimenting, already full of the promise of excitement, will almost certainly not come on some safari to distant lands. Training begins at home with very simple and perhaps home-made equipment, but with a spirit of enthusiasm which will be his best guide to this new form of escapism.

We remember our first blue tits photographed on the ledge of a window whose panes we had covered with black paper in which a hole had been made for the camera lens and another to serve as a peephole. The song and perky confidence of these little birds inspired us with the desire to go down into the garden and out into nature to observe other species. Pigeons, sparrows, blackbirds, swifts

Opposite, above: A group of giraffes (*Girafa camelopardalis*). This animal presents a particularly striking silhouette offering many interesting photographic possibilities when viewed from different angles.
Equipment: 35 mm reflex camera, 135 mm focal length.
Opposite, below: White bearded gnu (*Connochætes albojubatus*).
Below: The leaping gait of the graceful impala (*Æpyceros melampus*).
Equipment: 35 mm camera, photosniper mounting, 400 mm focal length.

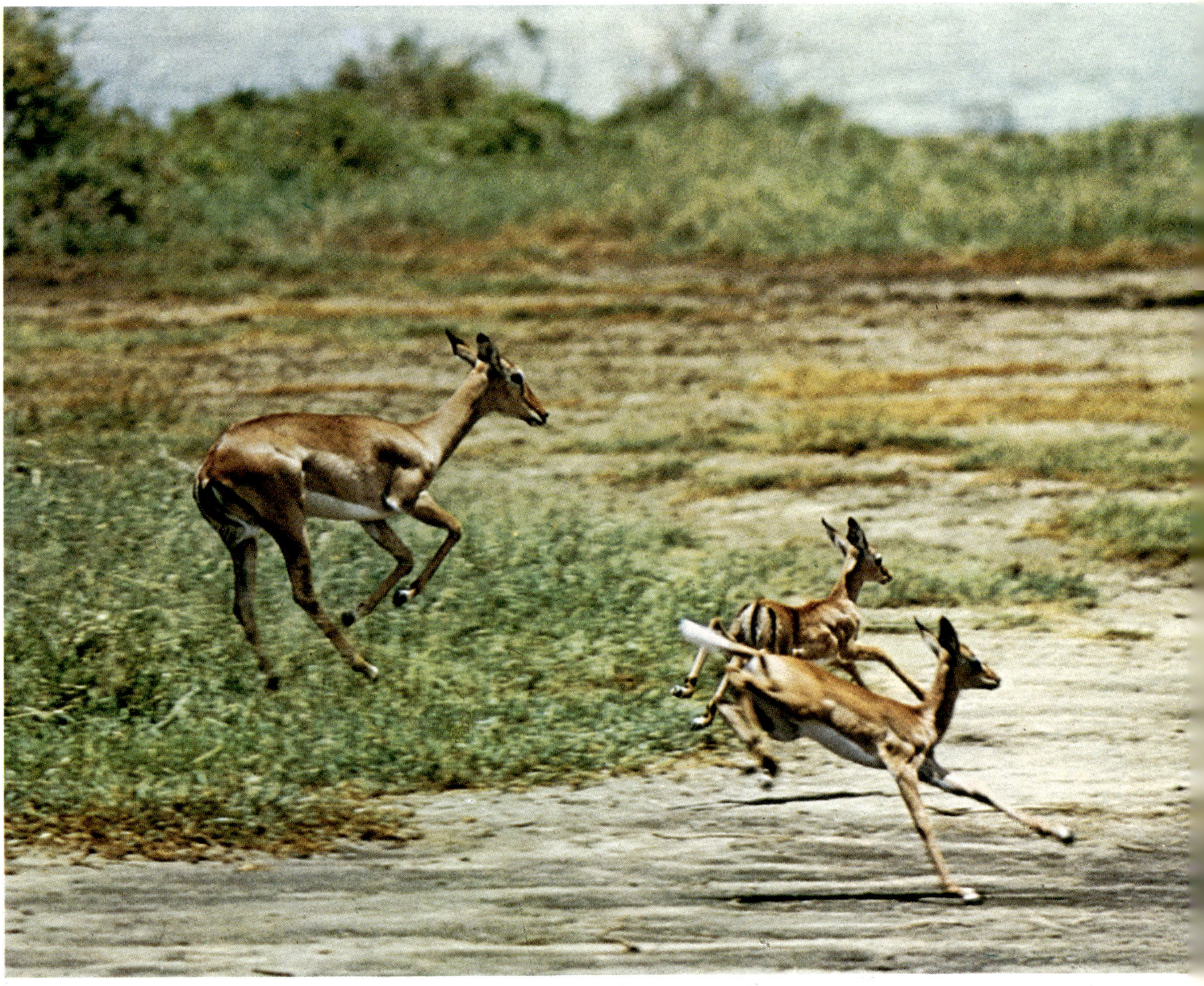

and bullfinches live and nest even in the middle of a town, and photographing these birds provides a good training school for learning to handle your camera efficiently and to react and think quickly. The squares and public gardens of your town are the home of hordes of insects–flies, bees, butterflies–and spiders, too, which provide plenty of scope for trying your hand at real close-up photography.

You can gain experience in the use of long-focus or telephoto lenses by photographing the waterfowl that live on or near the ponds, canals and rivers in and around your home town. The birds are constantly on the move and will present a real challenge to your skill in securing action pictures taken at exposures of 1/1000 second.

On the outskirts of the town you will find opportunities to set up your first hides, and if you are lucky enough to have access to a public refuse dump, it is well worth spending some hours there on sunny days. These are perhaps rather depressing surroundings which take some getting used to; but then the nature observer must learn to put up with a certain amount of discomfort. It is no worse than tramping about for hours in some stagnant foul-smelling marsh, where you will moreover be assailed by swarms of gnats while you wade perhaps waist-deep through mud, performing perilous acrobatic feats to keep upright–and sometimes all the reward you get for your effort will be just the glimpse of a swallow's tail.

A female vervet monkey (*Cercopithecus æthiops*) and her young, on which she lavishes much care and attention. These monkeys live in groups, with a preference for thinly wooded or savannah-type country. Each group contains individuals of all ages, and there appears to be no definite mating and breeding season.

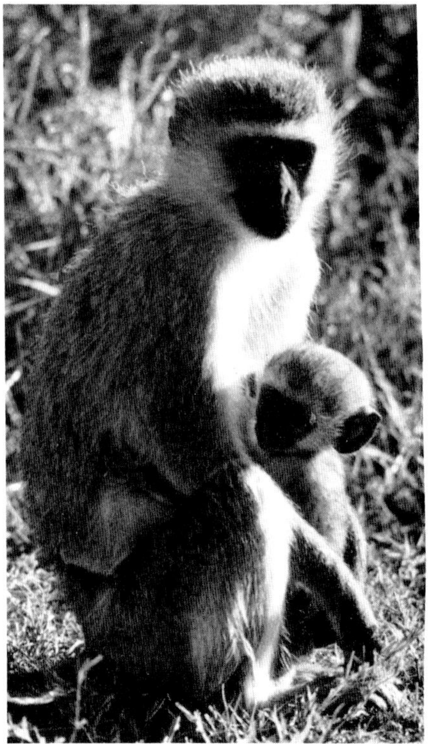

On a refuse dump you are likely to find rats, big, cunning, suspicious ones. To get a good photograph of one of these rodents can in itself claim to be quite an achievement. You will also find birds such as crows, jackdaws, blackbirds and magpies, which are likely to be less distrustful, perhaps because of the remoteness of the place. This is more particularly true of crows, which normally are very difficult birds to approach by stalking and are also difficult to photograph on account of their sombre colouring. In such surroundings as a refuse dump it can indeed be quite a problem to make an animal or bird stand out clearly from the background. But if you use high-powered telephoto lenses, which are a necessity for such work anyway, you should be able to get good pictures of the birds taking off, landing and in flight.

Beyond the outskirts of the town is the open country–'nature', but hardly in the sense of an environment where creatures live in total freedom. In the fifteenth century it was perhaps still possible to travel right across Europe from the south of Spain to the north of Denmark without ever leaving the forest. After the systematic destruction of forestland and the economic upheavals of the last three centuries, all that remain of those vast regions are a few relatively small wooded areas.

Truly virgin nature disappeared in Europe a long time ago, and such wild tracts of country that still exist are often subject to special restrictions on access or are privately owned estates (game preserves, etc.).

Nowadays you have to be careful about where you go, and you should make enquiries beforehand in order to be sure that you will not be trespassing. Otherwise you will risk being stopped by some forester or gamekeeper or you may arouse the suspicion of some over-zealous officer of the law who could take you for an undesirable prowler or even a spy! But if you patiently explain your purpose and show your equipment with the full enthusiasm of the dedicated naturalist, you will usually find that such suspicious-minded gentlemen become quite friendly and helpful–perhaps not without a tinge of slight amusement at this harmless crank, but generally with complete courtesy. And, incidentally, make sure you slip in some mention of a connection, however remote, that you are supposed to have with television broadcasting. It works like magic in opening the gateway to many a happy hunting ground.

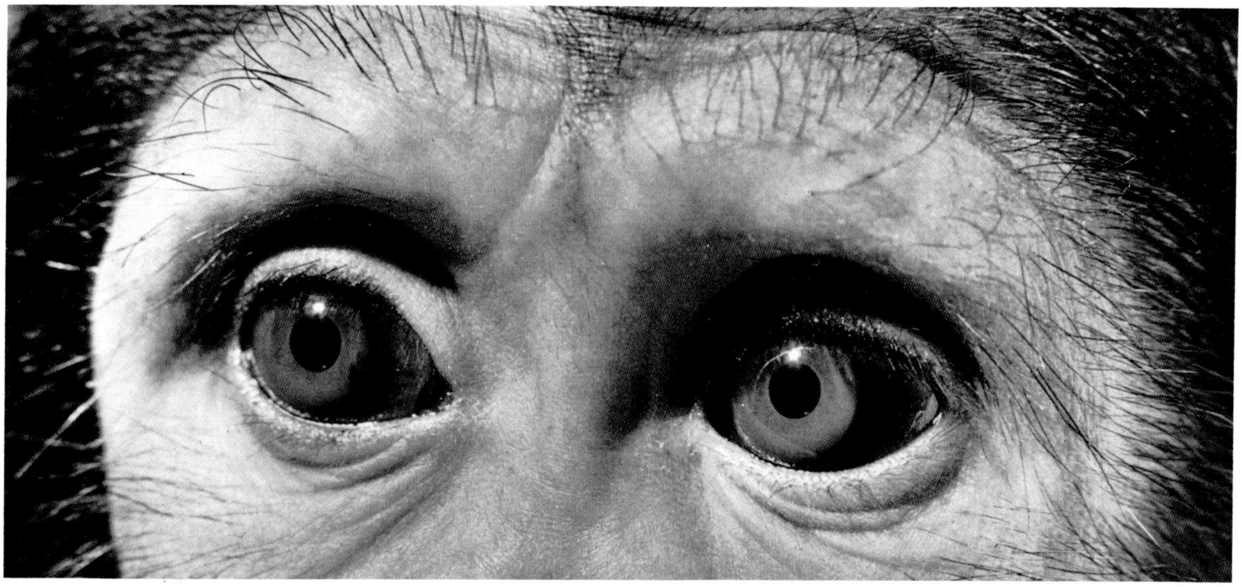

The 'almost human' gaze of a chimpanzee (*Pan troglodytes*). In the wild state these apes live in organized communities. They are very boisterous, passing their time chasing one another in the trees and searching for fruit and other food. It is difficult to get close to them, and it takes much time and patience to win their confidence and be accepted into the clan.
Equipment: Nikon and Micro Nikkor, 55 mm focal length.

It is absolutely necessary to get to know the *principles* that are being applied to govern nature protection and conservation in the area where you wish to operate and to acquaint yourself with the regulations in photographing animals.

In France, for example, the wildlife photographer will find that some sites or territories are classed as 'full reserves', where the natural environment with its plant and animal life has to be preserved. Access to these is strictly confined to a handful of scientists.

'Partial reserves' aim only at protecting one particular species of animal or plant, and application for permission to enter them must be made to the governors or to a scientific committee.

'Leisure zones and natural beauty spots' are populated and inhabited territories which are protected only from an excessive degree of industrial development. Access to them is free, subject only to a few restrictions as to motoring or camping.

Finally, 'national parks' are very extensive territories, certainly protected from all urban development and closely supervised, but unrestrictedly accessible to tourists and photographers in particular.

'Hunting and fishing reserves' are excellent places for photography, but special permission is needed for entering them.

As for the 'national forests' or 'communal forests', access to these is virtually unrestricted, except that visitors must conform to certain general rules, e.g. not to light fires or cut down trees. These few prohibitions, which are quite understandable precautions in the interests of conservation of such beauty spots and their animal and plant life, will certainly not deter you from carrying out your first experiments.

In the United Kingdom there are about 10 'national parks' with, on the whole, free access, and about 130 'nature reserves' with varying degrees of restriction of entry. There are many areas under Government control for other purposes (e.g. the plantations of the Forestry Commission) or other authorities (e.g. water-supply reservoirs) to which visits may be possible by agreement.

Similarly, there are 286 parks and reserves of one sort or another in the United States of America; these, as in other countries and regions, have parallel opportunities as well as restrictions. The intending traveller will often find it best to seek guidance from the appropriate State Tourist Agency, in advance, wherever in the world he intends to go.

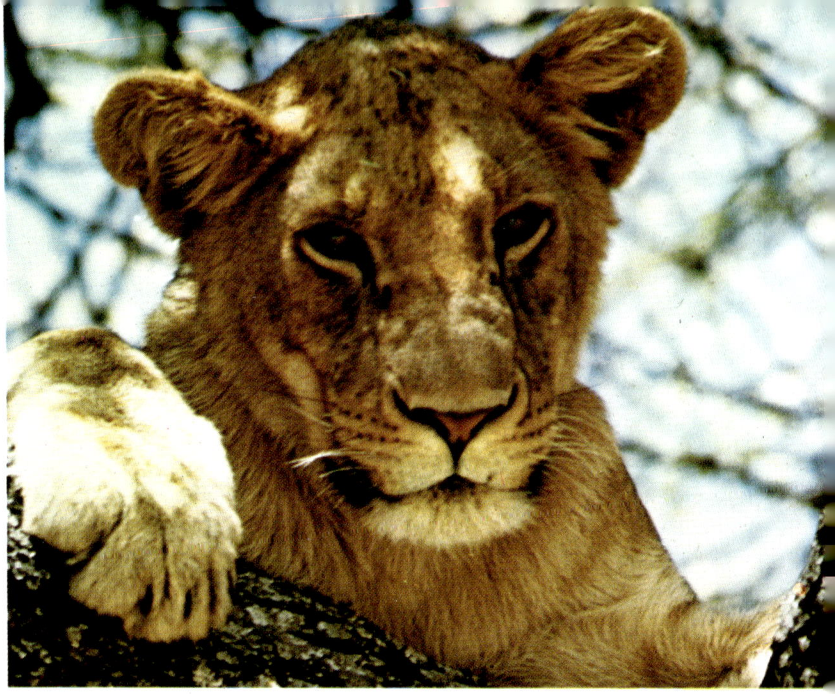

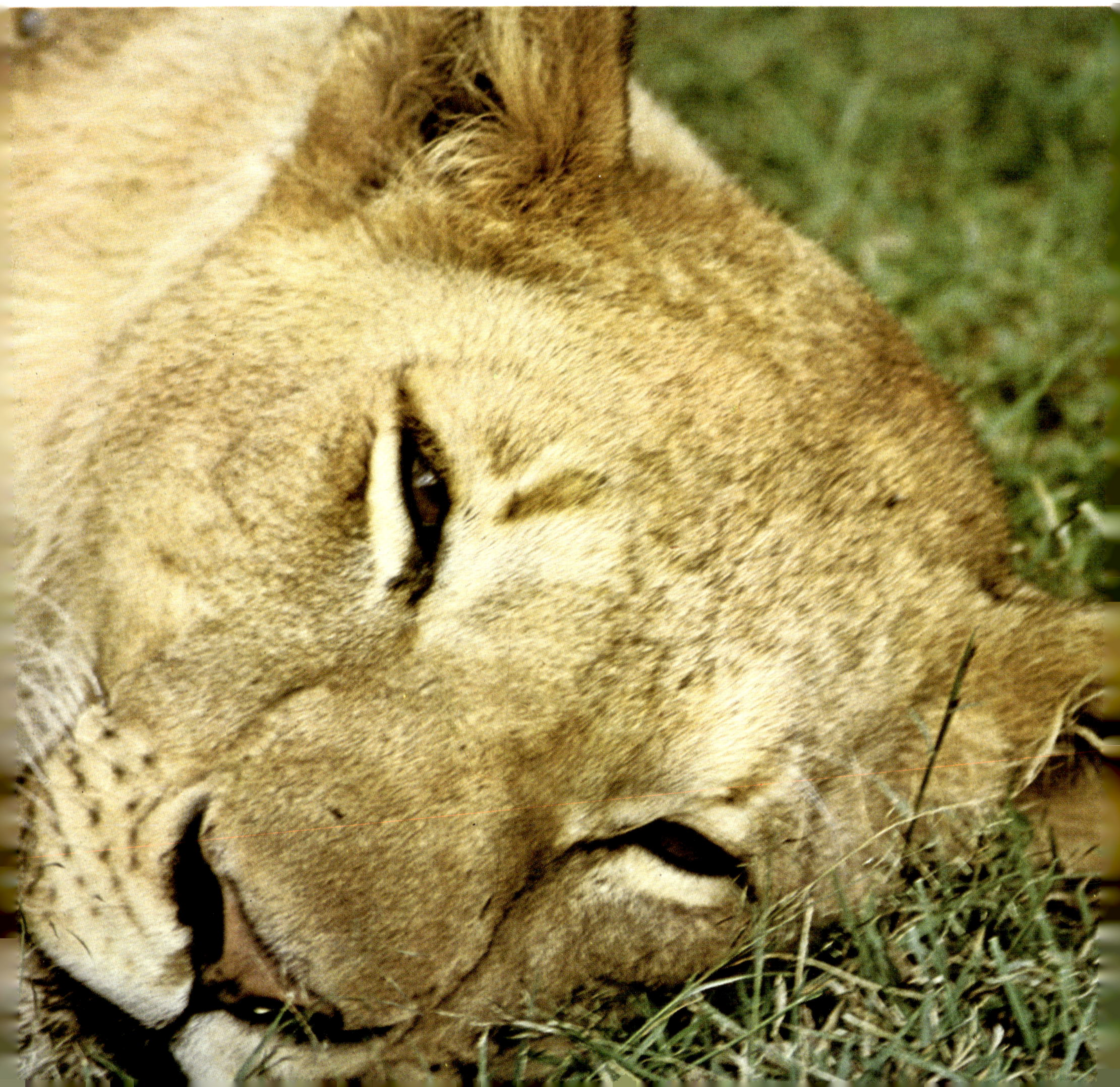

The sort of practice and experience you can gain in national parks and nature reserves will provide an excellent means of sharpening your wits and your interest, making you want to go farther afield and tackle more advanced and difficult things.

Before sallying forth into the field you should carefully prepare your expedition: choose the right time of year, find out all you can about the animals' habits, map out the amount of time you can devote to wildlife observation and photography, the techniques to use, etc. There then still remain some precautions to be taken with regard to the animal or bird and its environment.

Lions (*Panthera leo*) are fond of taking a nap during the hottest part of the day. The nimbler lionesses and cubs climb trees to get away from the hordes of flies that plague them at ground level.
Equipment: 35 mm camera, photosniper mounting, 400 mm focal length.

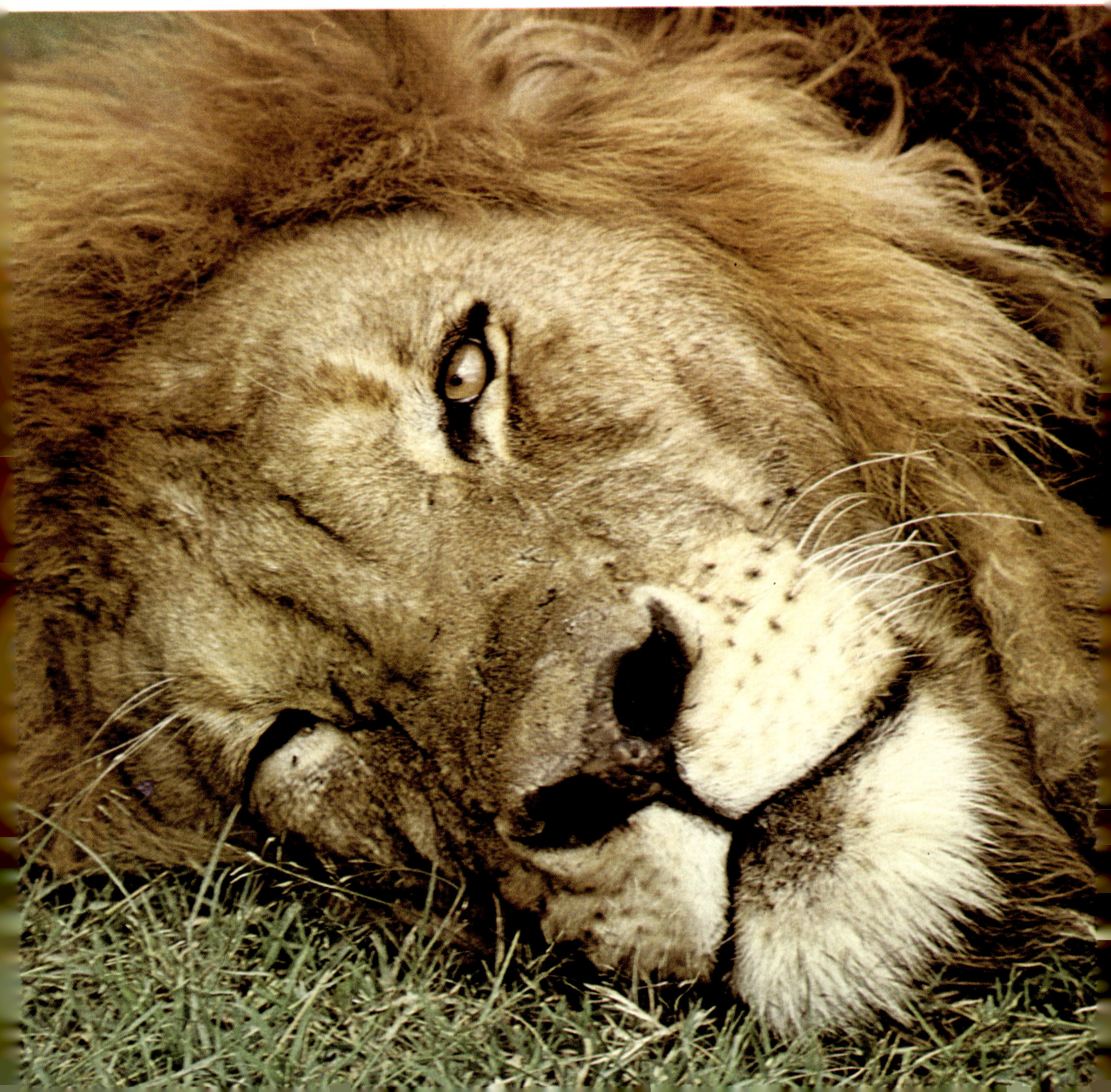

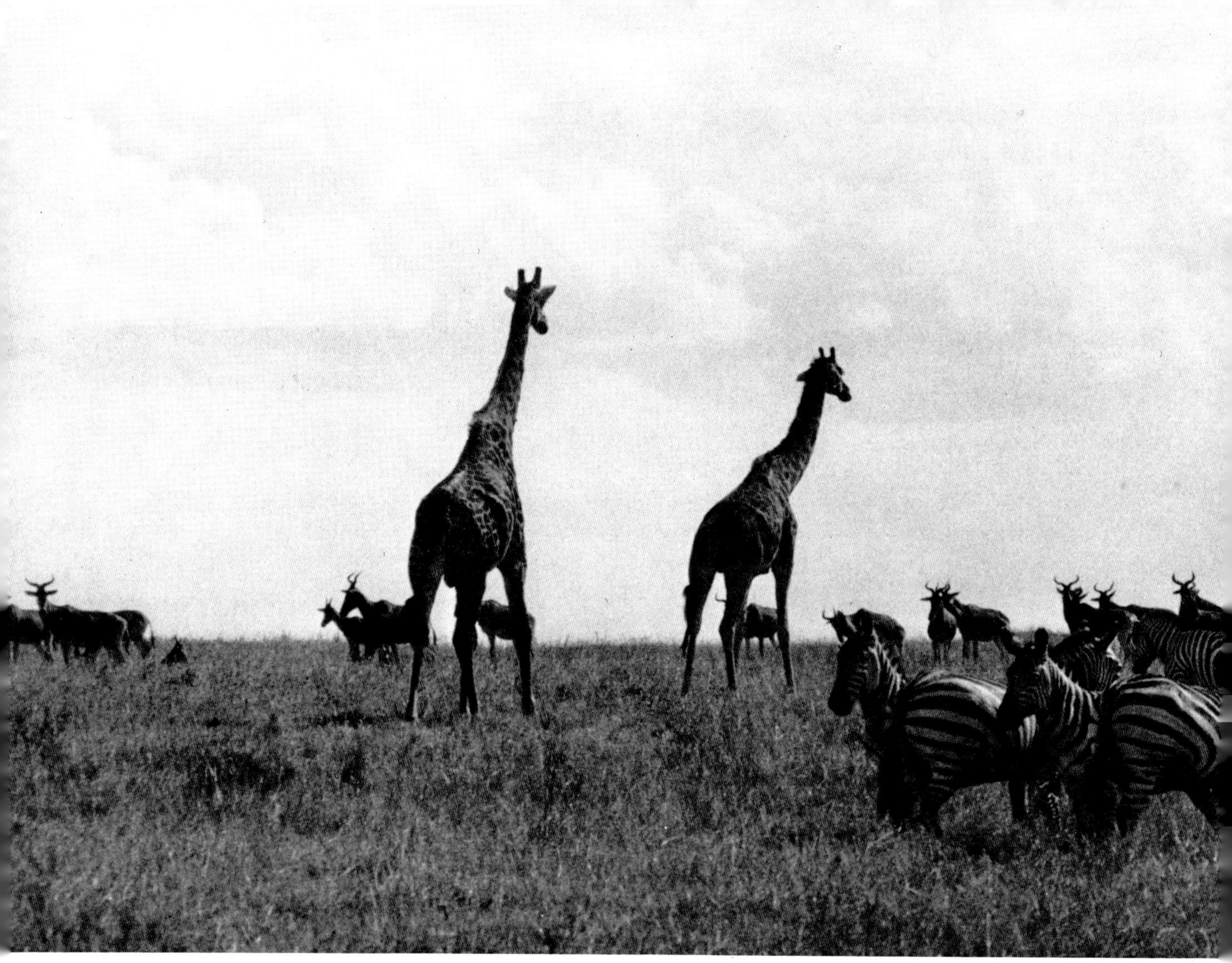

Groups of giraffes, bubals and zebras. In the great savannahs of Africa it is not at all unusual to find such composite associations of hoofed animals sharing a convenient feeding ground. The animal species that has a superior sense of smell warns those with better eyesight of the approach of danger, and vice versa.

Remember that a wild creature has its freedom, its rights and a territory which it regards as its exclusive own. If you install a hide close to a nest, for example, take care not to disturb the environment that the bird has chosen for its own special reasons–associated with climatic conditions or the amount of sunshine. Tall grass or plants around the nest should not be cut away; if necessary, they can be tied back temporarily until you get your pictures, but then you should restore them to the condition in which you found them. Such grass or plants provide shade for the eggs and thus protect them from excessive heat; they also conceal them from prowling predators in search of an easy meal.

But if the bird does not return to its nest within a reasonable time–which, according to the species, may vary from a quarter of an hour to several hours–you should dismantle your hide and withdraw quietly from the scene. For it will then have become fairly certain that the bird has spotted you and will rather abandon its eggs than come back to a place where it no longer feels safe.

Wherever you go, and whatever the season, the best method of getting about in the open country is nearly always on foot. It is slow but sure; but it does mean that you will have to carry all your photographic and other equipment on your back. Even if you cut down your requirements to the minimum, the burden is still likely to be too much for one man to carry for long distances. So, particularly on long expeditions, you need some obliging companion who

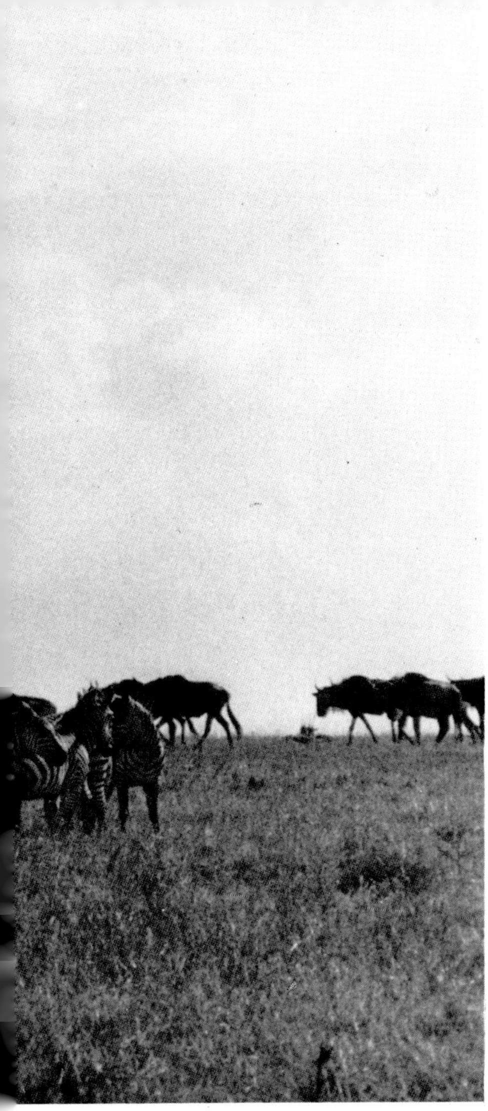

shares your enthusiasm–and your burden–and also understands the art of being silent. Then the weight of the equipment will not be a serious snag. You will perhaps even be able to take a bigger hide with you, which will make the process of waiting a little more comfortable.

A big beach parasol covered with easily transported camouflage netting can provide a hide large enough to accommodate even three people quite easily. It is particularly convenient in having only a single support, so that its height can be adjusted and in some cases it can even be moved cautiously towards the creature to be photographed.

To erect and use an observation tower or platform in the field require more complex organization and rather skilled team-work. For amateur purposes this is likely to be an exceptional technique. But it does go to show that if you are prepared to abandon the idea that wildlife photography is a solitary, private, even secret activity–and if you have adequate financial resources!–the inexhaustible potentialities of modern technology are at your disposal.

Stalking the subject with a team of photographers in constant communication with one another by means of walkie-talkie radio greatly improves the chances of catching up with a particularly shy or wily animal. But there is perhaps something rather unfair about the procedure of encircling the animal and systematically closing in on it. Anyway, this too must be considered a technique to be employed only where exceptional circumstances warrant it.

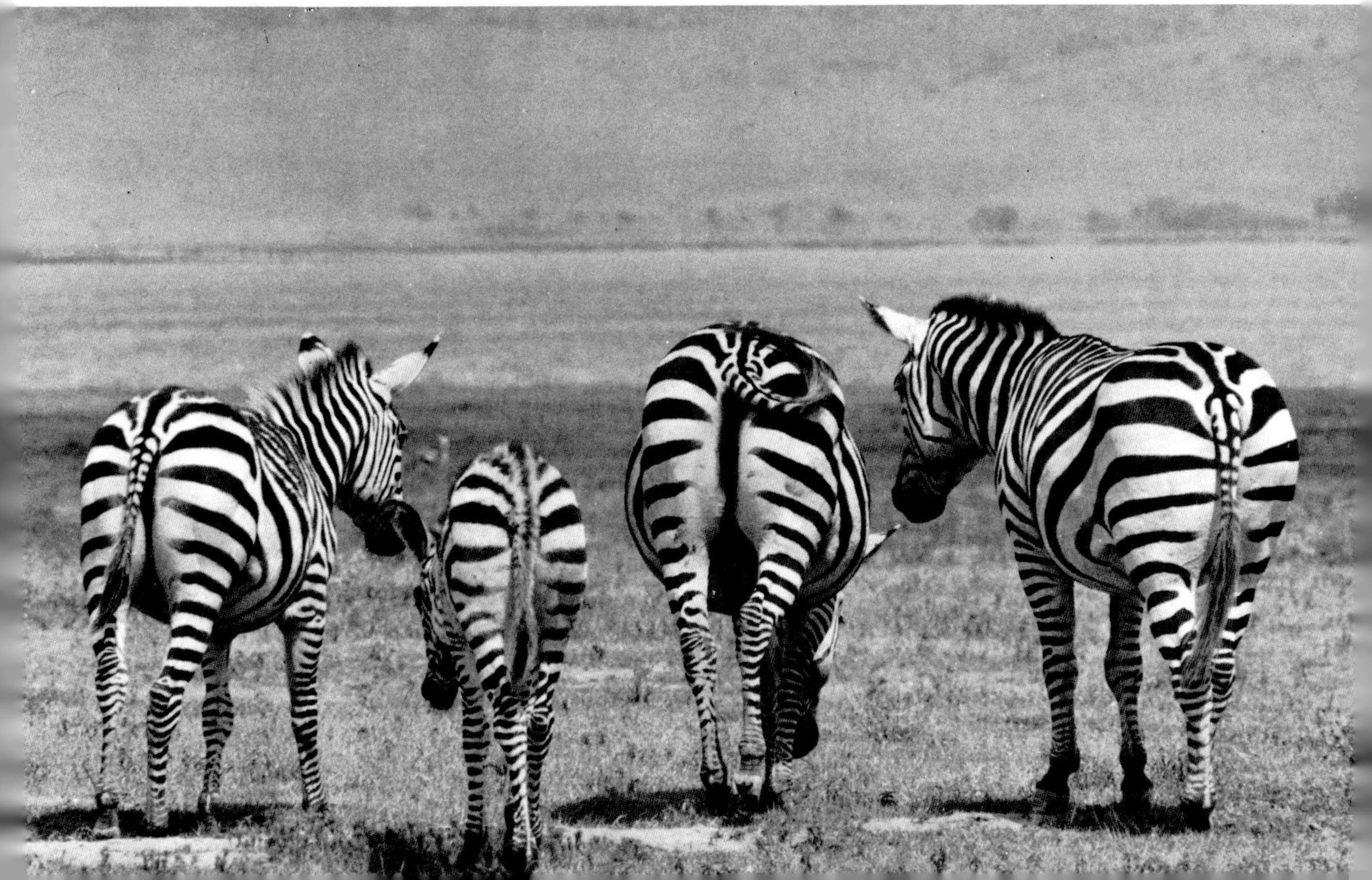

A herd of African elephants (*Loxodonta africana*) advances towards the photographer, led by the oldest member of the herd, with ears outspread as a gesture of intimidation. Stalking elephants in their natural environment calls for great skill and knowledge of their habits, for these animals, endowed with a very highly developed sense of smell, will scent an intruder a long way off unless he approaches from the downwind direction.

The lower photograph opposite shows two males engaged in combat.

Where aquatic creatures are concerned a more unobtrusive approach can be achieved in a boat propelled by an electric motor, whose gentle whirring, damped by the density of the water, is barely audible. The battery which powers the motor will have to be recharged after about two hours' service. When operating in regions where electricity from the public mains is not available, a generating set, driven by an internal combustion engine, will have to be taken along for charging the battery.

For scientific and documentary photography a specially-equipped motor vehicle may be used. This sort of conveyance, for professional rather than amateur use, has an observation opening in the roof, equipped with a mounting for a camera. Such vehicles are now extensively employed in the African nature reserves and wild animal parks where tourists are regularly taken on animal watching and photographing safaris. In a few hours' flying time you can be transported to entirely new surroundings and be confronted with animals living in complete freedom, scarcely taking any notice of the vehicle and its occupants – who are not allowed to get out, anyway.

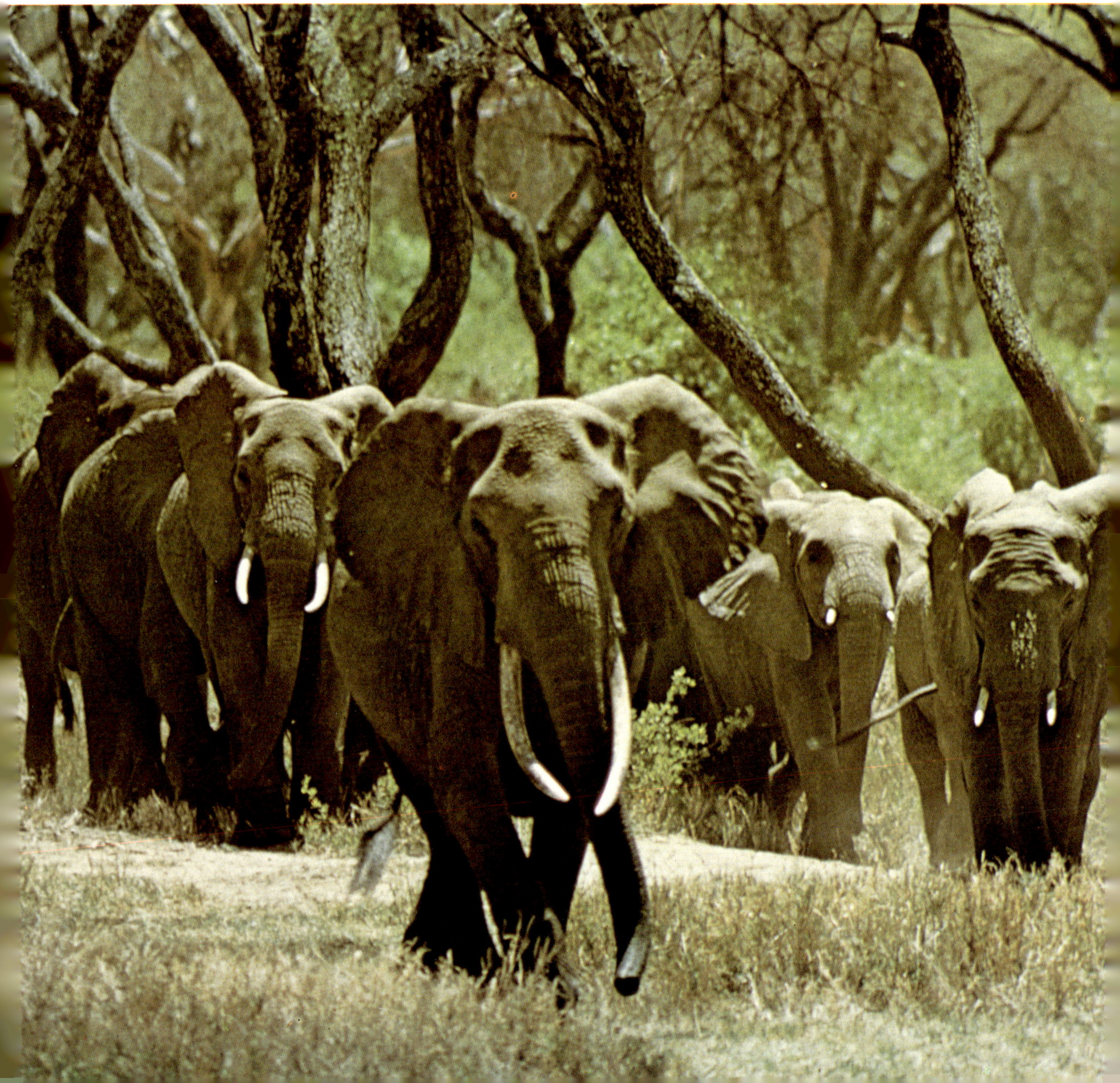

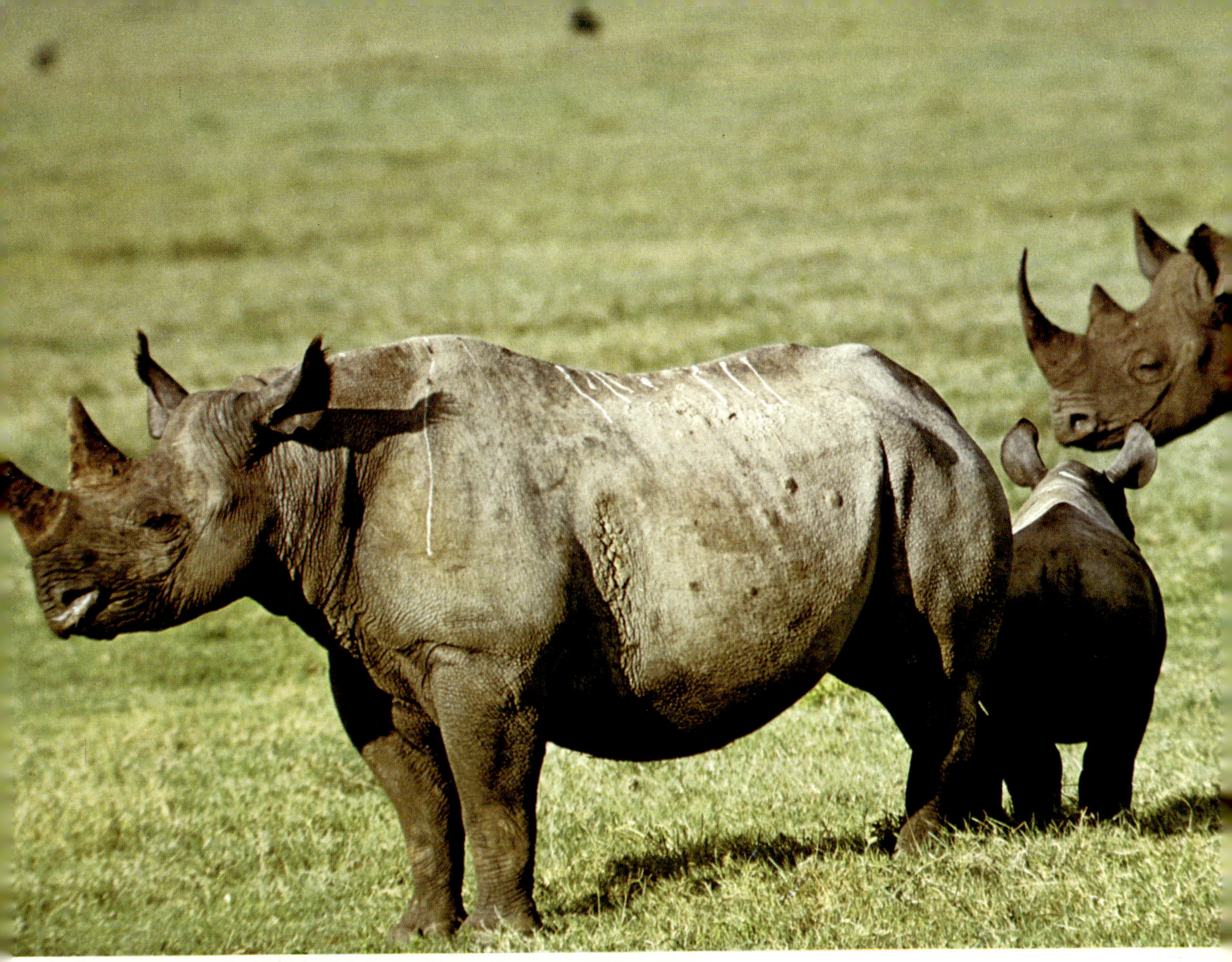

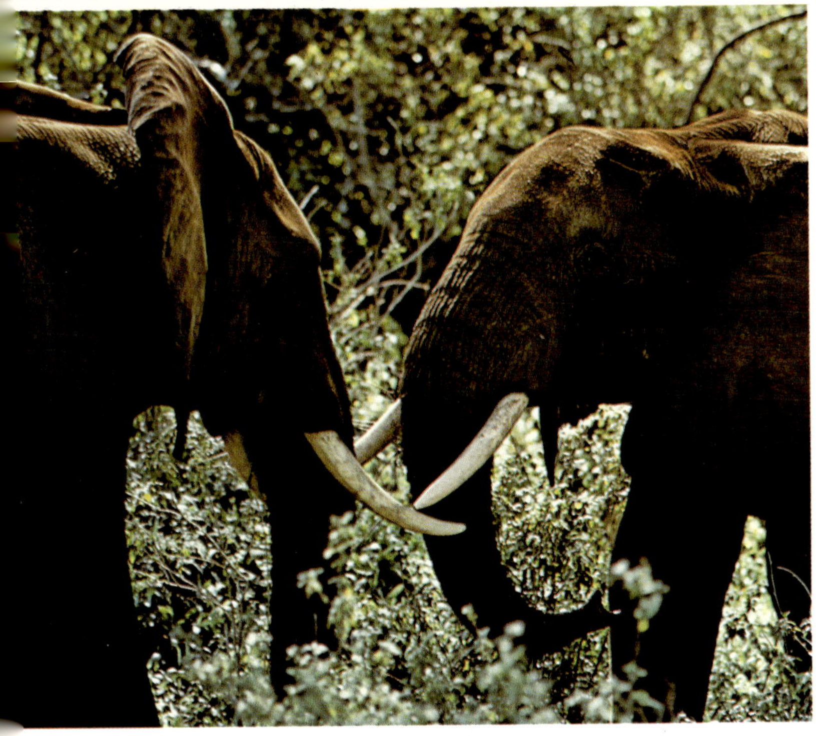

The black rhinoceros (*Diceros bicornis*) also has a very efficient sense of smell, but has poor eyesight. These irritable animals can be dangerous, especially in the case of a female accompanied by her young. The white streaks on the rhino's back are caused by the droppings of the ox-pecker birds (*Buphagus africanus*) which feed on parasites which they dig out of the crevices of the animal's hide.

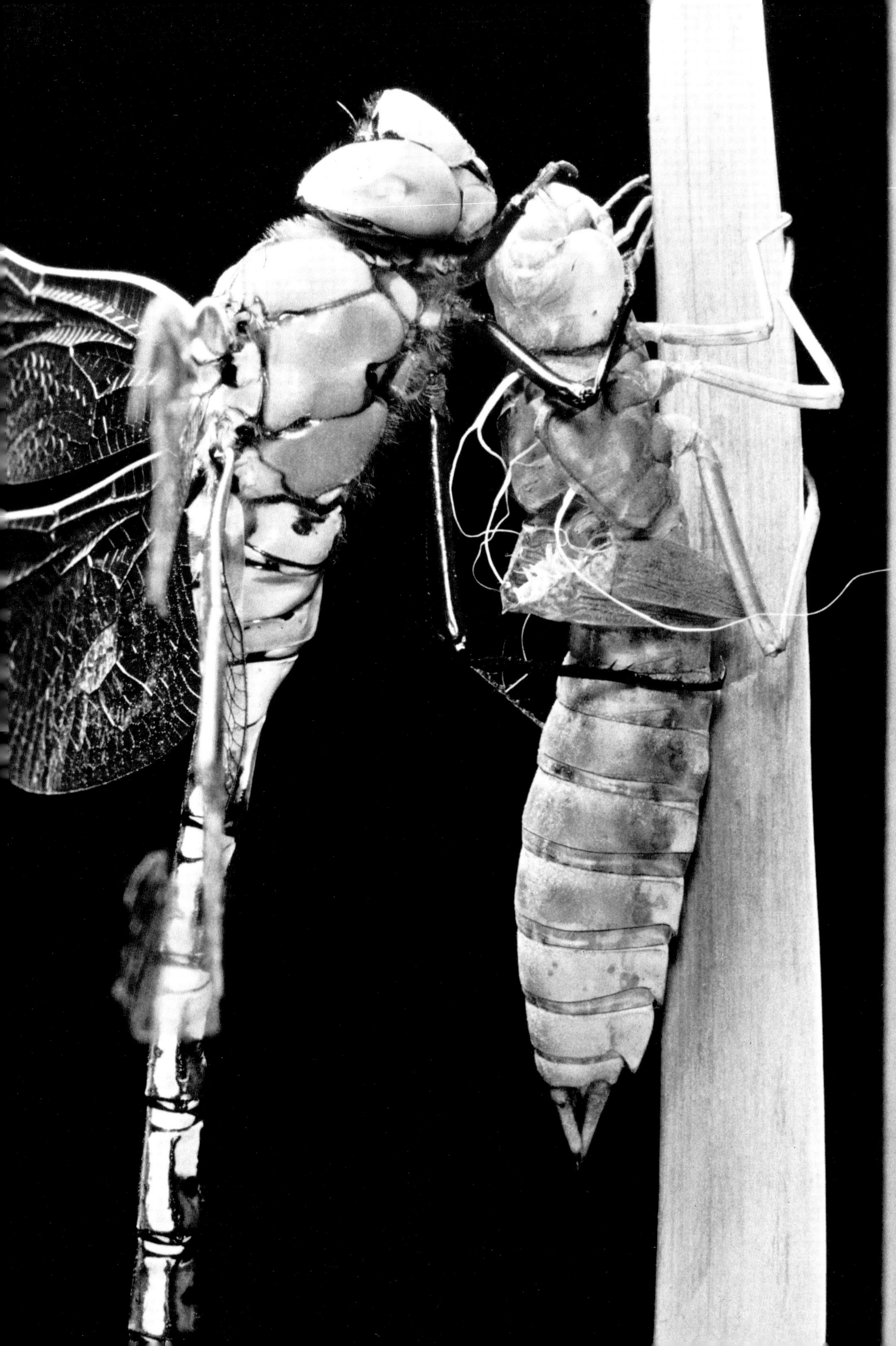

conclusion

Left: A dragonfly has just emerged from the fully-grown larva (nymph), which developed in the water of a pond or stream and finally climbed out of its accustomed habitat to undergo this transformation into its winged adult form. At first the newly-emerged dragonfly is a colourless creature with small crumpled-looking wings. But in a matter of hours the colours appear and the wings expand and harden. All stages of this final transformation can be observed and photographed.
Equipment: 6 cm × 6 cm reflex camera with lens of 80 mm focal length.

Below: This Madagascar spider spins magnificent rosette-shaped webs between big trees. Some species construct webs up to 7 feet in diameter, which are so strong that large and powerful insects and sometimes even small birds and bats are caught in them.
Equipment: 35 mm reflex camera, 135 mm focal length and extension adapter rings.

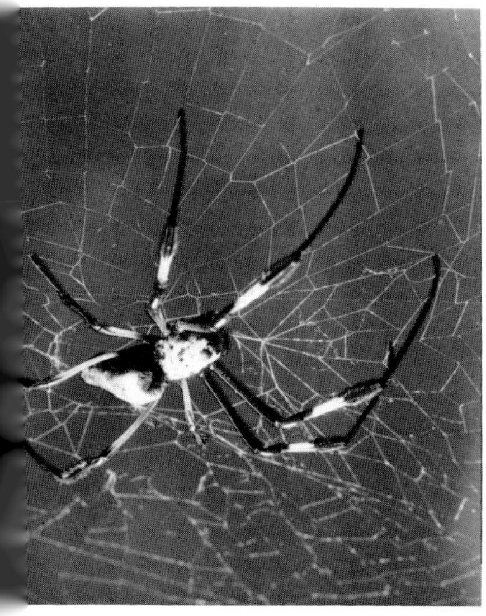

In our description of elementary principles and methods of wildlife photography we have intentionally confined ourselves to our experience in European countries. Farther afield, more particularly in Africa, the problems acquire quite a different order of magnitude. The distances to be covered, the climatic conditions, the size and population density of the animals, the vast territory in which they can freely roam—all these are factors which make so much heavier demands in terms of time and effort and involve the use of so much greater resources that it is seldom possible for the wildlife photographer to operate successfully alone and unassisted.

Although in recent years the setting up of a number of wildlife parks in which large wild animals roam about in a state of semi-freedom has made the 'photographic safari' something that can be enjoyed in miniature in one's own country; the 'real thing' still usually involves long journeys.

Before embarking on such an undertaking you should arm yourself with a substantial amount of solid information about the animal life, the terrain and the kinds of biotope you can expect to find. You must of course also provide yourself with the right photographic and other equipment and you should get to know about the habits and customs of the local population (their leisurely approach to life, the need to hand out financial inducements in the form of gratuities and gifts, etc.). And, last but not least, you should possess originality and inventiveness, for most of the subjects of which you will be going in pursuit have already been photographed many times before by tourists armed with expensive cameras and impressive telephoto lenses. To obtain results covering a sufficiently wide range of subjects, and of sustained interest, it is essential to operate in a team comprising a number of individuals, each with his own expertise or skill (photographers, zoologists, etc.).

In any geographical latitude the richness and abundance of animal or vegetable life will soon lead the nature photographer to concentrate on a particular species or type of subject best suited to satisfy his desire for closer observation of nature. The amateur prompted by healthy curiosity and interest based on a deliberate and free choice, but with only a limited amount of time to devote to his hobby, will select some well-defined field of specialization on which he will then concentrate in a precise and systematic manner.

There is certainly no lack of subjects. In Europe alone there are reckoned to be about 175 species of mammal, including, it is true, some very small creatures which are among the most difficult to observe in the wild state, such as mice, voles, dormice, etc.

So you must know the animals' habits and the kind of environment in which you are most likely to find them. You should also be able to detect and interpret the signs that can tell you whether a certain species lives in a particular place and whether there is any chance of getting sight of the animal at a particular time.

Broadly speaking, about 80 per cent of all wildlife photographers throughout the world are interested in birds. Is it because birds are so numerous and are relatively easy to observe against the background of the sky? Or is man's fascination of birds perhaps due to his age-old dream and desire to possess the power of flight and his admiration for creatures that can move about with such ease in this elusive element which it has taken his own species so long to conquer?

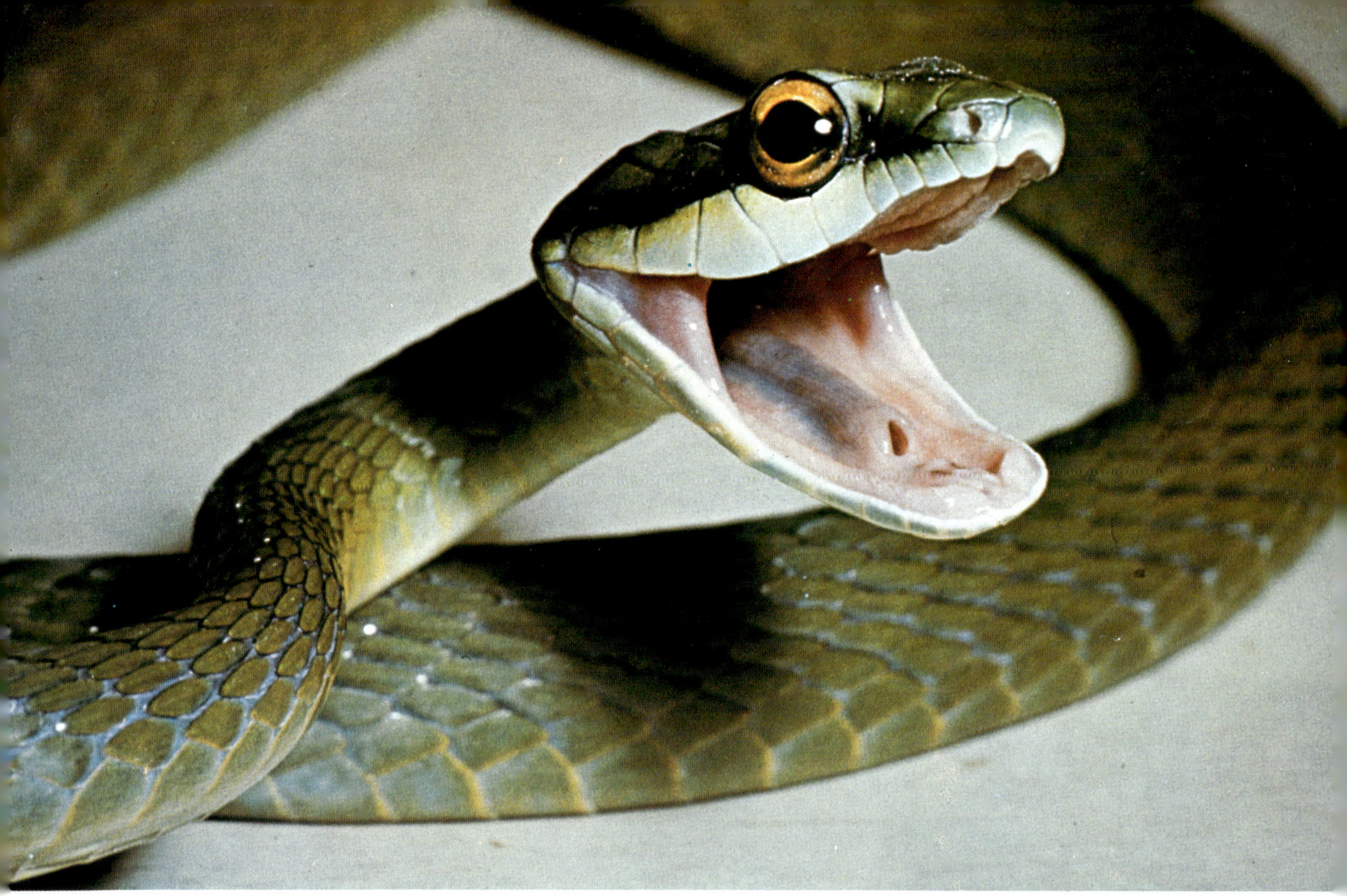

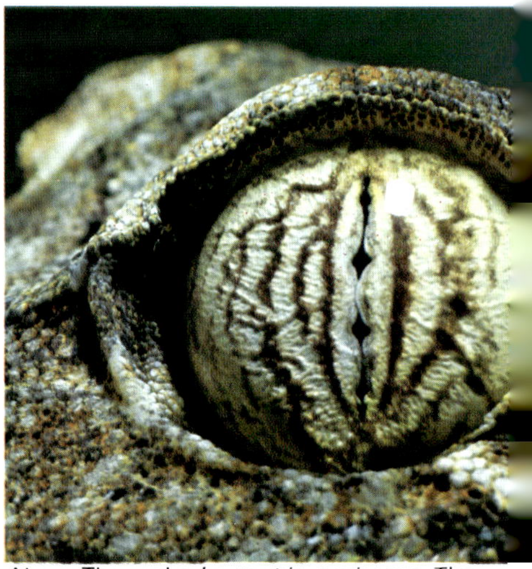

Throughout the world there are some 8000 species of bird. From spring until about midsummer the keen wildlife photographer will find innumerable opportunities for obtaining fine series of pictures of bird life. Through all stages of the reproductive cycle–the male displaying his plumage to the female, nest-building, brooding, the fledglings' first experiments in flying–each species provides endless new possibilities for observation and behaviour study.

But you should not forget the humbler creatures. Insects, in particular, with their staggering variety of forms and life patterns–there are estimated to be well over a million insect species throughout the world; some authorities put the figure much higher–and richness of colouring, provide ideal subjects for macrophotography.

And then there are the reptiles, including lizards and snakes, and the amphibians, notably the frogs, those cheerful creatures whose croaking often gives away their presence. The habits and behaviour of these groups of animals have not yet been exhaustively studied, and there is scope for original investigation.

The study and photography of fish and other marine creatures in their natural environment require rather sophisticated equipment, but are bound to attract and fascinate the properly trained skin-diving enthusiast.

All the year round, nature offers endless and ever-new opportunities for the naturalist and wildlife photographer, for whom the succession of the seasons will provide his most valuable guide.

In the pages of this book devoted to a peaceful hobby we have endeavoured, by means of comments, advice and impressions, some of them of an entirely personal kind, to point out to you the means of overcoming the technical barriers which often prevent the nature lover from making the right approach to his subject and also to inspire in you a desire not to stop at mere superficial curiosity about the creatures and things that share with us the world in which we live.

Above:The snake *Leptophis mexicanus*. The eyes of reptiles show considerable diversity of shape and appearance. The smaller photograph below is a close-up of the eye of a gecko (a species of lizard) whose pupil is reduced to a very thin slit.
Right: The eye of a chameleon (*Chamaeleo parsonii*). The eye is highly mobile and functions independently of the other eye. Thus the chameleon can, without moving its body, observe everything that is going on around it by swivelling its eyes in all directions.
Equipment: Hasselblad, 80 mm focal length.

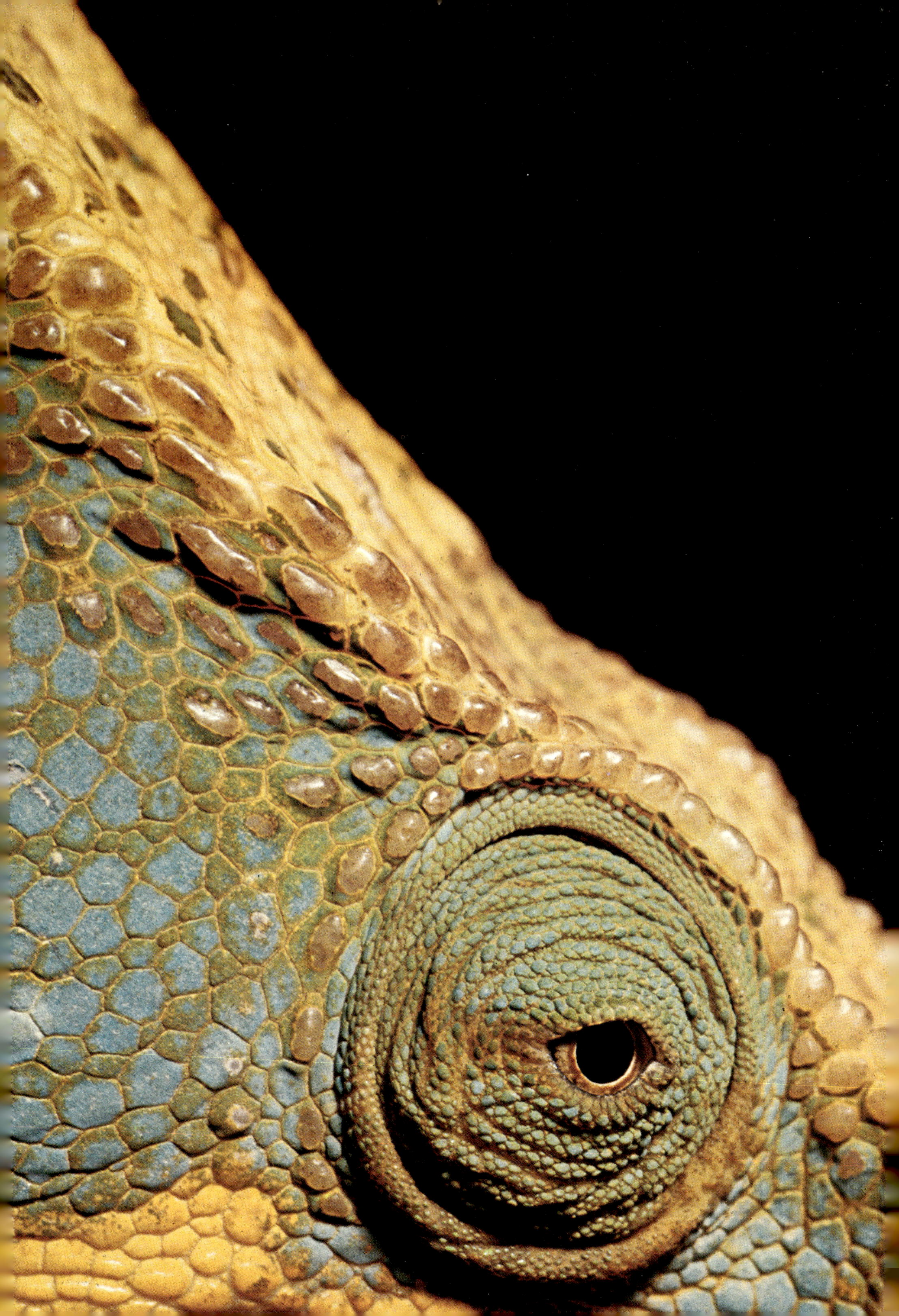

glossary

Bracken.

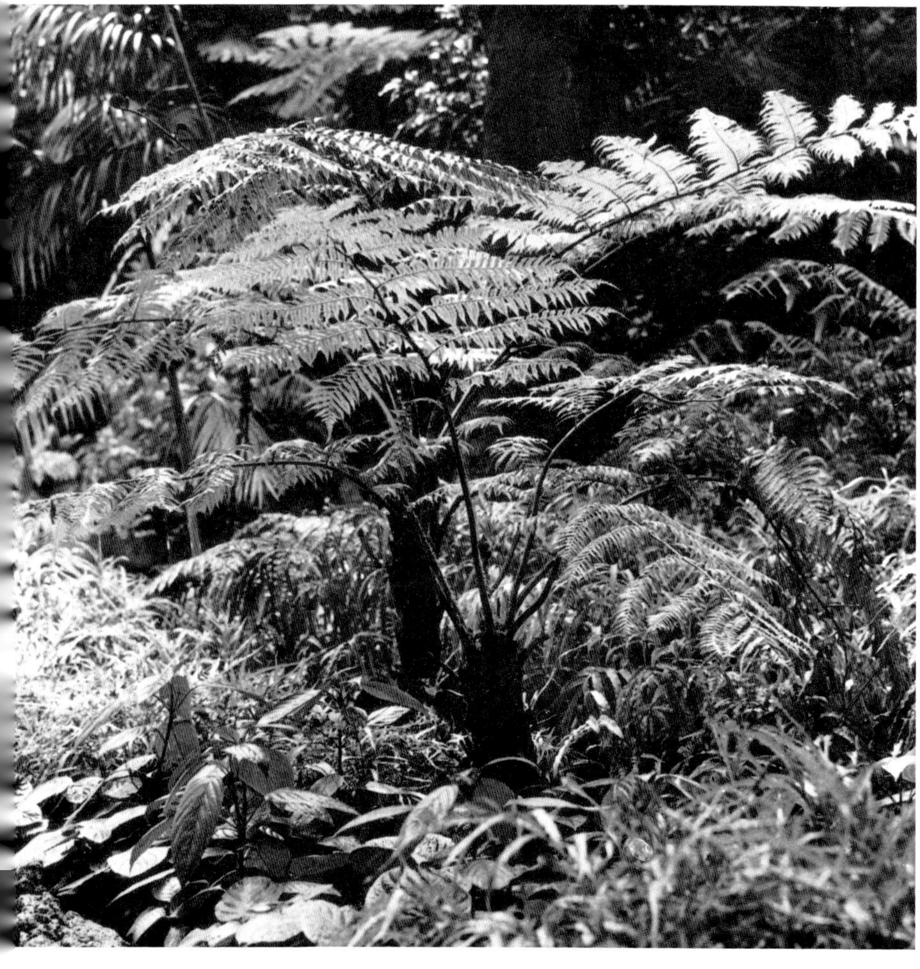

Anastigmat: A lens corrected for optical defects including astigmatism.

Angular field: The angle subtended at the lens by the largest object that the lens can image on the film.

Aperture: The term 'aperture' (more specifically: relative aperture) is synonymous with f-number.

Apochromat: A lens which has been corrected for the three primary spectral colours, as opposed to an achromatic lens which has been corrected for two colours only.

Astigmatism: An optical aberration which makes a lens reproduce a point light source as two lines at right angles in different focal planes.

Biotope: The whole set of distinctive factors that make up an animal's environment: other organisms, vegetation, soil, climate, etc.

Blimp: Sound-proof housing for a camera.

Bloomed lens: See 'Coated lens'.

Circle of confusion: A circle or disc of a diameter smaller than 0·01 inch appears as a point to the average human eye when viewed from a distance of 10 inches; it serves as a standard of sharpness in photography.

Coated lens: Coating or blooming is a thin film of a suitable metallic fluoride deposit on the lens surfaces to reduce the amount of light lost by reflection.

Colour sensitivity: The relative response of a photographic emulsion to light of different colours.

Colour temperature: The temperature (expressed in kelvins) to which a black body would have to be heated to emit light of the same colour as the light source in question.

Definition: The ability of a lens or of a photographic emulsion to resolve distinct lines. See 'Resolving power'.

Depth of field: The range, extending in front of and behind the focused distance, within which objects produce an image of acceptable sharpness on the film.

Diaphragm: Essentially any plate with a hole admitting light to the lens of a camera. In its simplest form the adjustable diaphragm (or adjustable stop) consists of a plate with holes of different sizes which can be moved into position in front of the lens. In the iris diaphragm the hole is formed by a set of thin metal blades which can open out or close to make the hole larger or smaller.

Diaphragm shutter: This type of shutter comprises a ring of interleaved thin metal blades which are pivoted at their outer edges, enabling them momentarily to open outwards. Diaphragm shutters usually have speed ranges from 1 to 1/500 second.

Ecology: The scientific study of the relationships between animals—or more particularly groups of animals forming biological communities—and their environment.

Electronic flash: The flash is produced by an instantaneous electric discharge in a gas-filled tube. The electric energy is stored in a capacitor (condenser), which is charged by the power supply. The tube can be used many times.

Emulsion: A photographic emulsion is the light-sensitive coating on a film: conventionally a suspension of fine particles of silver bromide in gelatin.

Ethology: The scientific study of the behaviour of animals in their natural environment.

Exposure: The combination of shutter speed and lens aperture to produce a satisfactory negative.

Exposure meter: An instrument which measures light intensity and indicates the correct exposure settings for a camera. Modern meters are mostly of the photo-electric type incorporating a barrier layer (which generates a small electric current when light falls on it) or a photo-resistor cell (which changes its resistance to an electric current flowing through it when light falls on the cell).

Extension bellows: Attachment for cameras with interchangeable lens, which provides a varying degree of lens extension (distance between lens and film) for close-up and macrophotography.

Extension tube: A tube of specific length to which the camera lens can be screwed and which is fitted to the front of the camera to increase the distance between lens and film for close-up and macrophotography.

Flash: See 'Flash bulb' and 'Electronic flash'.

Flash bulb: A source of artificial light generated by the rapid combustion of certain metals in oxygen inside a glass bulb, which is fired electrically and can be used once only.

Focal length: The distance from the plane in which a lens forms an image of objects at infinity to the centre of the lens.

Focal plane shutter: This type of shutter generally operates on the 'roller blind' principle and comprises a variable slit which moves across the surface of the film. The shutter is mounted as close as possible to the film, i.e. to the focal plane.

Format: The size of the negative taken by a camera.

f-number: The f-number denotes the relative aperture of a lens at a particular stop; it is equal to the length divided by the effective diameter of the lens (see 'Stop').

Frame: A single exposure on a cine film or a 35 mm film in still photography.

Grain: The negative image consists of black metallic silver (formed from the original exposed silver bromide particles) which is present in the form of finer or coarser clumps which present a more-or-less 'grainy' appearance when viewed under a microscope; the graininess can be an objectionable feature when the negative is enlarged.

Habitat: A place with a particular kind of environment inhabited by an animal, e.g. a rocky sea-shore.

Hide: A shelter of any kind in which wildlife observers or photographers wait in concealment at some strategic point to obtain a reasonably close-range view of a shy bird or animal.

Hyperfocal distance: The distance from the camera to the 'near limit' of the depth of field when the lens is focused on infinity. If the lens is focused on the hyperfocal distance, the depth of field extends from half this distance to infinity.

Illumination: The distribution of light over the subject being photographed and over the surface of the film.

Iris diaphragm: See 'Diaphragm'.

Macrophotography: The technique of taking life-size or larger-than-life photographs by increasing the camera extension and/or using supplementary lenses, but not producing pictures of such high magnification as those obtained by photomicrography.

Meniscus lens: A simple lens consisting of a single disc of glass, thicker at its centre than at its edges, with one concave and one convex face.

Miniature camera (35 mm camera): A camera using perforated 35 mm cine film for still photography; the size of the negative is normally 24 mm × 36 mm; in the so-called half-frame camera the size is 18 mm × 24 mm.

Mirror lens: An image-forming system using curved mirrors instead of transparent glass lenses.

Nanometre: One millionth of a millimetre (1×10^{-9} metre); the unit of length used for the wavelength of light.

Narrow-gauge cine film: Any film of smaller width than the standard 35 mm motion picture film. The most extensively used narrow gauges are 8 mm and 16 mm.

Negative colour film: A negative image is produced on the film for making prints on colour printing paper.

Photomicrography: Photography of very small objects through a microscope. Not to be confused with microphotography, which is the technique of making microscopically small photographs of objects by optical reduction.

Reflex camera: In the single-lens reflex camera the subject is viewed and focused on a ground-glass screen on which the image is formed by the taking lens of the camera. The twin-lens reflex camera has two lenses mounted one above the other, the upper lens being used for viewing the subject, the lower for taking the photograph.

Resolving power: The ability to reproduce fine detail. The resolving power (or resolution) of a lens is a measure of its ability to form distinct images of closed spaced lines. In the case of a photographic emulsion the resolving power depends on graininess, contrast and other factors.

Reversal colour film: With this type of film a positive image is produced directly; it is used for colour slides (transparencies) and amateur cinematography.

Shutter: See 'Diaphragm shutter' and 'Focal plane shutter'.

Speed: The speed of a sensitized material denotes its sensitivity to light. The three most widely employed speed systems are the ASA (American National Standards Institution, previously called American Standards Association); B.S. (British Standards Institution); and DIN ('Deutsche Industrie Norm' of the German Standards Organization).

Stop: Diaphragm settings are referred to as 'stops', each of which corresponds to a certain f-number. See 'Diaphragm' and 'f-number'.

Telephoto lens: This type of lens, actually comprising two groups of lenses (one converging, the other diverging), produces a larger image than a normal-focus lens without using more than the normal camera extension; it is shorter and more compact than an equivalent long-focus lens.

Triplet lens: A lens comprising three air-spaced elements, i.e. three single glasses mounted together to form an assembly.

Variable-focus lens: See 'Zoom lens'.

Viewfinder: A device which shows the photographer how much of the subject will be included in the picture, enabling him to compose his picture. Viewfinders range from a simple wire frame to the precision focusing screen in a reflex camera.

Wide-angle lens: Any lens which covers, across the diagonal of the negative, an angular field of view of 60 degrees or more.

Zoom lens (variable-focus lens): With this type of lens the focal length can be adjusted continuously by the movement of one or more groups of elements in the lens system. Originally developed for cine cameras and television cameras.

animals in dan

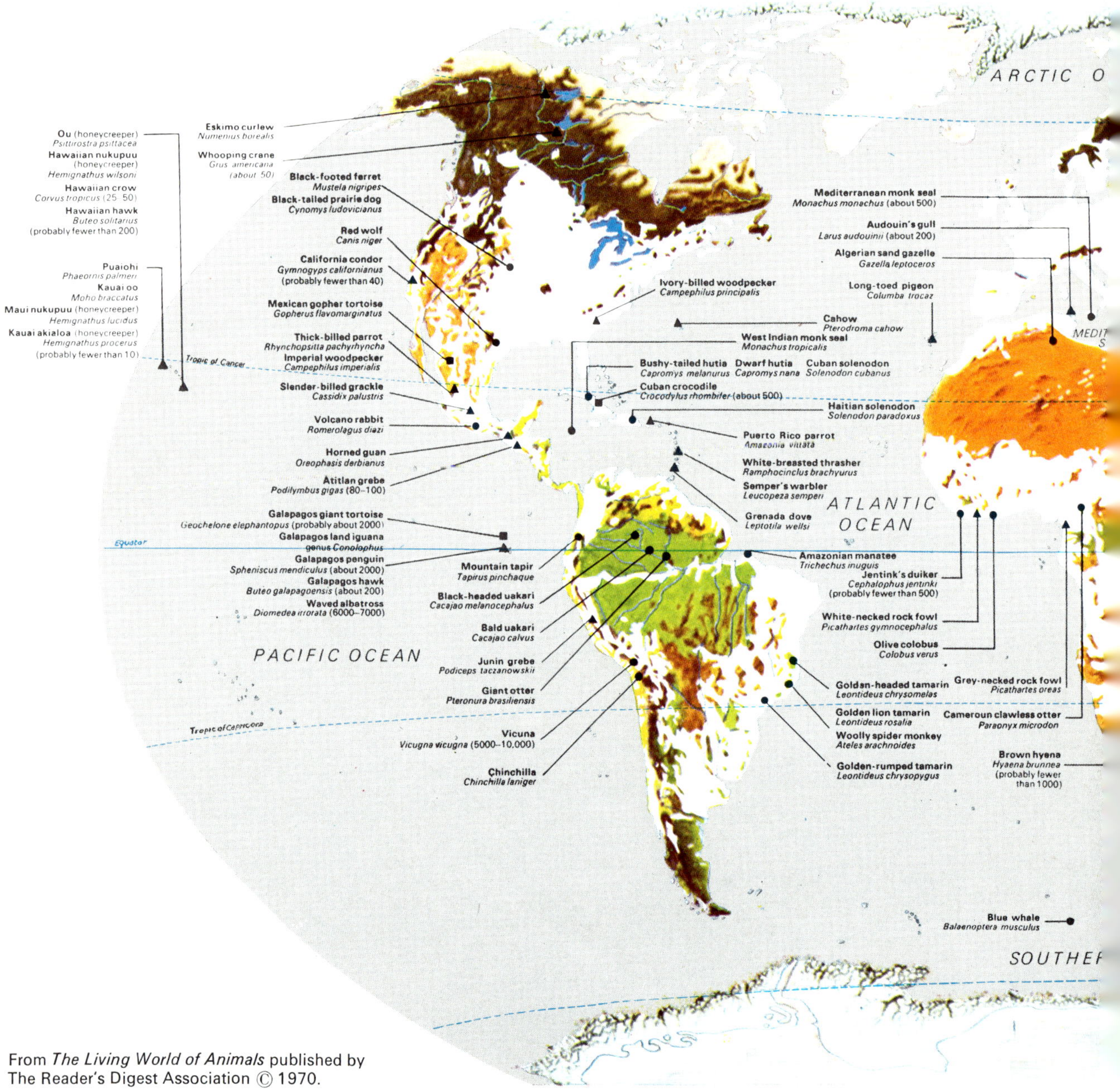

er of extinction

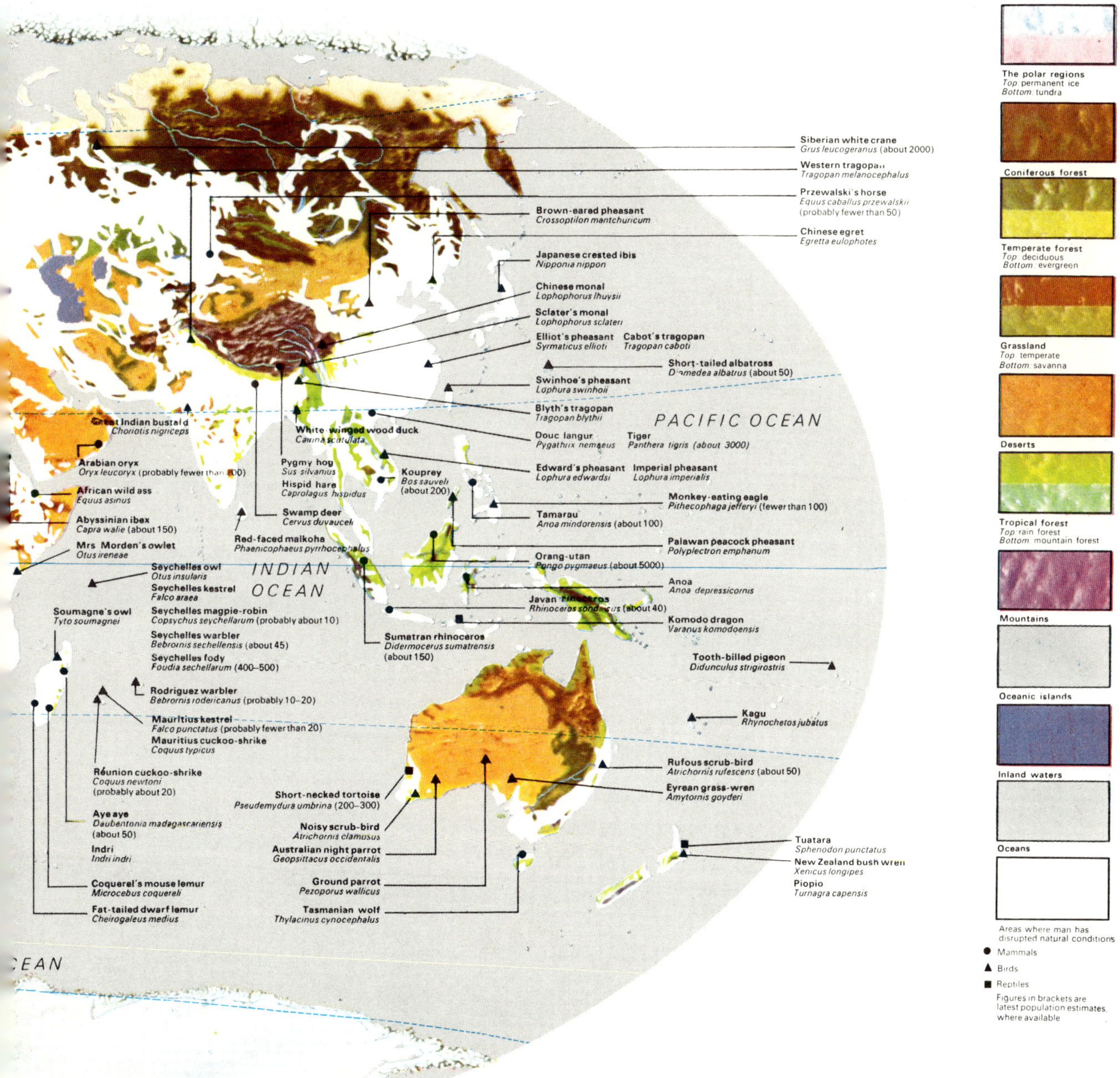

the world's parks and reserves

Introduction

As the wild and natural areas of the world continue to shrink and animals, birds and flowers disappear, much of the effort to save them is concentrated in the formation of national parks where all species and their habitats can be protected efficiently. Provision can be made for people to make scientific studies of them or merely to watch and photograph them. Many developing countries are becoming aware of the enormous advantages of creating safe and wild areas for people to observe and photograph their unique and beautiful wildlife.

It is extremely difficult to give more than a faint idea of the variety and profusion of the world's wild creatures to be seen in what is now an ever-growing network of parks and reserves throughout the world, but it is hoped that the following introduction to a few of them will encourage photographers to visit these places, whether it is to photograph Exmoor ponies in Britain or flamingoes in the south of France.

National parks have a widely varying status throughout the world. To some, access is free and unrestricted with nature trails, caravan sites or cabins. Others are areas of important scientific research, which are closed to the public or can be entered only with either an escort or a permit. Some parks—like the largest in the world, the Wood Buffalo National Park in Canada—extend for thousands of miles, while others consist of a few, but significant, acres.

A list of books which will give photographers an excellent and detailed account of what they can expect to see in the world's parks and reserves can be found on page 157.

Great Britain and Europe

The ten national parks in Great Britain are extremely accessible wild places for any visitor. If you have the stamina, you can roam the rolling heathlands of Exmoor and Dartmoor, keeping an eye open for the majestic red deer, otters and seals on the coast of the **Exmoor Park.** The **Peak District Park** is an area of open but sometimes precipitous fell country, while in the **Lake District** wooded hills alternate with areas of open water. Here you will see species like the roe deer, the pine marten, whooper swan, great northern diver and many kinds of duck. The **New Forest** in Hampshire, although not a national park, is an attractive area of natural woodland where badgers, squirrels, foxes and other animals live. It is one of the few nesting areas of the beautiful little falcon the hobby. You can also see the famous New Forest ponies. Ponies are an attractive feature of the **Snowdonia National Park** in Wales where you can also find mountain hares and wild goats living on the hillsides. The **Pembrokeshire Coast Park** juts out into the Atlantic and has much attractive wild, sea and cliff scenery. There are twenty-two national nature reserves, some of which you need a permit to visit. These include **Scolt Head,** Norfolk, an area of saltings with fluctuating and large colonies of terns, brent geese and wading birds. **St Kilda** is another NNR off the coast of Scotland which has some unique native species like the St Kilda wren and the Soay sheep. It also has the world's largest colony of gannets. Another island is **Rhum,** again off the Scottish coast, on which grow many rare plants and where red deer, grey seals and the spectacular golden eagle live. For an immense and beautiful variety of accessible birds, especially geese, swans and ducks, visit the Wildfowl Trust at **Slimbridge** in Gloucestershire, owned by Peter Scott.

Many reserves are owned by societies such as the Society for the Promotion of Nature Reserves and the Royal Society for the Protection of Birds; for these, entry is usually by permit only. Among them are the **Ouse Washes** in Norfolk, where there are many species of warblers, waders and wildfowl; and **Minsmere**, a reserve on the Norfolk coast, where avocets can be seen with their young at close quarters, as well as marsh harriers, bitterns and nightingales.

Foreseeing the land problems facing highly industrialized countries, those in Europe began establishing national parks and reserves soon after the turn of this century. Scandinavian countries, experiencing perhaps the least pressure, began establishing parks such as **Padjelanta** in Lapland Sweden. Here are valleys, lakes and glaciers, providing a home for the wolverine, arctic fox, brown bear and golden eagle, amongst many others. The **Linnansaari National Park** in Finland is a group of islands in the glacial Lake Saimaa, where ravines, often covered with forest, provide a sanctuary for red squirrels, blue hares and elks. The rare ringed seal breeds here and ospreys fish from the lake.

At the extreme south-west corner of Europe can be found a totally different environment. The Coto Doñana in Spain, an area of sand dunes and warm shallow lakes, lies near the mouth of the broad Guadalquivir river. Recently, with assistance from the World Wildlife Fund, the **Doñana National Park** was established. An unbelievable variety of species exists here, amongst them the rare Spanish lynx, wild boar and the Spanish imperial eagle. Flamingoes, herons, egrets, nightingales and eight species of lark are just some of the birds to be seen. Half the bird species in Europe visit the Coto Doñana during the year. A permit is necessary for humans!

An equally valuable wetland area lies in the mouth of the Rhône in southern France. **La Camargue,** with its warm lagoons and marshes, has, with the help of the World Wildlife Fund, become a national park. Although you need a permit to visit the central area, flamingoes, marsh and montague harriers, terns, avocets and many wader and wildfowl species can be seen and photographed by anyone walking through the tracks threading between the sea, the rushes and tamarisk shrubs. The semi-wild pale-grey horses and black bulls are always present wading through the shallow waters of the delta. Rare plants and the nimble chamois and ibex can be seen on the peaks and near the lakes of the **Vanoise National Park** in France which joins the **Gran Paradiso Park** of Italy. In the **Chambord National Reserve** are found red and roe deer and wild boar, as well as many species of waterfowl. Geese and cranes can be seen here on migration.

One of the most important parks in Italy is the **Abruzzi** in central Italy, a vast area of dramatic scenery formed by forests and valleys. Here can be found the brown bear and chamois, wolf, fox and wild cat and many species of rare birds. Situated on the sea is the **Circeo National Park** where wild boar, fox, pine and stone martens and fallow deer can be found.

The **Dümmer** reserve in Germany lies on a lake surrounded by reed beds in which breed tufted duck and red-crested pochard. The bittern, ruff, curlew and whimbrel also breed in this important area. Austria's **Neusiedlersee** and **Seewinkel** reserves boast a great variety of breeding birds. It is one of the best areas for seeing birds of prey in central Europe. The white-tailed and the imperial eagle are amongst those that inhabit the lakes. The grassy flats are a main wintering ground for grey geese. Ducks, waders, spoonbills and herons are also found here. On the border between Austria and Czechoslovakia is the **Marchauen** reserve. Here are nearly 3,000 acres of beautiful river forest landscape where creatures like the red and roe deer, wild boar, otter, pine and beech martens can be found. Different species of owls, woodpeckers, herons, pheasants, nightingales and birds of prey are also in abundance, as well as many beautiful and interesting kinds of flowers, shrubs and trees.

In the 14,000-acre **Hoge Veluwe** reserve in Holland you can see deer, mouflon and game birds living amongst the juniper, birch and oak trees or on the open wild heath.

The United States and Canada

Wisely, no attempt has ever been made to catalogue the hundreds of national parks, nature reserves and wildlife refuges in the United States and Canada. The world's first national park, **Yellowstone,** was established in 1872. Its creation reflected the quick reaction of Americans to the impact they themselves had made on the prairies and mountains of the north American continent. Some species were to become extinct and others, like the American bison, were being slain in thousands. Wild areas would no longer remain intact unless protected.

Stretching from the snows and lakes of Alaska to the volcanoes and tropical jungle of Hawaii, the parks extend throughout north America, although a concentration in what were once the emptiest and most dramatic areas is noticeable. Most of the protected wild areas of the United States and Canada are accessible and can be enjoyed by car, camping, canoe, horse-back or simply by walking.

Most of the species with which Canada is identified can be found in the **Wood Buffalo National Park,** probably the largest recognized park in the world. It stretches for 17,000 square miles between Lake Athabasca and the Great Slave Lake. It is a wild area of lakes and bogs, forests and grasslands. The largest buffalo herd in the continent is found here, 15,000 of them. Moose, elk, deer, and caribou can be found; black and grizzly bears too. Many smaller species enjoy a wilderness untouched by man, amongst them lynx and wolverine and the wolf, porcupines and squirrels. Canada, snow and white-fronted geese and many species of duck are found in the marshy areas.

Banff and **Glacier** national parks lie on the eastern side of the Rockies, and boast spectacular scenery, a great variety of wildlife and some conventional holiday attractions such as skiing and riding. Lakes, mountains, forests and canyons are accessible to all, as is the excellent opportunity of seeing elk, moose, mountain caribou, bears, beavers and white-tailed deer. One hundred and eighty species of birds can be found in **Banff,** Canada's oldest national park, and the total can be rivalled in **Glacier** where birds of prey, such as the golden eagle, as well as many song birds, are found.

Fundy National Park lies on the northern shore of the Bay of Fundy, New Brunswick, and has a spectacular coastline. Although it is a holiday resort as well as a wildlife area, there is no shortage of bears, moose, deer and beaver, raccoon and lynx or many other smaller mammals. Egrets, herons, sandpipers, loons and wild fowl are seen here. Maple trees, as well as beech, birch and poplar, ensure a brilliant autumn for visitors at this time of the year.

It is difficult not to introduce the parks of the United States with **Yosemite Park,** Wyoming, probably the most famous in north America. However, it is mainly the scenery that is the attraction here, although wildlife is plentiful. Tumbling waterfalls, hot springs, forests and mountain peaks are the most dramatic and photogenic assets of the park. Chipmunks, flying squirrels and golden-mantled ground squirrels provide lively attractions. The bald eagle, America's national emblem, may be sighted, as well as the rare fishing eagle, the osprey.

The **Haleakala National Park,** Hawaii, lies in the crater of a volcano. Rocks are coloured black, grey, yellow and red and many species of birds native to Hawaii can be found. Amongst them are the delicate iiwi, the apapane and amakihi and the very rare nene (Hawaiian goose).

The north-west state, Washington, contains mountains, glaciers, lakes and streams and almost semi-desert conditions in the **Olympic National Park.** Six thousand Olympic elk, as well as black bear, white-tailed deer and Olympic marmot, are readily seen. Well over a hundred species of birds, and innumerable wild flowers, fill the park in summer.

Wild flowers and trees are a major attraction in the **Glacier National Park,** Montana, which ranges from 3,000 to over 10,000 feet above sea level. However, the park also boasts over 200 species of birds as well as mountain goats, bears, hares, moose, martens, otters and lemmings, which live amongst the snows and mountain peaks.

The **Aransas National Wildlife Refuge,** Texas, is an area of tidal flats and bays hardly rising above sea level. This is the main wintering ground of the whooping cranes, which can be viewed through telescopes. Ibises, egrets, the rare sandhill crane and roseate spoonbill are some of the 300 kinds of birds seen here. White-tailed deer and armadillos are found and the American alligator lurks in the marshes.

The **Laguna Atascosa National Wildlife Refuge** is an area along the central flyway and therefore also well endowed with bird species such as Canada and snow geese, white-tailed hawk and white-tailed kite, doves and many kinds of wild-fowl. Cottontails, skunks and opossums are just a few of the animals living amongst the deserts and marshes of this Texas refuge.

The **Everglades** of Florida, the famous area of swamp, marshes and tropical forest, is a unique sub-tropical region. Mangrove, mahogany and sawgrass form a habitat for the saltwater crocodile, manatee, otter and opossum. The wood ibis, America's only stork, nests here, as does the very rare swallow-tail kite, bald eagle and snake bird. White and blue herons and the roseate spoonbill are often seen.

Mists floating above the dense forests of the **Great Smoky Mountains National Park** have given the park its name. Some of the highest points of the Appalachian Mountains form part of this virgin wilderness. Here you will find hundreds of wild flowers, fungi, mosses and lichens as well as a bewildering variety of trees and shrubs, amongst them silverbell, white ash, sugar maple, black cherry, cucumber trees and magnolia. Flying squirrels, mink and white-tailed deer can be seen as well as about 200 different kinds of birds.

Many miles of South Carolina's Atlantic coastline have become the **Cape Romain National Wildlife Refuge.** Islands, marshes and sandy beaches provide nesting and feeding grounds for thousands of water fowl and songbirds. Birds of prey, amongst them the bald eagle and peregrine falcon, inhabit the area, together with alligators, otters, turtles, wild turkeys, geese and innumerable waders such as the dunlin, turnstone, knot and marbled godwit.

Natural lakes connected by the White River of Arkansas form a valuable flooded plain in winter and spring for thousands of waterfowl. The **White River National Wildlife Refuge** is an area of cypress, gum, sycamore, maple, bitter and sweet pecan trees. Black bear, swamp rabbit and white-tailed deer are some of the mammals found here, and wood and white ibises, white pelican and wild turkey are only a few of the birds you might expect to see.

Only thirty-five miles from New York can be found the **Great Swamp National Wildlife Refuge** of New Jersey. Migrating geese and ducks find a resting and feeding place here where rhododendrons, cattail marsh, and laurel and oak trees form an attractive habitat also enjoyed by deer, red and grey foxes and striped skunks.

The **Montezuma National Wildlife Refuge,** New York, is another important wild fowl area on the Atlantic flyway. Canada geese, herons, terns, and wood, black and ruddy ducks, are a few of the species that take advantage of this 'stop-over' on their long migratory journeys. Wild millet, wild celery and specially-planted winter wheat, rye and millet provide much needed food for the many birds.

Africa

The wild animals of Africa are as familiar to us as our native species. People know as much or even more about lions, leopards, giraffes and rhinos as they do about the badger, stoat or otter. One of the reasons is that parks, without geographical barriers, have been established on a large and accessible scale, particularly in east Africa. Having arrived by air, a visitor can be at a reserve in less than two hours. It has been easier to establish national parks in the eastern and southern grasslands. The governments in central, north and west African countries have not made the same progress. Forest, mountain and wetland habitats and their many interesting species are less adequately represented in the national park network than the savannah grasslands.

Nairobi has a national park only 5 miles from its centre. Although it covers at present only 44 square miles, it is being enlarged. Lion, leopard, rhino and many species of antelope live amongst the trees and on the plains. Storks, ostriches and bustards are some of the more spectacular birds to be seen.

Lake Nakuru National Park is famous mainly for the thousands of greater and lesser flamingoes that move in rosy clouds over the blue sodium lakes. Over 400 other species are found on or near Lake Nakuru.

The **Masai Mara Reserve** is continuous with the **Serengeti Park** of Tanzania and lies to the south-east of Lake Victoria. It has the largest number of lions found in Kenya and the only herd of roan antelope in a Kenyan park. Thomson's and Grant's gazelles abound, as do leopards, cheetahs, Burchell's zebras, eland and gnus.

The **Tsavo National Park** is one of the largest in the world and lies in the eastern foothills of Mount Kilimanjaro. The area is mainly open grassland, dotted with acacia trees. It is the best place in Kenya for seeing elephant; the delicate gerenuk, the fringe-eared oryx and monkeys are further examples of the species with which the park is richly endowed.

A combination of lakes, volcanic craters and mountains attracts visitors to **Arusha National Park,** Tanzania. You can also see bushbuck, waterbuck, reedbuck, lions, eland and buffalo. Baboons, colobus and vervet monkeys are other attractive species to be found here.

The **Ngorongoro Conservation Area** lies in another crater, the floor of which is thick with game. Black rhinos, elephants, zebras, cheetahs and hunting dogs can be seen near the lake in the centre or in the bush surrounding it. Verreaux's eagle and the steppe and tawny eagle sail round the rim of the crater. Klipspringer, dikdik and impala also live in the grasslands of the crater.

Serengeti National Park is famous not only for its huge concentrations of wildebeest, which undertake their famous migration in early summer, but also the black-maned lion. About 180,000 zebras and half a million Thomson's and Grant's gazelles roam the park.

The **Murchison Falls Park** in Uganda has been given a reprieve—a dam stemming the magnificent falls will now not be built. One can go to the foot of the falls by launch and see a great deal of wildlife on the way—elephants, giraffes, hippos, lions or crocodiles (one of the biggest concentrations in Africa). Chimpanzees and baboons can be seen as well as black and white rhino.

Visitors might have to work rather harder to see animals in the **Lengwe National Park,** Malawi, as much of the park is covered with dense scrub which hides the shy and beautiful nyala antelope. They will also see the larger kudu, hartebeest, bushbuck and duiker. Bee-eaters, sunbirds, ibises and bustards are a few of the birds native to the park.

The **Luangwa Valley National Park,** Zambia, is one of the few places where you can go on a walking camera safari through mountains and across open plains to photograph animals coming to drink at the many lakes and pools of the Luangwa river. Thornicroft's giraffe is a creature unique to the valley and the largest number of black rhinos in Zambia is found here.

The **Gorongoza National Park,** Mozambique, teems with a wide variety of exciting wild animals and birds. The park offers many different types of habitat to species. Thousands of elephant, buffalo, impala, nyala and lion leopard make good use of the waterholes, palm jungle and open grassland. Hippos and crocodiles lie submerged (but not always!) in the pools and baboons scamper amongst the trees.

Rhodesia has twenty-five national parks and reserves. The oldest is **Wankie National Park** on the eastern edge of the Kalahari. Opportunities for viewing and photography are particularly good here. Part of the park is open to visitors, but some areas are devoted solely to conservation. White and black rhinos, about 7,000 elephants and black-backed and side-striped jackals are some of the species to be seen together with a wide range of antelope and gazelle, amongst them the magnificent gemsbok.

The **Victoria Falls National Park** lies above the plunging waters of the Zambezi—the river forms the northern boundary of the park. Hippos and crocodiles, cheetah, leopard and again a fine selection of antelopes can all be seen.

The depredations on South African game by settlers were to be repaired by the early establishment of national parks. The **Kruger National Park** is probably one of the most famous and spectacular parks in Africa. Wide plains merge into bush country and rivers cross the whole area, sometimes dropping through wooded gorges. Quagga and roan antelope are only two of the handsome antelope species that share the park with giraffes, red jackals, spotted hyenas and wild dogs. There are flowers, shrubs and trees, including bluegum, wild and strangling fig, sausage trees and the Transvaal ebony.

The **Golden Gate Highlands National Park** reaches 9,000 feet above sea level and in winter snow lies on the mountains. Steep valley edges reveal purple, red and golden rocks. The red hartebeest, white-tailed gnu and blesbok can be seen amongst the shrubs, mountain sage, wild olive and protea trees.

The **Etosha National Park** in south-west Africa is one of the wildest places on the continent. It borders the sea in the west and runs inland for 80 miles as a flat semi-desert area. It does, however, support thousands of animals and birds and, particularly in the east, a wide variety of trees, including wild fig, date palms and wolf's thorn. The innumerable species to be seen there include the gemsbok, brindled gnu and eland, cheetah, leopard and lynx. The aardwolf, honey badger and bat-eared fox are also found. Birds, including cranes, bustards, the ostrich, birds of prey and hornbills exist in bewildering quantities, relatively undisturbed.

Other parts of Africa are less well served with reserves. Protection measures are often haphazardly organized, and there is considerable scope for many countries in the north and the west to conserve the quickly disappearing flora and fauna of jungles, deserts and rivers. The hills and rivers of the **Mole Game Reserve** in Ghana support a fair variety of species, amongst them lion, leopard, roan antelope, waterbuck and Buffon's kob. Crocodiles, monitor lizards and river turtles can also be seen.

Deep gorges and wooded savannah country form part of the **'W' National Park** in Niger. Lion, leopard, buffalo, warthog and the caracal lynx are just a few of the species.

The wildlife of Ethiopia is celebrated if not always adequately protected. Perhaps the most famous park is the **Simien Mountain Park.** Giant lobelia form part of the vegetation and the park is known chiefly as the only habitat of the extremely rare walia ibex; the Simien fox and gelada baboon are other rare endemic creatures. The lammergeyer or bearded vulture is one of the most spectacular birds found here; ravens and choughs also exist in their mountain habitat. The river Awash, passing through several gorges, is a picturesque part of the **Awash National Park,** which lies east of Addis Ababa and consists otherwise of grassy plains and scrub. The beautiful beisa oryx, Grevy's zebra and Soemmering's gazelle are particularly attractive examples of the park's fauna. The endangered Somali wild ass and Swayne's hartebeest may be introduced into Awash. The lovely carmine bee-eater and proud kori bustard are also seen here.

Australia and New Zealand

Australia is one of the most thinly populated countries in the world and yet many of her species and habitats are endangered. Conserving them presents several difficulties, as many of them are both rare and widely distributed; some travel long distances and are inclined to trek out of any protected area. Laws vary from state to state and species protected in one state can be shot in another. However, parks are being established, although some of them are less conservation than recreation areas. Distances between parks are often vast, yet the internal airline system is sufficiently good to allow relatively easy travel.

Only 12 miles east of Adelaide is the **Cleland National Park** which has an abundance of acacias, grass trees and wild flowers. The stately brolga crane and endangered Cape barren goose can be found here as well as kangaroos, koalas and wallabies.

The **Flinders Chase Reserve** lies at the western end of Kangaroo Island in the St Vincent Gulf. Here you can see the curious echidna or spiny anteater, the duck-billed platypus, the koala and a race of the grey kangaroo. Emus, black cockatoos and brush turkeys are a few of the interesting birds to be seen.

Hattah Lakes National Park and Kulkyne State Forest consists of lakes, pine forests and gum trees with a good complement of wild flowers. Kangaroos, both red and grey, are to be seen, and the delicate honey-eaters, ibis, birds of prey and waterfowl gather in many parts of the reserve, which lies in the extreme north-west of the state of Victoria. A sandstone monolith over 1,000 feet high is the central point of the **Ayers Rock and Mount Olga National Park.** It is an extremely arid area but the bizarre landscape attracts many visitors each year. Bloodwood and ironwood trees help improve a rather bare habitat for dingoes, kangaroos and emus. The park can be reached from Alice Springs.

For people willing to make a journey by air or overland 350 miles north-west from Alice Springs, a wide variety of creatures is waiting in the **Tanami Desert Sanctuary.** It is generally arid, with sand dunes, but there is some vegetation in the form of spinifex and mulga trees. Red kangaroos, desert mice, foxes, dingoes and rabbit-eared bandicoots leap or scamper across the semi-desert. Geckos, monitor lizards, collared brown snakes and red-naped snakes slither along the ground. Above fly brown hawks, quail, shrike thrushes, wood swallows and, again, honey-eaters.

Although the **Cobourg Peninsula Sanctuary** requires a permit and some tenacity to reach, it nevertheless has much to offer. It lies to the north of Darwin and can be reached only by sea or air. Many of the species to be seen are descendants of introduced Asian animals, for example banteng cattle and Timor ponies. Many kinds of marine turtles visit the beaches and in the wide variety of habitat—sandy plains, rain forest and mangrove jungle—live innumerable mammals, reptiles and birds. The fawn marsupial mouse, brush-tailed possum and rare agile wallaby are some of the interesting marsupials found here. The dingo appears again as well as species of gecko, lizard and snake. The bird life is extremely rich: kestrels, ospreys, orioles, ibises, kingfishers and many wading birds inhabit the area as do lorikeets, cockatoos and bower-birds.

Woolwonga Sanctuary, to the east of Darwin, boasts many of the species found in the Cobourg Peninsula and is more accessible; even greater numbers of wildfowl can be found here. Chains of billabongs form **Goose Camp** where thousands of magpie and pygmy geese congregate. Another chain of palm-fringed billabongs called **Dreaming Waters** also attracts many species of birds.

The **Walpole-Nornalup National Park** near Perth has more scenic than faunal attractions. However, the magnificent stands of karri tree, a kind of eucalyptus, the innumerable wild flowers (about 7,000 different species), sand dunes and coastal hills are well worth seeing. You might also see the grey kangaroo or short-nosed bandicoot. Other interesting parks in the same region but with different attractions are worth visiting.

Heron Island lies off the coast of Queensland in the Great Barrier Reef. Wild poinsettias and palm trees flourish on this coral island. The bird life is varied and prolific and the surrounding habitat beautiful. Mutton birds nest in burrows and white-breasted sea eagles establish themselves when breeding in pisonia trees. Herons, cormorants, sandpipers and terns exist in large numbers and from spring to autumn thousands of green turtles drag themselves onto sandy beaches to lay their eggs. The coral formations provide a spectacular attraction, particularly on nearby islands and reefs.

Dunk Island, also off the Queensland coast, has secluded beaches, palm trees and thick rain forest. Rich golden butterflies flutter amongst frangipani and hibiscus blossoms. The marine life on the coral reef is rich and diverse. Reef herons and Torres Strait pigeons are a few of the birds to be seen.

The **Lamington National Park,** Queensland, is one of Australia's most famous. Luxuriant forest covers peaks and gorges and cloaks waterfalls. Tree ferns and extravagant orchids fill the jungle during part of the year. The rare rufous scrub-bird, Prince Albert's lyre-bird, the regent bower-bird, satin bower-bird and paradise rifle-bird might be seen amongst the trees.

The Snowy Mountains are a spectacular part of the **Kosciusko State Park.** Recreational activities are combined with a varied wild life. Skiing and camping are allowed. Many alpine flowers flourish amongst glacial lakes in the higher regions. The duck-billed platypus, echidna and grey kangaroos can be found as well as the brush-tailed rock wallaby. Lyre-birds, emus and cockatoos contribute to an interesting avifauna.

The virgin forests of the **Tidbinbilla Fauna Reserve** provide a habitat for many species of possum, including the sugar glider, pygmy glider and bush-tailed possums. Kangaroos and wallabies, wombats and koalas are seen amongst species of eucalyptus tree which include the broad-leaved peppermint, candlebark and snow gum trees.

Phillip Island can be reached from Melbourne and is famous for the fairy penguins inhabiting an area which consists of several reserves. Koalas, Australian fur seals, ibises and mutton birds are just a few of the many other attractions.

For many years introduced species threatened to do considerable harm to much of New Zealand's interesting flora and fauna, but as conservation areas have been established, the risk is diminishing; intriguing birds, such as the takahe and kea, and reptiles like the ancient tuatara, whose relatives became extinct 100 million years ago, will now be safe.

Very large, with a magnificent wild and mountainous landscape, the **Fiordland National Park** lies on the south-west corner of South Island. The edelweiss, gentians and orchids grow beside the lakes and waterfalls. Red deer and wapiti, and seals swimming in the waters of the fiords, are some of the mammals to be seen. The rare and flightless takahe and kakapo might be found. Penguins and petrels, shags, innumerable ducks and waders inhabit both the rugged coastline and the inland lakes.

In the north-west of North Island can be found the **Urewara National Park,** parts of which reach to over 4,000 feet. Here again the main scenic features are waterfalls, lakes and wooded hills. Introduced species, such as the brush-tailed phalanger, wild goat and pig and red deer, can be seen. The incomparable kiwi and the bell bird, although resident here, are very difficult to see, but other kinds of wildfowl are less elusive.

The kiwi might also be seen in the **Egmont National Park,** North Island, as well as the bush hawk, bush wren and bell bird. Snow-capped Mount Egmont rises in the centre of the park.

Birds are an important feature of the **Abel Tasman National Park** on the northern coast of South Island. Here, however, only camping facilities are available, but one's stamina is rewarded by fine scenery—beaches and coves, marshes and forest. The long-tailed cuckoo, white-faced heron, innumerable terns, petrels and species of skua, as well as the delightful little prions, can all be seen. Fur seals and sea-lions laze on the beach or plunge about in the sea.

The Exotic

For those in search of perhaps the more exotic, unusual or distant location for their viewing and photographing, there is an ever-increasing choice. South America, Asia, the Antarctic and the coral islands of the Indian Ocean can all be visited.

The vast and wild areas of South America, although threatened by man as elsewhere in the world, are probably still some of the least trammelled. The **Iguazu Falls** form a boundary point between Argentina, Paraguay and Brazil. The Falls are famous and beautiful and the surrounding jungle is full of wild animals, including jaguars, ocelots, pumas, monkeys and a rich variety of birds. The **Canaima National Park** of Venezuela is a mixture of steep valleys, waterfalls, rain forest and savannah; it covers nearly $2\frac{1}{2}$ million acres. Here again you can see the jaguar, lithe little tiger-cat, peccaries, armadillos, spider monkeys and innumerable birds including humming birds, toucans, woodcreepers, and birds of prey.

The Antarctic can now be reached by travelling on the *Lindblad Explorer* which visits this vast and lonely continent twice a year. There is much to interest travellers. Many species of penguins, amongst them the king, emperor, chinstrap, Adelie and royal penguins, can be seen in thousands. Mammals include the leopard, Ross, Weddell and crab-eater seals, the South American sea-lion and the southern elephant seal. Perhaps the bird life (nearly all of which is seen round the edge of the land mass) is the most exciting wildlife attraction the Antarctic has to offer. Apart from the penguins, petrels and albatrosses, gulls and terns swarm over the icy seas; and many of them breed in the Antarctic.

The parks and reserves of India are developing their viewing facilities and a rich variety of wildlife species can be seen from north to south India, and in Pakistan and Nepal. The **Gir Wildlife Sanctuary** in western India contains the last viable population of the Asiatic lion, whose numbers have dropped dramatically. Numbers now stand at about 300. Apart from lions you can see many species of deer including chinkara, sambar and axis deer. Wild pig are present in good numbers (the lions' main prey).

The Kaziranga Wildlife Sanctuary in Assam is one of the most important reserves in India and is the habitat of over half the world's population of great Indian rhinos, which have been hunted and killed until their numbers stand at about 700. The tiger can also be seen here as well as swamp and hog deer, leopard and wild pig. Bird life is also rich and varied—vultures, eagles, egrets and many kinds of waterfowl can all be found.

The handsome blackbuck and endangered barasingha or swamp deer can be found in the **Kanha National Park** in central India where the habitat consists of grassy parkland. Chital and sambar deer are also present as well as tiger, leopard, wild dog and the sloth bear. From watch-towers there is plenty of opportunity to see most species.

To the south of Delhi lies the **Sariska Wildlife Sanctuary** and here photographers have a rare opportunity to photograph tigers coming for bait. The reserve covers an area of valleys and hills sometimes covered with bamboo and flame-of-the-forest trees. Many kinds of gazelle and deer are also seen, as well as the caracal (lynx), leopard, palm and small Indian civet.

High sand dunes, lagoons and jungle in the south-east tip of Ceylon form the **Ruhuna National Park.** Here can be found a wide variety of species including the endangered Ceylon elephant, the delightful spotted axis deer, leopards and crocodiles. Birds are a particular attraction in this part and include orioles, quail, hornbills, flycatchers and peafowl. **Wilpattu,** on the western side of Ceylon, has a similar habitat and again a wide variety of species, including elephants, the very rare Asiatic buffalo, leopards and many monkeys. A large number of birds are attracted to the shallow lagoons and streams; amongst these are egrets, storks, herons, kingfishers and hoopoes.

In spite of the recent war, there is hope that the **Sundarbans Reserve** in Bangladesh will continue to exist. A vast area of forest and rivers, it holds probably the most important population of tigers in Asia, as well as many deer, wild boar and crocodiles.

The **Mount Apo National Park** on Mindanao Island in the Philippines is chiefly famous for its population of the severely threatened monkey-eating eagle which catches its prey by snatching monkeys from the branches of trees. The park is also famous for its impressive scenery. Mount Apo, the highest peak in the Philippines, rises from the park, where hot mineral springs, waterfalls and a volcano contribute to the scenic attractions.

The **Kinabalu National Park** in Sabah, Malaysia, is one of the few homes of the endangered orang utan, the only ape found outside Africa. The hills are covered with tea-trees, conifers, myrtles and innumerable varieties of ferns, providing an ideal habitat also for the gibbon, Sumatran rhino, civet and countless birds.

The **Seychelles** in the Indian Ocean should need no introduction. Typifying untroubled paradise islands, they are visited by more people every year. They have a unique and in many cases prolific bird life.
The magpie robin, the Seychelles kestrel and brush warbler and the Seychelles black paradise flycatcher are some birds you may be fortunate enough to see. However, sooty and noddy terns, boobies and frigatebirds are present in hundreds on some of the coral-fringed islands. Colourful frogs, lizards, fish and butterflies thrive and turtles will be seen in the crystal water.

The **Galapagos Islands** in the Pacific are volcanic and more rugged, but they too have much to offer with a rich selection of rare indigenous species. Amongst these are the strange marine and land iguanas, the several different races of giant tortoises, as well as sea-lions and penguins. Again the avifauna is extremely rich and plentiful, with many species, such as the red-footed booby, frigatebirds and storm petrels, present in vast numbers.

technical hints

Photographing through the glass of an aquarium

The angle of incidence of the beam of light from the light source should be approximately 45°. One or more lamps may be used. If the angle is larger, i.e. the beam is more nearly parallel to the glass, total reflection occurs, so that none of the light enters the water. If the angle is substantially less than 45°, too much of the light is reflected directly into the lens of the camera. Alternatively, the aquarium can be illuminated by means of a light source located above or to one side of it, but in that case the part of the subject facing the camera is likely to be inadequately illuminated. Movable partitions of transparent glass are used to keep the fish (or other creature to be photographed) within that part of the illuminated zone which is within the depth of field of the camera.

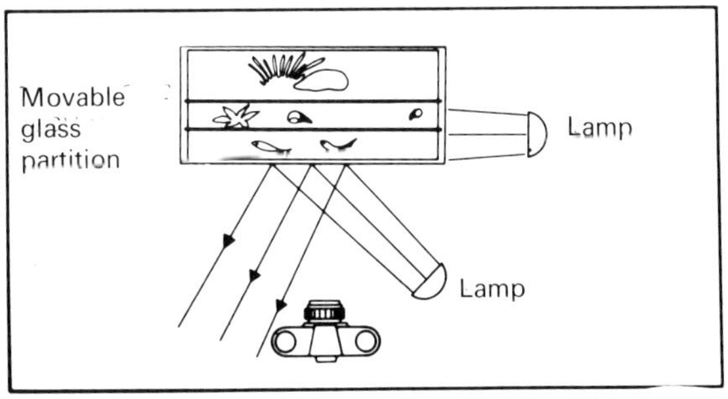

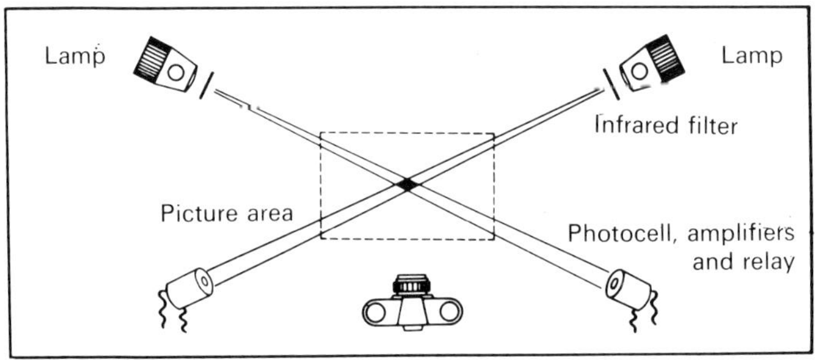

Photocells with crossed beams

To ensure correct composition of the picture and accurate focusing, it may be advantageous to employ an installation comprising two beams of light which can actuate coupled photo-electric cells which respond simultaneously. Only when the beams are both intercepted at their point of intersection, i.e. when the subject to be photographed enters a small well-defined area, does it become possible to release the shutter of the camera. The beams of light from the two spotlights each pass through an infrared filter and are thus made invisible. In order to obviate the time-lag due to the mechanical inertia of the shutter, it is preferable to use the so-called open flash technique (the shutter is left open in a darkened room) in conjunction with a relay having a response time of 1/2000 second, which directly operates the electronic flash.

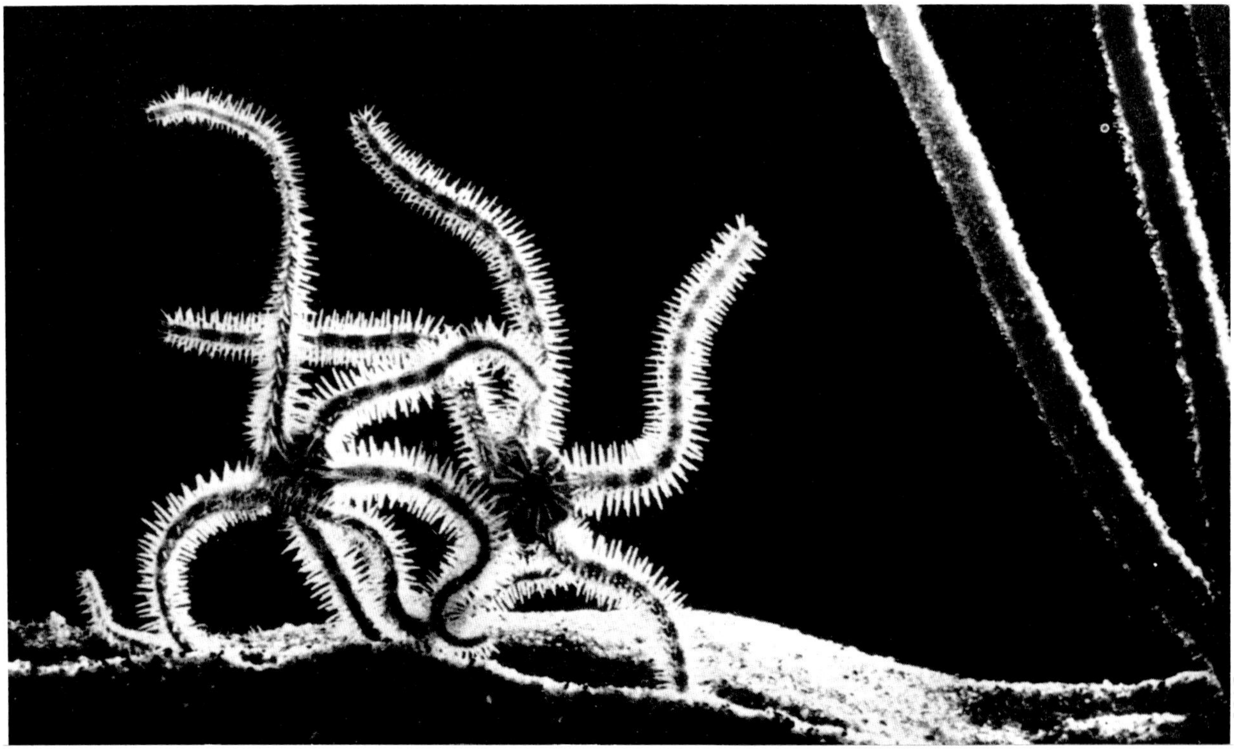

Two starfish, so-called brittle-stars (*Ophiura fragilis*).

TENT HIDES

Two types of portable hide in the form of tents which are easy to construct and inexpensive will be described here. It is advantageous to use a hide which is as low as possible. One could almost formulate a rule that the 'safe' distance which a wild creature strives to keep between itself and the hide is proportional to the height of the latter and to its prominence in the landscape. For this reason, too, it is best to use a periscope, even a very simple one, to scan the horizon from a crouching position.

TENT No. 1

Advantages:

1. You can stand erect in it and take photographs in all directions.
2. Several cameras can be installed in it.
3. Cameras and accessories can be attached to the framework of the tent itself (this can be very useful on wet ground).
4. It can be transported without having to be dismantled (it weighs only about 17 lb) and can be adjusted very quickly to increase or reduce its height (by adding or removing parts of the frame).
5. One or two persons can spend a fairly long time in it in reasonable comfort and protected from the weather (it has direct natural ventilation through its thin fabric; the roof should be waterproof, however).

Disadvantages:

1. It is nevertheless relatively heavy; it takes a rather long time to put up and requires a special tool for locking the connectors that join the parts of the frame.
2. The metal tubes of which the frame is composed are awkward (the longer units are at least 0·75 m in length) and noisy when accidentally knocked together.
3. Unless it is securely fixed, the fabric covering is liable to flap in the wind and thus act as a 'scarecrow'.
4. Although it is strong and serviceable, it is a somewhat conspicuous structure, and when dismantled it is rather bulky.

Framework:

Aluminium or duralumin tubes (20 mm diameter; units up to 1 m in length) assembled with T-shaped connectors. Four of these tubes are provided with points for driving them into hard ground; additional tubes serve as bracing and are useful as supports to which cameras and accessories can be attached.

Shape of the tent:

This depends on the nature of the ground and the scenery. By using tube units of different lengths many combinations are possible.

Camouflage fabric:

This is a coarse-textured neutral-coloured jute fabric (hessian). To facilitate erection, the two layers of material, of equal area, are not sewn together. The material is provided with slot-like holes with snap fasteners or some other quick-action means of assembly. Instead of ordinary fabric it is sometimes advantageous to use camouflage netting in two layers with meshes ranging in size from 5 to 10 mm.

TENT No. 2

Advantages:

1. Light (weighs only 9 lb) and compact; can be erected and dismantled very easily and quickly.
2. Unobtrusive in the landscape; wind cannot get much grip on it.
3. Completely watertight and can be fairly well ventilated.
4. Needs only one peg to secure it, and even this can be dispensed with if the guy rope is tied to a convenient fixed object.

Disadvantages:

1. You cannot look out in different directions (because the front of the tent faces in one particular direction).
2. You cannot stand erect in the tent, and it will accommodate only one person.
3. There is not enough room in it to have a wide range of equipment and accessories with you, and the tent cannot be transported in the erected condition.

Framework:

A single metal strut composed of one or more units (20 to 30 mm in diameter) is needed, which may be of telescopic construction, collapsing to less than 0·35 m when not in use. The extended strut is 0·70 m high.

Camouflage fabric:

Two materials are used for this tent: a triangular piece of neutral-coloured waterproof fabric and a piece of fairly fine-meshed camouflage netting. The latter may be rectangular or triangular and should be placed in double or triple layers in front of the opening of the tent. The angle of vision from such a tent is rather restricted (about 50°). The netting should be used on only one face of the tent, for it will conceal the occupant only if he has a dark or opaque background behind him.

TENT No. 1

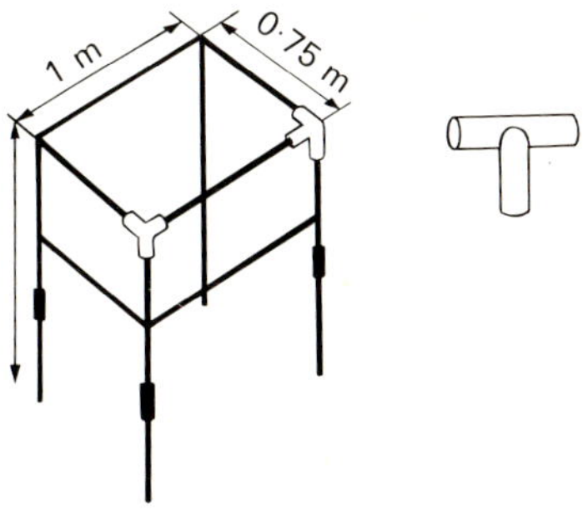

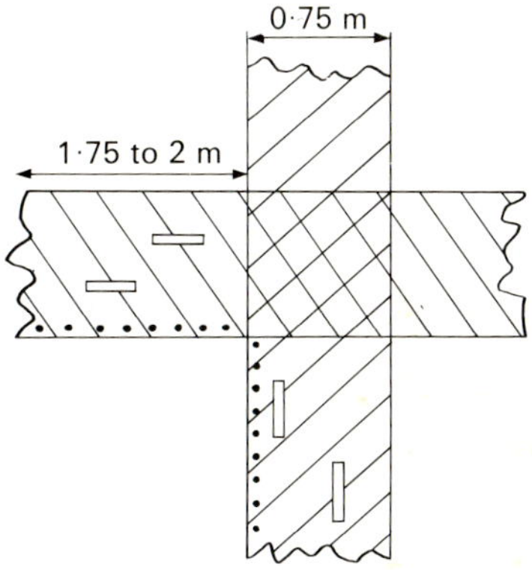

TENT No. 2

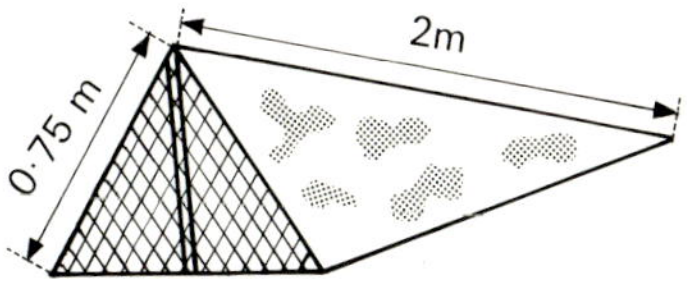

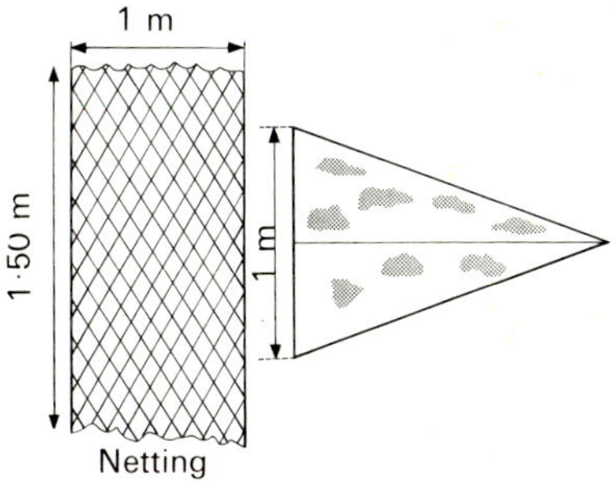

Testing and care

In practice, lens testing can be a particularly tricky operation, and you should therefore be very cautious in judging and interpreting the results.

In most cases a quick simple test will enable you to form a fair preliminary opinion as to image quality produced by a lens. This will take only a few minutes, and any reputable photographic dealer will undoubtedly let you try out a lens in this way before you decide to buy it

Using a film of medium speed, photograph the double page of an opened newspaper. The image of the newspaper should fill the whole picture area. From test shots at various apertures you can assess the amount of distortion (manifested by lines showing curvature along their whole length) or lack of covering power of the lens (image sharpness at the edges of the picture is not as good as at the centre). Also it will enable you to form an idea of the definition obtainable with the lens. A good method is to make comparative tests with another lens of known optical quality.

For more elaborate testing and in order to establish the intrinsic quality of the lens, independently of any conditions of use, there exist special test targets. These consist of multi-coloured patterns of lines and shapes. These test targets are supplied with full instructions for lens and camera testing; they are a very useful piece of additional equipment, and can be used by all enthusiasts—including the non-technical. To perform the test, the camera is set up before a panel to which test targets are fixed at the four corners of the image area. A fifth test target is placed at the centre of the panel.

Now a series of photographs of the panel is taken, using different diaphragm stops. The panel with its test targets should be evenly illuminated for the purpose.

After processing, the transparencies or negatives are examined so that the resolving power of the lens can be estimated in terms of the maximum number of lines per millimetre which it can distinctly record.

Incidentally, these test targets can also be used to provide useful information about enlarging equipment; films; film/developer combinations; and even the performance of colour materials.

Lenses should be carefully protected from knocks and jolts during transport by storing them in suitable boxes which should contain a drying agent to give protection from moisture. The surfaces of the lens should be kept scrupulously clean, but the delicate coated surfaces must not be wiped with chamois leather or very abrasive lens tissues. It is best to use a very clean soft hair brush, which has first been thoroughly washed in alcohol and dried, or a soft well-washed cotton cloth. To protect the outer surface of a lens, many photographers keep a haze filter permanently in place.

Kodak correction filters for colour photography

Kodak light balancing filters

Filter colour	Filter number	Exposure increase in stops*	To obtain 3200K from:	To obtain 3400K from:
	82C+82C	1 1/3	2490K	2610K
	82C+82B	1 1/3	2570K	2700K
	82C+82A	1	2650K	2780K
Bluish	82C+82	1	2720K	2870K
	82C	2/3	2800K	2950K
	82B	2/3	2900K	3060K
	82A	1/3	3000K	3180K
	82	1/3	3100K	3290K
	No filter necessary		3200K	3400K
	81	1/3	3300K	3510K
	81A	1/3	3400K	3630K
Yellowish	81B	1/3	3500K	3740K
	81C	1/3	3600K	3850K
	81D	2/3	3700K	3970K
	81EF	2/3	3850K	4140K

*These values are approximate. For critical work, they should be checked by practical test, especially if more than one filter is used.

Kodak conversion filters for colour photography

Kodak conversion filters

To convert	Use Kodak filter No.	Filter colour	Exposure increase in stops*
3200K to daylight (5500K)	80A	Blue	2
3400K to daylight (5500K)	80B	Blue	1 2/3
3800K† to daylight (5500K)	80C	Blue	1
4200K‡ to daylight (5500K)	80D	Blue	1/3
Daylight (5500K) to 3800K	85C	Orange	1/3
Daylight (5500K) to 3400K	85	Orange	2/3
Daylight (5500K) to 3200K	85B	Orange	2/3

*For critical work, check these values by practical test.
†Aluminium-filled clear flashbulbs, such as M2, 5 and 25.
‡Zirconium-filled clear flashbulbs, such as AG-1 and M3.

bibliography

Technical works

O. R. Croy, *Creative Photomicrography*, Focal Press, London; Amphoto and Hastings, New York.
R. L. Aspden, *Electronic Flash Photography*, Fountain Press, London.
G. A. Jones, *High Speed Photography*, Chapman & Hall, London.
D. F. Lawson, *The Technique of Photomicrography*, Newnes, London.
H. M. Malies, *Applied Microscopy and Photomicrography*, Fountain Press, London.
R. F. Saxe, *High Speed Photography*, Focal Press, London; Amphoto, New York.
A. Cox, *Photographic Optics*, Focal Press, London; Amphoto, New York.
T. Russell, *Lenses: How to choose them*, Bailey Bros, Folkestone; Amphoto, New York.
A. Ansel, *Camera and Lens, the Creative Approach*, rev. ed. Morgan and Morgan, Hastings, New York.
R. Kingslake, *Applied Optics and Optical Engineering*, 5 vols, Academic Press, New York.
D. H. John, *Photography on Expeditions*, Hastings, New York.
Photographing Nature, Time-Life Books, New York.
J. Sherman, *Camera on Safari*, Focal Press, London.
J. Warham, *The Technique of Bird Photography*, Focal Press, London.
D. Townsend, *Underwater Photography*, Stanley Paul, London.

General works on nature and conservation

J. Dorst, *Before Nature Dies*, Collins, London; Houghton Mifflin, Boston, U.S.A.
J. Fisher *et al.*, *The Red Book*, Collins, London; published as *Wildlife in Danger* by Viking Press, New York.
HRH Duke of Edinburgh and J. Fisher, *Wildlife Crisis*, Hamish Hamilton, London; Cowles, New York.
C. A. W. Guggisberg, *Man and Wildlife*, Evans, London; Arco, New York.
R. Carson, *Silent Spring*, Hamish Hamilton, London; Houghton Mifflin, Boston, U.S.A.
G. R. Taylor, *The Doomsday Book*, Thames & Hudson, London; World Books, New York.
B. Commoner, *The Closing Circle*, Jonathan Cape, London; Knopf, New York.
R. Fitter, *Vanishing Wild Animals of the World*, Kaye & Ward, London; Franklin Watts, New York.
D. Ehrenfield, *Conserving Life on Earth*, Oxford, New York.
V. Ziswiler, *Extinct and Vanishing Animals*, Springer-Verlag, New York.
J. C. Greenway, Jr, *Extinct and Vanishing Birds of the World*, Dover, New York.

Specialized works

R. T. Peterson *et al.*, *Field Guide to the Birds of Britain and Europe*, Collins, London; Houghton Mifflin, Boston, U.S.A.
K. Weber and L. Hoffmann, *Camargue*, Harrap, London.
C. A. Vaucher, *East African Wildlife*, Librairie Marguerat, Lausanne.
A. Carr, *Ulendo: Travels of a naturalist in and out of Africa*, Knopf, New York.
R. S. Arbib, Jr, *et al.*, *Enjoying Birds Around New York City*, Houghton Mifflin, Boston, U.S.A.
A. Leopold, *A Sand County Almanac*, Oxford, New York.
D. L. Serventy *et al.*, *The Handbook of Australian Sea-birds*, Reed, Artarmon (Australia).
V. Serventy, *Wildlife of Australia*, Nelson, London.
G. Mountfort, *The Vanishing Jungle*, Collins, London; Houghton Mifflin, Boston, U.S.A.
B. Vesey-Fitzgerald, *The Vanishing Wildlife of Britain*, MacGibbon & Kee, London.
J. and M. Teal, *Life and Death of the Salt Marsh*, Atlantic-Little, Brown, Boston, U.S.A.

Records

E. Mickleburgh, *Antarctica–A portrait in wildlife and natural sound*, Saydisc Specialized Recordings, The Barton, Inglestone Common, Badminton, Glos.
J.-C. Roché, *Oiseaux Méditerranéens*, Discourses, 34 High Street, Tunbridge Wells, Kent; just one of a series of birdsong recordings made all over the world.
BBC Wildlife Series, BBC, London; recordings of mammals, birds and reptiles from all over the world.
P. P. Kellogg and A. A. Allen, *Voices of the Night: The calls of 34 frogs and toads of the United States and Canada*, Houghton Mifflin, Boston, U.S.A.
R. S. Payne, *Songs of the Humpback Whale*, CRM Records, Del Mar, Calif., U.S.A.
Robert Redford (narrator), *The Language and Music of the Wolves*, Natural History Magazine, New York.
P. P. Kellogg *et al.*, *A Field Guide to Bird Songs*, Laboratory of Ornithology, Cornell University, pub. Houghton Mifflin, Boston, U.S.A.

Wildlife and conservation magazines (available throughout the world)

Biological Conservation, Switzerland.
Animals, London.
World of Birds, London.
The Ecologist, Richmond, Surrey.
World of Wildlife (part-work: editions available also in French, German and Spanish), London.
Bêtes et nature, France.
La vie des bêtes, France.
Das Tier, Switzerland.
Audubon, New York.
Natural History Magazine, New York.

Publisher's Note

The work of the World Wildlife Fund has helped the survival of many of the species and habitats described in this book. Ten years old in 1971, this major conservation organization, dedicated to saving the world's wildlife and wild places, now has seventeen National Appeals in different countries. Together with the International Union for Conservation of Nature, whose operations it helps finance, it supports ecological surveys of endangered species, protection measures for animals and habitats, and the creation of national parks throughout the world. (For further information write to: Director General, World Wildlife Fund, 1110 Morges, Switzerland; the Fund has an office in the United States at Suite 619, 910 17th St NW, Washington, D.C. 20006.)

The preparation of pages 148–53 and 157 of this book was helped considerably by reference to *The World Wildlife Guide* (Threshold Books, London). This is a vital companion for anyone visiting the world's parks and reserves as it gives all essential information to would-be travellers.